BUSTER KEATON

CUT TO THE CHASE

ALSO BY MARION MEADE

Biographies

Free Woman: The Life and Times of Victoria Woodhull
Eleanor of Aquitaine
Madame Blavatsky: The Woman Behind the Myth
Dorothy Parker: What Fresh Hell Is This?

Novels

Stealing Heaven: The Love Story of Heloise and Abelard
Sybille

BUSTER KEATON

CUT TO THE CHASE

MARION MEADE

HarperCollins*Publishers*

Grateful acknowledgment is made for:

2 letters from Joseph Keaton to Gerry Society (1900); 19 words from Joseph Keaton letter to Harry Houdini (1900); 50 words from Buster Keaton interview with Columbia University Oral History Project (1958); 15 words from Louise Keaton letter to Mary Anderson in Muskegon; 12 words from Harry Keaton letter to Mary Anderson by permission of Eleanor Keaton.

16 words from Joseph Keaton letter to Harry Houdini (1901) by permission of Harry Ransom Humanities Research Center, the University of Texas at Austin.

2 letters from Joseph Keaton to Gerry Society (1900); 23 words from Gerry Society case file on Buster Keaton as amended and corrected May 4, 1995, by permission of the George Sim Johnston Archives of the New York Society for the Prevention of Cruelty to Children.

9 words from interview with Buster Keaton (1956) by permission of Joseph Laitin.

61 words from Rohauer transcript; 40 words from Dugas interview; 254 words from "Search for Buster Keaton" by permission of Kevin Brownlow, Photoplay Productions.

35 words from unpublished manuscript entitled "Buster" by permission of Alan Hoffman.

50 words from Buster Keaton, Pop Art Series I, No. 322, Vol. VI, Pt. 2, by permission of Dr. Ronald Grele, Oral History Research Office, Columbia University.

16 words from interview with Marion Mack by permission of Rick Vanderknyff.

4 words from taped interview with Buster Keaton (exact date unknown) by permission of Studs Terkel.

HarperCollins books may be purchased for educational, business, or sales promotional use. For information please write: Special Markets Department, HarperCollinsPublishers, Inc., 10 East 53rd Street, New York, NY 10022.

Designed by Nancy Singer

Library of Congress Cataloging-in-Publication Data

Meade, Marion, 1934–
    Buster Keaton: Cut to the chase, a biography / Marion Meade.
      p. cm.
    Includes bibliographical references and index.
    ISBN 0-06-017337-8
    1. Keaton, Buster, 1895–1966.   2. Comedians—United States—
Biography.   3. Motion picture actors and actresses—United States—
Biography. I. Title.
PN2287.K4M43   1995
791.43'028'092—dc20   95-21390
[B]

95 96 97 98 99 ❖/HC 10 9 8 7 6 5 4 3 2 1

For Ashley Elizabeth Sprague

CONTENTS

Photographs follow page 216.

FADE IN

The blare of automobile horns rumbles through the streets of Times Square. On an unseasonably cold March day in 1917, a young man, all by himself, is pushing through the noontime traffic. He is twenty-one years old but looks younger, with a solemn, pretty-boy face and a shock of straight dark hair.

When he hears his name called, his head snaps around to see a man stepping toward him, a comic he knows from vaudeville. Looking surprisingly prosperous, the vaudevillian reports that he retired from the stage to manage a movie studio. "You've never been in the movies, have you?" he says.

Absolutely not. His family disdains motion pictures. In fact, a lucky break has just won him a role in a Broadway musical comedy. In his mind there is no comparison whatsoever between a Shubert musical and second-rate enterprises like movies.

But when he is invited to see for himself how a comedy is made, he agrees to go along.

Walking east on Forty-eighth Street, they cross Fifth Avenue, pass under the Third Avenue El, and stop just short of the East River at an old warehouse. At Colony Studio, observing the action on a country-store set, the young man gets his first glimpse of filmmaking. He watches all afternoon, completely transfixed, not by the story, not by its star, Roscoe Arbuckle, but by the camera. How does it work? What drives the film through the camera? How are the pieces of celluloid assembled?

By evening he is still there. He's even played a customer who buys a bucketful of molasses. As the crew prepares to leave, he turns to Arbuckle. May he borrow one of the cameras?

In his room that night, he dismantles the Bell & Howell. All the spools and discs and spindles are spread out before him. After his curiosity is completely satisfied, he reassembles the camera. The next day he quits his job in *The Passing Show of 1917*.

Nineteen ninety-five celebrates the hundredth anniversary of Joseph Frank Keaton's birth. Born into a family of touring medicine-show performers, the baby fell down a flight of stairs and became known as Buster. The nickname stuck to him for the rest of his life.

In movies, Keaton's universe keeps collapsing: houses crash on him, rocks chase him down hills, boats sink beneath his feet. Fearless Buster in his pancake hat copes with havoc, hilariously. His private life was also full of endless indignities: the anguish of a rough, battering father and an ice-cold mother, his loss of an education, alcoholism, problems with the Hollywood system, profound depression, broken marriages. But Keaton was a fighter. He despaired, then continued on. In the end he triumphed through courage, perseverance, and obsession with work.

One of the true geniuses of American cinema, Keaton seems to be untouched by time. There was no one like him. He was the complete filmmaker, who conceived, wrote, directed, edited, and starred in ten silent feature films and nineteen short comedies. His masterpiece, *The General,* continues to be praised as one of the greatest films of all time.

He was the best comedy director in the business, a director's director. Luis Buñuel was a great fan. Sergei Eisenstein—and Woody Allen and Leni Riefenstahl, Billy Wilder and Martin Scorsese—found him delicious. Today he is primarily honored as a legendary independent filmmaker. But the full scope of his artistry is breathtaking. He was a superb athlete who created incomparable physical comedy in such films as *Cops* and *The Navigator.* He was a magnificent actor whose impassive facial expression—he was called Deadpan and Stoneface—is misleading. He didn't need a smile to convey his thoughts or feelings.

Keaton became the lyric poet of silent films. His stories are about the special worlds of newsreel cameramen, Civil War railroad engineers, butterfly collectors, Roman charioteers, movie projectionists, gallant cowboys, prizefighters, and debonair play-boys. They are also about himself, with slivers of Joseph Frank "Buster" Keaton embedded in every character he played.

In *Sherlock Jr.* Buster walks down the aisle of a theater and enters the movie screen. In *The Playhouse,* nine Busters perform together. But that's not all. By multiple exposures, he becomes every member of the orchestra *and* the audience. Offscreen, he was not an ordinary person either. Practically his entire life was spent in the limelight. At the age of five he made a sensational debut as a vaudeville comic. His stardom lasted a lifetime. For Buster, celebrity was never a goal, it was a childhood accident.

By his death on February 1, 1966, enthusiastic film aficionados had begun calling him a genius. Such reverence made him terrifically uncomfortable: "No man can be a genius in slapshoes and flat hat." He preferred to be remembered as a performer whose career lasted almost seven decades. "I work more than Doris Day," he joked. Hollywood Boulevard's Walk of Fame honors him as a two-star celebrity, for his work in movies and television.

This book focuses on Buster's personal life. In recent years several fine books about his films have been published, so I saw no reason to plow the same field. By exploring the various events of his private life, my aim is to reveal a more detailed picture of the artist, which perhaps will further illuminate his art.

Keaton's legacy is twofold: as master of the sight gag he was one of the most sublime film comedians of them all; and as a master film director, his work behind the camera cannot be rivaled for its sheer visual brilliance. By exploring the camera's possibilities, he helped advance cinema into a sophisticated art form.

1 CHEROKEE STRIP

Summer lingers like death on the prairie. It had not rained since spring, and by September the heat had burned cattle trails and dried creek beds. Underfoot the crust of the earth was cracking. A hot wind tumbled past skeletons of abandoned houses, their hulks framed by fences about to keel over. Off to the north, amid the tallgrass of Kansas, nature was syrup sweet and the voice of the turtledove swirled throughout the land, but in the north-central Oklahoma Territory there was no sign of people, not even tombstones.

The Cherokee Strip was a slice of land sixty miles wide and two hundred miles long just south of the Kansas border and west of the Arkansas River. In earlier years the country had been considered a wilderness fit only for prairie dogs and Cherokees, who along with the Chickasaws, Choctaws, Creeks, and Seminoles inhabited the region until they were shoved westward by the government to make room for homesteaders. Sections of the Oklahoma Territory, not a state for another fifteen years, had first been opened in 1889 under the Homestead Act. Four years later the Indians were paid to vacate, and their six and a half million acres was declared open for white settlement. Anyone hardy enough to stake a claim, pay the modest administration fees, and farm for five years would own a 160-acre tract.

All six and a half million acres were claimed on the day of the last great land run, Saturday, September 16, 1893. A hundred thousand pioneers enticed by the promise of a free farm or a lot in one of the four already platted town sites had been crowded into makeshift camps that week, suffering in the 100-degree heat as they prepared to race into the territory on covered wagons, bug-

4

gies, buckboards, carts, and surreys, or on the backs of horses, ponies, and mules, even on bicycles or on foot. Masses of United States cavalry straddled the border at regular intervals, as if they feared a monstrous traffic jam.

At high noon the Strippers were stretched in a line across the prairie for as far as the eye could see. To the din of trumpeters and soldiers firing their guns into the air, with a gigantic yell, they stampeded across the border in search of the best land. By night-fall every acre, every lot, every blade of grass had been taken.

In the following days, on the heels of the Strippers, came droves of brew peddlers, powdered dancing girls in feather hats, amateur banjo players, thugs and con artists, faro and shell-game men, and gamblers galore. Among them was a troupe of Iowan actors and musicians who had spent the summer working the small towns south of the Cherokee Strip. The Cutler Comedy Company was a family Indian medicine show, comprised of Frank Cutler, an imposing man of forty-three who enjoyed writing poetry, and his wife, Elizabeth, and two adolescent children, Burt and Myra. The versatile Cutlers provided a variety of entertainments—miniversions of *Uncle Tom's Cabin* or *The Drunkard,* banjo solos, magic tricks, and the staple offering of all medicine shows, blackface comedy featuring Sambo or Jake in slapshoes and oversized trousers held up by elastic suspenders.

The Cutlers arrived from Edmond, thirty-five miles to the south. Just as soon as their caravan appeared on the government square, a man stepped up to speak with Cutler. He was a young roughneck with very long legs, who stood with a slouch that one day would be associated with Gary Cooper and hordes of other movie cowboys. He told Cutler how he had staked a homestead claim on behalf of his father. Then he asked for a job. Cutler asked about his experience, and the young man said that he could sing and make clownish faces and he could also do "flip-flaps," back-ward somersaults, though he admitted he had never performed before a paying audience.

Cutler could see that Joe Keaton was a drifter. He claimed to have ridden boxcars all the way from California, determined to reach the Cherokee Strip in time for the land run, not for his own gain but to win a farm for his parents. Still, the young man seemed eager to learn the medicine-show business, and Cutler needed somebody to double as a stagehand and bit performer. He offered Keaton three dollars a week and meals.

Joe Keaton lied about staking a claim. When his father arrived seven months later, he had to fend for himself.

Joe accomplished as little for himself as he did for his father. He did, however, develop a repertory of Bunyanesque tales, such as his account of his trip from Truckee, California, on board a boxcar, from which the crew threw him into forty-foot drifts of snow, leaving him to die.

Tales of his exploits as a hobo, told with a raconteur's skill, captivated pale, dainty, dark-haired Myra. Frank Cutler's daughter weighed barely ninety pounds and looked like a china doll. Sixteen in March, she was a wisp of a thing who stood four feet eleven. Her face was unremarkable. The mouth was thin, she had a noticeable overbite, her chin was weak, her gaze remote. Onstage these shortcomings were overshadowed by a lively manner and her musical accomplishments. Myra could play the piano, cornet, bull fiddle, and saxophone. Moreover, her singing and acting were passable, and from a distance she looked cute as a button.

Joe Keaton's grandiosity impressed Myra, who was too young and naive to see that his stories were complete invention. Her father, however, eyed the newcomer with hostile vigilance.

The town of Perry, a collection of tents and clapboard shanties, shot up. It was a raw place. The streets were carpeted with floury black dust that sifted into everything, even the food. At dusk, after the wind died down, the tang of gin hung over the streets. Inside darkened tents, law-abiding citizens anxiously listened for gunfire, a nightly occurrence, and bedded on the ground to avoid stray bullets.

People had money to buy amusement, but they preferred drinking, gambling, and sex to the less participatory pleasures offered by the musical stage. The Cutler Comedy Company had to compete with a half-dozen saloons, as well as gambling establishments and dance halls offering around-the-clock refreshment along with fiddle and piano music.

In some respects, Cutler's business was a typical medicine show of the late 1800s, which exploited myths about Native Americans possessing special healing powers. There was nothing particularly "Indian" about Indian medicine shows. They were simply a means of combining entertainment with the selling of "patent medicines," which were not even medicines. Free singing and dancing pulled in the customers and warmed them up for "Doc" Cutler's sales pitch. Joe Keaton, the show's newest employee, practiced a blackface monologue and a couple of songs, then worked up a specialty dance number that featured fancy high kicks. But Cutler, along with the public, was not impressed. Keaton once even secretly brought in his own claque to applaud his performance. Ernest Jones, a lawyer who was present that night, remembered, "All the applause Joe got for his bum work came from a bunch of rounders who had been brought in by Joe as boosters." Cutler also saw through the move, and Keaton was demoted to lugging scenery around.

Keaton believed Cutler had an ulterior motive. "I was a useful all-around performer," he said, "but the manager didn't like the idea of me paying attention to his daughter, and the result was I was notified to quit."

And that—not his atrocious performing—was basically the truth of the matter. The Cutlers wanted nothing to do with a loudmouth hustler who frequented saloons and whorehouses and consorted with the lowlifes found in such establishments.

Unlike many medicine shows, which were nothing more than motley rambling bands of troubadours, the Cutlers were well-fixed merchants, industrious, ferociously conventional, devoutly Republican, upstanding and civic-minded.

Frank Luke Cutler traced his ancestry to three English brothers who immigrated to the Massachusetts Bay Colony in the 1600s, then later moved north to Vermont. Generation after generation, Cutler men were strong, scrappy, independent, and known for their exceptional physiques—all developed into giants standing well over six feet and weighing more than two hundred pounds. Frank's grandfather and eight great-uncles joined up to fight with Ethan Allen's Green Mountain Boys during the Revolutionary War. In 1855 Frank's parents abandoned their tidy dry goods store in Erie, Pennsylvania, for the hardships of a farm and sod house in Cass County, in the new Nebraska Territory. Frank was four years old.

In his twenties Frank followed his brother Charles north to the tiny town of Modale in Harrison County, Iowa, about twenty-five miles north of Council Bluffs. Charles was operating a general store. The town's most successful businessman, he also served as mayor and postmaster. Young Frank clerked in the family store selling groceries, patent medicines, shoes, and clothing. Before long he married Sarah Elizabeth Shaffer.

Cutler's interests would always lean toward the artistic and intellectual. A lover of music and the stage like the rest of his family, he dovetailed his skills in merchandise with his interest in entertainment by organizing a traveling tent show. When summer came he took to the roads with his bottles of patent medicine. Medicine shows were often the only entertainment people in small towns got a chance to see, and if they were snared into buying products of dubious worth, who could blame them? For many the annual visit of families like the Cutlers was eagerly awaited, and the merchants became local celebrities.

There is no question that the cultural interests of Myra's family awed Joe Keaton, but Frank Cutler looked down on him, and that made him feel unworthy. Before long, he came to despise Myra's father and his patronizing attitudes.

By Frank Cutler's standards, Joe was a raw fellow who didn't look as if he'd ever amount to much. Sensing trouble ahead, Cutler gave him the boot. The Cutlers dismantled their tents and moved on. As soon as the weather turned cooler, they headed home for the winter.

In the months following the Oklahoma land run, Myra mourned her lost love. Just to be on the safe side, her family sent her to relatives in Lincoln, Nebraska, a distance of some three hundred miles. But Frank Cutler had not seen the last of Joe Keaton.

Joseph Hallie Keaton was born in 1867, seventeen miles outside of Terre Haute, Indiana, in Prairie Creek Township, where his father owned a gristmill. The Keatons, like Plantagenet kings, believed in economy of Christian names, and for five generations each firstborn son had been named Joseph.

A few years later, Joe's father got tired of grinding grain and bought the Henderson House Hotel in downtown Terre Haute, where he moved his family from the country. When Joe was growing up in this busy little city in the 1870s, powerful dreams were stirring. On the banks of the Wabash River, flanked by rolling green hills containing rich deposits of coal and iron ore, Terre Haute stood poised to become the Pittsburgh of the Midwest. In the space of two decades its population ballooned by nearly 300 percent.

But by 1893 Terre Haute's boom had evaporated. Still, Joe Keaton's ambitions, like those of such other local boys of his generation as Eugene Debs and Theodore Dreiser, had been formed by the energy and optimism that had built Terre Haute.

Joe had a million plans, but succeeding in them was another matter. Still floundering at the age of twenty-six, he was handed $100 and a gun by his disgusted father, who sent him off with instructions to make something of himself. Joe headed for the frontier.

In writing letters and articles about events that shaped him, Joe presented his life as a series of mythic tableaus: Davy Crockett becomes a cocky Joe battling snowdrifts forty feet deep; Pecos Bill as Joe nabbing crooks in a Denver poker game. His mulligan stew of all-American-boy fantasies pointedly failed to mention sundry details like employment, as if he also imagined himself pampered and monied. This was hardly the case. In every respect, the Keatons were plain people.

Joe Keaton was the end product of seven generations of a gentle religious sect that embraces nonviolence as a way of life. The beginnings of the Keatons in America can be found in William Hinshaw's monumental *Encyclopedia of American Quaker Genealogy,* with its relentlessly detailed abstracts of births, deaths, and marriages, its minutes of meetings, separated by sex, its picture of independent, sober-minded men and women who had fled religious persecution.

Founded in midseventeenth-century England by George Fox, a preacher dissatisfied with the Church of England, the Religious Society of Friends were people who refused to take oaths, bear arms, or own slaves. They treated women and men as equals and believed church clergy had no special authority. For these beliefs— and because they rejected all ritual and sat silently in worship waiting for God to speak directly to each one—they were ridiculed, jailed, some even executed. Quakers began arriving in the colonies in 1656. The Keatons, if not among the very first wave, were close behind.

The first Keaton to appear in Quaker records was Henry Keaton (sometimes spelled Keton). The name, which means shepherd's hut, can be traced back to the eleventh century and the Leicestershire village of Ketton. By the 1690s Henry Keaton was an industrious small farmer, planting tobacco and corn on his two hundred acres in the northeast corner of North Carolina, at Newbegun Creek in swampy Pasquotank County (later called Symons Creek). By 1700, when the Society of Friends had become the most important religious group in the colony, Henry Keaton was a respected figure among the Quaker settlement. With two of his friends, he distinguished himself by building a meeting-house in 1706 at Symons Creek, now historic as the first church of any denomination in North Carolina.

For almost 150 years Henry Keaton's descendants continued to prosper and multiply, always marrying, as their religion required, within the Society to Scotts, Bundys, and Truebloods. After the Revolutionary War, a conflict the Quakers opposed on religious grounds, their influence began to decline, although Henry's great-grandson Joseph was elected to the North Carolina State Senate in 1788.

In the first three decades of the nineteenth century, a number of the Keatons and their kin joined the exodus to the new state of Indiana, whose constitution forbade slavery. By 1833, Joe Keaton's grandfather, Joseph Zachariah Keaton, had established himself as a farmer in Prairie Creek Township, Vigo County, Indiana, where he married his neighbor's fifteen-year-old daughter, Margaret Trueblood, and proceeded to sire ten children.

This Indiana Joseph Keaton, the first about whom there are significant personal details, was apparently an adventurous man, sometimes impulsive, a dreamer liable to be carried away by sudden fancies and extreme solutions. In his forties, he left his wife to tend the farm and raise their surviving nine children as best she could while he went to California to prospect for gold. He absented himself for seven years, forced home only after the Civil War broke out. His adventures in the West were to fuel the fantasies of his grandson Joseph Hallie, who did not believe that putting up guests at the Henderson House Hotel was his destiny.

With a temperament too volatile for regular work, Joe Keaton dreamed of getting away from Terre Haute. He earned a reputation as the town bad boy and proved a disgrace to his parents' household and the memory of his meek Quaker forebears. He received practically no schooling because his teachers couldn't control him.

"I had fought every kid that ever looked like a fight," Joe proudly recalled, "and had carried more black eyes than all of them put together, which gave me the nick name of 'Dick Dead Eye,'" from Gilbert and Sullivan's villainous sailor in *H.M.S. Pinafore*. "I became the pride of Wabash Avenue," he said, "and continued to play 'hooky' and fight all comers." At home, around his younger sisters and brother—Rosa, Birdie, and Jessie Bert—he blustered and bragged about his plans to run away and join the circus. But although he was the kind of unmanageable kid whose parents might have felt secret relief if he had run away, he never carried out his threats. Instead, Dick Dead Eye hung around the pool halls shining shoes.

For all his aversion to school, Joe learned to read and write, and he also came across as articulate in conversation and seems to have been equally expressive in his literary composition. Actually, he had a gift for confessional journalism—a complement to his gift for self-promotion—and published a number of highly diverting articles about himself and his family. Later on, he would peck out his prose on a Blickensderfer, the first portable typewriter, which he taught himself to operate and hauled along wherever he traveled.

By the spring of 1894, Joe Keaton, the bad boy of Terre Haute, was drifting about in Kansas or Nebraska, content to pick up menial jobs or drive a hack.

One day as he returned to his lodgings the desk clerk stopped him: "There's a lady in the parlor waiting to see you."

Nobody could have been more startled than Joe when he saw Frank Cutler's peanut-sized daughter in the sitting room. What she had to say was more shocking still: The little girl whom he had not laid eyes on for eight months had journeyed alone all the way from Lincoln just to find her true love. Myra reminded him of their promise never to forget each other. She had burned her bridges in order to become his wife.

Like a thief who finds himself about to be hauled off to jail for a crime he can't remember committing, Joe was flabbergasted. He had never intended to marry Myra. He couldn't even afford to buy himself a square meal. How could he support a wife? Instead of admitting this, he tried to persuade her to go home.

Myra was willful. "The little girl," as Joe thought of her, declared that "she was contented to be my wife and fight life's battles among strangers." They were married by a justice of the peace

on the morning of May 31, 1894. When time came to pay two
dollars, Joe fumbled in his pockets but could scrape together only
$1.90, all the cash he had in the world. The justice of the peace
reduced his fee to ninety-five cents and treated them to a wedding
breakfast of fried eggs and ham.

Back in Perry, people doubted that Joe could really love Myra.
There had to be another motive. "Joe afterward got even with
Cutler by marrying his daughter," the lawyer Ernest Jones
decided.

It is more likely that Joe calculated the newlyweds would be
forgiven and welcomed into the medicine show. It didn't work out
that way, though. Frank Cutler did not invite Joe and Myra to
return to Iowa. In fact, he sent word that the bride would not be
welcome in Modale, and that went doubly for the bum she had
married.

Joe was stuck with Myra.

But Myra was also stuck with Joe.

That summer she was not long in learning that she had thrown
in her lot with a man who seldom had a dollar in his pocket.
Becoming a husband did not turn Joe into a good worker—in
fact, he simply was not a worker at all.

He was a stranger to personal discipline, still a juvenile at
almost twenty-seven. When Dick Dead Eye's raging temper flared,
he would fight by kicking his opponent's head. With his long legs,
he could easily kick straight up to a height of eight feet, even
higher with a flying hitch kick that involved feinting with his left
foot, then jumping into the air before attacking with his right
foot. All of this took place so quickly that most people never saw
his foot coming.

"He never laid a hand on a man," Myra would recall admiringly. He never had to, because "that hitch kick could break a jaw."

Soon after the wedding, Joe's ambitions to become an actor
were rekindled by the affronts he had suffered from his father-in-
law. He bought a pair of slapshoes and determined to succeed in
show business, with or without the help of Frank Cutler. The only
problem was that he lacked talent and experience.

Myra had to rescue them. It is ironic that she earned money
from music and acting, using the very same skills she had turned
her back on when leaving home.

Practically destitute, they found work, according to Joe, "as regular medicine show actors." And while Myra acted, sang, danced, and played a grueling schedule of three shows a night, Joe never set foot onstage. He did bone-wearying manual labor, setting up, tearing down, shoving on to the next stop. He also helped the "doctor" hawk compounds that promised to grow hair overnight, make short people taller, and cure epilepsy, Saint Vitus' dance, convulsions, hysteria, rheumatism, sciatica, insomnia, and disorders of the nervous system. The active ingredient of these exotic mixtures was 50 to 70 percent alcohol.

Despite the promise of regular wages, the money was by no means assured, and Myra and Joe lived hand-to-mouth. Joe recalled that "many a time I had to take a club along when I went to get my salary and many a time I missed it by waiting a day too long."

Just as the medicine-show wagons thumped up and down the rutted roads of eastern Kansas, winding across the prairie from village to village, so did the Keaton marriage limp along. By most people's standards, the marriage was a failure. Though Joe's macho posturing colors almost everything he ever wrote, his account of their first year together cannot conceal despair. His little-girl bride, who had been brought up in middle-class, middle-American comfort, already was learning to bite her tongue. Even her silence must have been a reproach to him. In the months after the elopement Joe could see that her determination to become his wife had little to do with nesting or maternal instincts. Unlike other girls her age, she had no domestic skills, no interest in housekeeping, and did not learn to cook until she was in her thirties. One habit she did pick up early was smoking cigarettes, rolling her own from Bull Durham tobacco.

Nor was her eagerness to marry based on physical passion. She seems to have been rather prudish. Joe, ten years older, was sexually experienced, but his early activity probably had been with prostitutes, and later in life he continued to feel most comfortable with this type of sexual partner.

Nevertheless, in February 1895, after the Keatons had been married eight months, Myra became pregnant.

Myra and Joe were homeless and dirt poor. Their few belongings were carted in sacks from town to town. The volatile Joe's

delight in kick-fighting often got them fired. They were never able
to save a nickel. Even after Myra's pregnancy could no longer be
disguised, she was forced to keep on working, playing two or three
shows a night, then riding a wagon over treacherous cow trails to
the next town.

Myra's rift with her family had not healed by the forthcoming
birth of Frank Cutler's first grandchild. The pregnant daughter
was not invited to come home for her confinement, with or without spouse, as was the custom. The Cutlers had virtually disowned
her.

That summer they visited Joe's family in Perry. His father, who
suffered from chronic Bright's disease, had sold the Henderson
House. Although Joe's sisters Rosa and Birdie were married, his
brother, Jessie Bert, continued to live at home. On that visit, the
couple went for a buggy ride that ended with the horse running
away and throwing Myra into the road. This was not the only accident she suffered during her pregnancy. In Cottonwood Falls,
Kansas, while employed by the Mohawk Indian Medicine Show, a
tent fell on her. In her ninth month, she stepped off the stage onto
a rickety chair, which collapsed under her. These accidents can be
accounted for, in part, as simply the routine hazards of touring.
But they also suggest her anxiety about motherhood; perhaps she
would have been relieved to be free of it. If one looks at Myra's
life as a whole, there can be no doubt that she lacked mothering
instincts.

Later on, for practical reasons, she would feel obliged to preserve appearances and stick up for Joe. It was lightning, not his
reckless driving, that caused the horse to bolt in Perry. Other
mishaps were conveniently attributed to acts of God. Across the
years these unfortunate incidents would be stitched together into a
quilt of lies and half-truths that made the Keatons sound pretty
much like a normal couple, when they were anything but. With
hindsight, those prenatal accidents seem due less to chance than to
pure and simple carelessness, a weather vane of the couple's com-
petence to care for children.

2. THE TRAINS OF WOODSON COUNTY

Woodson County, Kansas, was hay country, where grass shot up as high as a person's head and sometimes higher, whose county seat at Yates Center proudly called itself "The Prairie Hay Capital of the World" for its annual harvest of hundreds of thousands of tons. The fields were dotted with mowers whipping their scythes through the coarse grass, the hot roads crowded with wagons, their haystacks towering so high that they seemed about to topple over from the weight.

Buster Keaton was born on a wet autumn Friday night in Piqua, a railroad town with a population of two hundred. At all hours of the day piercing whistles blasted, brakes screeched, and bells clanged. Four passenger trains stopped there each day, bound for Wichita, and many freight trains stopped as well, mammoth iron machines lugging the precious wealth of the hay capital of the world. Even though it was surrounded by silent fields, the town vibrated with a racket almost symphonic.

The Mohawk Indian Medicine Show arrived in late September, when the leaves were beginning to turn. Short-funded, the company could not afford to stay in either of Piqua's hotels, so they camped in tents. Attendance at their shows was sparse. For one thing, they were competing with Ringling Brothers Circus, seven miles away in Iola.

The following week the weather turned cold and windy. Father Nicholas Fowler at St. Martin's Catholic Church gave permission to move the show indoors to the church hall. That's where Myra went into labor on October 4, 1895. She delivered across the street in a two-story, clapboard cube house, the home of a German-born carpenter named Jacob Haen and his wife, Barbara. The local midwife, Theresa Ullrich, attended the delivery. The baby had straight brown hair and popping dark eyes that reminded Myra of buttons.

His given name was Joseph Frank Keaton: Joseph in the Keaton tradition and Frank for Myra's stubborn father, who was still withholding his blessing from the couple. Joe later changed the middle name to Francis. No official acknowledgment was ever made of the infant's arrival. Piqua's doctor did not bother to report babies born in transit, nor did the local paper record the event. Joe and Myra also neglected to file a birth certificate, not surprising given the disorder of their lives. It took nine months for them to arrange a baptism. Joe Keaton later claimed that a brisk wind on the day of his son's birth was in fact a twister that "blew our tent away and almost wrecked the town." Buster took the tale further, rubbing Piqua off the map of Kansas. "Pickway itself soon afterward was blown away during a cyclone," Keaton insisted in his autobiography, *My Wonderful World of Slapstick*.

In fact, those early weeks in Piqua, with its train whistles and incessant commotion, would leave a curious imprint on Buster. Throughout his life he would feel a passionate love for trains. A number of his films would feature trains, most notably his master-piece, *The General*, whose title refers not to a military commander but to a Confederate locomotive.

A train steamed into La Ciotat station, Paris, on December 28, 1895. As it rolled closer and closer, the crowd began to scream. The train appeared to be rushing straight at them. People were frightened out of their wits.

The terrified spectators—thirty-three to be exact—were not actually waiting alongside the tracks at La Ciotat but were in fact watching images of the train projected on a white screen, at the Grand Café, 14 Boulevard des Capucines. It was Louis and Auguste Lumière's first paid demonstration of motion pictures, heady stuff that would become the prototype of cinematic thrills for a century to come.

The following spring, similar gasps would be heard during the first theatrical exhibition of motion pictures in the United States at Koster & Bial's Music Hall on West Thirty-fourth Street in New

York City. Thomas A. Edison's Vitascope projected hand-colored film fragments showing a scenic view of the ocean followed by a comic boxing match. Next was a tall blond dancer named Annabelle swaying almost life-sized on the screen. Patrons broke into cheers. "Wonderfully real and singularly exciting," marveled *The New York Times*.

While the French were shrieking at oncoming trains and patrons of Koster & Bial's were cheering colorful dancers, Joe Keaton had been hustling to feed three mouths. Had news of this novel technology somehow reached him, he would not have been the least bit impressed. Any actor who allowed his face to be projected ten feet high onto a blank screen was plainly stupid, he believed, a view he continued to hold for much of his life.

Less than a hundred miles southeast of Piqua, Kansas had been transformed by the discovery of coal and zinc some twenty years earlier. Mines worth hundreds of millions of dollars had been turning out a third of the nation's coal with imported labor from Eastern Europe. It was to these tough mining gulags that the Keatons roamed with their infant son.

Years later the walls of Buster Keaton's den would be covered with photographs. When visitors stopped by he proudly pointed out one particular picture of himself taken at the age of four and said that was the year he began drawing a salary in show business. "Before that," he joked, "I was a burden on my parents." Keaton in fact was at least five when the picture was taken. But the rest is true. It is easy to understand why he felt that he had been a nuisance.

Joe and Myra were poor parents. Before reaching his second birthday, baby Joe (the nickname Buster was yet to come) had brushes with death involving suffocation, incineration, falls, mutilation, and natural calamities. These crises Joe and Myra attributed to bad luck and force majeure rather than to their own neglect. For much of his first two years, little Joe slept mashed in a suitcase. He played backstage in the cramped, makeshift theaters of the mining towns. The family often roughed it in tents, and sometimes they were lucky enough to stay in boardinghouses. When they traveled to the next town, Joe bought a train ticket for Myra and the baby, and he walked to save money.

Myra was overwhelmed by the unending tasks of child care. She brought the baby along to the lodge halls and penned him backstage in a trunk. One day a stagehand accidentally brushed against the trunk and knocked the lid down. Myra later found her son half dead. Buster was kept tied up to a pole in the wings until it became impractical. Fearful of losing their jobs, Joe and Myra fed him sips of beer, but alcohol didn't quiet him. Nor did the back of Joe's hand.

Joe had no tolerance for childish behavior. The baby, he said, "would just butt in any old time. He would howl and make so much noise that the stage manager would have to let him crawl out on the stage." He would scuttle onstage and pop up between his father's legs while Joe was reciting a blackface monologue, generally drawing a bigger laugh than his father. Once Buster learned to walk, he toddled onstage whenever he felt like it and clung to Myra's skirt.

Buster was twenty months old when a storm struck the town where they were playing. From his bed on the second floor, he got up to investigate. A tornado sucked him out the window and up into a swirling black chute. His body rotated violently through space. Then just as suddenly he found himself on the ground again in a field. Or so he said. As did his parents.

Joe and Myra began to regard the boy as conspicuously different from other children, although his behavior seems perfectly normal for a child of two. His lungs seemed more powerful, his clinging more perverse, his accidents more troublesome. They felt he couldn't do anything right. The bad baby sounds much like a younger model of Joe himself. That must have pleased him immensely.

Buster tumbled down a flight of stairs, all the way from the top to the landing. In 1904, Joe remembered the incident occurring when his son was eighteen months old. Buster in subsequent retellings would push the date back to six months. Whichever date is correct, Joe was relieved to find the boy crying but unhurt. Making a joke out of it, Joe and an actor in their touring company complimented the child on his acrobatic skill and his indestructibility.

"Gee whiz," George Pardey, the actor, whistled, "he's a regular buster!"

"I'm going to call him by it," said Joe. And indeed, Buster served him well the rest of his life.

The first mention of Buster's nickname appeared some five

years after the accident in a newspaper interview. In this 1903 clipping Myra Keaton attributes the name to "a family friend" but did not mention Pardey by name. The following year Joe identified him in an interview with the *New York Dramatic Mirror*, a theatrical trade paper, by mentioning his name and profession—"an old-time legitimate comedian," he said. A small-time Midwestern actor, Pardey left no other footprints in theatrical history.

In his autobiography, Keaton changed the story: "When I was six months old, I fell downstairs and burst into tears. Houdini, who was nearby, picked me up, and said, 'My, what a Buster.'" However, when Buster was six months, the Keatons had not yet met Harry Houdini.

The first revelations about Buster's name appeared *after* Houdini had become an international star. Had he truly been the author of Buster's name, nothing in the world would have prevented Joe Keaton from saying so. The distinction would never have been conferred on a player so obscure as to be totally unknown to the readership of vaudeville's leading trade paper.

Although linking the Keatons with Houdini sounds like something Joe might have dreamed up, it was not his idea. It was in 1921 that Buster himself decided to install the magician as a cornerstone of his legend (although it could have been the work of Hollywood's shrewdest press agent, Harry Brand). This fiction, recast with a bankable star replacing a dress extra, must have sounded a great deal more interesting to Keaton, who at that time was standing on the brink of movie fame.

Still, in all likelihood, Keaton came to believe his own family fable, layered like lasagna with bits of melodrama, prairie miracles, and dime-novel plot twists. Houdini himself never objected.

Fabrications aside, Harry Houdini was a significant force in Buster's life. He was the great model of the fearless male, defying fate, executing impossible escapes. While others idolized Theodore Roosevelt after his charge at the Battle of San Juan Hill, Buster's hero was the master mystifier, for whom no fall would be dangerous enough, no stunt sufficiently life-threatening.

Joe was delighted with the new name: Buster sounded manly and feisty, a perfect description for Joseph Keaton the Sixth, and would eventually lead Joe to bill Buster as "The Little Boy Who Can't Be Damaged."

At that time, *buster* was a word with at least two meanings: one was a destructive natural force, the other a sturdy child, tough and full of beans. Five years later, Hearst cartoonist Richard Felton Outcault created a comic strip about a blond boy named Buster Brown and his faithful talking dog, Tige. In each strip mischievous Buster Brown gets into trouble and receives the punishment he deserves. The cartoon Buster, dressed in a sailor hat and foppish Little Lord Fauntleroy suit, was a more refined version of the character created by Joe Keaton, but the similarities between the two Busters were undeniable. Outcault continued the popular strip until 1920, eventually licensing merchandising rights to a number of enterprises, including a children's shoe company, two of which continued to survive into the 1990s.

When Joe Keaton was challenged in 1907 about which Buster was the original, he declared—inaccurately—his son had the name since the day he was born. Outcault insisted that the characters of Buster Brown and his friend Mary Jane were based on his own children. Nevertheless, Joe Keaton was right. His Buster came first.

It was a July morning—wash day. On the shady porch of the boardinghouse, the Keaton baby watched the hired girl trot back and forth between the clothesline and one of the tubs where she kept feeding wet clothes into the wringer. He was fascinated.

Finally he ventured down the porch steps, approached the machine, and stared for a few seconds before reaching up to poke at the rolls with his right index finger. Without warning, the steel pressure springs burst open and snapped shut, catching his finger. The rolls of solid white rubber began to suck his fingertip into its jaws.

Hearing his outcry, the servant flew across the yard. She tried to yank his finger loose, but the wringer refused to open its rollers and give it up. The girl then raced to the theater to fetch his parents. The wringer had to be dismantled, screw by screw, and by then the finger was shredded into bloody pulp.

They sent for a doctor, who amputated the finger at the first joint.

This accident took place in the summer of 1897. In his autobiography more than sixty years later, Buster recalled that on that same day, a short time later, he went outside again, only to be hit by a falling brick that gashed his temple. Only hours later came the twister that blew him out of the bedroom window—altogether "a pretty strenuous day" for a child of eighteen months.

Keaton's disfigured finger would never become a handicap. In 1961 the wringer accident would be re-created during a *Twilight Zone* episode titled "Once Upon a Time," in which Keaton played a janitor who uses a clothes washer to wring out a wet pair of trousers, apparently having no hesitation about using the wringer as a prop to get a laugh. Keaton never tried to hide his loss, unlike Harold Lloyd, who as an adult lost several fingers in a bomb explosion and always wore a glove in films.

In the summer of 1897 Joe turned thirty and Myra was twenty. They were doing as badly as performers as they were as parents. They had no particular act, no decent sketch they could call their own. There was nothing special about a woman cornet player or Joe's knockabout dancing and acrobatics—or about the blackface Sambo routines that he had mastered at long last.

The impoverished Keatons continued to soldier on, their lives full of daily hardships, their baby's health fragile after the amputation of his fingertip. Since the constant traveling was too strenuous for him, he desperately needed someplace to settle for a while.

That summer they got work with a stock company at Forest Park outside of Pittsburg, Kansas, a twenty-year-old mining town. When the season ended, Joe took off with the J.T.R. Clark medicine show while Myra and Buster stayed behind in Pittsburg. Soon Joe wired that he had wangled an engagement for Myra and she should join him immediately. Since the baby couldn't travel, she turned to Guy Fritts, an actor whose family lived in the town.

Buster, as Fritts remembered it, "was sick and Mrs. Keaton couldn't take him with her. My mother took charge of the youngster and kept him until he got well enough to join his parents."

In December the Keatons returned to Pittsburg, where they found winter work with a road show called the California Concert Company. "Dr." Thomas B. Hill, the owner of the show, assigned the Keatons minor roles and allowed Joe to do a Sambo routine with an Irish brogue.

A few days earlier Hill had hired a bright young man named Harry Houdini and his singer wife, Bess, another couple who had been taking hard knocks. Houdini had plans to become the next Jean Robert Houdin, the renowned French magician whose name he took.

He was born Erik Weisz, the fifth son of a Hungarian rabbi, in Budapest in 1874, and grew up in the Yorkville section of New York. With his wife as assistant, Houdini developed a handcuff escape act and began billing himself as the King of Handcuffs. Handcuff acts were quite common, but others used fake cuffs and Houdini practiced with real ones. So far the act had met with limited success.

Joe got along extremely well with the twenty-three-year-old Houdini, whom he treated like a younger brother and affectionately called "Boots." By Christmastime, when the company was playing in Cherokee, the two couples spent all their time together. They had much in common. In a snapshot taken that winter—and later misdated by four years to prove that Harry Houdini had been present at Buster's birth—the couples pose outside a tent with Dr. Hill, the resident Kickapoos, and a pair of dogs. Myra and Bess are dolled up in frilly gowns and hats, but it is Joe who dominates the picture, slouching like one of the outlaw Dalton brothers, legs defiantly apart, one hand on his hip, hat cocked at a rakish angle, a half-smoked cigar held between his fingers.

The California Concert Company moved on to Columbus and Galena. In his diary, Houdini kept careful records of the company's itinerary, along with the size of the houses it played to, which had been fair. But after Christmas, business dropped off sharply. The worried Dr. Hill asked Houdini to stage a phony seance. Facing the prospect of unemployment again, he held one for a full house at Papp's Opera House in Galena. Even so, the California Concert Company folded, and the Keatons and Houdinis went their separate ways.

Meeting Houdini proved a major turning point for the Keatons. It forced Joe to confront his own squandered past, which strengthened his resolve to break into vaudeville with a professional act and decent clothing. He knew exactly what he wanted: white spats and patent-leather shoes, a fancy tuxedo, and suits that looked good "on and off the stage." As for the act, that was a problem.

3 KEEP YOUR EYE ON THE KID

Joe and Myra decided to try their luck in vaudeville. Risking their meager savings, they arrived in New York City in November of 1899. In spite of high hopes, they had much to learn about how big-league show business operated. The fall season was well under way, and bookings had been arranged months earlier. Without advance bookings, there was no work. Trudging around to the theatrical booking offices, Joe learned just how tough New York could be.

Seeking a shortcut to success, some Rosetta stone to open the doors of vaudeville, Joe watched other acts while he struggled to construct a novel routine that would separate him from the rest. He first worked up an acrobatic comedy routine, "The Man Who Broke Chairs," stolen from a kung fu acrobat. This was soon abandoned for "The Man with a Table." Dressed as a clown, he would dive onto a sturdy kitchen table, turn handsprings, and plunge headfirst to the floor. After stacking a chair on the tabletop, he jumped from the floor and landed on the chair seat, shattering the chair and bruising his shins. Myra, in her dainty yellow gown, provided the refined element with her cornet solos. For a finale, she posed on the table and Joe kicked off her hat.

Joe and Myra finally found work at Huber's, a dime museum on Union Square. It was not real vaudeville. Dime museums, first popularized by P. T. Barnum in the 1840s, supplemented their freak-show flea circuses and Siamese twins exhibitions with variety acts—comics, acrobats, magicians, song-and-dance teams. Generally dime museums were the lowest form of entertainment, on a par with medicine shows. Nevertheless, Huber's was one of the half dozen most important dime museums in the country, and it would survive until the 1960s.

The Keatons, in the least desirable opening spot, had to repeat their routine fifteen to twenty times a day, beginning at nine in the morning and ending at 11:00 P.M. The wages amounted to ten dollars a week for Joe and Myra together.

With his parents gone all day, four-year-old Buster would remain at their rooming house. At six each evening, in costume and full makeup, his mother raced across Fourteenth Street so that she could give him supper.

After a week at Huber's, Joe and Myra were let go. Variety halls had no use for repeaters.

Christmas was coming, and the weather had turned bitter. Joe continued to tramp through agents' offices and often took his son along for company. One day on Fourteenth Street he spied Tony Pastor, one of the best-known vaudeville producers in the business, climbing out of a cab. In despair, Joe collared him on the sidewalk outside his Union Square theater and began pitching his act as rapid-fire as a bottle of Kickapoo tonic. Pastor, a portly man of sixty-five, known to be notoriously softhearted, must have pitied Joe and the shivering little boy at his side. He promised Joe an audition.

On December 18, 1899, Joe and Myra made their debut on a bill with various established acts. Tony Pastor operated a continuous performance house, requiring the Keatons to do three, perhaps four shows daily, a grueling routine. As befitted newcomers, "Mr. and Mrs. Joe Keaton, sketch team" appeared next to last on the program, before the Vitagraph, a standard closing "act" consisting of film fragments projected on a screen. This device had been around for several years, since Koster & Bial had begun presenting Edison's films, and other vaudeville houses were quick to follow. Since movies had not yet learned to tell stories, audience interest seemed to be flagging.

The Keatons were terrible. Tony Pastor was not fussy about closing acts. He recruited the cheapest attractions, which meant greenhorns like the Keatons, because vaudeville customers began leaving after the headliners' curtain calls. Closing attractions always "played to haircuts," show business slang for telling gags to the backs of people's heads.

"The act didn't go," Joe admitted. "'Twas bad." Bad yes, hopeless no. Joe continued to hustle, and they managed to attract the notice of a talent scout for the blue-chip Proctor circuit, a big-time chain of a dozen theaters, four in New York alone, which offered them a week's engagement.

Officially in show business now, Joe shopped for last-minute presents that he had never expected to afford. He bought Myra an alto saxophone, which she would teach herself to play and eventually incorporate into the act. For Buster there was a fat round ball used in playing the recently invented game of basketball.

On New Year's Day, 1900, the Keatons began their second big-time engagement in New York in the Taj Mahal of the city's showplaces, the three-year-old, 4,900-seat Pleasure Palace, located at Third Avenue and Fifty-eighth Street. By now the city's theater district was inching uptown, from East Fourteenth to West Twenty-third Street, then to Herald Square on West Thirty-fourth, and finally to Longacre Square.

That first freezing Monday of the new century, Proctor's doors opened at noon with the usual mixture of acts—a humorist, a boy soprano, a pair of blackface comedians, and a Hebrew cakewalk team—which ran continuously until 11:00 P.M. The Keatons, now described as an "acrobatic comedy duo," did not rate a review. They were again one of the "chasers" who emptied the theater, before stereopticon slides displaying "Christmas Views" and Paley's Kalatechnoscope with its flickering moving pictures of the surf at Coney Island.

Coincidentally, headlining at Keith's Union Square that same week was Harry Houdini. In the space of two years he had leapfrogged from medicine showman to vaudeville headliner.

The Keatons survived the spring playing at beer gardens in Brooklyn and New Jersey. By early in the summer they were playing the piers in Asbury Park and Atlantic City. That summer was memorable for Buster. Vaudeville was a Felliniesque dream—surreal electric lights, Strauss waltzes, dressing rooms saturated with layer on layer of greasepaint, women with powder-dusted breasts and carnation-red lips, sumptuous meringues who fawned over him and cuddled him in their laps. Thrilled by the magicians and jugglers, he watched their split-second timing and listened to the reaction of the audience. It was an education.

On October 27, 1900, the Keatons and their "Man with a Table" act opened at Wonderland in Wilmington, Delaware. For some reason, perhaps only the novelty of it, Myra and Joe suddenly decided to bring Buster onstage during a matinee. He was dressed up in a tramp costume like Joe's, with a bald red wig, baggy pants, and big shoes, and instructed to station himself at the side of the stage with his legs crossed and watch his father and mother. Afterward the theater's owner, annoyed, told Joe to take Buster off.

"He's a handicap," warned William Dockstader.

He was right. Buster was a pointless detraction from Joe's routine. But a few days later Dockstader relented because there would be a lot of children in the matinee audience.

In that matinee Buster and his father performed a variation of the roughhouse that took place between them offstage, when Joe would toss the little boy up on a table or slide him down a wall. Then they began to improvise on the theme of a father attempting to discipline a mischievous son. Joe picked up Buster and walked him to the footlights. "Father hates to be rough," he said, giving him a kiss and turning away. The only way to raise kids, Joe confided to the audience, was to be gentle but firm. "Never let 'em walk over you." In a wink, Buster threw his basketball and knocked Joe flat on his face. Buster chased his ball, intrepidly stepping over his fallen father. The audience ate it up.

The rest of the week, Buster invented fresh ways to torment his father while Joe attempted to discipline him. Joe dropped Buster onstage, spun him around, and bounced him against a piece of scenery. As a finale, he swung him high up into the air, then hurled him into the wings. The audience waited in shocked silence. Several seconds went by before a stagehand came onstage carrying Buster, who was grinning impudently. "Is this yours, Mr. Keaton?" asked the hand. By then the audience had begun to laugh uproariously.

Little Buster was clever and uninhibited, a natural jelly-legged little clown. Joe realized that his boy might transform their ordinary act into something quite special. Dockstader had gladly paid an extra ten dollars for the child.

After Wonderland, the Keatons signed with the Burke & Chase road company and struck off for the Midwest: Toledo, Cincinnati, Chicago, and St. Louis. While on the road, Joe ran an advertisement in the *New York Dramatic Mirror,* which offered the Keatons "assisted by our little son, Buster, the world's smallest comedian." There were no takers. Joe did not realize the legal problems involved. Theater managers, Dockstader being an exception, were extremely careful about breaking protective laws regulating the work of child entertainers.

The state of New York specifically prohibited "employing a minor in a theatrical exhibition." No child under the age of sixteen was permitted to sing, dance, juggle, or perform wire work or acrobatics of any kind. No child under seven was allowed onstage in any capacity whatsoever. Children over seven could appear in speaking parts with a special permit, issued to parents by the Society for the Prevention of Cruelty to Children, also known as the Gerry Society, a private child-welfare agency acting as a law-enforcement arm for the state.

Organized in 1875 to look after the rights of children, the SPCC was known as the Gerry Society after its founder, Elbridge T. Gerry, grandson of the U.S. vice president who had originated the practice of "gerrymandering." A successful attorney, Gerry became obsessed with youngsters who were being either exploited in the workplace or mistreated by their parents at home. Well ahead of his time, Gerry believed this social problem to be shameful, but a majority of Americans did not agree. Since the idea of children having any particular rights was novel, Gerry was frequently classified as a fanatic. Although he condemned all parents who tried to profit from their children's labor, he took a particularly hard line on "stage" parents and called their offspring "child-slaves of the stage."

The man who took up the problem of five-year-old Buster Keaton was James Austin Fynes, Proctor's general manager. Fynes thought Buster was immensely talented and devised a strategy for outfoxing the Society for the Prevention of Cruelty to Children. He first advised Joe to add two years to Buster's age, making him seven, the legal age for speaking parts onstage.

Also at Fynes's suggestion, Joe wrote a letter to the Gerry Society.

December 27, 1900
The Gerry Society

Dear Sir:

I have a son age 7 years. That possesses great theatrical talent. And in as much as he neither sings nor performs any
Acrobatic Feats. Would like to arrange to introduce him
on the Proctor Circuit in February. . . . The boy is a *comedian*. And if you can encourage me in any way would call
as soon as we get into New York. And complete the
arrangements. Am willing to aid the Society in Any way.

> *Joseph Keaton*
> *624 G St. Perry, Oklahoma*

The Gerry Society mailed him a form letter instructing him to
fill out the proper application at its office forty-eight hours before
opening.

He wrote the Gerry Society again:

I must state again that our little son does not in any way
indulge in any dancing, singing, or acrobatic feats whatever. And that we have never exhibited him in New York.
But we have the opportunity now. And should he be successful we are perfectly willing to aid your Society in any
way. So kindly send me the proper blanks and will fill them
out as requested.

> *Yours Professionally Mr.*
> *and Mrs. Joseph Keaton*

P.S. "Our son's particular line of work is comedy."

The Society replied that he still had to apply in person.

By February, Joe was happy with his son's progress. Buster was
a natural. Joe fed him old and new tricks, as well as peppery dialogue: Buster from the outset was no silent partner. He was
immensely animated. Two sassy expressions—"Pos-it-ively NO!"
and "That's what makes me mad!"—would become famous catch-
phrases associated with their act. Joe created Buster's stage personality: the half-strutting, half-waddling walk, the innocent gaze, and

later the solemn expression. Later Keaton insisted that he owed everything to his father.

Before the Keatons hit New York, Joe took out an ad in the leading theatrical paper: "KEEP YOUR EYE ON THE KID." They unwrapped the new act at Proctor's in Albany, with the Kid and the Kid's dad strutting onstage in identical red wigs and white clown makeup, baggy pants, red galways, and white spats. So enthusiastic was audience reaction that the manager moved them three times during the week to better spots on the bill. The Kid made the difference; the Keatons had found the road to success at last. "The Keatons with Buster made a ten-strike," reported the *Dramatic Mirror.* Now the ads presented him as:

B U S T E R

The smallest real comedian.

Buster made his New York debut at Proctor's 125th Street on March 11, 1901. Triumphant, the Keatons moved on to Proctor's Palace and then during Easter week were booked at Tony Pastor's, where they were held over and graduated from three shows a day to two. The *New York Clipper* praised Buster to the skies, marveling over his precocious self-assurance: "The tiny comedian is perfectly at ease in his work, natural, finished, and artistic."

For the rest of his life, Buster would never get over his feeling of superiority that resulted from being the center of attention, a special little boy whom people made a fuss over. As the It boy of 1901 he developed a variety of skills that he would use throughout his life: how to make grand entrances and imperious exits, how to stop the show, how to give plenty of electricity. He became addicted to a potent drug that he would never be able to kick: excitement.

"Pop made me the featured performer of our act when I was five," he said. Joe may have featured him, but it was Buster who made himself a star. For as long as he could remember he had been the nuisance, always in Joe and Myra's way. Now, he said, "I was their partner." He was their meal ticket, too, but he didn't know it yet.

Practically overnight the Keatons' lives changed dramatically.

Their weekly salary shot up from about $50 to $225, more than $2,500 in current dollars. From a boardinghouse on East Fifteenth Street they moved to an apartment on Twenty-first Street. Offers of bookings rained down on them, to the point that they needed someone to handle the contracts and signed with a personal manager. Two months later Joe fired him and took over the management himself.

During these giddy weeks, Joe received a letter from Harry Houdini, who was touring in Germany. In his reply to "Boots, old fellow," Joe said, "I can truthfully say I never had an act before. This one is the *real thing*."

The Keatons rolled triumphantly through the spring of 1901. In May they played America's most notorious pleasure resort, Coney Island. After doing a twenty-minute show at the Steeplechase amusement park, Buster could ride the ferris wheel and merry-go-round for free, stuff himself with ice cream and cotton candy, and still have time for a nap and dinner before returning for the evening show.

One of Joe's biggest worries was that the act and its daring physical roughness would attract the attention of law enforcement authorities. Although the mayor's permit approved Buster in a speaking role only—no singing or dancing, no acrobatics—Joe bounced him around the stage. Sometimes he threw him as far as thirty feet. To many people this certainly looked a lot like acrobatics.

The sight of a Gerry Society officer at the theater outraged Joe. Were there no more kids peddling papers on the streets in rain and snow, no ten-year-olds toiling in factories, mills, and coal mines? Surely the SPCC had more important things to do. The Keatons were wholesome family fare, who had begun advertising themselves as the Tumblebug Family. Joe prided himself on the fact that they were a model family act, "refined," as he liked to bill it, ideally suited for the entertainment of children. Furthermore, his son was onstage a total of thirty-six minutes a day, which was not exactly hard labor.

At that time, more than two million children under sixteen years of age were a part of the workforce, a figure that rose steadily until by 1913 one out of five children would be earning their own livings.

For the next decade the Keatons and the Gerry Society would continue to spar. When the Gerries came backstage before a show, it was Buster they questioned. If his offstage performance failed to convince the agents of his age, the Three Keatons didn't go on. When he left the theater his mother suited him up in long trousers, a derby hat, and a cane and briefcase. "In this way," he said, "they fooled some people into believing I was a midget."

Today the Society for the Prevention of Cruelty to Children firmly denies ever harassing the Keatons. However, according to Buster's memories, the Gerry Society became the bogeyman of his childhood, lying in wait, chasing him as if he were a criminal when he had done nothing wrong. This theme would be echoed in his classic two-reel comedy *Cops*.

Buster Keaton pushed the age of his debut back farther and farther. He announced in a 1926 *Ladies' Home Journal* article that he signed up with the Houdini medicine show "at the age of two weeks." In the same article he stated, "Before I was three I toddled onto the stage."

A photograph taken before the turn of the century shows an adorable Buster wearing overalls and a straw hat and holding a banjo. He was a compact little boy, small for his age, with straight brown hair, a cherubic face, and shoe-button eyes. An essential part of the act's charm was Buster's size. Audiences gasped when the tiny lad made his entrance onto the very large stage of a five-thousand-seat theater. They responded by thinking he should be fast asleep. In no time they were riveted by the boy frisking nimbly around the stage in exuberant imitation of his father, all the while wearing a great baby smile. One of the problems of the act would be to keep him looking infantile for as long as possible.

Joe and Myra now ran regular ads in the trade papers. Their photographs were professional—Joe all legs, Myra decked out, Folies Bergère–style, in ruffled cancan petticoats, Buster looking like a little gentleman in business suit, bowler, and walking stick. They also ordered stylish custom-designed stationery that announced "Joe, Myra & Buster Keaton. Comedians" and included three photos and four sketches plus a description of the act: "A Good, Clean, Grotesque Comedy, Replete with Eccentric and Acrobatic Dancing, Real Comedy and Mirth-provoking situations. Concluding with the funniest routine of Chair and Table work in Vaudeville."

From the very first Joe had handled Buster boldly. Before long, Buster recalled, the act became increasingly rougher. In the 1950s he told a friend, "Of course the old man kicked me around a lot. It was part of the natural order." To make it easier for Joe to grab Buster, Myra sewed a leather suitcase handle onto the back of his jacket. If Joe wasn't getting enough laughs, he would just grasp Buster by the ears to lift him off the ground.

The stunt that drew the biggest audience reaction was when Joe grabbed the handle and hurled Buster off the stage, across the footlights into the orchestra. "When you go through the air," he remembered, "you use your head as the rudder." Wherever he crash-landed, he would scramble back up onstage.

When he got hurt, he was not allowed to cry. Nor was he permitted to laugh. "If I should chance to smile," Buster recalled, "the next hit would be a good deal harder. All the parental correction I ever received was with an audience looking on. I could not even whimper." Now Joe constantly browbeat him about controlling his expression, sometimes hissing "Face!" at him, sometimes whipping him onstage for misbehavior offstage. He learned to swallow his smile the instant he stepped before an audience. Eventually, he could not help thinking of himself as "a human mop."

Buster finally became an expert at tumbling and taking falls. The amount of physical punishment he had to sustain while learning the tricks was greater than he ever publicly acknowledged. Onstage and off, pain became a part of his life.

"Even people who most enjoyed our work marveled that I was able to get up after my bashing, crashing, smashing sessions with Pop," Keaton said proudly.

One night in Syracuse, New York, Joe lost his temper with an audience full of wise guys, who had greeted Myra's saxophone solo with disdain. He gripped the suitcase handle between the shoulders of his son's jacket. "Tighten up your asshole, son," he muttered. Buster felt himself hurtling across the footlights. His shoes landed on the face of one of the hoodlums and broke his nose. His father, Keaton said afterward, "had no fear of hurting *me*—I was just a handy ballistic missile." Instead of rioting, the audience remained glued to their seats.

At week's end, when Joe counted their salary, he was annoyed to find that Jule Delmar, the manager, had deducted the price of a hat. He stomped into Delmar's office.

"Now, look here, Joe," Delmar told him. "You can't use your son to club the spectators with. And besides breaking that fellow's nose, you ruined his new brown derby." Escapades like this gave Joe his reputation as a wild man.

During a matinee at Poli's Theatre in New Haven, Joe misjudged one of his hitch kicks, slammed Buster in the head, and knocked him out. He lay unconscious for eighteen hours. Next morning a doctor told his parents he was lucky his skull wasn't broken and ordered several days of bed rest for the eight-year-old. Scarcely two hours later, Buster was back onstage as usual. He never forgot that experience because it was the only time a stage injury caused him to miss a performance.

Joe's idea of Buster as "The Little Boy Who Can't Be Damaged" began to affect Buster's image of himself. He learned that he must never show physical weakness. Concussions, sprains, dislocations, to say nothing of colds and stomachaches, were luxuries not permitted to him. Sick or well, he was forced to work because his parents could not perform without him. Aside from the concussion, the only other accident that caused Buster to miss performances was when he stepped on a rusty nail at Chicago's Majestic Theater and a doctor warned of lockjaw if he didn't stay off the foot. The Keatons didn't perform for a week, their only such layoff in sixteen years.

Victorian society, which lived by codes of extreme gentility, thrilled to the anarchism of slapstick. The violence of the Keatons' act—its subversiveness—was precisely what appealed to their audiences. Moreover, violence against children was not just acceptable, it was amusing. When asked in 1956 to describe the family act on Edgar Bergen's television show, *Do You Trust Your Wife?*, Keaton smiled and said that "Father threw me anywhere he liked." The studio audience roared, just like the audiences of old.

Outsmarting investigators from the Gerry Society had become a family sport. Buster knew them by sight. Their modus operandi was to put in an appearance during Monday's matinee and if satisfied, they would usually never return. On Monday afternoon Joe and Buster were careful to present a toned-down version of the act. At the evening performance they would add more roughhousing, and by the end of the week things would get pretty wild.

Should the Gerry inspectors return unexpectedly, it was up to vigilant theater managers to alert the Keatons. Sometimes the SPCC would send unknown agents, who managed to slip past the security systems. This seems to be what happened in March 1903, when SPCC superintendent A. Fellows Jenkins refused to sign the permit for Buster's appearance and he had to be taken off the program. An officer was sent to Proctor's 125th to make certain Buster did not appear. The following day Joe took his case to New York mayor Seth Low, who himself made Buster undress and examined his back for black-and-blue marks. None were detected.

In May the Keatons were back at Keith's in New York with a slightly different version of the act, minus the roughhouse and also without Myra and her saxophone. It was just Buster and Joe doing songs, zany dancing, impersonations, and low comedy.

"You're a blockhead," Joe snapped.

"Well, I'm a chip off the old block," said Buster, who then began dashing circles around his dizzy father.

"What are you doing?" Joe wailed.

"Just running around the block."

Joe, desperate: "Can you read your ABC's?"

"I have never read them." (That was true enough. Buster couldn't read or write.)

"What have you read?"

"I have red hair."

The act played to capacity audiences. *The New York Times* praised Buster as "an excruciatingly funny little chap." It also demonstrated that Joe and Buster could do a first-rate act without violence. However, once they left New York Joe went right back to throwing Buster against the scenery.

Later in life Buster would refuse to see Joe's physical and emotional abuse of him as anything more than fatherly love. He could not bear to hear any condemnation of his father. Keaton insisted that it was actually Joe who got the worst of it. "Dad has had a sprained wrist for years from throwing me," he said in a 1913 interview. "I've only been hurt a few times." To protect Joe and to prove that he was a real trouper, "the little boy who could not be damaged," he boasted of never wearing padding. The reason their act had no imitators, he said, was "because they can't stand the treatment."

Over and over he would finesse suggestions of child abuse. Since physical discipline of kids was commonplace at that time, it is not completely fair to judge Joe Keaton by today's standards. In years to come, some would say that Joe's parenting was typical of his time, but his detractors would claim that he was sadistic. There is truth in both assertions. It is the nature of physical comedy to rely on violent gymnastics, which appear to be excruciatingly painful until the end of the act when it's clear nobody got hurt. Joe Keaton, however, pushed slapstick so far that it straddled the line between physical comedy and child abuse.

Even by the standards of Joe's own time, there was reason for concern about the damage he was causing his son. No medical files or court records document the case. The strongest evidence is what happened to Buster's personality during these years. It is troubling that the fearless, giggling five-year-old with the impish grin gradually became an entirely different child offstage. He began developing into a complicated, high-strung, nail-biting, hyperactive child who would have trouble functioning as an adult. By now his habit of concealing his feelings was a way of life, probably the greatest price he would have to pay for being Buster Keaton. In contrast to his father, who was a big talker, Buster spoke infrequently. The daily battering, the lies about his age, and the routine deceptions for the benefit of the Gerries would have a subtle but permanent effect, slowly redrawing his face into an appearance of frozen watchfulness. The blank face, at first a gimmick, was now automatic. More and more he went about his work wearing a vacant look.

Modern psychoanalytic thinking about abused children helps to explain his mournful face. Psychotherapist Linda Sanford points out that Keaton's case is consistent with a dissociative disorder in which the heart and mind go numb. She noted, "To survive that kind of physical abuse, onstage or anywhere, because people throw their kids against walls at home too, you have to do a mind-body split. The only way of surviving was to send his mind and spirit elsewhere, to a safer place. Being without expression is really the classic dissociative disorder."

In his studies of survivors of childhood deprivation, psychoanalyst Leonard Shengold concluded that sometimes survivors do draw strength from their traumas. Shengold observed of Keaton and his serious "Buster" face that "the praise for not crying would suggest a premium on *not* knowing and *not* feeling. This could be connected with the 'deadpan' affectless facade Keaton made use of in his comedy—a histrionic display of his defense."

Alice Miller, a psychoanalyst who specializes in the effects of child abuse, also dissected Buster Keaton's life in *The Untouched Key: Tracing Childhood Trauma in Creativity and Destructiveness*. Miller argues that if Keaton had realized how Myra and Joe had exploited and abused his body as well as his emotions, he would not have made a career of entertaining people. "In spite of remembering what happened to him, Buster Keaton undoubtedly repressed the trauma of being abused and degraded," she wrote. "That is why he had to repeat the trauma countless times without ever *feeling* it."

Throughout his childhood the proud Buster would continue to transcend humiliation by emptying his public face of all expression. His eyes kept half concealed under their lids, he was as expressionless as a basilisk.

In adulthood the strength of his spirit would prevail. Moving forward, he overcame early experiences that might have crushed another youngster. At the same time, the severity of that abuse should not be minimized. The damage permeated his entire life.

4 JINGLES JUNGLE

Insiders familiar with all the tricks of comedy couldn't help wondering how Buster survived his father's treatment. Percy Williams, owner of a large theater chain, watched nervously a few minutes and turned to his secretary, Frank Jones. Weren't the Keatons scheduled to play the Colonial shortly?

"In about six weeks."

"Well, you'd better book them for next week before the old man kills Buster."

Sarah Bernhardt once threatened to have Joe arrested for mistreating his son. Eddie Leonard, a popular blackface minstrel who played the same bill with Buster, said that "it looked as though his dad would break his neck." In 1935 during a hospital stay at Sawtelle Veteran's Hospital in West Los Angeles, an X ray revealed that Buster did in fact have cracked vertebrae. A callus had by then grown over the fracture.

In 1903 Buster's paternal grandmother was surprised to learn that the seven-year-old didn't know what to do with a pencil. What struck her as shameful was a matter of relative indifference to Myra and Joe. However, they promised to attend to the matter.

By this time most states had passed laws requiring children to attend elementary school, and as a result the country's illiteracy rate had fallen to lower than 8 percent. The Keatons were reluctant to let school interfere with their livelihood.

That fall, a few weeks after he turned eight, Buster entered first grade in Jersey City, a port town just across the Hudson River from New York, where the Keatons were playing at the Bijou

Theatre. One morning at 8:00 A.M., his mother took him to the school. Whether Myra and Joe now voluntarily complied or a truant officer finally caught up with them is debatable. No situation could have been more alien to Buster, who operated on theater time and ordinarily was fast asleep at that hour. Even though he had no inhibitions about appearing before an audience of two thousand, a class of children was a different story.

Buster had no idea how to behave. Being confined to a desk, surrounded by strangers several years his junior, and required to focus on geography and spelling was not easy for a child whose attention span measured approximately twenty minutes, the length of the act.

After lunch Myra came back and took him to the theater for the matinee. The next morning she did not bring him back to school, and he never returned. After their engagement at the Bijou ended, the Keatons quietly slipped out of Jersey City.

Vaudeville children often had poor—sometimes very poor—educations. In the 1920s, the two little Hovick sisters in "Madame Rose's Dancing Daughters" (later the burlesque star Gypsy Rose Lee and actress June Havoc) were asked to name the vice president under Woodrow Wilson. They had never heard of President Wilson.

In the 1960s Keaton would tell his friend Susan Reed that he was taught to read by actresses he met backstage. At other times he said Myra taught him in her free time. Actually, Myra had become a rabid card player whose free time was almost totally occupied with pinochle. Most likely he taught himself.

After Keaton's death, his business partner, Raymond Rohauer, expressed doubts about Keaton's ability to read. Whenever Rohauer presented a document for Keaton's signature, it was invariably returned unread. When Rohauer protested Keaton said, "Oh, I trust you." He would sometimes sign a contract "Buster," and Rohauer would have to remind him to write his full name.

In 1962, touring West Germany with a revival of *The General,* Rohauer had to read the superlative press notices aloud to Keaton "because he never read a paper and he couldn't understand."

As an adult, he would sign his name in a spidery, hesitant script to various applications, fan pictures, and book jackets. However, there is nothing to indicate that he could compose more than a simple letter. Among the few items in his handwriting that exist is a two-sentence note to gossip columnist Hedda Hopper, in which he misspells his granddaughter Melissa's name and is shaky on punctuation and grammar.

Rohauer was not the only one to wonder about Keaton's literacy. MGM producer Lawrence Weingarten thought he was shallow, "a child, with the mentality of a child." Weingarten questioned whether he was capable of functioning at all around educated people. Friends of Keaton suspected that he was more or less functionally illiterate, but they felt protective of him and kept quiet about it.

Sometimes Keaton sought the help of professionals and arranged for the unofficial services of ghostwriters as well as ghostreaders. Toward the end of his life, he worked with writer Charles Samuels on an autobiography, talking as Samuels took notes and typed. Keaton never glanced at the completed manuscript. When Paramount Pictures purchased the film rights to his life story in 1955, he refused to read the screenplay because "I don't need to grow an ulcer on my ulcer." After 1940, his wife, Eleanor, assumed responsibility for reading scripts and offered her opinion on their suitability.

Seldom did Keaton agonize about what might have been. "He used to say that he had absolutely no choice about what his life and career were going to be," Eleanor Keaton recalled in 1990. Despite Keaton's first-rate intelligence, he would always have the unread person's sense of inferiority around educated people. Yet lack of schooling was not a handicap in vaudeville. Child performer George Jessel spent a total of eight months in school; George Burns ended his schooling in fifth grade, Jimmy Durante in seventh. The only requirement for success in show business was talent, which Keaton never had to worry about.

In 1904 vaudeville box office receipts had never been better. And yet the handwriting had already appeared on the wall—three years later the whole country would be crawling with nickelodeons, some four to five thousand of them. Not theaters but simply converted mom-and-pop stores that seated fewer than three hundred customers, circumventing the need for amusement licenses, nickelodeons showed primitive movies for five cents. In these darkened stores with dirty floors, people would be thrilled by flickering life-sized cops chasing robbers, travelogues of the Eiffel Tower, silent galloping cowboys, and newsreels of auto races. Nickelodeons ran twelve to eighteen thirty-minute shows a day and made a good deal of money. Attendance was unbelievable: more than two million customers a day, a third of them children. Most patrons had never stepped foot in a theater or watched a vaudeville show. Many were immigrants who had not yet learned English. Many were poor, but was there anybody without a nickel to spend for magic?

Shortsighted vaudeville managers thought nickelodeons posed no threat to them. How could a machine ever compete with a flesh-and-blood performer?

In ten years of marriage, Myra at age twenty-seven had produced no further live babies or stillbirths. What is likely is she carefully avoided sex with her husband not by banishing him from bed but by bringing her son into it. Life on the road did not permit the luxury of separate quarters for children, and so Buster continued to sleep with his parents far beyond the age when such arrangements were desirable or healthy.

For the most part, the Keatons' marriage had developed into a practical arrangement. Like other vaudeville acts, they were business partners. To pass the hours between shows, Myra smoked, gossiped, and cultivated a passion for pinochle, on which she would eventually lavish more attention than on her family. Joe spent his free hours talking about the subject he knew best—himself—and drinking beer at saloons. W. C. Fields remembered getting into a drinking match with Joe one night after a show at Tony Pastor's.

Looking back, Buster remembered neither one of his parents as demonstrative, with each other or with him, "but not many children expected that of their parents in those days." It seemed perfectly natural to him.

Now that the Keatons were doing well financially, they decided to indulge in the luxury of more expensive sleeping cars when they traveled, which they did all the time. Joe and Myra took the lower berth, while Buster shared the upper berth with his mother's saxophone. Buster slept alone, probably for the first time in his life. Even worse for him, "the Pullman babies began arriving," as Keaton put it. In 1903 Myra became pregnant. The family was in

New York, at Ehrich's boardinghouse, when the Keatons' second child was born on August 25, 1904. They named the blond-haired, blue-eyed boy Harry (after Houdini) Stanley Keaton. When the baby was three weeks old, eight-year-old Buster carried him out to the footlights at Keith's during his curtain call. Even so, nothing made Buster more resentful than sharing applause with the Pullman baby. He had become a child who could respond to an ovation with a princely sweep of his hand for silence. He once said to an audience, "I thank you for this applause." Then, after a perfectly timed pause, he added: "I deserve it." This got him a huge laugh, but no doubt his words also came from the heart.

Before long, the baby got a nickname, Jingles, because he made such a racket playing with his toys. Joe now turned his attention to the new child, figuring that since his first son had unique comic ability, so would his second. He began grooming Jingles for life on the stage. First as a baby, then as a toddler, he would be sent on to provide a cute finish to the act. The Keatons believed he'd be just as good as Buster.

As if all the fuss over Jingles was not troubling enough for Buster, his mother became pregnant again in the winter of 1906. Joe got Buster a booking as Little Lord Fauntleroy. He spent his mother's pregnancy working in velvet pantaloons and a curly blond wig for a New England stock company.

On March 21, 1906, the *New York Telegraph* published a story with a Portland, Maine, dateline: "Tries to Kidnap a Child Actor. Man Seizes 'Jingles' Keaton in Portland Street and Then Jumps into Cab." The article reported: "A bold attempt at kidnaping was made in this city at 11:30 o'clock this morning when an unidenti-fied man . . . seized 'Jingles' Keaton, the year and a half old son of Joseph H. Keaton, the vaudeville performer, almost under the eyes of his father."

Jingles was found alone on a bench in the waiting room of Union Station, happily stuffing his face with candy. The kidnaper had fled and was never apprehended. For good reason. He was a prop man, whom Joe had hired for the job. Joe faked the abduc-tion for publicity. Myra's layoff had made him extremely nervous that the act might be forgotten.

Joe wanted another son, but on October 30, 1906, Myra gave

birth to a daughter in Lewiston, Maine. She was named Louise Dresser Keaton, after the Indiana-born vocalist who had made popular such ballads as "On the Banks of the Wabash" and "My Gal Sal."

In the Rivermont Casino in Lynchburg, Virginia, Buster shot his father in the face. The gun was a new addition to the act. Buster was supposed to fire a blank cartridge at Joe when his back was turned. But that night their timing was off, and Buster firing the gun gave his father a full charge of powder in the face. A newspaper account described Joe as "badly lacerated but not seriously injured."

In November 1907, the Keatons were in New York at their favorite rooming house on West Thirty-eighth Street, all five of them squeezed into a single room. The Five Keatons, like the Three Keatons, still had no permanent address.

The year was ending on a bad note for the economy. A few weeks earlier, a run on New York's Knickerbocker Trust Company sent tremors felt by smaller banks all over the country. Now the stock market had collapsed, businesses were folding, and workers were losing their jobs. The Keatons continued to roll along. Buster reigned as a royal prince of vaudeville, the most popular child comedian in the country, fawned over by the trades. "Young though he is," raved the *Clipper,* "he ranks with the funniest of his older brother professionals, and none can create laughter better than he."

Buster also produced money, hundreds of dollars a week. To make sure the gusher kept flowing, his father furiously promoted the act, cooking the family history as thoroughly as the dried-out pot roasts they consumed at theatrical doss-houses. Since family acts were generally well received on the circuit, Joe had begun touting his family as the most wholesome act in vaudeville. He dreamed of developing a kiddie act similar to the one that Eddie Foy would devise a few years later with his seven youngsters. For that reason he was determined to bring Jingles and Louise into the act as often as possible.

Soon after they arrived in New York, Joe began working out a deal with the *Dramatic Mirror* for a front-page feature about all five Keatons, the kind of publicity that money could not buy. To clinch the coverage with the editors, who had never seen the two youngest Keaton children onstage, Joe would have promised practically anything.

On Sunday evening, November 17, the Keatons took part in a benefit concert at Brooklyn's stately Grand Opera House. Joe arranged for the *Dramatic Mirror* to be there. Buster, Myra, and Joe did their regular act, and as a surprise finale, Buster burst into the wings and came back pushing a baby carriage. Three-year-old Jingles sprang out and went hippity-hopping around the stage, chased by his brother. Jingles lost most of his clothing when his father grabbed him and stood him on his head. For an encore, a bewildered Louise was carried on and urged to dance. Only twelve months old, she soon plopped flat on her face.

Two officers of the Gerry Society witnessed this brazen flouting of the child labor law. The next day Joe was arrested. Uncharacteristically meek, he admitted under interrogation that he had no permit for Jingles and Louise (whose names were recorded as George and Vera), nor did he bother to deny that he had knowingly violated the law. But, he told the police, it had all been done to oblige the *Dramatic Mirror,* and then he pulled out a postcard from John Springer, manager of the opera house, with instructions to introduce Jingles at the end of the act. As a result, Springer was arrested later that day.

It was not until the first week of December that the Keatons faced the judge in the Court of Special Sessions at Jefferson Market Courthouse. The Three Keatons were barred from performing in New York City for two years. It was, Buster would recall, "a cruel setback."

By this time the Keatons could well afford to hire capable caretakers. Frequently Joe boasted to reporters that "a first-class governess accompanies them so that the care and education of the youngsters is looked after as well as if they were located permanently in one place." Such teachers did exist—they had to be certified—but no governess, first-class or otherwise, was ever employed by the Keatons. Their governess existed only for the benefit of the Gerry Society. Joe was too cheap to pay for teachers, or any sort of child care.

As a twelve-year-old, Buster wound up bearing an inordinate amount of domestic responsibility. Not only did his talent support the family, he was also expected to arrange hotel bookings and train reservations and keep an eye on his two needy siblings. He began to give silent expression to his resentment by exuding an air of helplessness, an orphaned manner that made females, his own mother excepted, want to mother him. In Boston he accompanied his brother and sister to the Common to feed the pigeons. Bored and distracted, he failed to notice when Jingles moseyed away. When he left to hunt for his brother, Louise also got lost. They were all eventually picked up by the police.

His resentment toward Jingles had to do, in part, with Joe's ambition to mold him into a second child prodigy, even though Jingles showed no particular talent for comedy. Audiences loved Louise. One customer, Dorothy Dana Walton, said that Joe and Buster, two grungy tramps in baggy pants and battered hats, "looked filthy, just dreadful. Then Mrs. Keaton would come out in a fresh immaculate dress wheeling the little sister in a go-cart. When people saw the baby in a lovely little white dress, they would just applaud wildly."

Signs of emotional disturbance had already appeared in Jingles, a chronic bed wetter. He and Louise were slapped around by Joe and neglected by their mother. They had become exceptionally aggressive with other children. Jingles's backstage scrapes were reported in the trade papers. He fought with his sister so frequently the *Telegraph* ran a photo of them in boxing gloves, slugging it out.

On a rare trip to Iowa they visited Myra's family in Modale. A picture taken there opens a window on the private world of the Keaton children. It shows them in a summer yard with flower bushes and fruit trees, standing next to their aunt, a tall, smiling woman in a lacy blouse. The children, however, appear to be in a stupor. Buster, next to his aunt, stands rigidly behind the two smaller children with a grim expression on his face. His brother and sister look as if they had just been thoroughly whipped. Louise is staring submissively at the ground, while a woebegone Jingles tries to control his fidgeting hands.

Eventually Joe was forced to accept the fact that Jingles and Louise lacked their brother's talent. In due course they would be packed off to Catholic boarding schools in Michigan. More than once, Louise recalled, her father was late with the tuition.

*   *   *

During the next two years the Keatons went about their business, banished from New York, biding their time until Buster reached sixteen—actually fourteen—the legal age at which the Gerry Society could not touch him. They crisscrossed the country: the West Coast, the Deep South, the Midwest. Twice they landed one of the much-coveted cover stories in the *Dramatic Mirror.* "The only place that the Gerries had any real power was in New York," recalled Eileen Sedgwick, who first met the Keatons while touring with her own family's variety act, the Five Sedgwicks. "As baby Eileen the child wonder, I was always underage. We had so much trouble in New York that finally we just couldn't go there."

The Keatons made good money, $750 a week. Still, Joe and Myra were far from extravagant. They shunned luxury cars and lavish hotels, and they all continued to sleep in one room even though rates at the best hotels seldom exceeded $2.50 a night. It would be another three years before the glory of big-time vaudeville began to fade and managers slashed salaries.

On July 1, 1909, the Keatons set off for London on the steamship *George Washington.* Any act that played abroad could parlay the trip into bigger salaries and better bookings back home. The Palace Theatre offered them $200 for a one-week engagement, a quarter of their wages in America. It made no difference because the Palace was easily the most important music hall in the world.

On July 8, they docked at Southampton. From the first day nothing about London pleased Joe. He hated the hotel, the food, even the Palace. The Keatons were not listed on the billboard posters out front and were given the worst place on the program. The stage was full of splinters.

On Monday evening the house was poor and the audience did not respond to the Keatons' act. When Joe threw Buster around, nobody laughed. Worse, when Joe took his call, a number of affronted patrons began hissing.

The next morning the theater manager asked Joe, "Is that your own son? Or an adopted one?"

Joe thought he was joking.

"My word," sniffed Alfred Butt. "I imagined he was an adopted boy and you didn't give a damn what you did to him."

After their one contracted week, the Keatons went home.

*   *   *

Once troupers finished playing amusement parks, it was common practice to spend the remainder of their summers recuperating and relaxing. A few years earlier, the Keatons had been booked into an amusement park near Muskegon, in upper Michigan. Enchanted with the scenic beaches, they rented a house in the village of Bluffton. The following year they decided to return. Among performers, Muskegon was known as a good show town, a community hospitable to artistic people. Joe and several other vaudevillians got the idea of building a summer haven for actors in the shoreline area of Bluffton, and inviting their friends.

In 1908, the Actors Colony Club was established on a tract of land on the western shore of Lake Muskegon. It was subdivided into lots and sold to several dozen actors, eventually housing nearly two hundred.

After their England trip, the Keatons headed straight for their new Michigan home, a clapboard cottage with three bedrooms on Edgewater Street. A typical example of summer cabins built at that time, it had a generous veranda in front and an outhouse at the back. On the porch, along with five new rocking chairs, Joe hung a crudely painted sign, JINGLES JUNGLE. On the gasoline stove, Myra, at the age of thirty-two, finally taught herself to cook. Years later Buster would describe his seven summers at the Actors Colony as the happiest of his life. In almost every photograph there, he is smiling. After years of suitcases and railway stations, he reveled in the first home he had ever known, even making friends with children his own age.

Buster loved baseball. Finally, he had a chance to play on a sandlot team. With his exceptional athletic skills and superb timing, he had already shown enough talent, it would frequently be said, to have made a career in major league ball. Throughout his life, baseball would be his religion. Playing shortstop for Dickie's Colts, he spent long hours on the field with his new friends Lex Neal, Vince Edlund, and Dick Gardner. Afterward they would head over to Cobwebs and Rafters, and if no one was watching, sneak a beer from the clubhouse kegs.

The social life of the colony centered around the Keaton family, its most famous and perhaps most eccentric residents. Myra shocked people by not only smoking cigarettes but rolling them herself. Usually she spent her time with pinochle. Joe, founder and president of the Actors Colony Club and a member of the Muskegon Elks Club, purchased a secondhand twenty-five-foot steam launch, which he christened *Battleship*. Buster easily replaced the old boiler with a two-cylinder gasoline engine. Although he had no previous experience with machinery, it came naturally to him.

Joe could be found on his boat fishing, wearing an admiral's hat. Otherwise he was at a favorite hangout, Bullhead Pascoe's tavern on Beach Street, which served heaping platters of succulent fried perch, crispy from being rolled in cornmeal, along with crackers and a stein of draft beer.

All the Keaton children would get into their bathing suits in the morning and take them off at bedtime. Bluffton was, Louise would remember, "that most wonderful little town" where she spent "unforgettable days."

5 THE PROVIDENCE
FURNITURE MASSACRE

That fall of 1909, the Keatons swept onto the New York City stage for the first time since they had been banned two years earlier. On October 4 Buster celebrated his sixteenth birthday—actually his fourteenth—with a gleeful ad in *Variety*:

Today I am a Theatrical Man—Goodbye Mr. Gerry!

Two weeks later the Keatons made a triumphant comeback at Hammerstein's Victoria. *Variety* said, "Buster improves with every show, and the youngster will undoubtedly be a better comedian as a man than he is as a boy, which is saying something."

Buster was in love. Before the family left for England, he had seen an automobile in Macy's toy department, a shiny black roadster with bicycle wheels and a three-horsepower single-cylinder engine, which could do eighteen miles per hour. The price tag on the Browniekar was hefty—$250—but thirteen-year-old Buster wanted it so badly that he refused to leave the store without it. Joe and Myra purchased the floor model and took it on tour with them, hauling it around in the baggage car, along with the trunks and Joe's Blicksenderfer typewriter. By the time Buster was eighteen, he would own adult machines, a Peerless Phaeton and a Palmer Singer. By then the Browniekar had been shipped back to Muskegon for nine-year-old Jingles, not only a dubious gift but a major headache because the baby car kept breaking down and replacement parts were difficult to obtain.

While Buster exhibited more passion for cars than for anything else, the same year that he purchased the Peerless he lost his virginity in Muskegon. Given the intimacy of backstage life and the theatrical boardinghouses where the Keatons stopped, what is surprising about his first sexual experience is its late date. Since the age of five he had been kissed and nuzzled by glamorous stars like Lillian Russell and Anna Held. Few small boys had as comprehensive a repertoire of sexual jokes and dirty songs as did Buster Keaton. He later said that growing up in vaudeville left him without fear of women. But despite numerous crushes, one on swimming star Annette Kellerman, the Esther Williams of prewar vaudeville, he was not sexually precocious.

During Buster's sixteenth summer, upon their arrival in Bluffton, his father gave him a serious lecture about sex. Joe absolutely forbade touching any of the local girls. The last thing Joe wanted was a shotgun marriage with some nice Muskegon girl. He also warned that street chippies would send Buster to a hospital for life. When he was ready for sex, he should visit Della Pritchett's whorehouse in the red-light district of Muskegon. Joe could vouch for its safety from firsthand experience.

One afternoon Buster was visiting the home of a Muskegon friend named Bob when a neighbor—one of the forbidden local girls—stopped by. Bob's family was away. They went into the kitchen to make molasses taffy. After a while, they moved on to more exciting pastimes. As Keaton later recalled, the girl was "cute as a bug's ear and dying for experience." The boys took turns having intercourse with her. Afterward, they went to a soda fountain and ordered banana splits.

As the boys sped along the road to Bluffton in Buster's Peerless, they were nearly overtaken by a souped-up Model T Ford bearing the girl's mother accompanied by the sheriff. Buster managed to lose them. For two terrifying days he holed up in a cabin in the woods.

When he returned home, he discovered that his pursuers had cornered Joe at Bullhead Pascoe's tavern. Joe pretended to be outraged. He challenged not only the daughter's morals but the mother's as well. The sheriff finally laughed and walked out; the mother, outshouted and outmaneuvered, gave up and went back to Muskegon. Joe's defense of his boy in no way diminished the scolding he later gave him for disobeying his orders. That summer the Keatons cut short their vacation by six weeks in order to play an August 15 engagement at Hammerstein's Roof Garden in New York.

One day during the summer of 1915, Buster started to experience worrying sensations in his genital area. The next day, in real pain, he confided his problem to one of his father's friends, who informed him that he had the clap. The best cure was a flaxseed poultice. By the time the flaxseed meal had been mixed with water and boiled into a thick paste and the hot poultice applied to his penis, the news leaked to Joe. He was furious that Buster had been so stupid as to hire a streetwalker, precisely the sort of prowling he had warned about. Why didn't he use one of Della's girls? Buster insisted that the prostitute he had met on the street worked at the brothel.

Joe held the madam responsible for his son's gonorrhea. Herding together his friends from Pascoe's, he formed a vigilante committee that gathered outside Della's front door, where they began to shout and throw rocks. After they shattered a window, Della Pritchett called the police and the vigilantes retreated to Bluffton.

In the following days Joe treated Buster's problem with patent medicines and favorite home remedies solicited from friends. The intimate details of Buster's clap were spread throughout the colony. In the era before sulfa drugs and penicillin, there was no cure for gonorrhea. Doctors usually prescribed potassium permanganate, but more popular continued to be self-treatment—of the very sort Joe was administering—which consisted of a variety of antiseptic salves and herbal concoctions.

It was not one of Buster's happiest summers.

Motion pictures were tailor-made for a slam-bang, knockabout act like the Three Keatons, but Joe failed to grasp the possibilities. In 1914 William Randolph Hearst wanted to turn the popular George McManus comic strip "Bringing Up Father" into a series of two-reelers. Since McManus's domestic comedy had much in common with the Keatons' act, Hearst offered Joe and Myra the roles of Jiggs and Maggie.

Joe angrily replied, "What are you *saying?* You want to show the Three Keatons on a bed sheet for ten cents." The Keatons were not freaks to be exhibited to every Tom, Dick, and Harry with a dime. He derided movies as nothing but toys made for the amusement of children. In truth, movies frightened him. For too many years he had labored to achieve professional success and place in the vaudeville community. A few performers such as Trixie Friganza and Blanche Ring did film their vaudeville acts. That the Keatons did not is unfortunate because they might have left more of a visual record of their stage work.

In those years, Joe's low opinion of the new medium was common. Film producers were reluctant to identify actors to the viewing public for fear they might become too well known and demand more money. Actors, on the other hand, nervous that any association with movies might jeopardize their stage careers, didn't want to be recognized. Now all this was rapidly changing.

In 1906, the *New York Dramatic Mirror* inaugurated a cinema department. It warned theater owners to add moving pictures to their programs, because that's where the big money would be made. The *Dramatic Mirror* also began to review films, mainly simple plot synopses. New rival theatrical paper *Variety* also cut back on coverage of vaudeville and eventually shifted variety news to its back pages. *Variety*'s first reviews of moving pictures, the Pathé film *An Exacting Honeymoon* and Edison's *Life of a Cowboy*, appeared in January 1907. More and more, the front sections of the theatrical bibles were devoted to motion pictures and their box office grosses, and rising stars such as Mary Pickford.

At this time, a typical bill would be made up of several one-reel films, each running ten to twelve minutes. With each passing year, films improved technically and their length increased from one- and two-reelers to feature length. In 1912, Mack Sennett opened a comedy production company named Keystone, and cameraman Billy Bitzer and director D. W. Griffith developed technical methods such as close-ups, fades, and backlighting. The following year, *Variety* reported an amazing statistic: Thirty thousand movie theaters were in operation, with an estimated total investment in the picture business of more than one billion dollars.

Joe Keaton did not believe that anything could replace vaudeville.

Buster Keaton had been seeing movies regularly since he first arrived in New York at the age of four, though he always liked to give the impression that he was naive about films. He claimed he stepped into his first film knowing practically nothing about the medium.

The fact is that vaudeville managers were already combining live entertainment with silent movies. Keaton played on the same bill with a movie. For instance, in a typical week, May 17–22, 1915, the Keatons headlined at Loew's American Roof in Times Square, in a program that concluded with Charlie Chaplin's *The Floorwalker.* Buster might have seen *The Floorwalker* twelve times that week.

In 1913 Buster began paying closer attention to the films of D. W. Griffith and the slapstick comedies of Mack Sennett. While Sennett's earlier work had seemed crude to Buster, he loved the Keystone Kops and began to recognize the possibilities of movies. One of the first films he admitted enjoying was *Tillie's Punctured Romance,* Sennett's feature-length comedy about a country girl who loses her money to a con man, starring Mabel Normand, Marie Dressler, and Charlie Chaplin. Earlier comedies were one or two reels. Sennett broke new ground with this six-reeler, which was hugely successful and made Chaplin a household name. Buster saw *Tillie's Punctured Romance* four times, mostly out of curiosity. He considered Chaplin talented, but Will Rogers was funnier, in his opinion, and so were a half dozen other comics.

But now Chaplin's career had exploded. In less than two years his take went from $1,250 a week to the stupendous sum of $10,000 a week.

Buster did not believe *Tillie's Punctured Romance* had any special influence on his choice of a film career. He credited *The Birth of a Nation* as his greatest inspiration. On March 3, 1915, Griffith's three-hour epic of the Civil War opened an extended run at the Liberty Theatre in New York. Based on Thomas Dixon's 1905 novel *The Clansman,* it was about a white southern family during Reconstruction. Buster joined thousands of New Yorkers who stood in long queues to pay the unheard-of admission price of two dollars a ticket. A masterpiece grossly flawed by racism, *The Birth of a Nation* was denounced as "aggressively vicious and defamatory. It is spiritual assassination." Black Americans were outraged; the NAACP picketed theaters. Hisses heard at some performances were drowned out by thundering applause from audiences who were overwhelmed by the movie's cinematic techniques. The picture would earn tens of millions of dollars.

During its forty-four-week run in New York, Buster saw *The Birth of a Nation* three times. "From then on I was sold," he recalled. "I was a picture fan." *The Birth of a Nation* also gave him the vision to make a Civil War picture a decade later, a masterpiece that some argue is the most authentic such work ever filmed. In 1977 members of the American Film Institute voted for the fifty best American films of all time. The five silent pictures they selected were Griffith's *The Birth of a Nation* and *Intolerance,* Chaplin's *The Gold Rush* and *City Lights,* and Keaton's *The General.*

Buster was almost full grown, so that the point of the Keatons' act—a father making his son obey—had long since grown blunted. A more serious problem than Buster's size was his state of mind. He had become a bored, restless adolescent who felt constrained by the rigid routines of touring and family life. For the first time he began turning in sloppy, indifferent performances. Reviewers who had supported him for a decade were suddenly less kind: "It is not an enlivening spectacle to see two grown persons in support of a lad of sixteen and Buster is not as clever as he was five or six years ago," sniped the *New York Dramatic Mirror.* "He should make an effort to put more enthusiasm into his work."

Joe himself was more often than not out of control. His temper tantrums gusted up like tropical storms, sudden and deadly. Myra felt relieved to see him go off and drink beer after the shows. One night Joe got into a barroom fight with three college boys and threw one through the plate-glass window. He was locked up and held on $250 bail. When someone arrived to inform Myra, she was playing cards. Waving the messenger silent, she played out her hand. Only after collecting her winnings did she dig into her bag for the bail money. Then she said, "Deal the cards."

More and more Buster was on the receiving end of his father's anger. During a matinee at the Grand Theatre in Pittsburgh, Joe threw a punch that sent Buster reeling upstage, then slammed him into the floor and into the scenery. The set fell over. Finally, Joe smashed a kitchen chair over his head. Buster learned to hit back for the first time. As a result of their onstage fight came a new routine, in which they bashed and slapped each other with brooms, trading powerful blows in time to the music of the "Anvil Chorus." Audiences loved it.

Turning to Myra for help was useless. As usual she offered neither protection nor solutions, only excuses for Joe's rages. He was mad at the world, she said. Some men just couldn't take getting older. When Buster smelled liquor, he prepared for the worst. In a classic alcoholic family scenario, he discovered that he could cover up for his father so that theater managers and audiences never caught on to the fact his timing was off.

Now it was up to Buster to keep the balls in the air, but he could not help wondering how much longer the act could last.

In the spring of 1916 a penny-pinching manager in Providence gave the Keatons flimsy old chairs instead of the sturdy kitchen chairs the act required. The chairs kept breaking and had to be replaced. At the end of the week, management deducted the price of the new chairs from their wages. Backstage, Joe went berserk and in a one-man riot smashed all the theater's prop furniture including a costly French sofa. Moving on to New York's Palace Theatre for the week of April 24, the Keatons were preceded by gossip about the Providence furniture massacre.

For vaudevillians, the Palace on Broadway and Forty-seventh Street represented Mount Olympus. If the theater was legendary, so was its manager, Martin Beck, who as general manager for the Orpheum circuit also controlled the booking of all big-time vaudeville for the western United States.

To oversee his vast theatrical empire, Beck used spies and secret reports to build dossiers on performers, including information on private peccadilloes. He must have collected a sizable file on the personal life of Joe Keaton, who for fifteen years had been constantly proclaiming—to anyone who would listen—his contempt for Martin Beck.

When the Keatons showed up at the Palace, they were chalked in as number three on the program, not a bad spot. But after the Monday matinee, as often happened, the bill was rearranged. The Keatons were notified that they were being moved up to number one, the spot traditionally reserved for jugglers, acrobats, and such, the so-called dumb acts because no talking was required. It was an insult for a comedy act to be in this position, and Joe redoubled his derogatory remarks about Beck.

Martin Beck seemed not to pay attention. But during one matinee the showman appeared beetle-browed in the wings, arms folded over his pouter pigeon chest. In the middle of the act, Joe happened to glance into the wings and noticed Beck.

"Okay, Keaton," he taunted. "Make *me* laugh!"

Buster remembered his father's face turning purple. Suddenly Joe streaked toward Beck, who ran through the backstage area, out the stage door, and along West Forty-seventh Street toward Sixth Avenue. Joe went after him but finally lost him in the crowds on Sixth Avenue. Buster, alone onstage, started to sing, then in desperation he recited until his father returned to the stage.

Trouble escalated when Beck asked some of the acts to shave a few minutes in order to maintain the program's tempo. Joe swore at Beck and refused to pare the act by one second. In the end he complied, in his own way. He brought onstage an alarm clock, which he elaborately set for twelve minutes and then placed on the floor. When the alarm buzzed, he and Buster halted midact. Joe picked up the clock and off they went, providing Palace audiences with more entertainment than Beck had intended.

Martin Beck ignored the alarm clock incident, and the Keatons completed their week. But Beck made certain that Fun's Funniest Family never played the Palace again, or any other theater in two-a-day big-time vaudeville.

The Keatons finished out the season, then headed back to Muskegon for the summer.

After the meltdown at the Palace, the only work the Keatons could get in the fall was on the small-time Pantages circuit, playing tank towns, a terrible comedown after big-league show business. They again had to do three shows a day.

Buster, now twenty-one, couldn't take the physical punishment of the act. His father began drinking before shows, whiskey instead of beer, which further impaired his timing. By the time they reached the West Coast, the act was embarrassing. Buster begged and nagged his father to shape up, even threatened to walk out. But Joe no longer seemed to care.

"Joe Keaton was a terrible disastrous drunk," said James Karen, who was close to Keaton in years to come. "I think Buster truly disliked him, but he would never admit it because he thought it was un-American to dislike your father. And if you said one word against Joe, or any member of his family, you were persona non grata." Ten years later, while filming a scene in *The General*, Buster knocked his father off a flatcar onto the railroad tracks, which hardly made up for years of manhandling. "He could take all sorts of abuse without saying a word," said Karen.

When the Keatons arrived in San Francisco in January 1917, Joe spent all his offstage moments drinking. Buster warned his mother that he was leaving the act. This time Myra, who had always defended Joe, agreed to leave with him. On Saturday night, following the final show, they slipped out of the hotel and instead of going to Los Angeles, where they were scheduled to open the following Monday, they boarded a train to Michigan.

"We didn't even leave him a note," Buster recalled.

Abandoning his father made Buster feel tremendously guilty. He had killed the act and left his parents without a livelihood. To atone for these crimes, he would exaggerate the story and paint himself in the blackest colors. He never tried to defend his actions: fleeing without a word; leaving his father drunk in San Francisco; snapping the umbilical cord to become a movie star. But escape from the Three Keatons proved more difficult than he had anticipated.

Scarcely three days later, Joe showed up in Muskegon. Having reached Los Angeles only to realize that both his wife and son had left him, he wasted no time in chasing them back East. He found a defiant son who complained that even though he had been working for sixteen years, he hadn't a dime to call his own.

Joe decided to humor Buster for the time being. If he was determined to work by himself for a while, Joe would not stand in his way. On top of that, he was even going to escort him to New York to consult with their agent, Max Hart. Buster and his father boarded the train to New York on Saturday, February 3, 1917. Except for a three-day stopover in 1919, Buster would not return to Muskegon for more than thirty years.

6 TOYS

Max Hart was a good-natured little man who made his living earning fortunes for comics. Reputed to be the ultimate talent agent, he represented an impressive stable of headliners who owed their careers to him, including Will Rogers, W. C. Fields, Bert Wheeler, and Eddie Cantor.

Hart understood that Buster Keaton lacked a track record in musicals or solo comedy. Still, the starmaker never had a doubt that he could sell him. Little Buster had grown up into a manly twenty-one-year-old with finely chiseled features, high cheekbones, and liquid, dark, unblinking eyes. His hair was combed smoothly back from a high forehead. No more than five feet six, he was very sturdily constructed, slender and athletic. His teeth were extraordinarily even and brilliant when he smiled. On top of all that, he had a reputation in the business as "a fine boy always, modest, ambitious, courteous, and self-respecting," in the words of the *Telegraph*.

That very week, the Shubert brothers—J. J. and Lee—were auditioning for the new edition of *The Passing Show*, a stupendously successful girlie revue now in its sixth season. The stars of this edition, with music composed by Sigmund Romberg, were singing comedienne Irene Franklin and De Wolf Hopper, a dapper matinee idol famous for his comic portrayals in Gilbert and Sullivan operettas; Charles "Chic" Sale, the rube monologist, was an old friend of Joe's and a frequent summer guest at Jingles Jungle. A cast of one hundred, most of them gorgeous women, would prance around as horses or Manhattan cocktails.

That morning Max Hart sent the Keatons to the offices from

which the Shubert brothers guided their theatrical empire. The Keatons were ushered in to see J. J. Shubert, a pudgy, neckless man, and his casting director, E. R. "Ma" Simmons. Keaton would later recall that Simmons inquired if he could carry a tune but mentioned no audition. Shubert, he said, signed him up on the spot for $250 a week with instructions to develop a skit—they would leave the rest entirely up to his judgment.

In fact, Buster had to test for a part, like anyone else unproven in musical comedy. J. J. Shubert did not cast unestablished people in such a casual fashion. The $250-a-week salary seems to be another creative revision of Keaton's life story. Shubert's skinflint reputation was legendary, and for this reason turnover was high, as top artists seldom spent more than one season with him. He had even lost the incomparable Marilyn Miller, whom he had more or less discovered, in a salary dispute when his refusal to meet her price threw her into the professional arms of his rival, Flo Ziegfeld.

Whatever figure Shubert offered Keaton, it satisfied both Joe Keaton and Max Hart, who knew the value of a Shubert showcase. In 1916 Shubert had picked Marilyn Miller and Ed Wynn. In 1918 it would be Fred and Adele Astaire, and later George Jessel, Marie Dressler, and Joan Crawford. Joining *The Passing Show* would take Buster across the frontier from vaudeville into Broadway musical comedy.

In the same week, the papers reported that America was expected to enter the war any day. Already German U-boats had sunk more than two hundred American merchant ships, and President Wilson had just ordered all vessels to carry arms. Joe lingered in New York. He presented Buster his slapshoes, in the old stage tradition of a father handing on his shoes to his son. At his favorite Times Square taprooms he spun nostalgic tales about his twenty-two years in show business. Then he went home to Michigan.

The turmoil of recent months and the break with his family left Buster feeling wretched. Throughout his life any sort of family strife would make him physically or emotionally ill. Now separated from his family for the first time, he took his meals alone at Child's, a chain specializing in pancakes with Log Cabin syrup, the closest approximation of a farm-boy breakfast available in Manhattan. In the evenings he slogged through the melting snow in Times Square to see Broadway shows with Sarah Bernhardt, Nazimova, Maude Adams, and Laurette Taylor.

On Lake Muskegon, the deserted Actors Colony was sighing under winter. Snowbound, holed up in Jingles Jungle, which had no furnace or plumbing, Joe Keaton struggled to come to grips with the loss of his boy. That winter his family was scattered, Myra visiting friends in Detroit, Louise at nearby Ursuline Academy, and Jingles in Kalamazoo. For the first winter in two decades, Joe was out of work, though the Keatons could have continued to perform, had they chosen.

Not without Buster, of course.

It was snowing on Monday, March 5, when rehearsals for *The Passing Show* got under way at the Winter Garden Theatre on Broadway at Fiftieth Street. The program for that show lists a variety of comedy sketches in such settings as a railway dining car, Trinity Church, and the Yale Bowl, along with the names of a half dozen comedians who had roles in ensemble skits. Only one comic, Chic Sale, was singled out for a solo bit, and he would steal the best reviews along with a talented comic dancer, vaudevillian Johnny Dooley. None of the other comics attracted the critics' notice.

A cold drizzle was falling on Wednesday as the Boston train pulled into Grand Central. On hand was a gaggle of film executives and exhibitors, newspaper reporters, and movie fans, all waiting to greet Roscoe Arbuckle, the country's leading comic film star after Charlie Chaplin. Known as Fatty, Arbuckle was an overripe man weighing 275 pounds, five feet ten, with blond hair, sleepy blue eyes, and rosy scrubbed cheeks. He was popular with adults and children alike.

Arbuckle's image of a good-humored, lovable fat man belied a violent temper, problems with alcohol and drugs, and a habit of suicidal driving. Six months earlier he had gone through tough times—breaking with Mack Sennett and struggling to kick heroin and morphine.

He had spent the past three weeks on a marathon cross-country promotion tour for Paramount Pictures in a private railway car lent by Evalyn Walsh McLean, owner of the Hope diamond. Two weeks shy of his thirtieth birthday and suddenly a very hot commodity, Arbuckle struggled to stay emotionally laced as the train stopped at two dozen cities along the route. He had to emerge from the train in each city, flash his big buttery grin, then get back on the train.

The previous night in the Back Bay section of Boston, Arbuckle had been the guest of honor at a banquet thrown by leading Paramount executives, including Adolph Zukor, Jesse Lasky, and Hiram Abrams; also attending was Marcus Loew, the biggest movie exhibitor in the country, together with a smattering of local politicians. At about eleven, Arbuckle left the banquet room at the Copley Plaza with his wife and his manager, dropped in at a nearby club for a nightcap, then retired for the night.

Shortly after midnight, Paramount hosted a stag party at Mishawum Manor, a whorehouse in suburban Woburn. Sixteen film VIP's were invited, in whose honor madam Brownie Kennedy had orchestrated a special entertainment. A silver tray was brought in. Its lid was lifted to reveal a "party girl" garnished with a few sprigs of parsley. She was immediately joined by fourteen other party girls. Fifty-two bottles of champagne were consumed by the guests. In the small hours of the morning, Hiram Abrams settled the bill: $1,000 for the parsley girls and $50 for hat checking. To Zukor and the other Paramount chiefs, the arrangement of sex orgies was nothing extraordinary. It was show business.

The next afternoon in New York, Paramount convened a news conference at Grand Central Station to announce that it would be releasing a new line of Comique comedies produced by Joseph Schenck and starring Roscoe Arbuckle. After making some two hundred films for Sennett, Arbuckle would be starring in and directing his own comedy shorts, a deal that included complete creative control and an annual salary of $250,000 plus bonuses that would bring him roughly a million dollars a year. The megadeal would make him the second highest-paid comedian in pictures.

In mid-March, two weeks after rehearsals had begun at the Winter Garden, Keaton was walking through Times Square when he bumped into Lou Anger. Keaton had often appeared on the same vaudeville bill with the chunky Anger and his singer wife, Sophy Bernhard. For ten years Anger had grubbed a mediocre living by playing a German soldier who recites a stream of hard-luck stories. Anger's act, never more than third-rate, died the night a German submarine torpedoed the *Lusitania*.

Now a successful-looking Anger told Keaton that he had left vaudeville to become a theatrical agent and was associated with Joseph M. Schenck in producing movies. The previous year Anger had pulled off a major agenting coup: After Roscoe Arbuckle, along with his nephew Al St. John and wife, Minta Durfee, had signed a contract with Max Hart for $200,000 a year, Anger had secretly convinced Arbuckle that he could get him more, and persuaded him to break his contract with Hart. Anger steered him over to Schenck, who offered a deal too sweet to refuse: his own comedy unit and a brand-new Rolls-Royce. Not for another twenty years, not until RKO in 1941 gave Orson Welles total artistic control over *Citizen Kane,* would a director win such freedom from a studio.

On account of Arbuckle's personal difficulties, production schedules on the first Comique film had slipped. In the week since his arrival, his marriage of nine years had broken up. After a nasty fight in which he smashed mirrors and vases in their Hotel Cumberland suite, he moved to the Friars Club, and then to the Bayside, Queens, home of Joseph Schenck.

Lou Anger invited Keaton to come along and visit the Comique set. Colony Studio was situated in a warehouse at 318–320 East Forty-eighth Street, in the gritty neighborhood east of the elevated subway tracks near First Avenue. On the ground floor, the Norma Talmadge Film Corporation was in full swing filming *Poppy.* It was the second feature Schenck had produced for the twenty-two-year-old former Vitagraph actress he had married six months earlier. Near the precariously built set, a violinist was attempting to put Norma in the proper mood for a love scene with Eugene O'Brien. On the second floor at Colony Norma's sister was hard at work on her new picture. Constance Talmadge, eighteen, was a bouncy blonde who had first gained attention in D. W. Griffith's *Intolerance.* She was now establishing herself as a light comedienne.

Keaton took special note of Schenck's boutique comedy unit tucked away on the third floor. He saw flats lashed together and painted to depict a village general store, with a trolley ladder and shelves piled with canned goods. Arbuckle was warming up with Al St. John, his bony-faced, elastic-legged second banana, and an

English bulldog named Luke. Arbuckle recognized Keaton and motioned him over with a friendly grin. Would he care to do a bit in the next scene? Keaton declined, because the year before Arbuckle had swiped two of the Keatons' best vaudeville gags—the "Anvil Chorus" broom bash and Buster's "Hidden Adversary" routine—and used them in *The Waiters' Ball.*

Ignoring the rebuff, Arbuckle invited him to stay and see how silent films were shot. Two rivals for the same girl are working in the store, St. John as a clerk selling coffee (ground by the bulldog trotting along on a treadmill) and Arbuckle as the butcher. He staggers out of a refrigerator wearing an ankle-length fur coat and a bowler hat and starts a free-for-all with cleavers and sausages. Arbuckle and St. John were practitioners of bash-and-bop comedy.

By this time Keaton's curiosity was piqued—not by the story or by the loopy gags, which he had been doing all his life. He could not take his eyes off the camera. He was dying to know how it worked. Mounted on a collapsible tripod was a Bell & Howell operated by a cameraman who wore his cap backward so that its peak would not hamper his looking through the viewfinder.

What would always intrigue Keaton most about motion pictures was the technology. All he wanted to do, he recalled, "was to tear that camera to pieces. I had to know how that film got into the cutting room, what you did to it in there, and how you made things match and how you finally got the picture together." During a break, Arbuckle was happy to show him the cutting room, where pieces of film were spliced together, and the screening room, to watch the unedited film shot the previous day.

Keaton told Arbuckle he would like to do a scene after all.

The plots of Fatty films ran pretty much to formula, with Fatty as the romantic, although slightly kinky, lover who woos and wins the girl. All two-reeler comedies consisted of one long series of gags, mostly made up on the set, or as Keaton put it, "things just started happening." At Keaton's stop at wardrobe, he was outfitted with baggy overalls, a clip-on tie, and a flat porkpie hat. In vaudeville he and Joe wore identical soft felt caps. The hat that would become his trademark, as familiar as Chaplin's mustache or Clara Bow's mouth, was initially selected that day, either by himself or Arbuckle or even the wardrobe department. (The porkpie originated as a woman's hat in the 1850s.) Keaton said in 1964 that he made the porkpie his signature "the first time I went out on my own as a comedian." In 1917, Chaplin, Arbuckle, even pre–straw hat Harold Lloyd, indeed nearly every film comedian was wearing a derby hat. Keaton "decided to get a hat that was my very own."

On the grocery-store set, Keaton was handed a tin pail and instructed to shop for molasses. In his first screen appearance, he is seen from the back as he moseys into the store. In contrast to the other actors, his performance is dignified and crystalline. Movements are deceptively economical. Whenever he is in a shot, he rivets the audience's attention. Although he smiles twice, his expression is serious. In the store he walks up to the counter and pulls a quarter from his pocket. He tosses the coin in the air, catches and kisses it, and lobs it into the pail, which he then deposits on the counter, along with his hat.

While Arbuckle is pouring the molasses, Keaton wanders over to a stove, where old men are playing checkers. Arbuckle asks for payment. Keaton, absorbed in the game, indicates the money is at the bottom of the bucket. When he is ready to leave, Keaton walks back to the counter for his hat and pail. Unbeknownst to him, Arbuckle has poured molasses into his porkpie hat, fished out the quarter, and then poured the molasses back into the bucket. As Arbuckle tips his bowler in farewell, Keaton attempts to do likewise, but of course the porkpie is stuck to his head.

Keaton, increasingly agitated, tries to yank off the hat, and Arbuckle helps him. In the struggle Keaton drops the pail and spills the molasses, and his feet become glued to the floor. Arbuckle parboils his feet with boiling water to free him, then picks him up and whirls him into the street. Keaton liked this routine so much that he would use it many times thereafter, particularly on television.

It was close to midnight when Arbuckle called it a wrap. As they were leaving, Keaton asked Arbuckle if he might borrow a camera and bring it back in the morning. Almost a half century later, Keaton would tell a friend, James Karen, that he had not only carted home the camera but had actually taken it apart. Then he knew that he wanted to be in movies.

The next morning Keaton showed up at Max Hart's office to announce that he was leaving *The Passing Show* and going into motion pictures with the Schenck organization. According to

Keaton's recollection, Hart assured him that it was a wise choice. Movies were the future. Keaton claimed that Hart tore up his contract.

Perhaps the termination of their relationship did not happen exactly that way. Hart, who had other motion picture clients, did not offer to continue representing him. Despite what Keaton wished to recall, Hart may not have taken his defection so lightly. For the second time within a year, one of his clients—first Arbuckle and now Keaton—had been raided by Joseph Schenck and Lou Anger.

Toting the Bell & Howell, Keaton returned to East Forty-eighth Street, got into his overalls and porkpie hat, and went to the grocery set, where Arbuckle was setting up for a fight scene with Al St. John.

"You're late," Arbuckle said.

Aside from St. John, his partner and nephew, Arbuckle had decided to engage no other regular actors and to invest his money in writers. It was easy to wind up with players who couldn't function as a team. Apparently he had no reservations about Keaton.

Brown paper bags had been filled with flour, tied up, and were stacked on the set. Arbuckle warned Keaton that he was going to brain him with a bag of flour and not to duck.

"How am I going to keep from flinching?" Keaton asked.

"Look away. When I say 'Turn,' turn. It'll be there."

And it was. Arbuckle's powerful throwing arm knocked Keaton into the air in a thick cloud of flour dust. Arbuckle, Keaton recalled, "put my head where my feet were."

At the end of the week, he went to collect his pay. Since asking about salary had not occurred to him, he was surprised to receive only $40. Money was something he seldom considered because he always had plenty of it and Joe and Myra took care of the family finances. He complained to Lou Anger, who claimed that the wage was all his budget could manage.

Keaton sent part of his paycheck to his mother, who had joined Joe in Bluffton. Myra returned the money. They didn't need it. As for his new job, she would delay breaking the news to Joe. When he was finally told of his son's movie debut, Joe almost cried out of disbelief and disappointment.

By the spring of 1917, motion pictures were strangling vaudeville. The trades devoted their coverage mainly to such superstars of the picture business as Charlie Chaplin, Roscoe Arbuckle, and the Talmadge sisters. Leaving *The Passing Show* was a shrewd business decision, perhaps the only one Keaton would make in his entire life.

At Comique, the man whose workday had once amounted to thirty-six minutes was now putting in ten- to twelve-hour days, but he didn't mind the long hours. The physical violence upon which all the early comedies depended made it seem as if he had never left the Three Keatons. Keaton remarked to a reporter that anybody who had pitied him being batted around by his father should see him with Arbuckle, who could "slam him about harder." The *Telegraph* article was headlined "Papa Joe's Worthy Successor."

Roscoe Arbuckle weighed fourteen pounds when he was born prematurely in north-central Kansas, near the Nebraska border. Since his wife almost died giving birth to her youngest and suffered poor health afterward, William Arbuckle developed an intense dislike of Fatty and slapped him around more often than the other offspring. Fatty was told that he had practically killed his mother.

Two years later the Arbuckles moved to Santa Ana, California, south of Los Angeles, where William Arbuckle then abandoned the family. At the age of eight, Fatty hung around the local opera house. He earned his first money as a performer when a touring stock company hired him to play a "pickaninny," which required him to smear his body with black greasepaint. After his mother died, Fatty lived for a while in the home of his sister Nora and her husband, Walter St. John, a vaudeville team. Then he was shipped to his father, who had remarried and was living in the Santa Clara Valley. Fatty washed dishes and scrubbed floors at his father's restaurant, kept his mouth shut during William Arbuckle's drunken rages, then went out in the evenings to compete in amateur nights at local theaters.

He had a fine tenor voice. With encouragement from his sister he got work as a featured singer at Grauman's Unique Theatre in San Jose. At fifteen he attracted the attention of vaudeville impresario Alexander Pantages and eventually went out on the circuit with his own act.

In April 1913 Arbuckle stepped off a Pacific Electric red car in the Los Angeles suburb of Edendale, a community of truck farmers that had been colonized by a multitude of movie companies. Clutching a portfolio of photographs under his arm, he trudged down Alessandro Street to apply at Keystone Film Company, a comedy studio just eight months old.

Since there was no guard, Arbuckle strolled around the open stages and shops. A door opened, and a man in undershirt and suspenders stepped outside. It was Mack Sennett (a Canadian, born Michael Sinnott, a boilermaker by trade), the George Washington of film comedy. He was a big, athletic man in his early thirties with a thatch of wild graying hair. He chewed tobacco and was constantly spitting, even though there was seldom a spittoon around.

Arbuckle was decked out in white: crisp white trousers, glossy cream-colored pumps, a straw hat, and a navy-blue jacket. He smelled of soap and cologne. Sennett aimed a stream of tobacco juice at Arbuckle's immaculate pants and said, "You, big boy, be here tomorrow morning at eight." Then Sennett slammed the door.

Three years later Arbuckle had become one of the most popular figures in motion pictures, playing a lovable country boob also named Fatty, a happy-go-lucky innocent who always went off in the last reel with a sexy girl. His fans didn't care that he was fat. They thought he was adorable. Arbuckle learned how to make personal appearances, how to give interviews, and when the studio handed him a script for his revised life story, he memorized it—he told reporters that he was an alumnus of Santa Clara College, where he had been a football star and had sung in the glee club.

During those years, in part due to the success of the Fatty series with Arbuckle and his talented partner, Mabel Normand, Keystone rose to become the world's foremost comedy factory. With such talented comics as Mack Swain, Chester Conklin, Charlie Chase, Marie Prevost, and Minta Durfee, it turned out a comedy a week. In 1914 Charles Chaplin arrived at the studio and made thirty-five films that year, including the smash hit *Tillie's Punctured Romance*. Audiences loved the hilariously incompetent Keystone Kops, and the shapely Bathing Beauties provided the first cheesecake on film.

Chaplin was earning $175 a week at Keystone when Essanay lured him away in 1915 with an offer of $1,250 a week plus a $10,000 bonus. Arbuckle, who had begun writing and directing many of his own films, saw his earnings climb to an excellent $500 a week. Still, by 1916 Chaplin was getting $10,000, plus bonuses.

Arbuckle was twenty-nine years old when he met Joe Schenck.

Norma Talmadge called her husband Daddy, and he called her Child. They could have been called Beauty and the Beast. Norma was acknowledged as one of the loveliest females on earth. Joseph Schenck, a square, stocky man, had heavy jowls, a lumpy nose, chilly blue eyes, little hair, and many gold fillings. He was so homely that some people felt sorry for him.

Schenck's main interests were money, gambling, and women. He never seriously considered marriage, preferring to play the role of sugar daddy to a string of gold-digging showgirls. He was known to favor rough-and-tumble sex, but the only way he could sleep with Norma Talmadge was to marry her.

Thirty-seven years old in 1917, Schenck was born on Christmas Day in the Russian village of Rybinsk. Arriving in New York as a twelve-year-old, he worked in factories and sold newspapers, enrolled in a pharmaceutical course, and got a job at Doc Hornick's drugstore at 111th Street and Third Avenue. He and his younger brother, Nicholas, bought the store two years later.

On Sunday mornings in the summer of 1901, the brothers used to ride the Amsterdam Avenue trolley all the way up to Fort George, near the northernmost tip of Manhattan. There like thousands of New Yorkers they could escape the heat, but otherwise there was nothing to do. They decided to rent a beer concession. That summer they cleared $1,200 in a few weeks. The next year they offered free vaudeville and made $16,000, which was more profitable than peddling pills, opium, and morphine, as they did on the side. By 1910 they owned a controlling interest in Palisades Amusement Park on the New Jersey side of the Hudson, which made them a fortune. The Three Keatons had appeared at Palisades many times. There is some reason to believe that Keaton's professional association with Schenck did not begin by chance. He may have set out to recruit Keaton by sending Lou Anger, just as he had done in raiding Arbuckle.

On several occasions in the twenties Keaton told national magazines about his switch to motion pictures, always singling out Schenck as the person responsible. "I had a visit from Joseph M. Schenck who suggested that I make a series of two reel comedies under his management." By 1926, Arbuckle had become a pariah in the picture business and Keaton may have been reluctant to associate himself with his former mentor for readers of the *Saturday Evening Post* and *Ladies' Home Journal*. On the other hand, this revelation may have been an accurate account of what actually took place.

Whatever the truth, Arbuckle's second banana, Al St. John, had never shown star potential. One of the original Keystone Kops, St. John was a comedian of mediocre talent and grotesque appearance. He was not only the son of Arbuckle's sister Nora but also the husband of Minta's sister Flora. Arbuckle's hiring of Keaton when he already had his nephew as a partner implies that it was Schenck's suggestion.

Schenck had begun his motion picture deal-making in 1913 when he recognized a woman aboard a ship returning from a trip abroad. She was the beautiful, notorious Evelyn Nesbit, whose millionaire husband, Harry Kendall Thaw, had shot and killed Stanford White, one of the nation's leading architects and Evelyn's former lover. Schenck hurried over to pitch her a deal, a starring role in a movie based on her own life. He had a fertile imagination and a genius for recognizing the commercial possibilities in high trash. Nesbit epitomized high trash, and *Redemption* broke records at the box office. Schenck raked in $200,000, launching his career as an independent film producer and supplier of product for major distribution companies such as Paramount and Metro.

On April 23, 1917, the first Comique comedy, titled *The Butcher Boy,* opened in two hundred theaters across the country, including the Strand in Times Square. The film did well at the box office and with critics, who singled out Keaton as a talented newcomer in his bit role as the village pest: "Newcomer Keaton can take a fall and still come up swinging for laughs." Keaton visited the Strand and paid admission to watch himself on a big screen.

Comique's second comedy was released a month later. *A Reckless Romeo,* with exteriors filmed at Palisades Amusement Park, is about a henpecked husband (Arbuckle) who indulges in a flirtation with a young woman (Alice Lake) and is captured on film by a strolling cameraman. In this film Keaton is not easily found. He may play the woman's boyfriend, but he is more likely the camera operator. Another sequence, shot at a Broadway night-club, included its entire staff of artists, chorus, orchestra, waiters, plus three dozen extras. These scenes, which took days to film and cost $10,000, were eventually scrapped. None of this was lost on Keaton, who ever after took it for granted that a good visual gag was worth any amount of money, and directors should not be concerned about costs. He would do anything for a good shot and always defined "creative control" to mean spending lavishly to get what he wanted.

War had been declared on Germany on April 6. Shortly afterward the War Department announced a need for five million men to fight the war in Europe. Then another catastrophe, this one from the Woburn stag party, rattled the executive suite at Paramount. The Woburn madam had been arrested because some of the party girls had been minors. Boston mayor James Curley tipped off Paramount about an investigation now under way in the office of district attorney Nathan A. Tufts. Tufts, who seemed to think the stag party a disgusting crime and sprinkled his conversation with anti-Semitic slurs, told Paramount that an indictment could be expected.

Zukor and his chiefs eventually anted up $100,000, including five hundred shares of Paramount Famous Players–Lasky stock.

The scene of *The Rough House,* Comique's next release, is a seashore resort. The film includes several touches that are pure Keaton: vegetables being sliced by an electric fan, Arbuckle's unconcerned reaction when his bed catches fire, and St. John catching knives in his teeth. Later he and Keaton appeared to jump into the picture from nowhere and then vanish just as miraculously, achieved by reverse-action photography. Today *The Rough House* is chiefly memorable for the scene in which Arbuckle, at breakfast, jabs forks into a pair of dinner rolls and walks them around the table, mocking Chaplin's famous waddle. Chaplin would later appropriate this for a magical moment in his 1925 feature *The Gold Rush* when he makes dinner rolls dance. In this film Keaton got bits as a bearded gardener, a grocery delivery boy, and a cop. He was learning his craft.

On May 18 the Selective Draft Act was signed into law and Keaton registered. By the end of June three million men had been called up, in addition to another million who had volunteered. A great deal more important to Keaton was his salary, which had been raised to $75 a week. Roscoe began teaching him the technical side of filmmaking—how to set up shots, how to perfect the framing and composition, how to operate the camera, splice film, and put the sequences together. The Chief, as Keaton called him—never Fatty—seemed incapable of jealousy or meanness. He was generous with advice as well as money, too generous, Keaton thought. Unlike Keaton himself, who would make sure he got most of the laughs when he became a star, Arbuckle didn't care who got them, actors or animals. In *The Butcher Boy,* Arbuckle loved the performance of Minta's dog (who at Keystone had been earning $150 a week). "Why doggone it," he said, "Luke is trying to steal that picture. We have to watch that bird." If he realized that Keaton, too, was stealing many of his scenes, he never let on.

In midsummer, as American troops began arriving in France, Joe Schenck decided to move the Comique company to the Biograph studio in the Bronx.

The undercurrent of kinkiness that runs through many of Arbuckle's films is especially prominent in the next comedy. At Koff & Kramp Druggists, Fatty is a clerk who is working hard either cheating customers or trying to keep from being cheated. To discourage women from spraying themselves with the store's expensive perfume, he replaces the scent with chloroform. An attractive woman enters the store and sprays herself, then passes out. Furtively looking around, Arbuckle fondles and kisses the unconscious woman, then revives her with smelling salts and sends her on her way.

Arbuckle is engaged to be married. Keaton, as a delivery boy, brings the wedding gown to Arbuckle's fiancée (Alice Mann) and finds himself modeling the dress in her bedroom as she does last-minute alterations. While still wearing Alice's gown he is abducted and spirited to a justice of the peace, where it seems he will be forced to marry Al St. John. By the end, he has fallen into the clutches of Fatty. In drag, Keaton is wickedly funny—and completely dignified, even while wearing lace and satin. The picture was titled *His Wedding Night.*

The next two films were back to business as usual. Since no print of *Oh, Doctor!* is known to have survived, it can only be described sketchily from reviews. Arbuckle plays a doctor with a passion for the horses. Keaton, his son, takes charge of the office after his father gallops out to collect a five-hundred-to-one bet. For the first time Keaton gets second billing, above Al St. John. In *Fatty at Coney Island,* Keaton suddenly dropped the dignified demeanor that had made his debut in *The Butcher Boy* so refreshing. He adopts the frenetic pace of Arbuckle and St. John: he mugs, he cries when St. John steals his girlfriend, he giggles while being vamped by a fat bathing beauty (Arbuckle), he practically winks at the camera. The idea of making a trademark of a frozen face has apparently not yet occurred to him. But he does wear what would become his signature porkpie hat. He bought Stetsons for $3.50, cut them down, then stiffened the brim with sugar water.

Much of his time was spent tinkering with Comique's camera equipment. Sometimes Arbuckle stationed him alongside the camera as codirector—"I directed when he was in the scene," Keaton recalled—and sometimes he brought him into the cutting room as well.

On the warm summer nights, after working from dawn to dusk, Keaton and Arbuckle navigated the city in Arbuckle's new Rolls-Royce. Roscoe had plenty of money to spend. One of their favorite hangouts was Reisenweber's, a lobster palace on Columbus Circle, where they would be escorted to a front table in the vast red-carpeted main dining room. Mingling with celebrities, they listened to a new kind of music being called jazz and Arbuckle drank champagne; Keaton did not drink. However, he did eat well, and was now learning to savor fine cuisine.

Arbuckle took him to weekend house parties where he got his first glimpse of upper-crust glamour. In Bayside, Norma Talmadge and Joe Schenck held gatherings at their waterfront estate on Little Neck Bay for their blue-chip friends from the city: big-name Broadway folk like John Golden, closest friend of Joe's youth Irving Berlin, suburban bankers, film actresses, and fat-cat businessmen. They played noisy games of croquet, sailed on Long Island Sound, and gorged on massive barbecues that their host prepared himself. He stood over the grill in an apron and cooked each guest's steak or chop to order.

From the first time he walked into the Schenck compound, Keaton knew what he wanted for himself someday: a huge main house with a Japanese butler, a guest house, a driveway lined with gleaming motor cars being polished by their chauffeurs, rolling lawns, and backyard vegetable gardens. Not to mention the Talmadge "girls," as the sisters were known, with their Pomeranian, Dinky, and their graceful friends, men in white flannels and smart, laughing beauties weighted down by diamonds.

The memory of Joe Schenck barbecuing mutton chops on the lawn of his Bayside estate would always symbolize to Keaton everything that a man might aspire to in life. But Keaton's biggest inspiration was his new friend, Roscoe. With an unending supply of flashy cars and handsome women, the Big Guy was a flabby Jay Gatsby, a voyager who had washed up on the shores of paradise, against all impossible odds a millionaire who made his own movies. In Keaton's career, there would be only one artistic influence—not Griffith, not Sennett, not Chaplin, but Arbuckle.

7 THREE SISTERS

Natalie Talmadge was a member of the Comique production team. In 1917 a pretty, slender woman of twenty with fussy brown hair and brown eyes, she had two sisters who were movie goddesses. Although her mother told people she was the youngest, actually she was the middle sister between Norma, who was twenty-two, and Constance, eighteen, whom everybody called Dutch because she had been an uncommonly chubby blond child. Natalie's nickname—Nate—was predictable.

Her mother made a special point of insisting that Nate had never shown any interest in acting. Peg Talmadge explained to the Cleveland *Plain Dealer,* "I told her that she must take up or at least learn some kind of work so as to be self-supporting, so she studied bookkeeping, stenography, and typewriting."

Despite Peg's advanced notions, Nate was not an emancipated woman aspiring to a career. She was on the payroll as script girl, at a good salary, because she was family. Her main duties were to answer her sisters' fan mail and autograph photos.

From the first day she met him she hit it off with Keaton, and soon invited him to her home. He must have been impressed by her plush apartment at the Ambassador Hotel on Park Avenue, where she lived with her mother and sister Dutch and where Norma and Joe occupied the honeymoon suite. The family spent weekends at the Schencks' country house in Bayside.

Peg Talmadge, a large, fat woman in her midfifties, with hair matted like a bird's nest, was the antithesis of her daughters. An astute businesswoman, Peg ascribed to the philosophy "Get the money and get comfortable." That is, love is nice, but a diamond ring lasts forever. Anita Loos, in her *Gentlemen Prefer Blondes,* would paraphrase many of Peg's wisecracks in the lines of Dorothy, Lorelei Lee's unrefined girlfriend. One evening in Paris, for example, Loos was attending the Folies Bergère with the Talmadges and Schencks, when Joe wondered about the age of a beautiful nude showgirl. Loos guessed eighteen. Peg scoffed: "No girl could get her knees that dirty in only eighteen years."

In large part, the Talmadge women occupied a woman's world without men because Peg's husband, Fred, an alcoholic, had abandoned her. On afternoons when they were not filming, the three sisters liked to lounge around the Ambassador suite. As Peg slugged shots of Irish whiskey with her tea and rounds of champagne cocktails were passed, the banter was spirited and unrefined. All four women had a taste for gossip, the more vulgar and bitchy the better. Natalie struck Keaton as the most subdued member of the family, which led him to think of her as an old-fashioned woman of delicate disposition. Standing five feet two and weighing one hundred pounds, Nate bore a slight resemblance to Norma. All three sisters were blessed with spectacular complexions that they said came from their mother's Spanish blood. Over time, Norma had matured into the kind of rose who makes other women feel drab. Dutch, too, developed into a long-stemmed beauty with expressive brown eyes rimmed by dark lashes. People were less apt to notice Nate. Over the years, her features became slightly compressed, "as if she harbored the same genes that produced her radiant sisters but had simply failed to blossom into full, lush bloom," wrote Anita Loos.

The Talmadges had not always lived in high style. Peg's origins remain murky. Anita Loos reported that she was a plumber's daughter from Jersey City, but Loos was unreliable about such facts. Peg concocted a much grander lineage, telling her daughters that she had been born in Madrid into a distinguished Castilian family, a story they never believed for a second. Margaret Jose, born in 1861 in Spain, longed to become an actress. Joining a Brooklyn amateur group, the Amaranth Dramatic Society, she was thrilled to receive a role that called for her to speak seven words. On opening night she forgot them. So ended her acting career.

How and where Peg passed her youth—what she did before

meeting Frederick John Talmadge at the age of thirty-two—was information she chose to conceal.

Fred Talmadge was a descendant of Robert Talmadge, who established himself in New Haven, Connecticut, in 1644. His immediate family suffered a succession of misfortunes. His father, John Tallmadge, a fervent Republican, attended a political rally in Hartford and suffered an eye injury when his railway coach was stoned by a gang of rowdy Democrats. He felt lucky to retain his sight. His younger brother was killed just months after the beginning of the Civil War. In 1864 outside of Petersburg, Virginia, "another Democrat on the Confederate side sent over a shell which bursted and injured my Eye," he wrote on a pension claim. After the war, he married Martha Culver and moved to the tiny town of Plainville, Connecticut. In May 1868 the couple had a son, Frederick, named after John's slain brother.

Fred was twenty-five years old when he met Peg Jose. Her parents didn't approve of him. He was seven years her junior and had two noticeable vices: drinking and gambling on the horses. As a result, he had trouble holding down a job. When he worked, it was as a traveling salesman for a company manufacturing souvenirs for carnivals and circuses. Peg married him anyway, and they eventually settled in an undesirable area of South Brooklyn, near the shipping piers. Peg soon became pregnant.

Marriage to an alcoholic meant no real peace of mind for Peg. She never knew what would set Fred off, when he would come home roaring drunk, or how much money he would give her to run the house. Eventually her rage would boil over into global contempt. Her barbs were deadly.

Despite Fred's frequent absences from home, Peg gave birth to three babies in four years. She later told Anita Loos how each and every one of her children had arrived by accident despite her best efforts to abort them by riding the Bump-the-Bumps at Coney Island.

When Norma was seventeen, Peg heard about a photographer who was paying models five dollars a day to pose for the illustrated song slides projected in movie houses during audience sing-alongs. Norma had a photogenic face that looked as if it should be adorning a chocolate box. Peg got her a job, then she lowered Norma's age to fourteen and began trundling her around to movie companies. Thanks to Peg, just four years later Norma had her own film-production company and was receiving a thousand dollars a week from Joe Schenck for their first feature, *Panthea*.

From the start, Joe was clearly eager to sleep with Norma. But he hadn't reckoned with Peg, who never permitted him to be alone with her daughter if she could help it. Still, the romance played out. In October 1916 Norma told her mother that she and Schenck were going to be filming late that evening and arranged for Peg to attend the theater with Irving Berlin. During the show, Joe and Norma drove to Stamford, Connecticut, found a justice of the peace to marry them, then sped back to the city. By the time Berlin brought Peg home, Norma was in bed asleep.

At a private preview of *Panthea* on Christmas Day, Joe's birthday, it was clear that the picture would be a huge success. Peg hugged Schenck and said, "Joe, you wouldn't make a bad son-in-law at that."

"I'm glad you feel that way," he replied. "I've been your son-in-law for over two months."

All the Comique Film Corporation needed in order to grind out a picture every two weeks was a camera, a handful of actors, and good weather, since all comedy companies used outdoor locations for roughly 80 percent of their scenes. In September 1917, with six films in the can and a New York winter looming, they packed up and moved to Southern California. The minute Joe and Myra heard about the move west, they pulled up stakes and joined their son, leaving Jingles and Louise behind in school in Michigan.

Arbuckle decided to lease low-rent space in Long Beach, a port city twenty miles south of Hollywood. He had pleasant associations with the town, where he had met and fallen in love with Minta. He also negotiated a good deal with Herbert and Elwood Horkheimer for space in their Balboa Amusement Producing Company.

Long Beach was a city of nearly 55,000, a good theater town that supported eight movie houses and two stock companies. Owing to its protected location—facing Catalina Island—it offered superb conditions for outdoor filming, with clear air year-round and seven miles of broad beaches. It was also a pleasant place to live. Arbuckle rented a big balconied house on the bluffs, about two miles south of Balboa, and shared the house with Herbert Warren, the company's scenario editor, and his wife. Keaton moved into a modest apartment with his parents.

Their first production at Balboa, *A Country Hero,* went over budget. One scene called for a locomotive to wreck two Ford cars, a sequence whose cost soared over $20,000 after numerous retakes. The film has been lost, but reviews indicate that it took place in a small town where a blacksmith (Arbuckle) and a garage owner with a short fuse named Cy Klone are at each other's throats over the local schoolteacher (Alice Lake). Cy Klone is played by none other than Joe Keaton, after Arbuckle offered him the opportunity to preserve his hitch kick on celluloid. Directing Joe proved to be tricky, however, because he wasn't used to taking orders. Joe contributed his special martial-arts touches to two more Comique films—*Out West* and *The Bell Boy.*

Among those accompanying Comique from New York was Natalie Talmadge, now promoted, on paper, from script supervisor to Comique's secretary-treasurer. In *Out West* she even received a writing credit. Keaton, like everyone at Comique, took care to be especially nice to Nate. Although he refers to her in his autobiography as his girlfriend, his regular girlfriend in 1918 was Alice Lake, formerly one of Arbuckle's leading ladies at Keystone and now with Comique's repertory company. The exuberant twenty-two-year-old Brooklyn-born comedienne was a dropout of Erasmus Hall High School, just like the Talmadges. Alice was a brunette of medium height, with well-shaped legs and mismatched eyes, one brown and the other gray, though the contrast did not show in black and white. Known at Keystone as "The Laughing Lady," she was a free spirit fond of frisking about the studio topless, and sometimes bottomless as well. She was a typical playmate for Keaton, a sexually rambunctious, undemanding woman who was not thinking of marriage as she exited the boudoir.

Every six weeks, another picture got under way. In November the company began filming *Out West* in the burned San Gabriel Canyon, where they built a mining camp out among the cacti. The picture, a lampoon of William S. Hart's ultra-realistic westerns, is chiefly memorable for its sadism and cold-blooded murders. It did well at the box office.

The next four films—*The Bell Boy; Moonshine; Good Night, Nurse;* and *The Cook*—saw Keaton taking Al St. John's place as Arbuckle's colead. As he evolved his own ideas about comedy, friction developed with Arbuckle. Keaton pushed for more subtle, less overworked gags, while Arbuckle worried about changing his Keystone-style slapstick, which he considered a proven formula.

Before long a more basic disagreement developed between the two men. Like Sennett, Arbuckle did pure physical comedy, while Keaton was primarily interested in mechanical comedy and would achieve his most memorable laughs with exotic camera effects involving houses, trains, and boats. These differences were illustrated in *Moonshine,* released in May of 1918, a burlesque of stage melodramas with virginal maidens, mustache-twirling villains, and implausible escapes. Keaton and Arbuckle are government revenue agents patrolling the backwoods of Virginia (the San Gabriel Canyon) in a limousine, trying to bring to justice a band of moonshiners. After the car stops they hop out, and Keaton whistles to the car, even though he and Arbuckle are obviously alone. Suddenly the car doors open and out springs a revenue agent, followed by another, and another, until more than fifty agents have exited the vehicle in one continuous long shot and are lined up in rows. *Moonshine* was shot in multiple exposure: One side of the camera lens was masked and the scene shot, then the film was rewound and the other side of the lens covered.

Arbuckle later objected to the picture's costuming and set decoration: The moonshiners dress in tuxedos while their daughter (Alice Lake) is wearing a haute couture gown. Furthermore, the brewers' gentrified lair features a parlor that looks like a Victorian drawing room. Such touches, Arbuckle believed, were altogether too sophisticated for average moviegoers. They only wanted to laugh.

Arbuckle was constantly lecturing Keaton about movie audiences being children under twelve or their adult equivalent. It was true that an important segment of their audiences were children, but Keaton believed moviegoers were a good deal smarter than twelve. He told Arbuckle that anyone who couldn't accept that idea would probably not last long in motion pictures.

In addition to his technical contributions, Keaton was developing considerable skill as a gag man. Comique's original gag team included Herbert Warren, a former vaudevillian and now Comique's scenario editor, and Jean Havez, a songwriter. In Long Beach two talented newcomers were added: Mario Bianchi, a pudgy little man who as Monty Banks would become a comedian and comedy director; and Clyde Bruckman, a former sports editor on the *Los Angeles*

Examiner. Bruckman would work on a half dozen of Keaton's features, including *The General* and *The Cameraman,* then go on to write for Harold Lloyd, Laurel and Hardy, and W. C. Fields.

In July 1918, Keaton enlisted in the army. The night before he was to board a troop train Comique threw a farewell dinner. Entertainment featured a minstrel show with Arbuckle, Al St. John, and Eddie Cline. Keaton's going-away present was a wallet containing $100, since his monthly pay would soon be reduced to $30. The next morning he was on his way to Camp Kearney, outside of San Diego, for basic training and assignment to Company C of the 159th Infantry, 40th (Sunshine) Division.

Despite his many war-bond drives, Chaplin was criticized for not enlisting. Detractors claimed that he paid off the right people in Washington and made a million dollars a year at home. Arbuckle tried to join up, but the army rejected him for being one hundred pounds overweight. He entertained marines training on Mare Island and made an anonymous donation of a trainload of Bull Durham tobacco.

In August Keaton's outfit was shipped east to Camp Upton in Yaphank, Long Island, a training camp on ten thousand acres of swampy, mosquito-infested land, today the site of Brookhaven National Laboratory. Irving Berlin composed the song "Oh! How I Hate to Get Up in the Morning" during his months there.

Before shipping out Keaton telephoned Natalie Talmadge in Bayside. At age twenty-two, she was retired. She filled her days staying in bed late and going to shows and browsing Fifth Avenue landmarks like Hattie Carnegie and Cartier. When she heard from Keaton, she offered to drive to Camp Upton in her brother-in-law's chauffeured Packard.

"She looked gorgeous," Keaton remembered. "So did the Packard."

This was Nate's second visit to the camp. She and her sisters and Anita Loos had stopped by to visit Irving Berlin, who had been stationed at Upton since the spring. Berlin had a crush on Dutch, which she did not reciprocate.

Natalie arrived alone to see Keaton. After spending the entire day together cruising around in the Packard, they ended up in western Long Island at fashionable Long Beach. They dined and danced at a romantic restaurant called Castles in the Air, owned by

Vernon and Irene Castle. What Keaton remembered best about the day was the food, how hungry he had been for a good meal and a cup of real coffee after two months of canned beans and corned beef. Natalie picked up the check.

Three days later, Keaton found himself in a convoy of troop ships on the Atlantic. From England he crossed the Channel on a boat so jammed that he had to stand up. He was stationed in Amiens, south of Paris. Neither the French countryside nor the town had much appeal. It was cold and muddy, and it rained continually. He had to sleep on the ground, either in cellars or in barns and stables. By his birthday on October 4—his twenty-third—he had come down with a hideous cold and an ear infection.

Keaton's family spent the rest of the war living in a rented apartment in downtown Muskegon. Jingles and Louise, now withdrawn from their boarding schools, lived at home and attended public school. Joe applied for work in a munitions factory and obtained an assembly-line job making artillery shells. On every shell he chalked the message "Give 'em hell, Buster," even though Buster was in the infantry. As it happened, the Keatons received extra money from an unexpected source—Joe Schenck, who sent them a $25 check each week.

One night in Amiens, Keaton was returning to his quarters after his regular poker game with a group of officers who played at a nearby château. He had a special pass to get past the sentry.

In the darkness, he heard the metallic click of a shell being snapped into the firing chamber of a rifle. He stopped in his tracks, spun around, and threw up his hands.

"Friend!" he yelled, though no one was visible. Through a curtain of rain marched a sentry whose rifle was pointed at Keaton's heart. The soldier furiously cursed him. He had demanded the password, but Keaton had paid no attention to that or to two further warnings. The sentry had been set to shoot. Terribly shaken by this close call, Keaton began to worry about his hearing.

As a result of a chronic ear infection, he had become virtually deaf. He fell back into the role of the little boy who can't be damaged and tried to ignore the problem. Superiors had to shout their orders at him. He was lucky that the armistice was declared only a few weeks later.

In France, Keaton thought of food day and night: bloody sirloin steaks, rib roasts, great swirling hills of mashed potatoes drowned in gravy, bacon and buttery fried eggs. When he wasn't dreaming of food he was combing the town in search of it. With his first paycheck he marched into an inn and gorged himself on a meal of rare beefsteak, french-fried potatoes, and wine straight from the carafe.

After the armistice Keaton was transferred to a small town near Bordeaux where a legion of restless soldiers waited for transportation home. The Sunshine Division organized entertainment. Keaton, now a single-stripe corporal, offered to direct a variety show using a thirty-six-piece regimental band. Among the acts was a blackface minstrel show with banjo, barbershop harmony, and dancing. Keaton himself performed, in drag, a solo harem dance with a snake. Carrying a string of frankfurters for the snake and wearing a bra made of dog tags and a skirt of knives, spoons, and mess kits, "Princess Rajah" did bumps and grinds. The skit was a terrific hit, but it also proved to be a mistake. The army recognized just how valuable his show business services could be, and he had to stay in France long after his friends had sailed. Not until March 1919 did he return home.

At the veteran's hospital in New York, Keaton's first visitor was Joe Schenck, who was shocked to see him looking so thin, ill, and depressed. Joe's solution to most problems was money. He reached for his wallet and showered its entire contents onto Keaton's bed. After Schenck left, he hurried out and treated himself to a new pair of shoes. Keaton would never forget his generosity.

While in New York he had dinner one night with Natalie Talmadge. He was surprised to learn that Nate was preparing to make her screen debut in Norma's next movie, *The Isle of Conquest*. Her mother confided to the Cleveland *Plain Dealer* that Natalie "doesn't want to be outdone by her sisters." It was only a question of time, she predicted, until Natalie would have her own motion picture company like Norma and Connie. She was already being groomed by the steely Beulah Livingstone, Schenck's New York publicist. Livingstone told reporters that while Norma was "the motherly type" and Connie a good-time Sally, Nate had a style best described as "thoughtful, quiet, and inquiring." That summer fan-magazine photographers would be invited to Bayside for a peek at all three Talmadge girls dressed in gym suits performing calisthenics on the lawn. According to *Picture Show Magazine,* Natalie "possesses the talent for which the Talmadge sisters are noted."

There is no evidence of any romantic link between Keaton and Natalie at that time. Peg said, "He used to come home with her for dinner now and then, and all three girls were quite devoted to him, but I cannot remember that I ever thought of his comings and goings as of any special import." Keaton, then earning $40 a week, was unsuitable. Peg was fully aware of his success in vaudeville and probably had seen the Three Keatons perform, but she looked down on variety artists as contemptuously as Joe Keaton had turned up his nose at movie people. Keaton himself had no illusions. He was not good enough for Nate, and that was that.

The army sent him to Johns Hopkins University Hospital in Baltimore for further evaluation of his hearing problem. He wrote in his autobiography that his hearing had improved so greatly that Hopkins released him after three days. If so, the improvement was only temporary. Throughout his life Keaton would have to contend with periodic hearing loss in both ears. Each time he caught a cold he would be deaf until the infection cleared up. Conversing easily, especially with educated people, had always been a problem, and this made it even harder.

In April he was discharged from the army. Due to a clerical error, he was obliged to travel from Baltimore to Camp Custer, Michigan, because when registering for the draft in 1917 he had named Muskegon as his hometown. There Joe and Myra were thrilled to see him again, but he spent only three days with his family. Impatient to rejoin Arbuckle and his friends at Comique, he headed west for Los Angeles, the city he now considered his home.

8 HOLLYWOOD

Within hours of his arrival, Keaton was getting an exuberant reception at Comique, which had moved from Long Beach to Alessandro Street in Edendale during his absence. As a welcome-home gift, Arbuckle handed him a beautifully wrapped box. It blew up in Keaton's face as he pulled off the wrappings.

If the Big Guy's fondness for practical jokes had not changed, it was nonetheless just about the only thing to have remained the same. Alice Lake had left the company to pursue dramatic roles at Metro. Al St. John was moving on to star in his own comedy series for Warner Bros. Most surprising of all, Arbuckle was talking about quitting two-reelers and making feature-length comedies, a step that not even Chaplin had dared to take.

It must have been gratifying for Keaton to find out that the picture industry had not forgotten him. Both Warner Bros. and the William Fox Company offered him jobs paying $1,000 a week. Instead he rejoined Comique and "the best friend I ever had" at his prewar salary of $250. As he later explained, he had accepted the lower salary because he felt indebted to Joe Schenck, a "square shooter" who had been kind to his family during the war.

Aside from gratitude, there was another reason for Keaton's loyalty to Comique. As he learned from Arbuckle, important changes were about to take place. If he stuck around, there would be opportunities for him.

Keaton moved into the Hollywood Hotel, where he shared a room with Ward Crane, a twenty-eight-year-old actor who had recently arrived from Albany, New York, and whose most memorable role would be Keaton's rival in *Sherlock Jr.* New York actors tended to lodge at the Hollywood until they found a house to rent or went back East. What passed for nightlife in Hollywood took place at dances in the hotel's lobby.

In April Keaton joined the Comique company on location in the hills near Glendale, but he did not appear in *A Desert Hero*. The next comedy would be permeated by the Keaton comedy style and contain a blueprint for *The Playhouse* and later pictures. *Back Stage,* the first color-tinted two-reeler, is a love song to vaudeville. Keaton is a stagehand at a variety theater, and Arbuckle is his boss. Here is the backstage life both of them knew so well: the frantic rehearsals, rowdy audiences, monologists who complain about their dressing rooms, male stars who bully chorus girls. Arbuckle even bounces Keaton off a heckler's face just as Joe Keaton had done years earlier in Syracuse. In a scene that foreshadows *Steamboat Bill Jr.,* Arbuckle is serenading Molly Malone on a balcony when the scenery topples over and frames him in the second-story window.

While *Back Stage* is among the best of the Arbuckle-Keaton two-reelers, *The Hayseed* is set in a small-town general store and could serve as a sequel to Arbuckle's other overalls comedies such as *The Butcher Boy* and *His Wedding Night.* The clunky story has no surprises, the fight scenes lack Arbuckle's frantic energy, and there are no interesting effects. Even Keaton's performance as a bumpkin grocery clerk is perfunctory.

That summer their funniest material was done off-camera. Driving through the isolated suburb of Beverly Hills, they passed actress Pauline Frederick's mansion on Sunset Boulevard. Frederick, obviously at enormous expense, had finally produced a velvety green expanse running the length of her 150-foot lot. For Keaton and Arbuckle's taste, the lawn was a little too perfect. Early one morning, dressed as workmen, Keaton, Arbuckle, and actor Lew Cody drove a truck up to the door. Claiming to represent the Beverly Hills Gas and Electric Company, they told the butler about a reported gas leak. They began digging up the grass. Frederick's servants were screaming: Couldn't they see that a fortune had been spent on the lawn? The gas men shrugged. They were only doing their jobs. What if the house blew up?

Finally, a hysterical Polly Frederick galloped out in her bathrobe. She recognized them. "When she stopped laughing she invited us in and served us a breakfast fit for a king," Keaton recalled.

Keaton adored such escapades. He escorted Adolph Zukor and
Marcus Loew on a terrifying roller-coasterlike ride through downtown Los Angeles while pretending to be Arbuckle's chauffeur.
Most of all he enjoyed the camaraderie shared with Arbuckle. The
two men were inseparable. A day on the set ended with dinner
together, then a night of partying or cards. On weekends they
went hunting or fishing, or drove down to Long Beach, where
Arbuckle owned a beach house. For a change of scenery, they
made the ten-hour jaunt up to San Francisco, mecca of the
swingers' universe and one of Arbuckle's favorite cities.

That summer Comique moved again, from Edendale to the
Henry Lehrman Studio in Culver City. There was bad blood
between Arbuckle and Henry "Pathé" Lehrman, a former New
York streetcar conductor whom D. W. Griffith had derisively nicknamed Pathé after his boast of working for the French cinema pioneers. After directing Arbuckle's first three films at Keystone,
Lehrman refused to work with Arbuckle. Fatty, he complained to
Sennett, was a prima donna who wouldn't take direction and
deserved to be fired.

After Labor Day, Comique began filming *The Garage,* a vintage Arbuckle-Keaton collaboration. By now it is clear that if
Arbuckle had taught Keaton how to make films, Keaton had
showed his mentor how to make well-crafted comedies. Arbuckle
had moved away from meat-cleaver comedy and closer to Keaton's
dry humor. In *The Garage* two guys are operating the town's combination garage and fire station when the heroine's boyfriend
comes in wearing a spotless white suit. In the old days, Arbuckle
would immediately have squirted him from head to toe with
grease, but now, with Keatonesque delicacy, the white suit picks
up only a single black handprint. As Arbuckle tries to repair the
damage, the suit very slowly turns black. While the picture is full
of delicious Keaton humor, his own acting talent is wasted.
Arbuckle was the star, and Keaton could never be anything more
than a second banana. In all, he had made fifteen pictures with
Arbuckle since first walking into the Colony Studio in the spring
of 1917. After nearly three years, having reached a dead end, it
turned out that he did not have to leave Roscoe. Roscoe left him.

Conventional wisdom was that the ideal length for a comedy
should be twenty minutes. After that, audiences got restless.

Throughout the war, the picture market grew more competitive, and traditional wisdom was being tossed overboard.

By 1920, 33 million Americans attended the movies every week. A typical bill included a big five-reel drama, a two-reel comedy, a newsreel, and a batch of shorts. Vaudeville managers began to beef up live acts with first-run five-reel films, the very best they could find, shown on a big screen. Cinemas, accordingly, found it necessary to show double bills. The days of the two-reeler were numbered.

In the studio wars, Adolph Zukor, the chief of Famous Players–Lasky, was buying up virtually the entire industry. In his view, the field was becoming crowded, with too many small studios competing for too few movie houses. He ate profitable rivals and forced others out of business.

For two years Zukor had been distributing the Comique shorts, whose popularity had continued to soar at the box office. If Arbuckle's two-reelers made piles of money, even more could be made if he switched to feature-length films. In an unheard-of deal, Zukor purchased the remaining cash value of Arbuckle's contract with Schenck, got the rights to Arbuckle's next twenty-two pictures, and guaranteed him at least $3 million over the next three years. All of the pictures would be features.

Arbuckle left Comique after making *The Garage*. He had a great future.

California's perfumed air was as sharp and pleasurable in Keaton's memory as madeleines and lime-blossom tea were for Marcel Proust. Forty years later he remembered thinking that it smelled like wine. In his autobiography, those halcyon months of his twenty-fourth year are described in a chapter titled "When the World Was Ours."

During 1919 the film colony continued to be a pastoral, placid town of squat and undistinguished buildings where everybody knew everyone's business. In East Hollywood just off Hollywood Boulevard grew orange and lemon groves and freshly plowed bean fields; oil derricks dotted the wide open spaces of Wilshire. There were no museums or theaters or elegant restaurants. Since most actors lived unpretentiously in rented apartments and got up at five in the morning and turned in by ten at night, their workdays were too long to allow for wild nightlife. "Life was good," wrote

Adela Rogers St. Johns, Hearst "yellow" journalist and a chronicler of early Hollywood. "Our town was beautiful."

The transformation of Hollywood into a dream factory was symbolized by Keaton's best friend. When Buster had left for boot camp eleven months earlier, Arbuckle had been living an unassuming life in Long Beach and sharing a rented house. When he returned, Arbuckle lived in a twenty-room, six-bath Tudor mansion in a fashionable district of Los Angeles. The house had stained glass windows and a six-car garage for his collection of automobiles—the Rolls-Royce that Schenck had given him in 1917, a Stevens-Duryea, a Cadillac town car, a White, and a Renault roadster. Arbuckle had purchased the West Adams Boulevard property, previously the home of vampy actress Theda Bara, for a quarter of a million dollars in cash.

In the drawing room of Arbuckle's opulent new home hung a crystal chandelier festooned with a thousand candles; the $15,000 front door was imported from Spain, and the bathtubs were plated with gold leaf. His bureau drawers were stuffed with hundreds of monogrammed dress shirts. His basement was stocked from floor to ceiling with thousands of bottles of fine imported wines and liquors, which were essential, since he threw sit-down banquets, teas, breakfasts, motor outings, house parties, and lawn fetes, once even a dog wedding, for which his bulldog Luke served as best man.

Arbuckle liked to keep his house full of people. At his Fitzgeraldian parties, large numbers of friends as well as the uninvited came to cadge free scotch. The only people who did not appreciate the all-night revels were his neighbors, who whispered of his vulgarity and complained that excessive drinking, rowdy guests, and a six-piece jazz band blaring at all hours made rest difficult.

Sometimes Arbuckle grumbled about how he hated extravagance. He would remind people that splurging was not his idea, but an order from Joe Schenck, who believed living well and behaving like a real movie star was important. Despite his complaints, Arbuckle relished being a rich and famous superstar who could make people happy.

Upon his return to Los Angeles, Keaton rekindled his relationship with Alice Lake. A few weeks later he met an actress friend of hers who was a rising comedienne at Metro. Viola Dana was four foot ten, ninety-six pounds, with green eyes and dark curly hair and the sexy and perky manner of a cheerleader. Keaton asked Vi out—to Alice's annoyance, no doubt—but he had annoyed women before and didn't take her displeasure seriously. Alice promptly began dating Arbuckle, and they made a foursome.

Dana was one of three sisters. Just as Keaton had been drawn to the Talmadge girls in New York, now he fell for a second troika of acting sisters.

Viola Dana was born in Brooklyn in 1898. Her father was a printer and her mother a frustrated actress who began hauling her girls around to Broadway casting offices before they were five years old. The Flugrath sisters, as they were christened, would be known professionally as Edna Flugrath, Viola Dana, and Shirley Mason. The eldest, Edna, danced with Anna Pavlova's company and as an adult became a screen actress in England. Vi appeared on Broadway in Ibsen's *When We Dead Awaken,* and Shirley was a stage veteran by four.

John Hancock Collins, the casting director for Thomas Edison's film company, discovered Vi when she was thirteen and arranged for her screen debut in Charles Dickens's *A Christmas Carol.* They were married a few years later. However, Collins died in the 1918 influenza epidemic, leaving Vi a twenty-two-year-old widow.

Keaton adored the Flugrath family. They were likable, good-humored folks who didn't put on airs, as opposed to the Talmadges, whose pretentious lifestyle had always intimidated him. This did not mean the Flugraths lacked elegance. Vi had just paid $10,000 for a new sable cape lined with gold brocade woven with silver poppies. Still, by the standards of the Hollywood elite, Viola Dana was riffraff, like Mabel Normand, another popular actress who failed to make the A-list party circuit. Such distinctions meant nothing to Keaton. He began spending most of his spare time at the Flugraths' Beverly Hills home. Viola Dana's niece, Sheila Kaufman, does not believe their involvement was sexual. "Vi was quite a cutup, the wild, impulsive one of the three sisters. But I don't think there was an affair with Buster because she was so very prudish about sex. She had a way of turning men into her friends."

That summer, Keaton turned into an enthusiastic party boy.

Nightlife in Hollywood was quickly changing. Buster and Vi, the romantic couple of the moment, had been regulars at the Hollywood Hotel's dances, but more and more the place to go was Vernon Country Club, a gin joint nestled among the beet fields and chicken farms in the San Fernando Valley.

Since Vernon Country Club observed no set closing hours, it attracted serious drinkers. Situated beyond the city limits, it could serve whomever it wanted and became an all-night hangout for scroungy Keystone Kops and pretty underage bar rats like Adela Rogers and Mabel Normand, both in pigtails and hairbows. Vernon also drew underworld characters who gave the club its special sleazy cachet. For those bored with unlimited amounts of whiskey and sex, the next thing was cocaine or heroin.

Narcotics were everywhere: at home, at Vernon, even at the studios. This was especially true at the comedy companies, where physically grueling work demanded large amounts of energy and stunts caused chronic injuries. Several of Keaton's friends had problems with drugs. Arbuckle had become hooked on morphine and heroin. After undergoing a difficult two-week cold-turkey withdrawal, he was now straight and back on the workingman's drug—booze. Mabel Normand was not so lucky. A well-known cocaine addict, her career would soon sink like the *Titanic*.

That fall Keaton attended a stag party at Arbuckle's home in honor of Joe Schenck. In a few days Arbuckle would be leaving on a European vacation, and when he returned would begin filming his first feature at the Famous Players–Lasky Studio. His successor had not been named, but Keaton seemed to be in line. After dinner Schenck took Keaton out to the porch and told him of his decision to turn over the Comique comedy unit to him. The deal was concluded then and there on the porch, sealed by a handshake.

Keaton signed his first agreement with Schenck on December 23. He contracted to make eight two-reelers a year for the Comique Film Corporation, each picture to cost no more than $30,000. The comedies were to be released by Metro Pictures, a studio recently taken over by Marcus Loew, whose Loew's theater chain was the biggest in the country. Metro agreed to pay Comique 70 percent of the gross box office receipts, payable each Friday. Keaton was to receive a weekly salary of $1,000 (the equivalent of $10,000 today), plus 35 percent of Comique's annual net income (the same arrangement as Arbuckle's). It was a substantial sum of money, although it did not approach Arbuckle's new seven-figure salary or the amount that a star like Harold Lloyd was pulling down.

Later Keaton said that Schenck gave him complete artistic control over his work and "just turned me loose." Joe, he declared, "never knew when I was shooting or what I was shooting." This was not exactly the case.

Schenck preferred calling the shots from New York and made only occasional trips to the Coast. Comique was policed by Lou Anger, who reported everything to his boss. Schenck had people watching his enterprises for him. He knew what kind of money Arbuckle spent on a scene, what happened in script conferences, whether Keaton was sleeping with Alice Lake or Viola Dana or both, who visited the studio. In the early days of filmmaking, financiers had tended to trust the director to come in on schedule with a picture. But Schenck had instituted the system of supervisors, his soldiers on the set every day to make sure his will was carried out. He also relied on stool pigeons, mostly actors who didn't mind spying on their colleagues to stay on Schenck's good side.

Freedom to control every aspect of his films was extremely important to Keaton. He assumed he would receive the same kind of autonomy as Schenck had given Arbuckle. This turned out to be an illusion.

Schenck seldom put his cards on the table, a fact Keaton never got through his head. Schenck allowed him a measure of artistic control—but within closely defined limits. Keaton failed to understand that even though Arbuckle had trouble keeping his production costs down, the comedy unit invariably made money. In Keaton's case, Schenck would follow the same policy: As long as there were profits, he would allow him control and remain in the background. It was very nearly possible for Keaton to forget him entirely.

Schenck courted Keaton by promising him tantalizing perks that not even Arbuckle had managed to squeeze out of him. In the past Comique had rented space wherever it happened to get a good deal. Keaton's Comique was to have a real studio of its own, and it would be called the Buster Keaton Studio.

During the holidays Keaton moved out of the Hollywood Hotel and rented a bungalow at 4011 Ingraham Street. It was comfortable, the equivalent of a two-bedroom apartment, but certainly not splashy. He was not a movie star yet.

The Buster Keaton Studio, formerly the Lone Star, was located across the street from Metro, on the corner of Lillian Way and Eleanor Avenue. Once it was the studio where Chaplin had made *Easy Street* and other films. At that time Lone Star boasted the largest stage of any producing unit in Hollywood, but for the past two years the lot had been empty.

His first sight of the studio filled Keaton with wonder. "So I had a city lot there, a good-size block, for my studio," he crowed to film historian Kevin Brownlow, even forty-five years later still awestruck over the recollection of having his own personal playground. Studios of the time tended to look like archaeological excavations, with their heaps of girders and canvas shacks. Lone Star was not like that. At the center of the property was a huge open stage, with canvas side walls and draped linen diffusers overhead. Since it was big enough to handle street scenes, it would cut down on unnecessary location work, although much of Keaton's shooting would always be done on location. The administration buildings included a film lab and projection room, business offices, scenic workshops, and property rooms. There were also twenty dressing rooms.

Long afterward, it seemed to Keaton that Chaplin and Lloyd were smarter businessmen than he because they had formed their own shops, produced their own pictures, and retained control of the rights. He himself had been nothing more than a sharecropper on Schenck's plantation, working his forty acres in exchange for a weekly wage and a percentage of the profits.

But in 1920 Keaton felt fortunate to be taking home 35 percent profits from a company whose main stockholders included the Schenck brothers, Marcus Loew, banker A. H. Giannini, and Irving Berlin. Even more important, Joe Schenck was relieving him of all business worries.

The only haggling between Keaton and Schenck was over picture length. Keaton wanted to go into features like Arbuckle. Chaplin and Lloyd, he argued, would soon be making features too and he could get a leg up. Schenck said that features were too costly. Very likely he had qualms about Keaton's ability to carry a full-length film.

*   *   *

With the opening of the Buster Keaton Studio, Joe and Myra sold their lake cottage and bought a touring car. In late January 1920, the family began the drive to Los Angeles in the new Cadillac chauffeured by fifteen-year-old Jingles. Except for the long weekend after Buster's army discharge, it had been three years since Louise and Jingles had seen their brother. Bounced from parochial boarding schools to public schools, now uprooted from the only security they had known, Louise and Jingles had difficulty adjusting to Hollywood. As Jingles would lament much later, "Keatons all agree, the greatest times we ever had was in Muskegon." With the move to Los Angeles, the Keaton children's education ended at thirteen and fifteen. Myra and Joe never placed much value on education. Louise and Jingles had already spent more years inside the classroom than the rest of the family combined.

At first Jingles showed up at the studio almost every day to watch the shooting. After a while he stopped coming. While other members of the family—especially Joe—occasionally acted in Keaton films, Jingles would be conspicuously absent. More and more both he and his sister fell into their old roles of homebodies who provided companionship for their mother.

Although the five Keatons supposedly shared the house on Ingraham Street, Buster was seldom there. He slept either at Arbuckle's or the studio, where his dressing room doubled as a small apartment with kitchen facilities. For the rest of his life he continued to support everyone in his family, without complaint. He considered it his duty. Given his habit of denying unpleasant situations, he may not have wished to see the problems shaking his family. In any case, he had his hands full preparing to film his first comedy.

9 HOME TEAM

In January of 1920, shortly after his family arrived in Hollywood, Keaton began working on his first film, *The High Sign*. For his story he reached into his father's history. In the opening sequence he plays a drifter, a bum who gets booted off a train near a fairground and is nosing around for a job, exactly Joe Keaton's situation when he bumped into the Cutler Comedy Company in the Cherokee Strip. After that, Keaton turns to fiction. Passing himself off as an expert marksman, Buster finds work in a shooting gallery, which actually is a front for an underworld gang. When the Blinking Buzzards attempt to shake down a wealthy local businessman, the businessman's daughter enlists Buster as a bodyguard. The Buzzards, meanwhile, initiate him into their organization, then they assign him the job of bumping off the businessman. The climax is a chase through a maze of corridors and trapdoors in their hideout.

Keaton inherited some of the cream of Arbuckle's company, with whom he had worked before: cameraman Elgin Lessley, cutter J. Sherman Kell, and a brilliant mechanic and designer, thirty-nine-year-old technical director Fred Gabourie, who did sets and special effects. As codirector Keaton signed a former Keystoner who was among the most sought-after in the business, Edward Cline. Although Keaton joked about only hiring good ballplayers, he went about building his production team with the greatest care.

Silent motion pictures required a high level of technical skill. Photography and lighting, stories and faces combined to create believable effects for the audience, whose imagination had to supply the missing sounds. Artistically lettered title cards were also used to explain the action and substitute for spoken dialogue. But silent films were never really silent. Most pictures were released with music cue sheets. Some people said they went to movies just for the music, which could range from a modest piano and violin to first-class orchestras and gigantic organs in the grand movie palaces. Sound effects—gunfire, thunder—were also added by technicians who sat in the orchestra pit or behind the screen.

The Keaton studio did not work from a written script; continuity was developed orally. Keaton later recalled that he and his writers would talk about a story, lay out all their ideas, then pull the scenario together. "The way we worked then, everybody knew what they were doin', so what the hell ya put it on paper for. We *never* bothered about a middle. After we had a good start, we'd work on a really great finish, and the middle sort of took care of itself."

After *The High Sign* had been cut down to twenty minutes, Keaton decided that it was nowhere near as funny as it should have been. In a scene near the middle Buster notices a banana peel lying in the middle of the sidewalk. Instead of slipping, as expected, he walks by the camera, turns to the lens, and thumbs his nose at the audience, as if to say, Sucker! Fooled you, didn't I? This gesture bothered him because it seemed to insult the viewers. In fact, he disliked the entire film.

The High Sign, an example of mainstream 1920 comedy, isn't half bad. It contains one of his priceless sight gags, in which he sits on a bench and opens a newspaper. But as the paper unfolds and engulfs him, he wanders endlessly among the maze of want ads like Theseus threading his way out of the labyrinth. Finally he falls backward off the bench, his head poking through a hole in the paper. That surreal joke alone is worth the price of admission. And yet Keaton was correct in judging the picture ordinary, made out of spare parts from old Arbuckle shorts. Since this was Keaton's first independent film, he wanted it to be special.

At this point, with *The High Sign* soon to be released, major revisions were out of the question. Keaton warned Schenck that the gags lacked punch and asked him to pull the picture. Schenck's exasperation can well be imagined; Metro had been promised eight shorts in 1920. He could not scrub a picture because Keaton happened to dislike a couple of scenes. Moreover, since the picture was far better than Keaton would ever admit, Schenck probably pushed for releasing it. In the end, Schenck acquiesced, and Lou Anger advised Keaton to take a few days off.

Frustrated and disgusted, he fled Hollywood. Piling guns and tackle into his new Buick, he invited his family to drive north to the Sierra Nevada, where Arbuckle was shooting *The Round Up,* his first feature for Paramount. In the wilderness Keaton relaxed a little.

Keaton's name had been mentioned during a dinner at the home of Douglas Fairbanks. A visitor from New York, Broadway impresario John Golden, was talking to Metro about filming his 1913 hit, *The New Henrietta.* On the stage the starring roles in this drawing-room comedy had been played by Fairbanks and William H. Crane. For the movie version the distinguished white-haired Crane was set to repeat his role as Nicholas Van Alstyne, the "Wolf of Wall Street" who makes a fortune from his Henrietta gold mine. Marcus Loew wanted Fairbanks for his part, the millionaire's coddled son Bertie, a playboy so effeminate he was nicknamed the Lamb. But Fairbanks had already used the Bertie character in his first motion picture. And in any case, he was now under contract to United Artists. He suggested Keaton.

Keaton was always a bit awestruck by Fairbanks. For the rest of his life he dined out on the story of how Dougie tapped him for his old role. "That could have been," allows Douglas Fairbanks, Jr. "There's nobody around to say nay now." Nevertheless, he doubts such an idea would have occurred to his father because there was no resemblance between him and Keaton. "They were different types." John Golden in fact may have first heard the idea from Joe Schenck, a dear friend and his next-door neighbor in Bayside.

Whoever was responsible, the idea of dressing up Keaton in white spats and top hat struck everyone as brilliant. As Schenck knew, critics did not always pay much attention to two-reelers. So for Keaton's coming out, he shrewdly decided to change his image, to strip him of his bumpkin overalls and porkpie hat, and market him to movie audiences by launching him first as a dandy in a high-quality feature film.

The New Henrietta was rewritten with Keaton as the central character and renamed *The Saphead.* Still, it remained a filmed play, stagy and long-winded, running seven reels, but with elegant production values and excellent acting. When it opened on

October 18, 1920, critics were quick to praise Keaton's performance. *Variety* called him "a cyclone" whose "quiet work in this picture is a revelation." With his dark, sensitive looks, his face in repose evoking years of quiet contemplation, he resembled a mixture of Buddhist monk and fashion model. He offered the ideal face and acting style for motion pictures, proving that less is more. He would become a master of knowing when to do nothing at all. *The Saphead* also gave him the recipe for an aristocratic character that he would enjoy playing in so many of his films. In the future, his costuming would be split between the porkpie hat and baggy pants and the top hat and stylish evening clothes, reflecting both his working-class origins and his desire to live like a prince. Yet, after *The Saphead* he would never again be completely happy in overalls.

While filming *The Saphead*, Keaton had continued his hunt for another film subject. Finally he decided to go with a parody of *Home Made*, a Ford Motor Company educational film on portable housing. In June, he hired Sybil Seely, an unknown actress, and began shooting. When asked years later how the idea of *One Week* had come to him, he would say that it spoofed *Three Weeks*, a shocking 1907 sex novel by Elinor Glyn. He never mentioned, or perhaps had forgotten by then, *Home Made*, a noncommercial, obscure film.

In *One Week*, a newlywed couple is presented with a vacant lot as a wedding gift, along with a build-it-yourself portable house and instructions for assembly. On Tuesday it is clear that something is wrong. A rival suitor has changed all the numbers on the various sections, and the house can only be entered through its windows. From Wednesday to Friday, the situation continues to deteriorate: The roof is noticeably smaller than the house; the chimney topples into the bride's bath; the kitchen sink is attached to the outside wall. At their housewarming party, a howling storm causes the house, which is built on a turntable, to start spinning madly. Saturday a building inspector says they have built on the wrong lot and must move. By Sunday they have propped the house on barrels and are towing it down the road. It gets stuck on some railroad tracks. Soon a train comes tearing toward them, but they jump back and it roars past. They are hugging each other when a train coming from the opposite direction demolishes the house. After placing a FOR SALE sign on the remains of their honeymoon cottage, Buster trudges away, then rushes back to leave the instruction manual.

One Week opened just in time for the Labor Day holiday to excellent reviews. In the weeks that followed it was clear that it would be one of the most popular comedies of the year. Keaton had demonstrated that he could deliver the goods. On the basis of a twenty-minute picture, he bolted overnight into a position comparable to that of the Talmadge sisters. A year-end tally of the top grossing pictures of 1920 did not include a single one of their films, though *One Week* was included.

From time to time, Natalie sent news of herself to Keaton. As he was aware, her attempts to become an actress had not worked out. Critics had looked down upon her clumsy screen debut in *The Isle of Conquest*. A few months later Dutch gave her a supporting role in *The Love Expert*. In this story a subdeb named Babs and her fiancé, Jim, must postpone their marriage until Jim finds husbands for his two unmarried sisters. Nate, as one of the spinster sisters, was incapable of injecting humor into the part of Dorcas. She was not mentioned by reviewers.

In the spring she was shoehorned into the cast of Norma's new picture, *Yes or No*. This time, *Variety* said, "The third of the Talmadge sisters, Natalie, has a comparatively small role in this production—hardly enough of a part for one to form any definite opinion as to her chances for success as a screen actress."

After *Yes or No,* Peg gave up on Natalie's film career. She had never pushed Natalie to succeed in pictures the way she had promoted Norma and Dutch. Perhaps she recognized that her middle daughter simply lacked the special incandescence that caused the other Talmadge girls to light up the screen.

Throughout most of 1920, life presented no great excitement for Nate. She was still very much attached to her mother's apron strings and more frustrated than ever.

During the same period, Keaton was riding a wave of success. Every one of his comedies had received fabulous notices. Confident that he was on the right track, he raced from picture to picture. In *Convict 13* he is a socialite golfer who knocks himself out with a ball, then hallucinates that he is a convict about to be hanged. *The Scarecrow* is a charming technocomedy about a pair of farmhand roommates (Keaton and Joe Roberts) living in a bachelor's pad equipped with a phonograph that doubles as a stove and a bed that converts to a piano.

All of his films were economically cast: his regular heavy, Joe Roberts, Eddie Cline, Joe Keaton, and Arbuckle's dog, Luke. Ingenues were hired as needed. Sybil Seely played the lead in *One Week, Convict 13,* and *The Scarecrow,* Bartine Burkett in *The High Sign.* Both women were clever, competent unknowns, whom the studio could pay bargain basement wages. Bartine Burkett recalled getting paid $25 a week. "I was supposed to be the costar," she said.

That summer, Lou Anger decided it was time to put an actress under contract. Keaton's main requirement was her height, because he liked to give the impression of being taller than his five feet six. In the twenties some of the biggest heartthrobs were actually of modest stature: Douglas Fairbanks was five feet seven inches, John Barrymore five feet eight, and Chaplin five feet five. Keaton thought that Sybil Seely, approximately his own height, was too tall. He wanted a woman short enough to stand under his outstretched arm.

In September, Anger selected Virginia Fox, an alumna of the Mack Sennett Bathing Beauties. She seemed perfect: only five feet tall, eighty-nine pounds, with black hair, rosy cheeks, and the physique of a child. Her shoe size was 1½.

Virginia Fox made her debut in *Neighbors,* Keaton's tale of a tenement Romeo and Juliet. Anger compared the new leading lady to Gloria Swanson and Mabel Normand and predicted that she too had the talent to graduate from the Sennett swimming-pool line to starring roles. There was no doubt that she had refined manners and breeding. She arrived at the studio each morning chaperoned by her grandmother. On and offscreen, Virginia's manner tended to be aristocratic. She was "a rose with a very strong stem," in the words of her daughter, Darrylin Zanuck Pineda.

Three years later, Virginia married Darryl F. Zanuck, a Warner Bros. writer, and retired from the screen. "We never knew our mother had once been an actress," said Darrylin Pineda. "It wasn't considered important."

Out of these early pictures, completed in a few months, evolved the screen personality "Buster." Unlike Charlie Chaplin, who claimed that the inspiration for his tramp burst full-blown from his costume and makeup—the derby and cane, the big shoes and baggy pants, the mustache—Keaton's character seems to have been more carefully thought out. Building on the unique stage personality that his father had devised for him as a child, he now was able to compose for the screen a rich, complex character, then design a chaotic universe in which to place him. Buster was a well-designed construct, as fastidious a creation as the Sistine Chapel ceiling. He played the ancient role of the stoic, always braced for catastrophe in an indifferent cosmos.

When Buster gets thwacked by life, he hits the ground, but in the next instant he is on his feet. When he is hurt, he never flinches. In contrast to a comic like Stan Laurel, whose character cries when he is confused, no circumstance whatsoever could make Buster cry or turn helpless. As director Frank Capra once observed, streetwise "Charlie" outwitted trouble, beleaguered Harold Lloyd used speed to outrun his tormentors, and Harry Langdon tended to trust in God to get him through tough times. But Keaton, said Capra, "*suffered* through them stoically." In fact, he does not submit to trouble raging around him so much as he stands in disbelief and processes absurdities with unblinking direct-ness.

Keaton's screen persona was no more the real man than the real Charlie Chaplin was a tramp who waddled like a penguin. From vaudeville Keaton retained the reserved expression that now would become his screen trademark. Though he had laughed in the Comique films, in his own comedies he chose to be serious—and he would be the only screen comic who did not smile. His melancholy expression would give rise to such nicknames as Deadpan and Stoneface.

He kept one prop from Comique days, the flat porkpie hat. Otherwise, there was no trace of the various characters he had played in the Arbuckle films.

His screen character did incorporate certain aspects of his own personality: his unerring eye for the ridiculous, the taciturnity that drove some people wild, a mixture of cool intelligence and little-boy cleverness, cynicism, and deep sadness. The personal traits that he omitted from Buster were mostly flaws—his indifference to people, his extreme egotism, and his preoccupation with work.

In creating Buster, one of his biggest problems was that he got no help from his appearance. He wasn't fat, awkward, childish, or nearsighted. He had a classical profile that would remind film critic Penelope Gilliatt of a Picasso drawing, admirable eyes, excellent posture, and a mouthful of the most glorious teeth in pictures ("all his own," reports Eleanor Keaton, "except one that was knocked out by a steel cable").

Keaton, like so many doughboys, began smoking cigarettes during the war. Throughout his life he would average three to four packs of Camels a day. Now during the first year of Prohibition he became a regular drinker as well. Once alcohol became illegal, everyone in Hollywood drank. The new liquor laws had no effect on business at the Vernon Country Club, where cocaine continued to sell briskly. Keaton was also a regular at the Sunset Inn. At its weekly "Photoplayers Night," he was one of the actors who packed the restaurant with impromptu entertainment. Diners had to reserve tables two weeks in advance to see Keaton do his Salome dance in a costume made of kitchen utensils, or the equally famous skit in which Viola Dana and Alice Lake played strip poker and Roscoe Arbuckle was the Keystone Kop who broke up the game. Typically Keaton got only a few hours of sleep, but he always arrived at Lillian Way ready to work.

Keaton and Vi had broken up when she fell in love with stunt pilot Ormer Locklear, but they remained friends and he went back to dating Alice, though it is not likely that he was faithful to her. He picked up women wherever he happened to find them. Women who were clearly concerned about their virtue did not attract him. Around nice girls who lived with their parents and obeyed curfews, Keaton behaved like a big brother. He escorted Bartine Burkett to dances at the Hollywood Hotel, made sure her dance card was filled out, then disappeared. "He went upstairs to drink in Viola Dana's room," she guessed. At eleven thirty he would return to the dance in time to take her home.

One night he drove Bartine to Arbuckle's house, where a party was under way, then realized that a good girl like Bartine would be absolutely out of place there. He got out on West Adams Boulevard and handed her his car keys.

"But, Buster," she said. "I've never driven. How am I going to get home?"

"I'll teach you," he replied. "Here's low gear, here's second, and there's the brake. See you in the morning." She managed to get home without an accident, but her family, she recalled, "nearly died."

Now that Keaton had become a star with his own studio, it was necessary for Lou Anger to hire him a press agent. Harry Brand, a former sports reporter from the *Los Angeles Evening Express,* would become an important behind-the-scenes figure in Keaton's life. He was a born promoter, a New Yorker by birth. He worked as a newspaperman, as secretary to Los Angeles mayor Pinky Snyder, and as publicist for Warner Bros. (He had also gone to jail over a phony film company, the Harry Brand Advanced Motion Picture Company, whose investors never saw their money again.) Decades later, after Joe Schenck and Darryl Zanuck formed 20th Century-Fox and Brand became Fox's director of publicity, he would mastermind campaigns that made Shirley Temple the most famous child star in history, Betty Grable a GI Joe "pinup girl," and Marilyn Monroe a sex goddess. Buster Keaton was his first attempt at packaging and marketing a star.

From the start, Keaton felt comfortable with the twenty-five-year-old writer, who was exceptionally easygoing and engaging, a regular guy and one of the wittiest men in town. They shared a love of sports and had also suffered childhood accidents that left them with physical injuries: Keaton's amputated finger and Brand's crooked knee.

Brand began trolling Keaton's past for promising material. He exhumed the Keaton family's brief association with Harry Houdini, who was now a household name synonymous with power and daring. Thus, the Keatons' two-month job with the California Concert Company became shamelessly exaggerated into a long-term business partnership between Joe Keaton and Houdini. Then Brand eliminated the obscure George Pardey and made Houdini the person who had named Buster. Houdini did not object.

Keaton had a part in fabricating this mythology. In one of his first interviews, the new authorized Keaton story was trotted out for a reporter from *Motion Picture Classic.* Accompanied by a blizzard of exclamation points, the article "Poor Child!" breathlessly recounts practically every one of what would become Keaton's beloved fairy tales: deadly cyclones and vanishing towns, wizards in the form of Harry Houdini the Hand Cuff King, ogres shaped like Gerry Society officers. The article also included the Houdiniesque myth of Keaton's physical indestructibility.

As a result of Harry Brand's enterprise, Keaton's childhood traumas involving violence, brutishness, and alcoholism—all the psychic scars that had helped to form his perception of the world—were gone. Keaton would never refer to them again, and if others did, he quickly offered denials. But in doing so he also pushed further into exile his true self.

For a very long time Myra Keaton had been trapped in a violent marriage. From the back roads of country Kansas to the backwaters of northern Michigan, she had put up with beatings and booze. Now, after almost thirty years together, she broke up the marriage. But she never divorced Joe.

If Keaton was upset, he gave no sign of it. Relations with his father continued much the same. Almost every day Joe showed up at the studio to have lunch with his boy, still refusing to admit that there was anything good about motion pictures. During the next few years he would completely remodel his life, forming a relationship with a Christian Science practitioner who helped him achieve sobriety.

For Myra there would be no man but Joe. On their fiftieth wedding anniversary she put on her prettiest dress, rode the bus downtown to his hotel, and brought him a home-cooked dinner.

For now, emancipation meant loneliness, which she fought by clutching her youngest children to her breast. For the rest of her life, she never let go.

10 HONEYMOON EXPRESS

Joe Keaton moved downtown to the Continental Hotel in the theater district. The residential hotel catered to ex-vaudeville and carny performers who tap-danced in the elevator and kept the lobby cloudy with cigar smoke. They endlessly relived their palmy years.

Joe Keaton was content to spend his days in the Continental lobby chewing on a fat cigar. He delighted in describing the gasps of the audience when he had picked up his boy by the seat of the trousers and hurled him against a backdrop, how he had changed Buster's age in order to fool the law. Upstairs, his room was papered with photographs of seven-year-old Buster in top hat and cane.

Joe had never felt so comfortable. Not only had his boy made good, but Hollywood was full of his relatives. Both of his sisters lived close by, Birdie in Culver City and Palm Springs and Rosa in Hollywood. He had no financial worries; every month his son mailed the Continental Hotel a check for the room.

Hit followed hit: In 1920 *One Week* was succeeded by *Convict 13*, *The Scarecrow*, and *Neighbors*. By Christmas three more films were in the can waiting to be released. Keaton continued to drive himself to exhaustion. At the age of twenty-five he was experiencing the same thrill of being special and famous as he had at five. In the movies, unlike in vaudeville, his face was enlarged to the size of a four-story building.

At Christmas he was previewing *The Haunted House*. He plays a bank teller who discovers that another teller is part of a counterfeiting gang hiding out in a mansion, rigged up as a "haunted house" to throw police off their trail. He ended the film with a dream sequence: Buster is hit on the head and knocked out. In the afterlife, he climbs up a long staircase to heaven, but in Keaton's heaven there is no God, and Saint Peter is a snarly old guy who slams the pearly gates in his face. He finds himself barreling down a chute like a piece of lost airport baggage, and finally lands at the feet of the devil, who welcomes him to his rightful fate with a playful jab in the rear with a pitchfork. Building the staircase was the greatest fun Keaton had had since he got to wreck the house in *One Week*.

After the new year, he began *Hard Luck*. In this he is a zoo attendant who, after losing both job and girlfriend, decides to do away with himself. He discovers that it is not so easy to control one's own fate. He tries everything: hanging, drowning, walking into traffic. Nothing works. Then he drinks a bottle of scotch in the belief it is poison and finally winds up at a country club pool with a bunch of bathing beauties. Scampering to a high diving board, he sticks out his chest, spreads his arms, and sails through the air. He misses the pool and plummets straight through the marble tiling, leaving a deep hole in the ground. The bathers peer into the chasm, but Buster has disappeared, achieving his dearest wish at long last.

That scene, Keaton recalled, was "the greatest thrill of my life." His crew covered over part of a swimming pool with wax paper to look like tiles. The problem was that from the top of the board, he couldn't distinguish the fake tile from the real. "I was so scared that if I hadn't lost my balance due to a sudden wind, I would never have left that platform."

The best gag of all was an idea of Eddie Cline's. Many years later, the club is shuttered and abandoned, its lawn overgrown with weeds and its swimming pool dry, although the hole in the tiling remains. Buster is seen emerging from the moss-covered hole dressed in a kimono and followed by his Chinese wife and their two Chinese-American children. "They laughed so hard that when the next feature came on, they laughed all the way through the credits and halfway through the first reel." It was his "biggest laughing two-reeler," he said, as well as his all-time favorite.

Shooting on *Hard Luck* concluded on the morning of January 9. After lunch the crew began setting up for the opening shots of the next picture, *The Goat,* in which a vagabond is mistaken for the escaped murderer Dead Shot Dan and must flee from the police. Keaton was under pressure to deliver. He had now made seven pictures, eight if he counted *The High Sign,* since going solo. In 1921 he was supposed to complete eight more, each one containing almost a hundred comic bits, many of them highly complicated. Luckily he remembered funny visual gags from his years in vaudeville, but he still worried about running out of ideas. Like every other comic he knew, he was becoming an expert recycler of old material. Pretty soon, he joked, he would have to start stealing from himself.

He had little time or energy for his personal life. Nevertheless, thanks to his lithe good looks and cool style, he was one of the most eligible bachelors on the screen. If there was no shortage of women in his life, there were no strong attachments either. He still saw Alice Lake, but their affair had grown stale. Of all the women he had known, the only one to cause a bubble of passion was Viola Dana, and their liaison had lasted only a few months. It would be falsely said that there was not a woman in Hollywood whom Keaton didn't try to bed. He was selective, preferring leggy but petite showgirl types. For the most part, he kept his relations with the opposite sex superficial and gave husband-hunting women a wide berth. For companionship he preferred the company of men.

In New York, twenty-two-year-old Constance Talmadge and her best friend, Dorothy Gish, known as Doates, were sitting in a New York restaurant with their boyfriends, businessman John Pialogiou and James Rennie, Gish's leading man. For three years Dutch had been enamored of Pialogiou, but he had shown no interest in marriage, which only fueled her obsession with him. Over lunch, Pialogiou finally agreed to marry her. Connie decided they should elope immediately. She began teasing Gish and Rennie, daring them to come along and make it a double wedding.

On the day after Christmas, Dutch and Doates slipped out to meet their boyfriends and drove to Greenwich, Connecticut, where they were married by a justice of the peace. Afterward they informed their families. The Gishes were shocked. Dorothy's sister Lillian believed that if not for Dutch's bad influence Dorothy would never have married Rennie.

At the box office, Connie and her sister ranked among the top ten female stars along with Gloria Swanson, Mary Pickford, Mabel Normand, and Mary Miles Minter. Recently F. Scott Fitzgerald had rated Connie as a flapper deluxe associated with Fifth Avenue and diamond rings, while Norma was his archetype of noble beauty. For Norma, the gilt and the glitter that accompanied being a star surrounded by adoring fans were still very important. Constance cared increasingly less about her career and wanted to take it easy.

Connie's elopement infuriated her mother. For a second time one of her girls had run off to marry without Peg's permission. After her marriage, Connie moved out of her mother's apartment to settle with Pialogiou's family at the nearby St. Regis Hotel.

Natalie, the only unmarried Talmadge girl, began to panic. Both of her sisters had careers and husbands, but she had nothing. At twenty-four, she felt consumed by the futility of her life. As usual, Peg devised a plan. She believed idleness to be "the curse of many New York girls." That winter, she redoubled her efforts to keep the unhappy Nate busy. A bit role was found for her in Norma's current picture, *The Passion Flower,* but Natalie's acting had not improved. Afterward, she was sent back to her old job of autographing Dutch's fan photos: "Merrily yours, Constance Talmadge," although her sister encouraged her to write, "Screw you, Constance Talmadge." Peg told Anita Loos that Nate was so dumb "her brains rattle." In fact, Nate was immensely insecure. Her granddaughter Melissa said, "She had a demure, feminine air about her, a lot like the character she portrayed in *Our Hospitality.* But there seemed to be little self-confidence and I don't think she had ambitions of her own."

In the eyes of the public Natalie was famous for being the nonacting Talmadge sister, whose picture appeared in saccharine rotogravure stories of celebrities at home. When Nate finally had her hair shorn into a fashionable Dutch bob, it was an event. With Connie holding scissors, pretending she had done the trimming, the sisters posed for *Photoplay.* But aside from autographing photographs and acting as her mother's traveling companion, Nate had little to do.

After Connie's elopement, Natalie and her mother migrated south to Palm Beach. In January Nate wrote Keaton a letter. According to his autobiography, she told him flat out that she was the only daughter left at home and "if you still care about me all you have to do is send for me."

He had not even seen her for two years. He knew virtually nothing about her. The one thing he did know was that she had a boyfriend, a Chicago businessman who often visited New York. Known as the dairy king of the Midwest, Owen Gilman was twenty-eight, pleasant-looking, and reportedly a millionaire. He and Nate were frequently seen together at parties and theater first nights. Peg immediately dubbed him "the butter and eggs man," a witticism that soon made its way into the gossip columns. Four years later, George S. Kaufman wrote a hit comedy called *The Butter and Egg Man,* in which his rich yokel from Chilicothe, Ohio, is just dying to invest his savings in a Broadway show. Natalie was not serious about her butter-and-eggs man.

On February 3, news of Keaton's engagement to Natalie Talmadge found its way into the papers. Harry Brand was no doubt the source of the leak. Keaton was quoted as saying that there had been an understanding between them for some time "and the consent of Mama Talmadge has been duly received," which most certainly was not the case. Peg had been scanning New York and Palm Beach for suitable men. According to *Variety,* no wedding plans had been made because Keaton was so busy. He was starting a new picture about a modern, high-tech all-electric home, and he was busy building an escalator.

Scooped by Keaton's publicity man, Beulah Livingstone, the Talmadge girls' publicist, passed along to the New York dailies a wire from Nate in Palm Beach: YES, THE REPORT OF MY ENGAGE-MENT TO BUSTER KEATON IS ABSOLUTELY TRUE AND I AM VERY HAPPY.

Meanwhile, Keaton had thrown himself into work on his next comedy, which was to be his most technically elaborate picture so far. Graduation day at State U finds Buster getting a degree in botany, but the diplomas get switched and he winds up with a sheepskin in electrical engineering. Invited to install electricity in the home of the dean (Joe Roberts) while he and his family are on vacation, Buster follows directions in a textbook, *Electricity Made Easy.*

Keaton turned this plot into an opportunity to create a futuristic house: moving stairs, an automated bed, a bathtub on tracks, smart appliances that wash, rinse, dry, and put back china on the pantry shelf, a swimming pool that fills and drains automatically.

On the day after his engagement announcement, he was doing a scene on the escalator when it speeded up for no apparent reason. One of his slapshoes caught between the risers. He yelled for the stagehands to turn off the electricity. But before they could pull the switch there was the sound of bone snapping, the shoe was torn from his foot, and he fell ten feet. When he tried to stand, he fainted and was taken to Good Samaritan Hospital. He had broken his leg.

He had always believed himself to be indestructible. Now the doctors told him that his right leg would have to remain in a cast for seven weeks and after that he would have to walk with a cane. It might be months before he could return to work.

Two films—*Hard Luck* and *The Goat*—were ready for release. He would also dust off *The High Sign*. Discharged from the hospital and caged up with his family on Ingraham Street, he hobbled around on crutches and tried to think of ways to fill his time. He had never been good at doing nothing.

Buster and Natalie were married at five o'clock on Tuesday, May 31, on the porch of the Schenck mansion in Bayside. The veranda was covered with bouquets of delicate pinky white snowballs and baskets of hothouse roses. Keaton's former roommate, Ward Crane, was best man, and Constance Talmadge matron of honor. Among the guests were the bride's family and friends, assorted business friends of Joe Schenck's, Anita Loos and her husband, director John Emerson, and Lou and Sophy Anger. Noticeably absent were Fred Talmadge and Keaton's entire family, who either had not been invited or chose not to make the long journey.

Although Natalie was a practicing Catholic, Keaton had no tolerance for organized religion and did not care to be married in the church. The civil ceremony was conducted by a New York City judge.

On her wedding day, Natalie wore an outfit chosen by Norma and Constance, a flouncy ruffled dress made of white organza with a hemline just below the knee. Keaton looks listless, standing beside her without the aid of crutches or the gold-tipped walking stick he had purchased at Tiffany's. In some of the wedding photos, the bride is clutching her bouquet, her sisters are smiling, and the groom is gazing into the distance with his hands folded. In others he is rolling his eyes. Looking most unhappy of all is the mother of the bride. In recent days she had never left Nate's side, even at the marriage-license bureau.

No honeymoon had been planned. After six weeks at the Hotel Biltmore, Keaton was itching to get home and back to work. This seemed so disgraceful to Peg that she later improved on the facts and gave her daughter a wedding trip "spent motoring from New York to Los Angeles with occasional stopovers."

On the day after the wedding, the newlyweds left New York on the *Twentieth Century Limited,* accompanied on the five-day trip to Los Angeles by Lou and Sophy Anger.

Among the wedding gifts were two favorites: from Connie a Belgian police dog that Keaton named Captain; and from Norma and Joe a deluxe-model Rolls-Royce, a $10,000 car delivered to them in Los Angeles.

Years later Keaton had rewritten the event. He told biographer Rudi Blesh that fear of losing Natalie to the butter-and-eggs man made him seriously pursue her. Yet in another account, he said that Natalie had pushed him to set a date for the wedding when he wasn't ready.

Keaton would never completely make peace with himself about marrying Nate. There were practical reasons for his decision. He was physically attracted to her and had as much feeling for her as he did for any woman. He was also ambitious and understood that marriage into the Talmadge-Schenck family could not help boosting his career. *Motion Picture Magazine* pointed out that "one of the most interesting and least mentioned features of the Keaton-Talmadge marriage is that it completes what is perhaps the most powerful oligarchy in pictures today." Joe Schenck's influence was far more reaching than most people suspected, Norma was at the peak of her career, Constance was still rising. But "Buster has just begun. They are all world-famous, all earners of fabulous salaries. It is quite certain that in aggregate wealth they outstrip even the famous Pickford-Fairbanks combine."

The Talmadges had some trouble adjusting to their newest member. Connie's first reaction to the marriage was to laugh and call it a "mail-order romance." Her mother simply didn't like Keaton. Nor did she care for the idea of her daughter living thousands of miles away in California. Nate proposed that her husband move back East and produce his pictures at the Colony Studio. He flatly refused.

Peg told her friends that Natalie "didn't develop along sexy lines." For that matter, none of her girls were wild about sex, according to their mother. She preferred to believe that Norma avoided intercourse with Schenck as if he were "a swamp." As with any of Peg's tales, this one may have had a kernel of truth, but both Norma and Dutch, sexpots on-screen, appear to have had active sex lives offscreen.

At the outset of her marriage Natalie had problems with sex, but there may have been a simple reason: She was inexperienced. Keaton, on the other hand, felt that he was an expert on the subject, not even able to count all the women he had been with. He and his buddies were always passing along odds and ends of sexual lore. For example, an ice cube pressed against a drunk woman's genitals was the fastest way to sober her up. But his experience meant nothing to Nate, who found sex disappointing and treated it as something she owed him but hoped would be over as quickly as possible.

During the trip to the Coast, they had their first real disagreement, over where they were going to live. Keaton didn't like being hemmed in by houses and packs of motor cars. He wanted a ranch in the San Fernando Valley, where there was plenty of undeveloped land going for less than a hundred dollars an acre. He suggested a working farm with cattle, chickens, and orange groves. At first they could hire a farmer to run the place, but once it showed a profit, they would build a ranch house with stone fireplaces and beamed ceilings. In the meantime, they would rent an apartment in town.

When he had finished talking, Nate said that they would find a house in Los Angeles, which is what they did.

The house they finally took was located at 855 Westchester Place, even though Keaton thought it was too big. The minute they moved in, reporters and photographers descended. In an interview in the *Los Angeles Evening Herald,* Keaton joked that he had already learned there were two sides to every argument— "your wife's and her mother's." Natalie was no happy vacuumer and floor waxer, even though she put on an apron and posed in the kitchen for photographers. She was obsessed with clothes shopping, a passion that she had contracted from her sisters.

Their new dog, six weeks old and two pounds in weight when they got him, had begun sleeping on the bed, but Captain was growing and the bed was getting crowded. Sleeping with pets has never been particularly conducive to good sex. A window into their uneasy relationship was captured in a *Photoplay* gag photograph taken three weeks after their wedding. They posed side by side on a bench. Nate is giving her husband a wary glance and clutching a rolling pin. Keaton's right ankle is fettered by a ball and chain, and he is wearing a funereal expression.

Keaton believed he was a star because his pictures made people laugh. But when he returned from New York he was no longer Buster Keaton. He had become Buster Keaton the husband of Natalie Talmadge. Naturally, Harry Brand publicized the celebrity nuptials, and movie magazines were eager to help.

A reporter from *Motion Picture Magazine* found Keaton in a bad mood. He poured out a stream of angry remarks about straitjackets and henpecked husbands. In his household, Keaton said, he would come and go as he pleased, at whatever hour he chose, without apologies. When pressed for details about his marriage, he clammed up. "I've only been married three weeks," he said. By the end of the interview, he had completely alienated the reporter. The article, "Only Three Weeks," included insensitive remarks about Natalie and portrayed Keaton as egotistical and arrogant.

Keaton was indifferent to the press; all he owed audiences were laughs, and he didn't much care what they thought of him personally. Following a three-month layoff he was facing a ferocious schedule. His new film could include few physical stunts because he still had to be careful of his leg. In place of gymnastics, he turned to special effects and made a technical masterpiece, one of the most inventive films ever produced. In *The Playhouse* Buster buys a ticket at the Buster Keaton Opera House. Inside, he discovers that every person in the theater is an exact replica of himself: the conductor tapping his baton, the musicians in the pit, the stagehands, the nine-man minstrel show, even the people sitting in the audience. In a box, a man (Keaton) reading his program notices that every performer and technician is Buster Keaton. He remarks to his wife (Keaton in drag), "This Keaton fellow seems to be the whole show." What's more, he is the entire audience as well. "The audience laughed like hell at that," Keaton later recalled.

The multiple-image effects were achieved by placing the camera in a special light-proof box with a lens mask that blocked out the entire frame except for a narrow slit in which Keaton was performing. After each sequence, the film would be rewound and the process repeated. Cameraman Elgin Lessley had the tricky job of hand-cranking the camera at exactly the same speed for each exposure; for the nine minstrels, the film had to be rolled back nine times. Delighted with the results, Keaton knew that his innovation would be immediately copied by other comedy companies and warned his crew to keep the process a secret.

"Keaton ranks third among screen comedians," *Photoplay* said after screening it. "You know the other two."

Keaton did not enjoy laboring in the shadows of Lloyd and Chaplin, especially Chaplin, with whom he felt a secret but sharp sense of rivalry. Keaton and Chaplin first met in 1918 after Comique moved to the Coast. What Keaton resented most was being confused with Chaplin. "Buster" bore no resemblance to Chaplin's "Charlie" tramp, a lovable charmer but basically a bum who was liable to steal anything not nailed down, a quality that horrified Keaton. Buster was a conformist, a practical, law-abiding citizen striving to do the right thing. Like his Kansas-born creator, Buster was a son of the heartland with its traditions of working until your tongue was hanging out. The celluloid Buster would no more condone anarchism (with *Cops* being one exception) than the real-life Keaton would parade down Fifth Avenue waving a banner on May Day.

In public Keaton was careful to genuflect before Chaplin as the greatest comedian who ever lived. Not only did he dislike Chaplin personally, but he also despised his Communist politics. He remembered drinking beer one night in his kitchen and listening to Chaplin, a recent convert, pound the table and extol the virtues of the Bolshevist programs. Keaton, not in the least interested, listened politely. Chaplin believed that communism was going to transform society by abolishing poverty and hunger. Then children the world over would have full stomachs and shoes on their feet. That was all he wanted, he said.

Keaton stared at him.

"But Charlie," he said, "do you know anyone who doesn't want that?"

Keaton had no use for politics. He never bothered to vote and never affiliated himself with any party. His antipathy for Chaplin was rooted in something a great deal more personal: Chaplin's intellectual pretensions inflamed Keaton's old insecurities stemming from his lack of formal education. In his opinion the trouble with Charlie was that "when people praised him as a genius, he believed it," he later told his friend Carol De Luise. With his high-flown discourses about the masses, Chaplin only succeeded in making a fool out of himself. Keaton suspected that Chaplin knew as little about history and economics as he did.

Throughout the twenties, indeed throughout his entire life, critics would deny that Keaton belonged in Chaplin's league. While Keaton and Harold Lloyd, too, were content to make people laugh, being funny was not enough for Chaplin. He wanted desperately to expand both his range and his image, and eventually succeeded in rising from slapstick comic to serious artist. One reason that critics adored Chaplin was his intellectual aspirations—the very aspirations Keaton condemned as phony.

The Blacksmith started out as a parody of Henry Wadsworth Longfellow's poem "The Village Blacksmith" and its sentimental picture of the small towns in which most Americans lived. Keaton's comedy has general stores, livery stables, clapboard houses, and barbershops but also reflects some of the personal preoccupations of a man living in an expensive house in Los Angeles with a difficult wife.

Under Keaton's spreading chestnut tree, the village blacksmith shop was a combination stable and auto repair shop. Joe Roberts is the thuggish shop owner who chases schoolchildren, Buster is his inept assistant, and Virginia Fox a horse-riding society dame whom Buster loves and finally weds. In an elaborate sequence a customer brings in a spotless white Rolls-Royce for minor repairs. Buster, who is working on a jalopy, accidentally shatters the car's windows with a sledgehammer, blowtorches its paint, and crashes an engine into its side. Did Comique's budget allot $10,000 for a brand new Rolls? Could this be the same Rolls that Norma and Joe had given him as a wedding gift?

In the concluding scenes, the eloping couple jump onto the observation car of a departing train and wave good-bye. The train puffs away and starts across a trestle, but it derails and plunges off the overpass. "Many a honeymoon express has ended thusly," read the title card, a message to Keaton's own spouse. There is a surprise ending that reveals the hero in his bathrobe, safely at home with his wife and baby. The honeymoon express is only a toy train.

The Blacksmith relies on Arbuckle-type horseplay and is not nearly so stylish as *The Playhouse*. Still, it was fast and funny, and exhibitor previews suggested it would be "another button-buster."

Keaton soon modified his bachelor behavior. He saw less and less of his former sidekicks. The nightly club-hopping with Arbuckle and the others in their gang—Lew Cody, Norman Kerry, William Collier, Jr.—was over. Arbuckle of late had no time for clubbing. During the summer he completed three feature films without a break. Not only did he work six days a week at Paramount and Sundays in script conferences, but he gave publicity interviews at lunch, usually dressed in pongee pajamas under a purple velvet dressing gown and bedroom slippers.

In July Arbuckle's name cropped up in the news, unconnected with motion pictures. In Boston, district attorney Nathan Tufts was prosecuted in state court on a corruption charge. Four years earlier Tufts had dropped his case against the president of Paramount Pictures after the night with the parsley girls in Woburn. At Tufts's trial, Adolph Zukor and several other Paramount executives were mentioned for their involvement in the orgy. Arbuckle was not named because he had no part in the incident, but the press identified the scandal as having taken place on his publicity tour. Tufts was found guilty of accepting a $100,000 bribe and removed from office. Arbuckle was not concerned by the revival of this scandal. The Paramount party had been a routine affair. In the picture business, a good party meant a wild party replete with good-time gals. He didn't figure that unsavory publicity might hurt him at the box office.

After working without a break for months, Arbuckle treated himself to a present: a custom-built Pierce-Arrow phaeton with leather upholstery and solid silver accessories. This monstrously long touring car cost $25,000 and featured a full bar and a foldaway toilet.

In April, en route to his wedding aboard the Santa Fe *Super Chief,* Keaton had bumped into Hiram Abrams, the forty-year-old president of United Artists, and his wife, Florence. Keaton and Joe

Schenck's brother, Nick, were invited one afternoon to the Abrams drawing room for a game of contract bridge. Since neither of them played, Abrams offered to teach and drew Keaton as his partner.

As a child, Keaton had picked up pinochle from his mother and had been playing it ever since. Bridge had never interested him. He was unable to get the hang of sacrificing his hand for the sake of his partner. Abrams became impatient with him and began shooting annoyed glances his way. The UA president, he remembered, "kept telling me that I was stupid and became more abusive as the day wore on."

At last Keaton threw down his cards and jumped up. "If you bawl me out once more I'll slap the taste right out of your mouth."

He could not help wondering if other people in the business also thought of him as a dumbbell in a flat hat. Probably they could not imagine him ordering a French wine or making a killing in an oil deal. They certainly wouldn't worry about losing to him at cards.

In subsequent months he would spend hundreds of hours learning to play bridge. Eventually he accumulated enough points to achieve master rank and become one of Hollywood's best players. The game would become as all-consuming a pastime for him as pinochle was for his mother.

11 THE LABOR DAY PARTY

In the last week of August 1921, Keaton had a call from Roscoe Arbuckle, who was thinking about the Labor Day weekend. His idea was to drive his new Pierce-Arrow to San Francisco and invite people for a party. Katherine Fitzgerald, his secretary, had already booked three large rooms at the St. Francis Hotel. He wanted Buster and Natalie to join him. There would great food and plenty of liquor.

For days Keaton had been shooting on location at the Bay of Balboa. By the time a morning haze swathed the marina, Fred Gabourie and his crew had been struggling for hours to sink a boat. This had been going on for days. First they had loaded it with a 1,600-pound weight made of pig iron, then they tried building a breakaway stern and collapsing it. They even bored holes in the bow. Yet the boat did not submerge completely. Filming was brought to a standstill. After three days they started from scratch and hooked an underwater pulley to an offscreen tugboat. At last the boat slipped under the water.

The Boat, a shorter version of his 1924 feature *The Navigator* and another of Keaton's personal favorites, contains one of the unforgettable moments in all of silent films. A man with a wife and two small sons is building a boat in the basement of his home. He appears to be a by-the-book Sunday builder, except that his boat is named the *Damfino* (Damned If I Know). Finally ready to move the *Damfino* to the harbor, he realizes that like a ship in a bottle the mast is too tall and the vessel will not fit through the basement door. After removing a few bricks, he attaches the boat to his

Model T and begins pulling it out of the basement, ripping open the side walls of his house. As his family watches, the house slowly collapses into a pile of rubble, an awesome sight gag.

At the marina, the master builder prepares to launch. Planting himself in the stern, he glows with pride. The *Damfino* slowly slides down the ramp into the water—but keeps going straight to the bottom of the bay, taking its builder along with it.

After a series of catastrophes, the *Damfino* is sunk by a storm and the family appears in danger of perishing. Buster and his family end up on some godforsaken shore, where they huddle together.

"Where are we?" asks his wife (Sybil Seely).

Buster faces the camera as he shrugs. "Damned if I know," he mouths.

Likewise, in his own life he was damned if he knew where he was.

All summer he had been trying very hard to please Nate. She had grown up in a family where contempt for men was considered a positive female trait. Educated to hunt for male faults, she paid little attention to his opinions and made no effort to hide her lack of interest in his films. "Peg had schooled Nate," Anita Loos believed, "to look down on her husband as a mere substitute for a career, but in my opinion the chance to wake up in the morning and look across a pillow at that fabulous face should have been fulfillment enough for any girl."

He tried to placate her with an expensive roadster and dinners at the Sunset Inn, where the menu featured a Buster Keaton shrimp cocktail. At the Ambassador Hotel they attended banquets for important film distributors. On Sundays they went swimming or fishing. Nevertheless, in Nate's eyes he did everything wrong.

Not that Keaton was an ideal spouse. With his self-absorption and almost pathological silence, he could be ungenerous. Monosyllabic moods locked him into separateness. There must have been many instances when he did not speak with her at all. Natalie could not break through that wall of indifference.

Away from New York, Natalie felt homesick and bored. Now that she had become a wife, she wanted to be something else. She sometimes made scenes about wanting to take on a film role, but he was firmly opposed to her working. The last thing he wanted was an actress wife.

Keaton found comfort in his dog. Captain eventually weighed 160 pounds. Keaton was so crazy about him that he took him along to the studio every morning. At night Captain continued to occupy their bed, his master and mistress sleeping squished into the corners. At the studio Captain was friendly, but he reacted when anybody laid a finger on his master. After Captain attacked Joe Roberts, Lou Anger ordered him to be tied up when they were shooting. Arbuckle, who also got knocked over, joked that it was just like Buster to own a dog that had no sense of humor.

Keaton's studio was his own private kingdom. His dressing room was a place he could live in, and he sometimes did. It had a kitchen, dining room, and bedroom, and someone always there to look after him. On the train to New York for his wedding, he had met a dining-car chef, Willie Riddle, one of the gourmet cooks who made traveling on the Santa Fe *Super Chief* as luxurious an experience as sailing on a deluxe ocean liner. Keaton relished Riddle's cooking. He also liked him immensely and offered him a job at the studio as his personal cook.

Willie Riddle became Keaton's cook and bartender, and he also took care of his wardrobe, shopped, telephoned, ran errands, wrote letters, made appointments, warded off pests, and attended to the hundred and one matters that helped keep Keaton functioning. In Keaton's dressing room Riddle operated an open bar throughout Prohibition. Friends could go into the kitchenette at any hour and count on getting a drink or a meal. For a dozen years he would be the glue of Keaton's daily life.

In years to come, certain friends of Keaton's concluded that he had actually accepted Arbuckle's invitation to go to San Francisco for the ill-fated Labor Day weekend. "He told me that he was supposed to go and help Arbuckle celebrate the finish of a picture," said James Karen. "But then something happened to stop him, something trivial at the studio. The reason some people believed him to be there was that he would describe the weekend as if he had been present. In his imagination he was."

Arbuckle's party did not sound like much fun to Natalie, who hadn't the slightest interest in one of Roscoe's rowdy outings, any more than she was dying to hang out at Vernon Country Club with her husband's gang. It is less clear how he felt about going. As a bachelor he would have jumped at the invitation. Several times a year he and Arbuckle were in the habit of taking off for San Francisco, usually on a moment's notice. While Arbuckle continued to be his best friend, it was no longer possible for Keaton to wander off with him and spend a weekend getting tanked up.

Instead of accepting Arbuckle's invitation, Keaton and Nate chartered a yacht and cruised over to Catalina, an island twenty-two miles off the coast, a more suitable way for a young couple to spend a holiday. The prospect of a four-hour crossing to Catalina did not thrill a queasy sailor like Natalie, but she agreed to go. At the last minute Keaton invited Roscoe to change his mind and join them, but he had promised people a party and couldn't back out now.

On Saturday the Pierce-Arrow nosed north with Arbuckle and two friends, actor Lowell Sherman and comedy director Fred Fishbach. It was dark by the time they reached the St. Francis Hotel on Union Square.

Labor Day was unusually hot. On the twelfth floor, Arbuckle was still in his bathrobe and slippers eating breakfast when people started to arrive. In all, there would be roughly thirty guests in suite 1220 by midafternoon. A number of local politicians stopped by. A Hollywood agent had in tow one of his clients, an actress named Virginia Rappe, whom Arbuckle had dated several times and was pleased to see. The rest of the crowd were strangers.

By the middle of the afternoon Arbuckle was sweating in his silk pajamas and robe, drinking highballs, and chatting with the chorus girls. As the guests became drunk, inhibitions lessened and couples sneaked off into the bedrooms and appeared later with their clothing in disarray. When Virginia Rappe complained that the party needed music, Arbuckle telephoned room service to send up a Victrola.

Rappe, who worked for various comedy companies, lived in Hollywood with her aunt. Three or four years earlier, Arbuckle had met her while leasing space at Pathé Lehrman's Culver City studio. At that time she was sleeping with Lehrman and hoping for marriage, but their relationship was stormy and Lehrman did not propose. She went out with other men, among them Arbuckle, with whom she had several weekend dates, Keaton said later. She was a tall, sleek young woman of about twenty-five with a mass of brown hair, so pretty and wholesome that her photograph had appeared on the covers of sheet-music scores, including that of "Let Me Call You Sweetheart."

After the Labor Day party, it would be said that Rappe was not an actress at all, but trash who had infected several actors with venereal disease at Keystone and forced Mack Sennett to fumigate the studio. In reality, she was no different from other Hollywood hopefuls. To conquer the business, even to get a walk-on part, they had to hustle and scheme and be sweet to the right people. Virginia had acted in several Sunshine comedies at Fox and in 1920 was excited to be starring in a feature, *Twilight Baby.*

At 3:00 P.M. Arbuckle went into his bedroom to bathe and dress. He was surprised to find Rappe on the bathroom floor vomiting into the toilet. According to Arbuckle, he handed her a cup of water, then carried her into his bedroom because she was too drunk to walk. A moment later, he said, he left to have his bath and when he returned to his bedroom found Virginia jerking on the bed, screaming, moaning, and clutching her dress and tearing off her stockings and black lace garters. Two of Virginia's friends rushed into the bedroom and tried to calm her down. What worried Arbuckle most was not Rappe's distress but the racket she was making. To revive her, Maude Delmont stripped off her clothing and immersed her in a tub of cold water, but it had no effect. When she was taken back to Arbuckle's bedroom, he remembered one of Keaton's folk remedies for hysterical drunks and suggested they apply ice. Obligingly, the women pressed ice against her forehead and abdomen, and Arbuckle held an ice sliver against her vulva.

"Shut up," he said angrily, "or I'll throw you out the window."

At three-thirty a hotel manager knocked at the door. Arbuckle told him that one of his guests had drunk too many orange blossoms; if the manager would take her away to a place where she might sleep it off, he promised to pay for the room. Rappe was taken down the hall to room 1227, and the party went on without her. At 8:00 P.M. Arbuckle dined with friends downstairs in the hotel restaurant and afterward went to the ballroom to hear music. When he came back to his room at eleven forty-five, a handful of stragglers were still there. Arbuckle sent everyone away and began packing his bags for the trip home in the morning.

On Tuesday Arbuckle paid his $500 bill and returned to Los Angeles by ferry, the Pierce-Arrow stowed in the hull.

The morning after the holiday Keaton returned to work, facing two more tough weeks if *The Boat* were to be wrapped on schedule. As usual, the studio was bustling with films at various stages of development: *The Playhouse* was already in New York awaiting distribution; Keaton and Fred Gabourie were doing final shots of *The Boat;* Eddie Cline was in the editing room preparing *The Blacksmith* for previews at the end of September; and the gag department was busy working out a story line for the next comedy, about a butterfly collector.

Keaton's summer release, *The Goat,* was performing strongly at the box office, as was Arbuckle's latest film, *Gasoline Gus,* which had opened two weeks earlier.

On Friday, September 9, Virginia Rappe died at Wakefield Sanitarium. Her death certificate listed the cause of death as "rupture of the bladder," complicated by "acute peritonitis." The words "due to external force" and "manslaughter" would be added shortly. Within hours of her death, Maude Delmont told newspaper reporters that her friend had died because Fatty Arbuckle had dragged her into his bedroom and raped her.

Arbuckle politely told reporters that the Labor Day affair was only a cocktail party and Virginia Rappe had been quite drunk. He denied there was violent sex, and said he had no idea why Maude Delmont should be "sore" at him. He even offered to return to San Francisco for questioning. That night Viola Dana was at his house with a film crew using his garage for a location shot. It was almost midnight when Roscoe walked in with Joe Schenck and Sid Grauman, a friend who owned several Hollywood cinemas.

"Now listen, kids," Arbuckle said. "I have to go up to San Francisco. I can't tell you why. But for God's sake, don't die on me."

Dana had no idea what he was talking about.

Joe Schenck took charge. After calling a top criminal attorney, he appointed Lou Anger to handle Roscoe. At the Hall of Justice in San Francisco, Arbuckle was grilled for three hours on Saturday before being arrested and fingerprinted. Bail denied, the police locked him up. On Monday morning he was indicted for murder in the first degree. The Big Guy was facing the death penalty.

Many who worked at the comedy studios, Keaton included, were acquainted with Virginia Rappe. She was a pretty girl, that was all. That she should be dead and Roscoe accused of her murder was unbelievable.

The judgment of the moviegoing public was swift and severe. Before the week was out, theater managers began yanking Arbuckle's films (as well as Virginia Rappe's). The case touched on larger social issues involving proper conduct for women. Before the war it would have been unthinkable for a well-brought-up young woman to drink gin, smoke, or go out joyriding with men. A revolution in manners and morals was creating a younger generation whose behavior seemed, to their parents, absolutely depraved. A year earlier readers had been scandalized by F. Scott Fitzgerald's best-selling novel, *This Side of Paradise*, which told what women were doing in parked cars.

What was said to have happened to Rappe was every mother's nightmare. "My mother snatched the newspapers away from me," said silent screen actress Lina Basquette, only fifteen at the time of the Arbuckle trials. "Those stories were not proper for me to read. Years later I met Arbuckle and found him to be a very common kind of person."

On September 25 Keaton finished *The Boat,* and Eddie Cline started to cut it. A preview was planned for mid-October. Three days later the murder charges against Arbuckle were reduced to manslaughter, and he was released on $5,000 bail. The next day the Keatons were at the Santa Fe station in Los Angeles to meet his train. They had to push their way through because hundreds of people were milling about. Before the engine had come to a full stop, the crowd rushed his car. The first person to step off the train was Minta Arbuckle, followed by her husband, who seemed a little wobbly but was nonetheless smiling. "Hello, folks," he said. That was all. Although most newspaper accounts of the homecoming carried headlines about cheering crowds, Keaton remembered it differently. He was shocked to hear people chanting "Beast," "Murderer," "Big fat slob." The frenzied way they were pressing forward made him think they wanted "to tear him to pieces," even though only weeks earlier he had been one of the country's most beloved screen stars.

On Saturday night Keaton stopped by West Adams Boulevard for a drink. The house was a hive of activity, echoing with the strains of ragtime. Arbuckle, calm, walked up and down the drawing room making sure glasses were filled. However, he served no alcohol, only soda and snacks because, he said, he had "learned his lesson." The friends who had gathered said it was terrible but everything would be all right. "Half the people there whispered and tiptoed around," Keaton remembered, "and the others laughed too loud." And so did he. "What could you say to the poor bastard?"

Keaton refused to believe that he might be convicted. "Certainly Fatty Arbuckle was wronged," Keaton said later. "He was no more guilty of that charge than I was." He offered to be a character witness at the trial to swear that Roscoe would never hurt anyone. He would explain that he had been the one who first told Roscoe about using the ice. But Joe Schenck forbade his testifying, or even showing his face in San Francisco. The trial was going to get dirty, and Keaton would have to stay out of it. Even Earl Rogers, California's foremost criminal attorney, refused to undertake Arbuckle's defense. He thought a thin comic would walk away free but the public would surely treat a fat man like some sort of monster. He predicted that Roscoe's weight would "damn him."

Although he continued to believe Arbuckle had nothing to worry about, Keaton stopped talking about wanting to testify. Nor did he attend the trial, scheduled to begin in November, because Roscoe had refused all offers of company and wanted nobody around except Minta and Lou Anger. It would be irresponsible, Keaton understood, to jeopardize his career and the livelihoods of a whole studio of people who were depending on him.

Another development also played a part. "Speaking of the Talmadges," wrote Cal York in *Photoplay*, "I hear that Natalie is very happy in her Hollywood home, that she loves to cook and keep house for Buster, and that there may be a new little Talmadge added to the family before long. Norma and Constance may be aunties."

At long last Natalie had achieved something that her sisters had not: She was going to be a mother. Not that Norma and Connie had ever wanted children. "None of the Talmadge women liked kids, beginning with Peg," said their friend Irene Mayer Selznick.

During the first six months of the marriage, a lonely Peg Talmadge had shuttled between coasts to visit her daughter. Once she learned of the pregnancy, there was no holding her in the East. "Peg came right on out and moved in with us, and the girls rushed their current pictures through," Keaton said. "They were converging on us like homing pigeons."

By now Connie's marriage to John Pialogiou had broken up, at the same time that she met Captain Alastair MacIntosh, a companion of the Prince of Wales who held a commission in His Majesty's Horse Guard. In November, divorced from Pialogiou but not yet married to MacIntosh, feeling at loose ends, Connie came to stay with Nate and Buster. Keaton found himself living with three women, each of whom distrusted men.

Although Keaton didn't care for Peg or Norma, he was fond of Dutch with her giggly enthusiasm, and they always got along well. Even so, he could see that she might turn out to be a bad influence on Nate, especially when it came to buying clothes. He was constantly astonished at how quickly his thousand-dollar weekly paycheck disappeared. Spend though she might, nothing seemed to satisfy Nate. She could not keep up with her sisters; in November Norma scored a new diamond ring from Joe that was, *Photoplay* reported, "so large that no insurance company would insure it."

No sooner had Keaton grown accustomed to having Peg and Dutch around than Joe and Norma blew in from New York. Since making pictures in California was cheaper, Schenck decided in November to move the Talmadge studio to Hollywood. All the Talmadges protested: They hated Southern California, and the approach of Christmas only heightened their complaints. The heat was miserable, the Santa Clauses and fake snow laughable, and the stores tacky and unreliable. By catalog, they ordered gifts from Bendel's and Hattie Carnegie, then at the last minute packed up and returned to New York for a white Christmas.

A few weeks later they were back. Norma and Dutch began to enjoy Hollywood's social swirl. "The Talmadges were much in evidence at all social functions," noted *Photoplay*. Norma and Joe, Hollywood's first mogul-superstar couple, headed everyone's priority guest list. Irene Mayer Selznick, daughter of upcoming mogul Louis B. Mayer, first met the Talmadges shortly after their arrival. "None of the Talmadges cared about being a hostess," she recalled. "Joe was worldly and sophisticated, at ease in any hotel in the world. He would be the one to say, 'Norma, we're having a party.' And Norma would say 'Fine, I'll attend.' She never knew who was coming or how many."

Once the family arrived, Keaton had to put up with comparisons between himself and Joe Schenck. Of course his brother-in-law's wealth dwarfed his. The Talmadges also patronized him, sneered at his opinions, and failed to appreciate his films on any but the most superficial levels.

In November he was working on a comedy with basically two characters, Joe Roberts and himself. *The Paleface* is about a butterfly collector who chases a specimen into an Indian reservation and eventually becomes the chief by saving the land from greedy oil speculators—not, however, before the tribe tries to burn him at the stake. Keaton thought nothing of jumping into nets or diving into pools. For a scene in *The Paleface* he planned to plunge into a net from a seventy-five-foot-high rope suspension bridge strung across an old mule-train road up in the Santa Susana Mountains. The day before shooting the scene, a technician making a test jump broke a shoulder and a leg. In Keaton's opinion, he had failed to hit the net properly. As Keaton stood in the same spot the next day, he thought about the man in the hospital and began feeling nervous. Later he admitted he almost didn't jump but "I didn't want to show yellow before my own gang." The stunt gave him a tremendous "kick."

On the first Sunday in December, Arbuckle's manslaughter trial drew to a close at the Hall of Justice in San Francisco. At noon, after forty-one hours of deliberation and twenty-two ballots, the jury announced it was deadlocked: Ten jurors had voted for acquittal, two for conviction. Annihilated by the press before the trial began, Arbuckle would now be retried. In Los Angeles, he sat in darkened rooms in his mansion and wept. When Keaton visited, Arbuckle demanded: Why was this happening to him? Why did everybody hate him? Why did the papers call him impotent and claim that he had raped Rappe with a champagne bottle and ruptured her bladder? He drank to forget the lies people had said about him, and that kept him drunk most of the time.

That winter was turning out to be one of the most terrible in Hollywood's short history. Suddenly the whole world was watching. Opening a special news bureau, the *Chicago Tribune* prepared for a mud slide of stories about alcoholism, drug addiction, and alarming sexual practices. So notorious had the picture business become—so many indiscretions had caught up with so many overpaid and overpublicized actors—that the word *Hollywood* was becoming a synonym for scandal. The public was shocked by its glimpses behind the scenes. For stars like Keaton, it was time to behave like a puritan. Virginia Fox told *Motion Picture Classic* that Natalie Talmadge accompanied her husband to the studio almost every day because she enjoyed being close to him. "They are the happiest couple!" she insisted. "We are just one contented family at the Keaton Studio." Not content to market his employer as a family man and straight-arrow citizen, Harry Brand turned Keaton into an all-American humorist by ghostwriting under Keaton's name a nationally syndicated newspaper column filled with Will Rogers–type homespun witticisms.

The consensus was that the San Francisco police had blown the Arbuckle case out of proportion. Had the party taken place in Los Angeles, Rappe's death would have been ruled accidental. Paramount would have been able to destroy evidence, create alibis, pull whatever strings necessary to protect Arbuckle, just as they would do in 1935 when Thelma Todd was murdered by Mafia boss Lucky Luciano, or when in 1932 Jean Harlow's husband was murdered by an ex-wife and MGM recast it as a suicide. In 1935 Virginia Rappe's death would have been one-day news. Studio moguls tended to be philosophical. Arbuckle's employer, Adolph Zukor, took the fatalistic view that the Big Guy's fame and money had worked against him and there was nothing he or anybody else could do about it.

12 COPS

Keaton watched Arbuckle's trial in horror. Just before Christmas 1921 he began filming a picture about the failure of the American dream: Hopes turn out to be nothing; talent and industry are irrelevant because life is only a lottery. For the first time, the established order generates indignation in Buster.

In *Cops* a penniless man has fallen in love with the mayor's daughter, an arrogant rich girl (Virginia Fox) who holds him in contempt because he hasn't succeeded in business. Buster sets out to win her love by making something of himself. After Buster finds a wallet full of money (which he pockets), a con man sells him someone else's furniture that has been piled on the sidewalk. With his remaining money he buys a wagon and a broken-down horse to haul away the hot merchandise. He gets tangled up in a policemen's parade and finds himself surrounded on four sides by men in blue uniforms. As his wagon moves toward the mayor's reviewing stand, he takes out a cigarette and hunts for a match. At that very moment a rooftop terrorist hurls a bomb, which lands on the seat next to Buster. After using the burning fuse to light his cigarette, he flips the bomb like a used match into the crowd of marching cops.

The centerpiece of the movie is the ensuing pursuit, with hundreds of cops swarming up and down streets, over fences, and across backyards to capture the bomber. Buster surrenders, only after the girl rejects him. The end title shows his porkpie hat resting on a tombstone.

Keaton's bombing scene resembled a gruesome act of terrorism in American history. Just two years earlier, thirty people were killed and hundreds more injured when a bomb concealed in a horse-drawn wagon exploded on Wall Street. As a subject for humor, anarchism seemed tasteless to twenties audiences. *Cops* presented a predicament for its distributor having to sell it as light entertainment. First National's marketing of the film stripped all of its political overtones. A Seattle paper said *Cops* was "abounding with gags, and plot will be conspicuous by its absence." Fifty years later a French film semiologist would place *Cops* alongside "The Waste Land" and *Ulysses* as one of the great works of art produced in the year 1922. Keaton did not agree. "Well, just running away from cops is a gag," he told an interviewer in 1956. He dismissed the plot as "hit and miss" and the chase sequence as "ordinary."

During the filming of *Cops* Arbuckle returned to San Francisco for his retrial. On February 4, as the whole country waited, the jury announced another deadlock. This time ten of the jurors had favored conviction. That same week two not entirely unrelated events occurred that made Hollywood appear sinful and decadent. William Desmond Taylor, a director at Paramount, was found shot to death in his Hollywood home, and two of Hollywood's biggest stars, Mabel Normand and Mary Miles Minter, were implicated in his murder. A few weeks later Wallace Reid, a popular film star, was hospitalized for the morphine addiction that would soon prove his undoing. Despite these scandals, attention continued to focus on the San Francisco sex trial.

In March the Arbuckle case was tried for a third time. On April 12, the jury stayed out only five minutes before returning a verdict of not guilty. The jury foreman described the defendant as "entirely innocent" and the victim of "a grave injustice." There was not "the slightest proof" connecting him with Rappe's death.

During the twenties the Keatons were occasionally invited to spend weekends at San Simeon, William Randolph Hearst's castle north of San Luis Obispo. One day Keaton found himself in conversation with Hearst and Joe Schenck when Arbuckle's name came up. He heard Hearst boast that the Arbuckle trial sold more papers than the sinking of the *Lusitania*. Keaton was deeply shocked and would never forget Hearst's words.

What happened in Arbuckle's hotel bedroom on Labor Day is still a mystery. He had the best defense that money could buy. His legal team hired Pinkerton detectives, among them future novelist

Dashiell Hammett, to investigate Virginia Rappe and Maude Delmont. Hammett concluded that Rappe had gonorrhea and Arbuckle had been framed. However, fat villains began to appear in his fiction.

In death Virginia Rappe was smeared as diseased and promiscuous, and Arbuckle was characterized as impotent. Arbuckle's lawyers argued that their client was a bighearted gentleman who wouldn't dream of drinking, fornicating, partying, or losing his temper. Despite what they said, he was no saint. As his friends knew, he drank too much and also tended to be a mean drunk. It is entirely possible that he and Rappe did have sex that afternoon, but under the circumstances this could never be admitted.

At the least, Arbuckle was guilty of living by the rules that governed Hollywood, which amounted to no rules at all. The Labor Day celebration epitomized the community's contempt for women on screen and off—and its acceptance of parties that permitted males to regard females as commodities, as interchangeable and disposable as the parsley girls in Woburn.

After a seven-month nightmare, Arbuckle got his happy ending. He wasted no time getting back to his house on West Adams and started to plan his next picture. But the last reel was still to come.

Monday, September 5, 1921, would be a date long remembered in Hollywood history. The main repercussion of Arbuckle's party was the establishment of the Hays Office and censorship, Hollywood's attempt to clean up its image, just as the Chicago White Sox bribery scandal in 1919 had led to the appointment of a commissioner to regulate baseball. In his new job as head of the Motion Picture Producers and Distributors of America, Will H. Hays, ex-postmaster general, attended to the Arbuckle matter at once. On April 19, exactly one week after Arbuckle had been exonerated, Hays banned him from the screen.

Although *Photoplay* published the full text of the jury's apology, movie fans appeared not to care. The public, said the film community, could no longer laugh at a man who had become a symbol of perverted sex. Sex trials would not always have this result. Twenty years later Errol Flynn would be accused of statutory rape of two teenage girls aboard his yacht, win acquittal, and become a bigger star than ever. But this was 1922, not 1942.

Several years later ex-King Alfonso of Spain was visiting

Hollywood and wanted to meet Fatty Arbuckle, one of his favorite stars. The scandal had to be explained to him. How unfair, Alfonso replied, it might have happened to anybody.

Keaton also believed that it could have happened to any of them, even to himself. He never faltered in his support of Arbuckle. In March, when Comique stockholders decided to change the name of the company from Comique Film Corporation to Buster Keaton Productions, he magnanimously agreed to give Arbuckle 35 percent of all future profits on his films.

Keaton bought one of Arbuckle's scenario ideas for a picture parodying Hollywood cowboy star William S. Hart. During the trial Hart had attacked Arbuckle in the press, and Arbuckle was itching to pay him back.

The Frozen North was filmed in the small northern California town of Truckee, not far from where the Donner Party had lost its way in 1846. As the picture opens, at the last stop on a New York subway line, a Canadian Mountie type emerges from the exit and finds himself knee-deep in the snowy wilderness of Alaska. Hart always played Dudley Do-Right characters, but Keaton plays Hart as a thief and a bully, a seducer and a murderer. It was a surprising and bizarre change of pace for him. Buster subjects his wife to shoves, curses, and infidelity, and when she retaliates by shooting him in the back, it was what he deserved. The closing frames, showing Buster asleep in a cinema and being woken by a janitor, soften the effect somewhat. Hart refused to speak to Keaton for years. The comedy also briefly satirizes Erich von Stroheim's evil count in *Foolish Wives,* but Stroheim took it good-naturedly.

With Norma and Joe at the Ambassador Hotel and Peg and Connie right in his house, Keaton began to feel claustrophobic. It seemed as if "the walls were bulging," he said. More and more the Talmadges made disparaging remarks about his being a comedian, and they also teased him about the new baby, which they had decided would be a girl. None of them wanted the baby to address them as Auntie or Grandmother. "Just plain Norma," Norma said. "Connie," said Dutch. "Peggie, I suppose," decided Peg, who wrote to Anita Loos her suspicion that Nate would have a boy. "If so, out it goes hot or cold."

Keaton's next picture was pointedly titled *My Wife's Relations.* A candy-shop clerk living in a Polish neighborhood is falsely accused of breaking a window and hauled before a judge by a vast and rugged Irishwoman. Unable to speak English, the judge mistakes them for a bride and groom. Before Buster knows it, he is married and meeting his new in-laws, a father and four brothers, a gang of remarkable greed. They examine him as would a poultry inspector and stamp him a reject: "He won't last a week in this family." After getting smacked around for two reels, Buster is seen relaxing on the observation desk of the *Reno Limited,* looking forward to a vacation in the divorce capital.

The picture allowed him to say many awful things about his in-laws. To their credit, the Talmadges took the film in stride. Whatever their shortcomings, they had always known how to laugh at themselves. Although Keaton won that round, he would not always be so lucky. He could never predict when the clan would give him a bloody nose.

Shortly before *My Wife's Relations* opened in May, Nate decided it was time to move. She had never really liked 855 Westchester because there was no swimming pool or tennis courts, no banquet hall or projection room. The move was accomplished without consulting Keaton. The twenty-room pseudo-Tudor house with pool was located on Westmoreland Place. One of their neighbors was Mack Sennett. There was a ballroom on the third floor, a useless amenity. Dutch used the space as an indoor track to ride her bicycle.

The nursery was filled with baskets of sweet peas and sprays of orchids artfully arranged in a miniature baby carriage. There were stacks of tiny, handmade garments and piles of receiving blankets. In the center of the room was a wicker cradle lined in pink satin, frilly lace, and streaming pink ribbons.

On Friday, June 2, shortly after 7:00 P.M., Natalie had a baby boy weighing seven pounds. He was named Joseph Talmadge Keaton. For his godfather, his parents chose William "Buster" Collier, Jr., one of Keaton's friends who was a movie juvenile and the adopted son of a well-known stage actor. *Movie Classic* assumed that the baby had been named for Joseph Schenck, while other fan magazines referred to him as the Talmadge heir and treated his father as superfluous.

At home Keaton's suggestions were a waste of breath. For example: the pink ribbons on the baby clothes. "Blue is for boys," he said.

"No," Nate insisted, "pink is for boys." Further conflict arose over the baby's name. She began to call him Jimmy.

At the studio Keaton could be a severe boss and his crew had felt his steely anger whenever he caught someone failing to do his job. At home he preferred to avoid serious conflict and often wound up swallowing his emotions, as he had done as a child.

Not long after the birth of Joseph, Keaton discovered that his relationship with Natalie was not going to change just because she had a baby. She continued to look down on him, belittling his abilities as a businessman. That fall she assumed responsibility for the family's finances. Keaton authorized Buster Keaton Productions to transfer to his wife "all monies due, or which may hereafter become due me, by way of additional compensation" and "to make payment of said sums as they may occur to the said Natalie T. Keaton." In other words, he would receive no remuneration for his work; his salary and bonuses would be paid directly to his wife.

This seemed perfectly normal to Keaton. In his family, it had been Myra Keaton who controlled the money, each morning doling out enough for the day's expenses, usually sending Buster to buy tickets and pay hotel bills. Buster never learned to manage the money, he only knew how to spend it. To him, financial chores were women's work, just like washing dishes and making beds.

However, his wife's financial experience was limited to shopping sprees on Fifth Avenue. Eventually Keaton engaged a professional business manager.

That summer Arbuckle went to China and Japan. Embittered by his banishment from movies, he told reporters that he was considering film production in the Orient. Or maybe he would appear on Broadway in a legitimate show. The Talmadges also left for several months to tour Europe.

The Keatons discovered Tijuana, a small town on the Mexican border that provided bread and circuses for Hollywood, in the form of gambling casinos, brothels, and dozens of bars. At the Tijuana racetrack, a breeder had named a two-year-old sorrel colt for Keaton. Together with Lou and Sophy Anger, the Keatons made the two-hour drive south to see this speedball run in the Debutante Stakes. To their delight, he broke the track record at three and a half furlongs. (After winning nine of his first ten races, Buster Keaton went lame in the eleventh and never raced again.)

For two years Keaton had been pressuring Schenck about moving from two-reelers to feature-length films. The big comedy stars were all going into features. Chaplin had made *The Kid* in 1921, the year after Harold Lloyd had produced *Grandma's Boy.*

That summer and fall Keaton was working at top speed turning out two-reelers. According to his contract with First National, he owed five more shorts, but he made only four. In addition to *Daydreams,* about another swoony man who gets into trouble pursuing success in the city, possibly codirected by an uncredited Arbuckle, the quartet includes *The Balloonatic,* in which a would-be lover looks for love and finds it after subduing a bear; a retooling of the abandoned *The Electric House,* with exteriors filmed at his own home; and *The Love Nest,* the most surreal of his short works, in which a tormented man struggles to attain peace of mind by going across the ocean in a silly little boat.

After *The Love Nest,* Keaton thought it was time to force a showdown with Schenck, who was due back from Europe with the Talmadges in November. At Natalie's suggestion, they decided to meet the ship. Arriving in New York, the glamorous young couple with their five-month-old infant drew the attention of the press. In photographs, Natalie, trim in a belted cape with fur boa and spiky heels, stands with her arms around Keaton in his impeccably tailored dark suit, white shirt, homburg, and beautifully polished boots. And their faces were as perfect as if they had just stepped off a movie set.

A reunion at the pier on November 26 was followed by a week of meetings with the stockholders of Buster Keaton Productions. Marcus Loew found no reason why Keaton should not do features, and everyone else agreed. It would mean higher rentals from exhibitors. The stockholders decided that production of two-reelers would cease immediately and the studio would close down for renovations. When it reopened Keaton would make two features a year, a spring and a fall release, and average about eight weeks for filming each one. The final subject was money. Keaton's fifteen-month marriage had left him painfully broke. His present salary of $1,000 a week plus 35 percent of the net profits didn't even begin to cover his expenses. Without argument, Schenck generously escalated him to $2,000 a week (and later to $2,500) plus profit sharing and bonuses.

During the fall and winter, First National released the last four comedies, and in March 1923 Keaton's final short comedy, *The Love Nest*, came out. By that time he had already made *The Three Ages*, a six-reeler that ran fifty-six minutes. Structured as a parody of *Intolerance*, D. W. Griffith's epic of bigotry and greed through the ages, it leapfrogs through time in three separate but similar stories set in the Stone Age, ancient Rome, and 1920s Los Angeles. In Jurassic times Keaton plays a caveman whose yearning for a mate is hampered by a rival suitor; he is a charioteer in ancient Rome, who finds himself in the lion's den; and then a twentieth-century man who winds up enslaved to a clotheshorse wife and a Pekingese.

The episodic approach allowed Keaton to play it safe. Unsure that his gags could be stretched to feature length, he figured that he could chop it into three shorts. As extra insurance, he passed over Joe Roberts and signed a well-known actor, Wallace Beery (who had recently played King Richard in Douglas Fairbanks's *Robin Hood*), to be the villain in all three stories.

In two reels Keaton could keep the audience laughing pretty constantly. In a six-reeler he had to stop the laughter and pick it up again, not an easy thing to do. He and Eddie Cline had been his gag department. Now he added three gagmen with excellent credits: Joseph A. Mitchell, who came from vaudeville and the legitimate stage; and a pair of former Comique writers, Clyde Adolph Bruckman, a twenty-nine-year-old onetime newspaperman, and Jean Havez, fifty-three, a veteran vaudeville song and sketch writer, who had left Arbuckle's writing department to join Harold Lloyd's studio.

The days of puny budgets were gone. Features required bigger crews and more elaborate sets. Fred Gabourie and his carpenters created sets for the Roman scenes by building a movie-set shell reproduction of the Colosseum's lowest tiers, then duplicated the upper tiers with tiny hanging miniature models. The Circus Maximus chariot race was shot on location of a recently closed Hollywood Exposition. The largest expenditure went for construction of a dinosaur. For a game of prehistoric baseball, played with rocks and a bumpy club, Keaton at bat tried to drive a hit into a foe's head. Take after take was rejected. "On the fifty-second take it worked just the way it was supposed to," said an actor in the film. "And it was worth all the trouble."

*   *   *

Margaret Leahy was a blond English girl who had returned with the Talmadges from Europe in November. She had been working as a dress-shop clerk in London when she won a beauty contest, one of whose prizes was a contract for a role in Norma's next picture, *Within the Law*. By the time they reached New York the Talmadges had adopted her as their protégée, calling her the most ravishing girl in England. They had no doubt that she would become a major star. In Los Angeles, a blizzard of promotion touted Leahy as "a true English type" who had played "in both French and English cinemas on the continent."

On the first shooting day of *Within the Law*, it was obvious that the beauty queen would need a great deal of coaching, which was not surprising, since she had no acting experience. The director, Frank Lloyd, tried to be patient, but Leahy rattled easily. The next morning he found himself reduced to near-despair, and by the third day of shooting, he was threatening to quit. Leahy was gorgeous, but she lacked the talent and the temperament for acting. She could not walk naturally. Or stand or sit. She was hopelessly awkward. Lloyd finally announced that either she went or he did.

After observing Leahy on the set, Schenck realized that Lloyd was right. Schenck didn't want her in *Within the Law* either. But he hesitated to fire her, lest she or her family sue him for breach of contract. So he decided to give her to Keaton.

Nothing had prepared Keaton for Joe Schenck's announcement that the English girl would be his leading woman in *The Three Ages*. He could not help hearing all about her problems. Now he was saddled with her.

The wily Schenck was prepared. "Comic leading ladies don't have to act," he assured Keaton.

Schenck's theory was preposterous. But his brother-in-law needed a favor, and so Keaton resolved to make the best of the situation.

Schenck's public relations people got Leahy chosen as a Wampas Baby Star, one of a dozen pretty faces predicted each year for stardom by an association of movie advertisers. The selection of a foreigner stirred indignant comments from the Hollywood press corps, who disparaged her as "the Talmadge English importation."

According to Keaton, Leahy was a disaster. The beauty queen

went around with a dazed look. Years later he distinctly remembered "the scenes we threw in the trash can! Easy scenes!" In the end he got a decent picture. "But my God, we previewed it *eight* times! Went back and shot scenes like mad."

Three months before its U.S. release, *The Three Ages* premiered in London on June 25 at a charity benefit screening before a distinguished audience that included Queen Mother Alexandra, Princess Alice, and other members of the royal family. Prime Minister David Lloyd George arranged for a private screening at his home later that week, as did President Alexandre Millerand of France. In the U.S. the *New York World* thought Keaton had made "the funniest picture of his career." In *Life* magazine, Robert Sherwood called him a national treasure capable of raising the spirits of the human race in the face of taxes, strikes, and Mussolini.

Eventually the picture would rack up $448,606 in domestic grosses, not bad for a first feature. It also played strongly in the foreign market. In Russia, where Keaton was a far bigger attraction than Chaplin, *Three Epochs* (as it was called there) inspired Sergei Eisenstein to imagine a film on economic development with "Lenin's analysis of the 'five epochs.'" Unfortunately, the Russians would rent a picture for one week from the Berlin film exchange, make a dupe negative, then distribute copies all over the country.

In many cities *The Three Ages* broke records. A navy lieutenant in charge of film programs for U.S. ships reported that "Buster Keaton is the most popular comedian in the American Navy."

But in Keaton's judgment *The Three Ages* was only "all right." It had enough laughs, but generally he thought it had misfired. In truth, it served as a warm-up for his next picture.

"The Talmadge girls were the fabulous three," said Elaine St. Johns, daughter of Adela Rogers St. Johns, who knew where all the Hollywood bodies were buried. "Constance came on as Miss Mischief, Norma was sexy and sultry, and Natalie stayed home and had babies. They were Hollywood's greatest sister act."

As Keaton was becoming a star in his own right, the popularity of Norma and Constance had already peaked and would soon begin to wane. "Norma Talmadge had quite a shock the other day when she heard someone refer to her as Buster Keaton's sister-in-law," commented *Photoplay.* "Such is fame!"

Norma, now pushing thirty, had never made truly unforgettable pictures—they have not been shown for decades—but she was a heavy hitter at the box office. In 1923 she was earning $10,000 a week (compared to Connie's $5,000). Fans worshipped her as the greatest emotional actress on the screen. "I used to be a very ardent fan of hers when I was thirteen or fourteen," said Douglas Fairbanks, Jr., a film princelet who got closer to her than most fans. "I had pictures of her all over the place." Young Fairbanks, like numerous moviegoers, tended to think of Buster Keaton as first "a fellow who was married to one of the Talmadge sisters" and only secondarily as a star in his own right.

Despite the success of *The Three Ages,* Peg Talmadge continued to regard her son-in-law as a second-string celebrity who would never eclipse her Norma. To boost her daughters' careers and satisfy the hunger of curious fans, Peg decided to publish a memoir about the family. This posed a bit of a problem: She was not a writer, and her story could not be the complete truth. (She could not, for example, mention a spicy detail like Connie's two failed marriages.) Supervising two teams of ghostwriters and a professional fan-magazine writer, Peg compiled a document that held few facts. A chapter titled "Natalie Marries Buster Keaton" paints her son-in-law as a pretty good comedian who was able to repair almost anything around the house with a penknife and a piece of string. The crowning indignity is a photograph of Keaton's house on Westmoreland, misidentified in the caption as "The Talmadge Home in Hollywood."

By the time *The Three Ages* was released Keaton already was doing postproduction on a second feature that would mark a leap forward in his filmmaking. Set during the 1830s, *Hospitality* was loosely derived from a true story about a legendary family feud. The Hatfields of Logan County, West Virginia, and the McCoys of Pike County, Kentucky, were two large clans whose hatred of each other dated back to the Civil War. In 1882, when Johnse Hatfield attempted to elope with Rosanne McCoy, armed warfare began and continued for a half dozen years, until Kentucky state troopers invaded West Virginia to seize several of the Hatfields.

Although the real-life feud had taken place forty years earlier, Keaton decided to move his story back still further to 1830, in order to coincide with the invention of railway locomotives. He was bewitched by stories involving mechanical characters, and no machine, in life or in films, enchanted him more than a train. He asked Fred Gabourie if it would be possible to reproduce one of those glorious early steam locomotives. When his art director didn't see why not, Keaton began growing his hair long.

Instead of reproducing De Witt Clinton's American engine, they agreed that an English import, George Stephenson's Rocket, looked much funnier. While the train was being built to scale at the studio, the creative department was assuring Keaton that every detail was authentic, a departure from most silent comedies.

Keaton plays William McKay, a New York dandy in elegant top hat and Johnny Walker waistcoat, who is summoned to the South to claim his dead father's estate. On the train ride back to his birthplace, he becomes friendly with a pretty passenger named Virginia. Unaware that she is a Canfield, the clan that killed his father, he accepts her invitation to come home for dinner. When Virginia's brothers learn that Willie is a hated McKay, they begin fingering their derringers. But their father (Joe Roberts) warns them that shooting Willie under their roof would violate the southern code of hospitality. They must wait until he leaves. Under the circumstances, Willie tries to stay as long as possible.

For the role of Virginia Canfield, Keaton began looking for an actress who combined old-fashioned southern-belle prettiness with the look of an innocent schoolgirl. He gave the role to the least obvious choice, a woman he would describe as "a frustrated actress." At the age of twenty-eight, Natalie was finally to get her opportunity. He was taking a risk. Insignificant though her previous roles had been, she nonetheless had managed to fail.

Though Keaton disapproved of her working, he must have sympathized with her needs and perhaps also understood her resentment toward her sisters. She was not a thrilling actress, but then neither was Virginia Fox or Sybil Seely. Nate, unlike them, lacked natural comedic talent, but she looked right for the part. He was convinced that he could act with her and direct her.

That spring they were getting along quite well. With a baby in the nursery, their marriage seemed to stabilize. Peg and Connie found homes of their own. In May Natalie became pregnant again.

An important character in the early sequences of *Hospitality* is a cantankerous railway engineer. He kicks off his passengers' hats and angrily flings wood at farmers living alongside the tracks. This was a perfect role for Joe Keaton. Now fifty-six, he had developed a paunch and a bald spot, and his face betrayed his years of heavy drinking. Though he could have had endless screen work, he was not interested. But he was more than willing to appear in his boy's films. (He played fathers in *Daydreams* and *Sherlock Jr.* and a Union general in *The General.*) Keaton also asked Joe Roberts, who had worked on most of his two-reelers and was practically a family member, to play the head of the Canfield clan.

To re-create the Shenandoah Valley of the nineteenth century, Keaton planned to shoot exteriors three hundred miles north in Truckee, the same gorgeous region near the Nevada border where he had made *The Frozen North.*

At the beginning of July a crew of twenty arrived in Truckee with a locomotive, three passenger coaches, thirty exterior sets, and the material to build several miles of narrow-gauge railroad track. Keaton played baseball with his crew and fished for Truckee's famous salmon trout with his father. The two Joes— Roberts and Keaton—speaking in shorthand, conversed endlessly about vaudeville. For Keaton, listening to them took him back to Muskegon.

Natalie threw herself into the part and proved to be a better actress than anyone had given her credit for. If there was any problem, it was that Nate was attractive, in a mournful sort of way, but lacked movie star glamour. In a few scenes an unflattering wig made her look a fright.

In the pleasant atmosphere of Truckee the Keatons enjoyed a family holiday, but there was tragedy on the set. Joe Roberts suffered a stroke. When he was released from a Reno hospital, he insisted on returning to Truckee. He did not look well and died a few months later.

Keaton's passion for daredevil stunts resulted in a disturbing accident. The film climaxes in a daring rescue of the heroine, whose boat is being swept downstream through the rapids. As usual, Keaton had refused to use a double. As a safety precaution, and to make sure he would stay within camera range, a holdback wire was attached to his body.

When the cameras started to roll, he plunged into the fierce current of the Truckee River and began to swim. A few seconds later, the wire snapped and he shot forward, tumbling over rocks and boulders, swallowing great mouthfuls of foam as he was borne toward the rapids. It took all his strength to maneuver himself to the river's edge so that he could grab an overhanging branch. When he was found ten minutes later, he lay in the underbrush along the riverbank facedown in the mud, his feet still dangling in the water. He did not move when they pulled him out. His first words as he lifted his head were: "Did Nate see it?"

Back in Hollywood, he completed the rescue sequence on the lot. A waterfall was constructed over the swimming pool. To create the distant valley below the falls, a miniature set was planted with hundreds of tiny trees. As Virginia's boat plunges over the falls, Willie uses a rope to swing out over the waterfall and grab her at the last moment. Although a dummy was substituted for Nate, Keaton performed the dangerous stunt himself. Hanging upside down underneath the waterfall, he swallowed so much water that a doctor was called to give him first aid.

The last important scene still left to shoot was the prologue. On a stormy night, a mother and her baby huddle inside their home; a bolt of lightning reveals two men battling with guns in the rain. The next lightning burst shows them lying dead on the ground. In the role of Baby Willie, Keaton cast his fourteen-month-old son. The baby's part was brief, but even so the klieg lights irritated his eyes so badly that he had to be taken off the picture. Nate, now in her fourth month of pregnancy, was showing and had to do her retakes behind bushes.

Retitled *Our Hospitality,* the picture played to sold-out houses. "Keaton is a comedian, dramatic actor, and acrobat par excellence," wrote the *San Francisco Call. Variety* said, "*Our Hospitality* classes as one of the best comedies ever produced for the screen and will set a new fashion in picture comedy conception." In *The New York Times,* Mordaunt Hall called Natalie "quite good in her part."

In domestic grosses, *Our Hospitality* would take in $537,844, topping *The Three Ages* by almost a hundred thousand dollars.

On December 24 the Keaton studio hosted a gala Christmas party attended by employees, friends, and legions of freeloaders. For a company on a hot streak with two successful films in release at the same time, there was plenty to celebrate, and it got a little wild.

On Christmas Day, which happened to be Joe Schenck's forty-fourth birthday, Keaton and Natalie entertained the clan at Westmoreland Avenue, where the drawing room was filled with a towering tree surrounded by toys imported from New York's finest stores.

Norma and Joe left to spend New Year on Coronado Island, where they entertained on their usual grand scale. Among their bejeweled guests was Theda Bara in apricot velvet, diamonds, and pearls. Even so, nobody outsparkled Norma, whose white crepe gown and embroidered Spanish shawl was topped off by a necklace of glistening rubies the size of pigeon's eggs.

The Keatons toasted the New Year with Connie and a crowd of their friends at the Biltmore Hotel. The year was ending on an exultant note. At twenty-eight, Keaton had even greater expectations for 1924.

13 HEARTS AND PEARLS

That January it felt as if everything Keaton touched turned to gold. His life at the studio had settled into a comfortable pattern: spring and fall releases, three-week vacations after each picture. His team—the best art director in the business, the best gagmen and cameramen, unit manager and cutter—all had stuck with him. There had been no failures. Only smash hits.

Shortly after New Year's Day 1924, he began shooting a film with the working title *The Misfit*. Set in a small town, the film relates the adventures of a motion picture projectionist who is a bright kid but bored. He wants to become a private detective and during work studies a book on the subject. His fiancée has been lured away by a rival who has stolen her father's watch, pawned it to buy her a deluxe box of chocolates, and incriminated the projectionist by planting the pawn ticket in his pocket. At work, after threading into the machine a melodrama called *Hearts and Pearls: Or, The Lounge Lizard's Lost Love*, the projectionist falls asleep. His dreams are projected into the film on the screen; people from his life replace the movie characters. His dream self leaves the projection booth, climbs over the orchestra, and walks into *Hearts and Pearls* on the screen. "This was the reason for making the whole picture," Keaton said afterward. "Just that one situation." It would take sixty years before a filmmaker repeated the idea. In *The Purple Rose of Cairo,* Woody Allen brings a celluloid character off the screen into the audience.

Some of the most exuberant moments take place when the poor projectionist gets whipped around in editing. He pounds on the front door of a house and suddenly appears in a garden. Sitting on a garden bench, he is suddenly in a street full of whizzing cars, which nearly run him down. He peers over the edge of a precipice only to find himself in a jungle staring into the hungry eyes of lions; then he is sitting on a rock in the middle of the ocean; and finally he dives into water that becomes a snowbank.

A celluloid character boots the projectionist headlong out of *Hearts and Pearls*—there is no projectionist character in the movie. He clambers right back into the screen, entering the body of "Sherlock Jr., the world's greatest detective." Immediately he is called in on a jewelry heist. He and his sidekick, Gillette, must foil an assassination plot, track down the criminals at their hideout, and snatch the stolen pearls.

After rescuing the kidnapped heroine, the projectionist falls off his stool and wakes up. At that moment, his fiancée bursts in to tell him she knows all about the rival's theft of her father's watch. Unsure what to do, the projectionist glances at the screen and the romantic fade-out of *Hearts and Pearls*. He copies the celluloid and kisses his fiancée. No picture of Keaton's celebrates his originality better than this one.

The Misfit was filmed on location in Los Angeles and at the Keaton studio. He cast Marion Harlan, who had done a bit in *The Three Ages*. With shooting several days to go, she became ill and was replaced by Kathryn McGuire, a Keystone player known primarily for playing opposite a German shepherd in *The Silent Call*, a Rin Tin Tin–type picture. McGuire, a Wampas Baby Star of 1923, was a pretty ingenue on her way up. Keaton chose his one-time roommate and best man, Ward Crane, to be the villain and Joe Keaton to be the girl's father.

For codirector he signed the blacklisted Roscoe Arbuckle. His only work—and it was uncredited—had been as director/writer for Educational's Reel Comedies. Now he was almost broke. His West Adams Boulevard mansion was finally sold to Norma and Joe, and his Pierce-Arrow, Cadillacs, and Rolls-Royce were memories. His legal fees alone amounted to $750,000, part of which he had borrowed from Schenck and other friends.

Arbuckle's real name could not be used on the screen, so they agreed on the pseudonym William Goodrich.

For several days Roscoe seemed to be his old cheerful self. Then Keaton happened to notice a mistake and offered suggestions for improvement. Arbuckle took it personally and became emotional. He started snapping at the actors. He screamed and got "flushed and mad," Keaton recalled. The terrible humiliation, Keaton couldn't help thinking, had "just changed his disposition." Arbuckle's outbursts made Keaton so uncomfortable that he decided to take him off the picture.

Arbuckle soon found work at Tuxedo Comedies directing Al St. John shorts. During the next decade he would direct more than fifty films, though not with his old flair. Under his pseudonym, William Goodrich, he also turned out one feature, *The Red Mill*. After that, he became increasingly bored with low-budget pictures.

On February 3, 1924, Natalie gave birth to a second boy, Robert Talmadge Keaton. For godparents, the Keatons chose their intimate friend Edward Brophy, a twenty-nine-year-old assistant director at Norma's studio, and his wife, Annie. Both of Keaton's sons were baptized as Catholics, even though Keaton himself "had no use for religion," his older son would recall. "He never had a religion and avoided church whenever possible." During the baptism, the center of attention shifted from the newborn to his twenty-month-old brother, who broke away from his parents and ran up the aisle pleading, "Wanta be kept! Wanta be kept!" What terrified him, it turned out, was the baptismal font. A few days earlier a litter of kittens had been drowned at their house and only one kitten was kept.

After Bobby's arrival, Natalie decided that she wanted no more children and moved her husband into a guest room. Keaton soon realized that her postpartum period of abstinence was being extended indefinitely. She no longer wished to have sex with him.

He was reluctant to blame Natalie. Instead, he suspected that her mother and sisters were responsible. Both Dutch and Norma, phobic about pregnancy, feared morning sickness, hemorrhoids, heartburn, varicose veins, and stretch marks, not to mention the horrors of labor. Despite the excuse of Catholicism that she fell back on when it suited her, Natalie could have followed the examples of millions of other women in the twenties; she could have been careful.

It took months for Keaton to accept the situation. Then he told his mother-in-law, "I'm not going without sex. I won't support a mistress, and I am not going to flaunt anything in public, but if I want sex I'll have it. And you might as well get used to the idea because that's the way it's going to be."

By banning him from their bed, Natalie guaranteed that he would find other partners. Women swooned over him. Maybe it was the dark eyes and husky voice, or his little-boy sweetness, or the athletic build and his sensational dancing. "Gals used to go for Buster," said Keaton's close friend William Collier, Jr. "That great smile—worth a million dollars because they never saw it on the screen." (For that matter, Keaton's smile charmed men too. "I was always delighted to see him smile," said Douglas Fairbanks, Jr.)

In his romances Keaton behaved circumspectly. He never carried on openly with women, and he avoided involvements with other prominent stars, though he apparently did not consider leading ladies off limits. Natalie was content to look the other way.

He was happiest when he arrived at the studio in his $3,000 Mercer raceabout. In his private gym, he kept in shape with daily workouts. Personal assistants catered to his every wish. As an assistant prop man he hired Ernie Orsatti, outfielder for the St. Louis Cardinals, whose off-season job was essentially to play ball with his boss. Every afternoon at four they broke for a game on one of the open stages.

In those moments when he could forget about his marriage, it was a grand life.

In a downtown freight yard, Keaton was running along the roof of a moving train. When he reached the last boxcar, he planned to leap and grab on to the spout of a water tank, which was supposed to slowly lower him to the ground.

Instead of the expected smooth descent, the ten-inch pipe suddenly released a flood of water that tore his grip loose and flipped him backward onto the tracks a dozen feet below. The back of his neck slammed against the steel rails. He fainted and was brought to with cold water. The camera kept rolling. Elgin Lessley didn't dare stop cranking until Keaton yelled cut. Later that morning, the pain became so intense that Keaton had to dismiss the crew. For weeks he suffered blinding headaches, but his incredibly high pain threshold allowed him to go on working.

In 1935 an X ray revealed that at some point Keaton had suffered a major injury. A doctor pointed to the callus that had grown over a fracture, next to the top vertebra.

"When did you break your neck?" a doctor asked.

"Never," Keaton replied.

Although the exact time of such an injury would be impossible to pinpoint in a person with his history, Keaton decided it had happened that day in the railroad yards.

Except in *College,* he refused to use a double and was proud of doing his own stunts. Furthermore, if a scene required one of his actors to fall, Keaton doubled him. However, on each of his feature films he experienced a serious injury or a close call. During *The Misfit* Keaton was riding a motorcycle that skidded, smashing two cameras and knocking over Eddie Cline, who was standing with a crowd of extras. Keaton crash-landed on a car and walked away with minor bruises.

In old age no memories pleased him more than reliving his stunts: awnings giving way, pipes breaking, rainspouts collapsing, safety nets two stories deep. Afterward the boys in the scenario department would gather in the screening room for the dailies and "get a thrill out of it," Keaton recalled.

Schenck forced him to take out a $1 million life insurance policy. On the application, Keaton stated that he was in excellent health, played baseball daily, and spent one to two hours a day in the studio gym. He also noted that longevity ran in his family. His paternal grandfather lived to the age of ninety-two (actually seventy-two), and Frank Cutler, living in Waco and still active at the age of eighty (he was seventy-three), drove his car and trailer all over Texas.

Of all the pictures Keaton had made, *The Misfit* was the most complicated because of camera effects. Some of the stunts that looked impossible were not camera tricks but very elaborate feats he remembered from vaudeville. For example, Sherlock's assistant, Gillette, disguised as an old woman peddling ties from a case suspended from a strap around her neck, is standing against a wall. As Sherlock runs from the gangsters, he dives through the woman's torso—into the tray actually—and disappears. Incredibly, the woman walks away. Keaton claimed this trick had been invented by his father and refused to reveal how it was done. In 1957, he performed it on Ed Sullivan's *Toast of the Town* on a fully lit stage. Afterward Sullivan pumped him, but Keaton refused to divulge the secret. The trick involved a small trapdoor in the wall directly behind the tray. The actor playing Gillette was suspended in a horizontal position, with his head and shoulders outside the wall and his torso inside. Keaton did really dive through the lid of the tray into the trapdoor, to the other side of the wall.

"We spent an awful lot of time getting those scenes," he recalled. The picture took four months to complete instead of the usual two, only to be followed by postproduction problems. The first preview turned out to be a catastrophe. The Long Beach audience gasped in disbelief at the special effects but did little laughing. Keaton took the film back to the cutting room. A second screening proved even worse. After further cutting, he wound up with a picture only 4,065 feet long, running about forty-three minutes. Schenck didn't think the five reels were releasable as a feature and asked him to add another thousand feet, but Keaton refused. *The Misfit* was retitled as the punchier *Sherlock Jr.* and released on April 21, 1924.

Reception was mixed. *Photoplay* called it "rare and refreshing." The reviewer for *The New York Times* thought that it had "one of the best screen tricks ever incorporated in a comedy." But most of the notices were not so good.

After being lavished with praise for nearly twenty-five years, Keaton got bashed by the critics. Innovations that would delight audiences fifty years later struck some of Keaton's contemporaries as out of step with high standards of comedy. *Picture Play* called it devoid of "ingenuity and originality." *Variety*'s reviewer sneered that *Sherlock* was as funny as "a hospital operating room." Edmund Wilson, writing testily in the *New Republic,* thought Keaton (and also Harold Lloyd) paid too little attention to character development and too much attention to high-tech gimmicks— "machinery and stunts"—in contrast to Chaplin, who continued to rely on old-fashioned pantomime.

Keaton was accustomed to critical success and hefty box office receipts. With the release of *Sherlock Jr.,* he tasted failure for the first time. In the end, the film made $448,337, just a few hundred dollars less than *The Three Ages.* Keaton would remember it as "all right," but "not one of the big ones."

The big one came about entirely by accident.

After *Sherlock Jr.* had finished shooting, Fred Gabourie didn't have much to do. The crew was on year-round salary and Schenck did not like to see his employees idle, so he found chores for them. Keaton's art director was loaned out to First National for a seafaring action picture, *The Sea Hawk,* set in Elizabethan England. Director Frank Lloyd needed a location scout to tour Seattle, Vancouver, and San Francisco looking for four-masted schooner hulls that could be fixed up to look like a fleet of Elizabethan war vessels.

Meanwhile, the mood at the studio was gloomy, since Keaton and his creative team felt under pressure to come up with a good story idea. After the discouraging reception of *Sherlock Jr.* they were not in a particularly daring mood. But when Gabourie returned to Hollywood, he was whooping with excitement. In a San Francisco boatyard he had been talking to a company about a ship they wanted to sell for scrap, a five-thousand-ton ocean liner, five hundred feet long, just sitting in a slip between Oakland and Alameda.

If they could get the boat, Fred told Keaton, they could tow it out into the ocean and do anything they wished. "Set fire to it if we want to," Gabourie suggested. "Blow it up. We can do anything we want." There was no time to waste because the owners wanted to get rid of it. Keaton could scarcely contain his enthusiasm.

He persuaded Schenck to charter the boat for $25,000, which included the wages of a skeleton crew as well as the cost of sailing it from San Francisco to Los Angeles. Schenck convinced Keaton that he could make a terrific picture without blowing up the ship, because afterward it was going right back to the shipping company.

Keaton's ocean liner had a sad history. The thirty-three-year-old *Buford* had been a military vessel carrying troops to the Spanish-American War and then to the war in Europe. During the Red Scare after the war, the U.S. government deported suspected subversives. In December 1919, the *Buford*—dubbed the "Red Ark" by the press—was dispatched to Russia with 249 of these exiles on board, among them two well-known anarchists, Emma Goldman and Alexander Berkman. Two hundred of the group may have been guilty of little more than foreign birth and leftist sympathies.

When the ship pulled in at the San Pedro docks that spring, its decks were flaked with paint and sheets of rust clung to the hull.

Keaton rechristened it the *Navigator.* He sent in a crew of painters, then moved in generators and lighting equipment. Next came the carpenters, and finally a gang of assistants and cooks. Altogether there would be a production crew of sixty, half of them his people and the rest sailors. Finally Keaton moved in and prepared to ride the resplendent S.S. *Navigator* out to sea.

On San Francisco's Nob Hill, Rollo Treadway glances out of his bedroom window one morning and notices a pair of newly-weds driving by. He turns to his butler.

"I think I'll get married," reads the dialogue title. "Today." Two steamship tickets are booked on a honeymoon cruise leaving the next morning for Honolulu.

Climbing into his limousine, Rollo has himself driven across the street to the home of his socialite sweetheart, Betsy O'Brien (Kathryn McGuire). When he suggests getting married that day, Betsy rejects him. Rollo isn't about to throw away the tickets. He has always wanted to see Hawaii. He decides to board the ship that night. He winds up on the wrong ship, a ship belonging to Betsy's father that is the center of international skullduggery and soon to be set adrift by foreign spies. Rollo boards the *Navigator;* so does Betsy, who has come to help her father. Next morning the ship is adrift at sea; they are its only passengers.

In this picture, Keaton finally got to play his adored *Saphead* character, a pampered, useless playboy surrounded by maids, but-lers, and chauffeurs, a man who can't shave himself and has yet to light his own cigarette.

For ten weeks Keaton lived at sea on board the *Navigator,* where the weather tended to be far calmer than at home. Much of the shooting was done off Catalina. At one time or another, most of his family came out to visit.

To shoot the dramatic spy scenes, Keaton decided to hire a codirector, which is strange considering his experience on *Sherlock Jr.* He offered the job to Donald Crisp, a British-born actor cele-brated for his portrayal of the brutal father in *Broken Blossoms,* who had only one directorial credit to his name. He was astonished to discover that Crisp had no interest in the dramatic scenes. "He turned gagman overnight on me!" Keaton said. His problems with Crisp made the news columns. *Variety* reported Keaton's "diffi-culty" on the set and his clashes with Crisp. One morning when Crisp arrived for work, Keaton notified him that the picture was completed. It was not. After Crisp left, Keaton reshot his scenes, much as he had done with Arbuckle's work in *Sherlock*. Crisp had allowed the actors to overact. If there was one thing Keaton couldn't stand, it was overacting.

Schenck and Keaton found themselves increasingly at odds over money. On this picture, Joe had been nervous about shelling out $25,000 for a single prop, though Keaton was right—the *Buford* was worth every cent. All that remained to film was an underwater sequence that, in the name of savings, would be shot in the Riverside municipal swimming pool. The only problem was that at its deepest end the pool was nine feet, while the mockup of the Buford's propeller measured twelve feet. Permission was duly received to extend the pool's concrete walls to twenty feet. When the new pool was filled, the extra weight of the water caused the bottom to cave in. Schenck had to rebuild the Riverside pool.

After this mess, the company packed up and moved to Catalina. They did not stay long because Keaton decided the water was too milky and he was not going to shoot in milky water. They would just have to find a better location.

The next stop was five hundred miles away at Lake Tahoe, where the water was crystalline clear but also bitterly cold. Keaton insisted he would go down himself. Even in a diving suit he could stay underwater for only fifteen minutes. Each time he came up he took a swig of straight bourbon, as did the cameramen who were going down in a diving bell. Getting a few minutes of film at Tahoe took several weeks. As expenditures climbed, Schenck began boiling with rage. It was a struggle between two people who wanted total control over every detail. Keaton ruled his studio like a monarch; Schenck was always trying to make him heel.

There were reasons Keaton was indifferent to Schenck's problems. Recently Joe had broadcast the news that he planned to spend $3.5 million (the equivalent of $140 million today) on nine features (primarily Norma's and Connie's), the heftiest budget ever mapped out by an independent producer. The money bought increasingly lavish production values for the Talmadge sisters' pictures such as *Ashes of Vengeance* and *Dulcy*. So why should Keaton scrimp?

One of Keaton's favorite friends was Jimmy's godfather, the engaging twenty-two-year-old actor William "Buster" Collier. A frequent visitor to their home during the midtwenties, Collier worshipped Keaton and felt fond of Natalie, though he thought she didn't have an ounce of personality, at least not compared to Connie, with whom he was having an affair. Natalie was "a very good mother and the two kids were very well brought up," but Keaton was simply not "a family man." As much as he loved his children, he "never stayed home much. He was always out playing ball or hunting and fishing."

In the opinion of Anita Loos, the boys were indulged by aunts who had no idea about what was best for children. They spoiled them with the most expensive items they could find. When most boys their ages were playing with building blocks or a jack-in-the-box, they were presented with miniature automobiles.

Natalie's standards of family life had been inherited: the turmoil of an alcoholic home, then a mother bringing up children alone and an absent father enshrined in family lore as a skunk. Lacking a helpful model for motherhood, Nate was unable to fit herself into traditional roles.

On Columbus Day 1924, *The Navigator* premiered at New York's Capitol, the biggest movie theater in the world, where it drew huge crowds. It was held over a second week, a rarity at the Capitol. The picture received almost unanimous praise. It turned out to be Keaton's biggest financial success. Despite the new swimming pool for Riverside and the $25,000 rental of the *Buford,* the film cost only $385,000 and its domestic gross would be $680,406.

This time Keaton had no reservations. He believed *The Navigator* was his best.

When he arrived in New York to plug the movie, his future had never looked brighter. Even before completion of *The Navigator,* Schenck had promised him a raise. In his pocket was a new three-year contract. For each of his next six films he would receive $27,000, and in the event of a third picture begun in any calendar year he would get a $13,000 bonus. In addition, he continued to share in the profits of his films.

Although accompanied by his wife, he spent little time with her. He attended the 1924 World Series at the Polo Grounds, where the New York Giants were facing the Washington Senators.

Then, following the Giants to Washington, he joined newspaper-man Damon Runyon for the deciding game, a twelve-inning classic in which the aging but still great pitcher Walter Johnson stopped the Giants, winning the Senators their one and only championship.

As Keaton soon discovered, Natalie had plans for his increased salary. Real estate was booming in Southern California, and she had found a new obsession: houses. Instead of sex they now clashed over real estate. After less than a year, the charms of Westmoreland Place and its third-floor ballroom had faded. At Nate's insistence they had moved out, embarking on what seemed to Keaton a perpetual quest for more elaborate homes at better addresses.

The Schencks had recently sold Arbuckle's mansion and were building a house in expensive Benedict Canyon, not far from the sixteen-acre site that Harold Lloyd had selected for his new estate and the twenty-four-acre villa of scenarist Frances Marion.

Keaton knew that it was senseless to keep throwing away money on rent. He had already moved his family out of Ingraham Street and bought his mother a comfortable nine-room bungalow on Victoria Avenue.

The Keatons' first home of their own was a large, tile-roofed house on Ardmore Avenue with a wonderful lawn and clipped yew trees. Keaton wound up borrowing the full $55,000 price from Joe Schenck. After only ten months, a period that Keaton would refer to as "refueling," Natalie decided it was time to sell again. Keaton didn't want to move, but to his delight he cleared $30,000 on the sale. After that he decided to stop arguing with Nate and began to regard housing as high-stakes gambling.

Although their new home on Muirfield Road was even bigger and fancier than the one before, what Nate really wanted was something completely new. That year Keaton purchased two choice lots in rustic Beverly Hills. On the smaller, he decided to design and build a three-bedroom ranch house, drawing up the blueprints himself with the assistance of Fred Gabourie and making sure the layout was suitable for children. He wanted to surprise Natalie. Only when every stick of furniture was in place would he take her to see it.

In early 1925 the house was finished, a pool dug, and the interior handsomely furnished. It was paid for. With landscaping, the total cost came to $34,000. The Keatons arrived with friends,

Eddie and Bernice Mannix. Keaton was exhilarated as they strolled from room to room. Bernice Mannix was crazy about the house, but Nate was silent.

"It has no room for the governess," she finally said. "Where would she sleep?"

He was flabbergasted. This was the first he had heard about hiring a sleep-in governess.

Nate continued. "We will need one bedroom for ourselves, the boys another, the butler and cook another." And of course the governess still another.

Keaton turned to Bernice Mannix and said, "If you really want it, Bernice, it's yours."

The Mannixes agreed to buy the house for $37,500, a 10 percent increase over Keaton's cost. They moved in a few weeks later.

After the box office success of *The Navigator*, it would seem that Keaton might have the power to film any story he wanted. That was not the case. Schenck routinely bought motion picture rights to fiction and plays that he thought might be converted into suitable vehicles for both the Talmadge sisters and Keaton (even though Keaton never broadcast this fact). One of Schenck's story properties was *Seven Chances*, a successful Broadway comedy by Roi Cooper Megrue, based on a short story by Gouverneur Morris. After a year's run in New York, David Belasco sent out several road tours, and eventually the show became a favorite of stock companies.

Keaton took an instant dislike to *Seven Chances*. He saw it on Broadway and thought it was a sappy farce. Probably what he resented most was Schenck's sneakiness. Behind Keaton's back he had paid $25,000 to director John McDermott for the rights, and he also promised McDermott that he could codirect.

Keaton submitted. By this time he owed Schenck a great deal of money. And lately he had let Schenck cut him in on investment deals: a $100,000 share in a San Diego housing development and a chunk of the Hollywood Roosevelt Hotel (whose investors had included Schenck, Sid Grauman, Irving Berlin, and Irving Thalberg). Later, all of these joint ventures would collapse once the Depression hit, and Keaton would be wiped out. "Whenever I made investments on my own, I came out all right," he recalled. "But when I went in with someone I lost my shirt."

In 1925 he was in no position to refuse Schenck a favor. He agreed to make *Seven Chances,* even accepting Schenck's director.

When shooting began at the beginning of January, Keaton's first order of business was to get rid of McDermott. As usual, Keaton did everything and made his codirector feel he wasn't even on the picture. McDermott soon complained that the studio was wasting thousands of dollars. Keaton agreed, and McDermott quit.

Seven Chances is about romance and greed. Keaton plays a briefcase-toting junior partner in a brokerage firm. He drives a Stutz Bearcat roadster. At noon on his twenty-seventh birthday, Jimmie Shannon learns that he will inherit $7 million if he is married by 7:00 P.M. that evening (a bequest that is urgently needed because the firm is in crisis over a fraudulent deal). Jimmie bears little resemblance to Keaton's Buster. He wears the rakish straw boater that Harold Lloyd had made his trademark. In fact, the rah-rah corporate personality seems much like Harold Lloyd's pushy comic identity. Even though Jimmie has a sweetheart, she turns him down. He then spends the afternoon proposing marriage to everyone he meets. Not a single one of the young ladies (among them Jean Arthur in a bit role as a switchboard operator) is interested. Desperate, Jimmie mindlessly continues proposing to a growing number of females, including a female impersonator and a barber's mannequin. Meanwhile, his business partner has advertised in the paper for a woman who might like to marry for money. Hordes of applicants in bridal veils, women of all shapes, sizes, ages, and races, flock to the church, and Jimmie is forced to flee.

Suddenly the streets of Los Angeles are swarming with five hundred would-be brides. Traffic is blocked, pedestrians are mowed down, parades are scattered, a football game is interrupted. Jimmie runs out into the countryside.

In *Seven Chances* Keaton got a chance to show off his athletic ability. The high-speed chase, one of his best since *Cops,* was stunning. Despite that, he disliked the picture, and the first preview confirmed his suspicions. The audience sat silent. Not until the very end did he hear anything remotely approaching a real laugh. To his surprise people began sitting up in their seats.

The next day they ran the ending slowly. The laugh was caused by a shot of Jimmie Shannon on a steep embankment scrambling to dodge three little rocks, which were chasing him down the hill.

Keaton ordered fifteen hundred papier-mâché rocks that ranged in size from golf balls to boulders eight feet in diameter. On Ridge Route in the High Sierras, workmen hauled truckloads of rocks to the top of a burned mountainside and started an avalanche. Keaton thought the rock chase saved the picture.

In February, after postproduction on *Seven Chances,* Schenck closed down the studio for two months. Keaton spent a few weeks hunting and fishing in Northern California with his men friends. Then at the beginning of March he and Natalie left the children with Peg and went East to attend the New York premiere of *Seven Chances.*

Despite the fact that they had not slept together for two years, Buster and Natalie Keaton seemed a loving Hollywood couple. Natalie made the obligatory small talk with reporters about their sons, hoping "the children will not break all the mirrors in the house and cut up the tapestries to make ships" in their absence. For publicity shots, they went up to the Biltmore roof and posed against the New York skyline, Natalie bundled in furs and listening attentively as her husband points out the sights.

One day Keaton rode a bus down Fifth Avenue with a reporter from *Motion Picture Magazine.* When they reached Washington Square, he was mobbed by law students from nearby New York University, who began yelling for autographs. "He wrote his name gloomily in an exercise book and fled before he could be asked to repeat," the reporter would write. If there was one thing he hated, it was crowds.

Seven Chances drew capacity crowds. Despite Keaton's dislike of the picture, it was a resounding commercial success that brought in $598,288 in domestic rentals, about $80,000 less than *The Navigator.*

Back in Hollywood, Keaton attended the wedding of Roscoe Arbuckle. Earlier that year Minta had agreed to a divorce so that he could marry Doris Deane, an actress he had met on the ferry returning home from San Francisco after the Labor Day party. During their four-year courtship he had tried to promote her career by pulling strings at Metro, Educational, and Universal. Keaton agreed to cast her as one of the first seven women who refuse to marry him in *Seven Chances.* Arbuckle and Deane were married on May 16 at her parents' home in San Marino. Keaton was best man and Natalie matron of honor. The wedding reception was held at the Keaton home.

In the summer of 1925 Keaton took Natalie and the children to the Duncan Valley Ranch, about sixty miles from Kingman, Arizona, in the northwestern region of the state. Mohave County, once known for its mining camps, offered spectacular vistas for a movie, but the heat made filming unbearable. Temperatures of 120 degrees threatened to cripple the electrical equipment, and the cameramen worried about the emulsion melting off the film. To protect the cameras, Elgin Lessley and Bert Haines chilled them with ice. From Los Angeles they had brought several dozen carpenters and extra electricians, all of whom had to be housed in tents with a portable kitchen. There was no relief from the heat for anyone.

Go West was a buddy movie. Keaton plays a drifter named Friendless who leaves "a small town in Indiana" to ride the boxcars and follow Horace Greeley's advice to go west and seek his fortune. On the Diamond Bar cattle ranch, the pale tenderfoot gets toughened up as he struggles to learn milking and herding. Then Friendless meets Brown Eyes, an outsider like himself. Keaton's costar and love interest is not the rancher's pretty daughter (Kathleen Myers). It is a pretty Jersey brown-eyed cow, who falls in love with Friendless after he removes a pebble from her hoof.

For the rest of the film, Friendless's sole objective is to keep the cow from going to the slaughterhouse. En route to the stockyards in Los Angeles, Friendless opens the cars and frees the whole herd. To get the shot, Keaton turned loose three hundred head of steer in the freight yards of Los Angeles's Santa Fe Depot and moved them up Seventh Street to Broadway. At the end, once the herd is safely delivered, Friendless and Brown Eyes ride off together in the backseat of the rancher's car. This is Keaton's only feature without a happy romantic fade-out between Buster and the woman he intends to marry.

Keaton put the cow through her paces by using a rope halter and feeding her tidbits. After ten days she was trailing him with only a length of black sewing thread tied to his finger. Then he had trouble keeping her out of his dressing room. Brown Eyes, who received $13 a week, was the most cooperative of all his leading women, he joked.

For *Go West* Keaton suddenly found himself without the creative team that had seen him through five pictures. On February 11, Jean Havez, who was fifty-five, died of a heart attack. At the end of February Joe Mitchell went to Universal for higher wages, and Clyde Bruckman was snapped up for Harold Lloyd's *For Heaven's Sake.* Bruckman would return, but Mitchell never did. Keaton learned the hard way that replacing his regulars would not be easy.

Keaton took credit for the cow-story idea and gave the writing credit to Raymond Cannon, a former actor at Paramount and subsequently a gagwriter for comedian Douglas MacLean. Another contributor was Lex Neal, thirty, one of Keaton's boyhood friends from Muskegon who had scant experience in films. Eager to help an old friend, Keaton put him on salary as a gagman and assistant director.

Some parts of *Go West* pleased Keaton, but overall "I didn't care for it," he said. "The cow is the whole show," *Variety* said when it premiered on October 25. For the most part, reviews were positive. *Life* called it "a soul-stirring tragedy." Even literary crab Edmund Wilson, normally not a fan of Keaton's, grudgingly admitted that he was "not entirely unresponsive to his newest picture."

While *Go West* was not a smash hit like Harold Lloyd's new release, *The Freshman,* it made just under $600,000, about the same as *Seven Chances.* It turned only a small profit, since it was expensively shot almost entirely on location.

On October 4, 1925, Keaton celebrated his thirtieth birthday. He had learned how to run a studio, handle stardom and parenthood, even how to survive pictures that failed. He still bit his nails down to the quick. What he had not yet figured out was how to relax and be happy.

14 POMP AND CIRCUMSTANCE

Keaton realized that no other star in Hollywood lived as modestly as he did. Everyone was scrambling to spend money on palatial homes. Joe Schenck said that the public had anointed all of them kings and queens and expected to see them living like pashas. In 1925 housing starts had become Hollywood's hottest topic of conversation.

Going all the way was Mack Sennett, who purchased a mountaintop in the Hollywood Hills east of Cahuenga Pass. On display in a Hollywood real estate office sat a model of his granite-and-marble mansion, which he boasted would be as permanent as the pyramids and as noble as New York's Pennsylvania Station. Sennett's Xanadu would never materialize, but plenty of other fantasies did: John Barrymore's seven-acre Belle Vista estate with its skeet range and private zoo, and Harold Lloyd's Greenacres, a forty-room Italianate villa under construction on sixteen acres in Benedict Canyon, a project that would include a nine-hole golf course.

On Sundays Keaton was a regular visitor at Norma and Joe's Santa Monica beach house. On the so-called Gold Coast, a community of two dozen houses, pastel oceanfront palazzi, had foot-thick stucco walls to keep out the heat. The Schencks' neighbors included MGM's Louis B. Mayer with his twenty-room, thirteen-bath house and Marion Davies and William Randolph Hearst, who owned a monstrous 118-room compound named Ocean House.

By 1925 Keaton had done well in real estate and various other investments. With Schenck and Lou Anger, he owned two oil wells paying substantial dividends. That year he commissioned the architectural firm of Gene Verge to design a neo-Italian Renaissance villa for his three-acre parcel of land located above

Sunset Boulevard, just off Benedict Canyon. Keaton's neighbors included Chaplin, Fairbanks, Lloyd, Tom Mix, Marion Davies, and the Beverly Hills Hotel.

Fred Talmadge died at the end of November 1925, his system finally succumbing to a lifetime of alcohol abuse. Four years earlier, when Norma and Connie moved west, he had been relocated from the Bowery to the Sunset Strip. In California his life was little changed; there still was no room for him in the lives of his busy, glamorous daughters.

Now for a few hours he got to be the star of a Hollywood funeral. Drunk though he was, he was the father of the Talmadge Girls and father-in-law of Buster Keaton and Joseph Schenck. A Hawaiian orchestra played "Aloha."

Even now Peg Talmadge could not forgive her husband for poisoning her marriage and then walking out on his family. Particulars about his corpse were included in her report for Anita Loos: The girls visited the funeral parlor three and four times a day, hovering over the coffin and staring down at the face on the satin pillow. Fred had been fifty-six but now looked thirty, thanks to an artistic embalmer.

That Christmas the Keatons were living with Peg Talmadge on South Plymouth Boulevard. After unloading the home on Muirfield Road for a sizable profit, they moved into her house while waiting for their Beverly Hills house to be built. Peg had trimmed a Christmas tree for the children, but the holiday was cheerless. Fred's death had left his daughters so morose that Norma and Connie talked about retiring from the screen. Disappointing box office reports for *Go West* made Keaton nervous, and he was on a strict diet in preparation for his next film.

Joe had acquired rights to a decent musical comedy with a hero Keaton happened to like. Alfred Buttler is a rich coddled brat, like Rollo Treadway in *The Navigator* and Bertie Van Alstyne in *The Saphead*. He looks as if he had just stepped out of Abercrombie & Fitch. We see him first in the family drawing room, where he is sipping a cocktail. His father looks disgusted. Why doesn't Alfred do something manly for a change? Take a hunting trip. Rough it. Kill a few animals. Next Alfred and his valet (Snitz Edwards) are seen in a palatial tent with a king-size bed, dining on French cuisine. Buttler transforms himself from a weakling into a boxer, who knocks out the champ. Keaton was fascinated not by Alfred's life of ease, but by his life in training for the ring.

Battling Buttler was a three-year-old English musical comedy that had run 288 performances on Broadway with Charles Ruggles in the leading role. Keaton's millionaire happens to bear the same name as a famous prizefighter, Alfred "Battling" Buttler, the world lightweight champion contender. To impress a young woman (Sally O'Neil), Alfred pretends to be the boxer. After their marriage, he is stuck being Battling Buttler and must train to fight the real Buttler's upcoming match with the champion.

Keaton dumped all the songs and dances and much of the plot as well, and subtracted one of the *t*'s from the name Buttler. In the stage musical the hero is reprieved at the last minute from having to fight the Alabama Murderer. Keaton knew that he couldn't tease an audience "for seven reels that I was goin' to fight in the ring and then not fight." Keaton's version would conclude with one of the most realistic boxing matches in silent pictures. When Martin Scorsese filmed *Raging Bull* in 1980, he remembered *Battling Butler* and made sure the camera stayed in the ring with Robert De Niro. During his childhood, Scorsese recalled being bored by filmed boxing matches shown at Saturday matinees because all the action was shot from the same angle. "The only person who had the right attitude about boxing in the movies for me was Buster Keaton," Scorsese said.

Keaton was a physical-fitness fanatic who kept himself in excellent shape. The only flaw in his physique, in his opinion, was his legs, which were short for his torso. Legs notwithstanding, he had no objections to showing off his body by wearing the skimpiest of costumes. For *Battling Butler,* he increased his daily exercise workouts by adding roadwork and began a special training diet.

To make the fight scenes realistic, he rounded up battered-looking fighters from gyms throughout the state. For the climactic scene, which is supposed to take place in Madison Square Garden, he persuaded Lou Anger to rent the huge Olympic Auditorium. Hundreds of extras were hired to fill the ringside seats; the rest of the crowd were people who were admitted free of charge to watch a movie being shot. Schenck was convinced that the picture would be a hit. Long before its release, MGM trade ads touted *Butler* as "the biggest Keaton of them all! And don't forget—KEATON MEANS KALE!"

Production was halted unexpectedly when Keaton fell from the practice ring and landed on his head. After a few days at home with head and body bruises, he returned to work. He was injured again on February 16 during a scene in which he was to leap back into the ring after being knocked out of it. Strained ligaments in his leg and back forced him to take off even more time. He finished the picture sore and limping.

Though Keaton would select *Battling Butler* as one of his favorite films, modern-day critics agree it is probably one of his weakest. There are noticeable changes in lighting from one sequence to the next, and mismatched suits during another scene, sloppiness that normally doesn't occur in Keaton's films.

The following summer *Battling Butler* premiered in New York at the Capitol. It turned out to be Keaton's biggest moneymaker, grossing nearly three quarters of a million dollars. In *Life*, Robert Sherwood wrote that it was unique, "just as funny as it ought to be." *Variety* applauded the direction, particularly in the fight scenes, and said that even though Keaton was on camera throughout the entire picture, he was "equal to the prominence."

Before Keaton began production of *Battling Butler,* Clyde Bruckman told him about a book he had read. Set in 1862, it told the true story of a group of enterprising Union officers who drew up a daring plan to infiltrate Confederate territory and cripple transportation and communication lines by hijacking a locomotive at Marietta, Georgia. The wood-burning locomotive, named the *General,* would be driven back north as the hijackers destroyed track, burned bridges, and cut telegraph lines along the way.

The Andrews Raid failed. In a sixty-mile-per-hour chase, two southern train conductors named Fuller and Murphy apprehended the raiders; nine of them were hanged and the rest imprisoned. One of the survivors, William Pittinger, published *Daring and Suffering: A History of the Great Railway Adventure* in 1863. Later it was republished as *The Great Locomotive Chase,* the edition Bruckman had seen.

Here was a story using Keaton's favorite prop. The subject was made to order for the screen because the heart of the tale was a chase. Keaton, nonetheless, thought the problem was that Pittinger told his story from the raiders' point of view; the Yankees were heroes and the southerners villains, which he feared movie audiences would not accept. Not only would the movie scenario have to represent the southern point of view, but to win audience sympathy the rescuers trying to recapture the *General* must be combined into a single individual. With these changes, Keaton thought the idea was magnificent. While he was willing to buy rights to the book, he was advised it was unnecessary because the material was in the public domain.

By the time *Battling Butler* wound to an end, Keaton had obtained Schenck's approval, and plans for *The General* began moving forward. Keaton was determined to be historically accurate. After learning that the original *General* locomotive was on display in the Chattanooga railroad station, he requested permission to borrow it for the film. A small logging railroad in eastern Tennessee was leased. The deal fell apart when the *General*'s owners, the Louisville and Nashville Railroad, realized Keaton's picture would be a comedy. Descendants of some of the participants protested, and the railway hastily withdrew its cooperation.

In April Keaton's location manager, Bert Jackson, found a small railroad in the heart of the Oregon lumbering region, amidst spectacular rustic scenery, quaint covered bridges, and picturesque rivers. The Oregon, Pacific and Eastern Railroad still owned two vintage locomotives just like the original engines used in the Civil War. Keaton and Natalie went up by train to inspect the location. It was exactly what he wanted. At a nearby lumber railroad he purchased a third engine, which would be remodeled into the *Texas*, the train to be wrecked in the climactic scene. The studio built passenger cars and boxcars on flat cars to match the old engines.

During the weeks before production, enthusiasm for the picture became so intense that it swept along even the usually tight-fisted Schenck, who proposed a budget of $400,000. Clyde Bruckman, with the assistance of two top writers, Al Boasberg and Charles Smith, worked out a scenario that focused on the engineer devoted to his locomotive. Keaton and Fred Gabourie talked of blowing up bridges. Keaton also began letting his hair grow long to play the role of Johnnie Gray.

For Johnnie's girlfriend, Keaton wanted an actress with long curls, a coiffure not easy to find in 1926 Hollywood. Norma Talmadge's hairdresser urged him to consider twenty-four-year-old Marion Mack, a Sennett Bathing Beauty and then a $100-a-week actress at Mermaid Comedies. Mack, who had just bobbed her hair, borrowed a wig. At the audition Keaton's face was expressionless, and he did not utter a word. Finally Lou Anger and Clyde Bruckman turned to him for a decision. Keaton nodded. She would do. Mack was hired at a salary of $250 a week.

On May 27, 1926, Keaton's crew rolled into Cottage Grove, Oregon, with eighteen freight carloads of Civil War cannons, passenger railroad cars rebuilt from discarded Pacific Electric Big Red Line trolleys, stagecoaches, wagons, houses built in sections, and a platoon of workmen. Camera equipment included three thirty-five-millimeter Bell & Howells, an Akeley specially made for wide shots, and several still cameras with four or five different lenses. The Bartell Hotel put itself at Keaton's disposal as both hotel and business headquarters and arranged to house the overflow of visitors fourteen miles north in Eugene.

Over Memorial Day weekend, Keaton drove Natalie and the children to Cottage Grove in his big Stutz roadster. He spent the holiday scouting locations with Fred Gabourie while his company went sight-seeing and picnicked along the Row River. On Monday, May 31, construction began on the town of Marietta, Georgia, guided by engravings from the Pittinger book. Almost all the scenes would be shot on location, including the indoor scene at the recruiting office when Johnnie Gray is trying to enlist.

The second floor of the town's biggest garage was leased as a costume and prop room. A commissary, run by Chinese cooks brought in from Los Angeles, was set up to prepare meals for actors and extras. Crowds poured into the casting office looking for jobs as extras. But there were not enough able-bodied youths to fight a war. To obtain soldiers for the battle scenes, the company brought in trainloads of Oregon National Guard units. Keaton photographed the moving trains by setting up the cameras on a rebuilt automobile that was driven along graded roads next to the track. When there were two parallel tracks, he lashed the camera car to a railroad flatcar.

Once filming began, regular train service to Cottage Grove virtually ceased. Every morning at 5:00 A.M. the line was closed down so the tracks would be free for the moviemakers. All day long, the movie trains clacked up and down the line. Despite such inconveniences the town could not have been more understanding. Keaton was spending a third of his budget there and employing some fifteen hundred local people.

On the first evening at the Bartell there was a party celebrating the Keatons' fifth wedding anniversary, and Natalie joined the film crew in the dining room. After that, however, she steered clear of them as much as possible and never ate downstairs again. In the Keaton suite she took care of the children and sewed needlepoint seat covers for the chairs in their new home. Later in the summer, she had company when her mother came up to visit. But generally she had no interest in socializing with other wives and actresses.

Filming began on June 8. Each morning at six o'clock Keaton left for the location by train with Bruckman, Willie Riddle, who was on hand to prepare his boss's hot lunch as always, and Marion Mack. Keaton had nothing to say to her and in many instances did not bother to direct her scenes. She felt "ignored and slighted," she said. "Buster just stuck to the job and to his little clique, and that was all." Sometimes shooting would be delayed for hours because "they stopped the train when they saw a place to play baseball," she recalled. As the weeks passed, Keaton warmed up and began making her the butt of practical jokes, usually an indication that he liked a person. She decided that his coldness was "mostly just shyness."

In the evening he continued with writers' conferences and scheduling for the next day. Every minute was filled with people. On Sundays he organized exhibition ball games that brought out the whole town. One town resident thought Keaton was "one of the best shortstops I've seen. He could have played big league ball. We just loved him because he was full of tricks. Once he loaded his bat with gunpowder and when the ball came across the plate, he took a swing and the bat blew up. The ball went about a mile and a half."

In the first week of July, Keaton's father arrived to play a Union officer. Appearing in cameo bits were a number of celebrities, including Glen Cavender, a retired Spanish-American War hero and winner of the French Legion of Honor, who played the leader of the hijackers. According to United Artists press releases, at one time there were about three thousand people on the payroll. While this sounds like an exaggeration, there is no doubt that Keaton's re-creation of the Civil War was adding up to a fortune. Cost of production time was estimated at $400 an hour.

By midsummer the picture business was buzzing with rumors

that *The General*'s costs had passed a half million dollars and now might even total $1 million, a shocking amount for a comedy. Word traveled that Keaton was completely out of control. Unable to find a suitable bridge for the highlight of the film, he decided to build one (a 213-foot-long trestle bridge across Culp Creek). If a river level turned out to be too low, he ordered a dam constructed. And so it went: railroad track laid, covered bridges built, and burned, and rebuilt, and then burned again for retakes.

Schenck went on the warpath, trying to rein in a runaway production. Keaton, struggling to get the shots he wanted, seemed supremely indifferent to Schenck's concern. He had major aggravations of his own. From the start, the production was plagued by accidents and the field hospital kept humming. Keaton himself was knocked unconscious when he stood too close to a firing cannon, and assistant director Harry Barnes was shot in the face with a blank charge. One of the train wheels ran over a brakeman's foot, which led to a negligence complaint and a $2,900 lawsuit.

The greatest problem was fires started by the movie locomotives. They were equipped with safety devices, but even so sparks from the wood-burning trains set farmers' haystacks ablaze, and the business office wound up paying $25 in damages for each stack. Soon there were dozens of forest fires, at least one of them raging out of control near Culp Creek. And each time a fire broke out, production stopped while the moviemakers rushed to douse the blaze. Getting clear, smokeless skies as background became more difficult.

At last Keaton was ready to film his most spectacular scene, in which the Union spies on the *Texas* chase Johnnie Gray in his recaptured *General* back to the southern headquarters. After the *General* crosses a burning bridge, the *Texas* follows, but the bridge collapses and the spy train flips over into the stream.

During the filming of this spectacular scene on Friday, July 23, Cottage Grove shut down as businesses closed their stores and declared a holiday. In the hot sun, an estimated crowd of three to four thousand assembled. The scene was scheduled for 11:00 A.M. Six cameras were in position when Keaton changed his mind and ordered them moved. The crash train then practiced several runs across the trestle while the specifics were worked out by the cameramen and an explosives expert. There would be no second takes.

It was 3:00 P.M. when Keaton finally gave the signal. The engineer who started the *Texas* rolling leaped down, leaving behind a dummy at the throttle. The timbers of the bridge had been partly sawed, and when the dynamite charge went off, the bridge snapped in half. The engine dropped into a twisted, steaming pile in the river. Because the dummy looked so lifelike, spectators began screaming. The crash set off the train whistle, which continued to screech. Afterward Keaton posed for still photos standing on the wreckage. He was as "happy as a kid," reported the *Cottage Grove Sentinel*.

The train-crash cost came to $42,000 ($1.7 million at 1995 price levels), making it the most expensive single shot in all of silent films. That figure did not include disposal of the wreckage. Not until World War II would the *Texas*'s rusty carcass be salvaged for scrap metal.

Over the weekend, Keaton filmed battle scenes that would be compared to Mathew Brady's Civil War photographs. In a belated effort to save money, he used his Oregon guardsmen for both Union and Confederate soldiers: "And put 'em in blue uniforms and bring 'em goin' from right to left, and take 'em out, put 'em in gray uniforms, bring 'em goin' from left to right. And fought the war."

During the battle scenes special precautions were taken to prevent forest fires: a stationary pump, portable equipment, and a water tank on a flatcar. Still, a huge fire, the biggest so far, brought shooting to a halt. The crew and guardsmen, nearly six hundred of them, fought side by side for hours. The equipment proved inadequate, and the troops were forced to battle the flames with blankets and the jackets of their uniforms. Keaton, in his underwear, used his pants to extinguish tiny brushfires. Natalie, coaxed out of the Bartell Hotel for her first public appearance in weeks, served refreshments to the firefighters. The total cost of the fire came to nearly $50,000.

By the following week, filming had become impossible. Thick gray smoke hung over the area. Because the interior scenes—the enlistment office, Anabelle's sitting room—were still to be shot, Keaton decided to leave. His purchasing agent, Al Gilmour, remained in Cottage Grove while the rest of the company returned to California on August 6. Less fortunate were the townspeople. Having no escape from the smoke, they could only pray for rain.

15 ITALIAN VILLA

On the knoll of a hill, overlooking a rolling lawn, the pale green stucco mansion rose like a fifteenth-century suburban house transplanted from the Venetian countryside. Against a backdrop of cypresses and palms a staircase of exactly sixty steps descended to a thirty-foot Romanesque swimming pool, flanked by classical nude statues and inlaid with mosaic tiles. The steep terraces had been landscaped by a gardener who once worked for Pope Pius XII.

In 1926 Beverly Hills was still open country, and from his hilltop Keaton could look straight across the valley to Valentino's estate. A driveway winding up from Hartford Way ended in a spacious cobbled courtyard and an ornate grillwork entrance door recessed in an arch of intricately braided mosaics. The two-story crescent-shaped main house boasted twenty rooms and six baths for the family alone. Above the garage was a three-room apartment for the gardener and his wife, the upstairs maid; in the servants' wing of the main house were additional quarters for the cook, butler, chauffeur, and governess, a staff of six in all.

The interior represented the golden age of the movie star. The sunken entrance gallery, tiled with a black-and-white marble tango floor, reflected the Valentino influence, and a nude statue graced a tinkling fountain of goldfish set amid tropical foliage. On the ground floor wide arches separated the rooms: the spacious drawing room with its baronial fireplace and grand piano, floral upholstered pieces, antiques, and bric-a-brac; the luxurious screening room; a formal dining room with beamed ceiling; and a salon whose walls were painted with murals. Along the rear of the house ran an airy glassed-in patio. All the rooms had marble or oak-wood floors and Oriental carpets.

Upstairs, Natalie's pale green master bedroom took up practically the entire west wing. It had a fireplace with an ornate gilt mantelpiece. Her oversize bathroom was tiled in pink, and her dressing room was ample enough to hold the hundreds of ensembles in her wardrobe. Keaton's bedroom was big enough for little more than a double bed and dresser. There were connecting doors between all the bedrooms and baths; to enter any of the rooms it was never necessary to go into the central hallway or to see the servants.

On the lower level a family room with fireplace and exposed beams functioned as a card and billiard room. The grounds were distinguished by ornamental flower gardens and a number of outbuildings, including bathhouses and columned pergolas in the pool area, an aviary, three tennis courts, and for Jimmy and Bobby a playhouse replicating the main house and battery-driven roadsters to tool around the grounds. A winding brook stocked with trout could be turned on and off at the push of a button.

It was customary for film stars to give their homes names, such as Falcon Lair (Valentino) and Greenacres (Lloyd). Keaton simply called his home the Italian Villa.

In the light of his earnings at the time, Keaton spent a fortune. The total value of the estate can only be guessed. He once said that the land and house cost $200,000, and he estimated the furnishings at another $100,000. These included imported chandeliers, gold-leaf fixtures in the bathrooms, even sinks and toilets lowered to accommodate a master and mistress whose heights were five feet six and five feet two. Kitchen appliances were of such high quality that they remain in use today. Furniture designed by Keaton himself included Natalie's bed and for his own room a matching carved bed and pair of traditional dark oak bureaus connected by a full-length mirror. Some of these massive pieces were built at the Keaton studio. His studio carpenters also were dispatched to the villa as needed for other work. Jack Coyle labored to build Keaton's trout stream. "My father was impressed by Keaton's extreme extravagance," said his son John Coyle. "Because to get it right the brook was built, torn up, then built again. It was something to be marveled at. Not the stream so much as the amount of money and time that was spent on a frivolous whim of creating an English gentleman's estate."

The decor of the house was "very ornate, very grand, and everything you think he wasn't," said Pamela Mason, who bought the Italian Villa with her husband, James, in 1949 and has occupied it for forty-six years. "It was a spectacular dream house that he built for himself. He must have seen himself as the king and her as the queen. But—and this is so typical of everything out here—the minute they built it they wrecked their lives and couldn't live in it."

By the end of August heavy rains had cleared the smoke from Cottage Grove. Keaton took a small crew back up and completed location work on *The General* in two weeks. This time no spouses were invited. On the day they wrapped, Saturday, September 18, a drinking and fireworks celebration at the Bartell Hotel threatened to spin out of control as rockets were lobbed down the main street of the town toward the church.

Back in Hollywood, Keaton was busier than ever. After finishing a week of studio work, he started the final edit. The world premiere was scheduled for the end of December in New York, followed by special showings in Tokyo and London.

At the Italian Villa, he sequestered himself in his new workshop assembling the picture from 200,000 feet of exposed film. Although there was a cutting department and excellent editors at the studio, he had always done much of his own editing and liked the idea of a home office. As usual, he edited by hand, holding the thirty-five-millimeter film to the light rather than using an editing machine. The cutting room was a tiny separate building, adjacent to the main entrance of the house. In size, it was scarcely bigger than an ordinary toolshed and so insignificant, especially when compared to the guest house across the courtyard, that subsequent owners would use it to store gardening supplies. In the rear stood a safe where he kept copies of his early shorts, as well as the negatives from *The General*.

After Christmas Keaton and Natalie drove to Mexico for a New Year's party hosted by Joe Schenck at Agua Caliente, a deluxe resort in development thirty miles south of the border near Tijuana. When completed, Agua Caliente would include a plush hotel and casino with a gold-leaf ceiling and a nightclub (its floor shows in the early thirties featured fourteen-year-old Rita Hayworth, nee Margarita Cansino, performing tangos with her father), as well as a racetrack and golf course. Schenck, a well-known gambler, was a major stockholder in the spa, which became a pleasure playpen for Hollywood's power elite.

Despite his Beverly Hills dream house, Keaton seemed unhappy. On New Year's Eve his angry mood was noticeable. Marion Mack remembered Keaton sliding across the casino dance floor on his stomach and coming to rest at the feet of showgirl Peggy Hopkins Joyce, the golddigger's golddigger and onetime girlfriend of Joe Schenck. "He pretended to get all mixed up and accidentally on purpose he tipped over her chair and spilled her all over the floor," Mack said. "I guess he just wanted to take her down a peg."

That sort of antic distressed Natalie, not for the first time either. Once at a horseback-riding party in Griffith Park, Keaton began trotting backward after a couple of drinks. Natalie publicly warned him "to stop acting like a fool," according to another guest, director Sam White. "But he fluffed her away, as if to say, nobody tells me what to do. Of course he liked to drink and was always lifting the glass."

A few weeks after the Agua Caliente celebration, Zelda and Scott Fitzgerald crashed a costume party given by Sam and Frances Goldwyn in honor of Connie and Norma. In Hollywood to write a scenario for Connie, Scott and his wife arrived at the Goldwyn front door on all fours, impersonating dogs. After being welcomed, Zelda went upstairs and ran herself a bath.

Keaton's unruly behavior at Agua Caliente was due to mounting apprehension. The American premiere of *The General* had been delayed until January, but test screenings and alarming word of mouth had already dispelled hopes for a box office success.

For Joe Schenck, too, there was little cause for celebration that holiday.

In the fall Norma had begun filming a lavish production of *Camille,* Dumas's soap opera about an ill-fated courtesan. To play the part of Armand, Schenck had chosen a newcomer, a twenty-one-year-old Mexican actor who combined the virile Latin-lover looks of Rudolph Valentino with his own distinctive swashbuckling dash. Luis Antonio Damasco de Alonso was born in Ciudad Juarez, Mexico, the son of a Basque bullfighter. In Los Angeles Luis and his four brothers dropped out of high school and worked at the Llewellyn Iron Works, later entering pictures as extras, wardrobe men, and production assistants. Coalescing the names of movie superstar John Gilbert and serial heroine Ruth Roland, Luis came up with the acting name Gilbert Roland. Luis had already managed to romance a number of prominent stars, most recently Clara Bow, to whom he had been briefly engaged. "Clara was my first love," he said.

During the filming of *Camille,* Joe suggested that Gilbert Roland escort his wife dancing, because, as usual, he was tied up with poker. If Gilbert Roland was not Norma's first extramarital lover, he was the first one she fell for in a big way. Schenck's initial response was denial. Before long, everybody in town was talking about the romance. Norma and Gil rode down Hollywood Boulevard in an open car with their arms around each other.

According to a widely repeated story, Joe ordered a member of his entourage who had connections with the mob to kidnap and castrate the youth. When this gossip reached Roland, he made an appearance at the all-male Hollywood Athletic Club, where nude swimming was permitted. He strolled around the entire pool before diving in. "My brother was a real character," Chico Day said.

Norma, who denied plans to divorce Daddy, told fan magazines that they were only living apart and implied that reconciliation was a possibility. Even Joe himself believed that Roland's novelty would wear off and Norma would come back. Joe accepted the blame by saying that he had paid her too little attention. Norma's true reasons for leaving Daddy were a combination of boredom and years of acquiescing to intermittent physical abuse and knockabout sex. In the end, the paunchy, balding Schenck could not compete with a worshipful twenty-one-year-old.

Peg Talmadge did her best to break up the romance. It was beyond belief that her thirty-two-year-old daughter was going to jeopardize her social position for the sake of a pretty face and alluring sex. Money was not an issue because Norma had made herself independently wealthy over the years, but a pretty boy who was great in bed could never substitute for the great advantages of being Mrs. Joseph Schenck.

The General had its first screening on New Year's Eve at two movie theaters in Tokyo. Its American premiere at the Capitol was now set for January 22, 1927. To publicize the film, the engine bell from the real *General* was shipped to New York and displayed in the theater lobby.

But for the first time in its history, the Capitol held over a film for a third, then a fourth week, creating a booking problem. It was the winter's most talked-about movie, *Flesh and the Devil,* starring Greta Garbo and John Gilbert. At the end of January, Joe Keaton accompanied his son to New York, only to find the premiere postponed. They headed back to the Coast because Keaton had to start a new picture. *The General* finally did open on February 5, on a program that included a short called *Soaring Wings,* a study of vulturous birds.

New York reviews ranged from lukewarm to savage. To the *Herald-Tribune,* the picture seemed "long and tedious—the least funny thing Buster Keaton has ever done." *Variety* labeled *The General* "a flop," placing the entire blame on Keaton: "It was his story, he directed, and he acted." The *Telegram* saw it as a rehash of old Mack Sennett shorts, while the *Mirror* critic flogged Keaton for being self-indulgent and no longer capable of producing a feature-length film. Between the lines the press suggested that this was a costly boondoggle, made to satisfy an egomaniac. *The General* seemed to be the *Heaven's Gate* of the twenties. Even Keaton's admirer Robert Sherwood said that "someone should have told Buster that it is difficult to derive laughter from the sight of men being killed in battle."

Not all the New York critics disliked *The General.* One described it as a moving daguerreotype. The *Brooklyn Eagle* gave the film a favorable review, but afterward the paper received letters of protest from moviegoers who had felt like walking out, and some who perhaps had. The Capitol gave the picture its standard one-week run. It was succeeded by *The Red Mill* starring Marion Davies, Roscoe Arbuckle's first directing feature. According to the *Exhibitors Daily Review,* the Capitol took in $50,992.80, an average intake and only some $15,000 less than the Garbo-Gilbert sizzler. It was not really a problem of moviegoers failing to show up. They did. But they left disappointed.

A number of theories have been put forward to explain the film's failure: the delay in opening, ineffective distribution by United Artists, and unfair notices from vicious reviewers. Louise Brooks, a friend of Keaton and an admirer of the film, believed that the trouble lay in the title: Moviegoers stayed away because nobody connected *The General* with the name of an engine. They thought the movie was about a Confederate general, or perhaps a comedy about the war. Insufficient time might have passed for Americans to make jokes about a national tragedy. Indeed, to people whose parents or grandparents had fought in the Civil War, it was still a highly charged subject.

The main reason for the failure of *The General* seems to be less complicated. People who paid their admissions to a Buster Keaton comedy expected it to be uproariously funny. But where were the big laughs? Where were the pratfalls? At this point in his career, it was impossible for Keaton to step out of genre and take his audience with him. Even though people could see *The General*'s extraordinary beauty and appreciate its dramatic power, they were unable to move past his reputation as a slapstick comic and accept him in the role of a fine director.

In the end, *The General* cost over $750,000, which was $365,000 more than *The Navigator* and $383,000 more than *Go West*. Its domestic gross of $474,264 was $300,000 less than *Battling Butler* and $400,000 short of being classified as a profitable film. The picture would not show a profit until it was "rediscovered" some three decades later.

In the seven decades since the film's release, Keaton's epic has come to be regarded as one of the monumental works of the silent film era. It is primarily this film that would lead serious cinephiles of the fifties and sixties to turn Keaton into the darling of *Cahiers du Cinema* and *Sight and Sound*.

Never did Keaton understand why *The General* scored so poorly. "I was more proud of that picture than any I ever made," he said in 1963. "Because I took an actual happening out of the . . . history books, and I told the story in detail, too. . . . I laid out my own continuity, I cut the picture, directed it. And I had a successful picture."

After the beating he took on *The General,* he retreated to safer ground.

Next Keaton chose to do a picture that required as little intellectually from him as possible. In the rainy winter of 1927 Keaton began filming *College,* his eighth feature and one of his weakest, though it is unusually rich in gags.

Keaton plays Ronald, a bookworm who dislikes athletics. At Clayton College, where he is working his way through school at various jobs, his sweetheart, Mary (Ann Cornwall), is susceptible to the attentions of Jeff Brown (Harold Goodwin), the school jock. Ronald tries and fails at baseball, then track. Finally he becomes the coxswain of the rowing team. The aquatic scenes, which Keaton enjoyed immensely, were filmed at Newport Bay. Not only did he turn over the writing and directing to others, but for the first time he used a double for a stunt. To vault into a second-story window, he hired Lee Barnes, Olympic pole-vaulting champion from U.S.C. "I could not do the scene," Keaton said, "because I am no pole vaulter and I didn't want to spend months in training to do the stunt myself." He had trained for months to do *Battling Butler*, but this time he was tired. When the picture opened the following September at the Mark Strand in New York, *Variety* predicted that *College* would do decent business "because the Keaton name assures that, but many pictures of this grade will find him marking time rather than advancing."

Thirty-two years old, Keaton was still exceptionally handsome and in excellent physical condition. But how much longer could he sustain his youthful look? It is curious that instead of selecting roles appropriate for his age he chose to be a juvenile once again.

In March Joe Schenck had rented klieg lights, rounded up a handful of stars, among them John Barrymore and the Talmadge sisters, and held a first-class Hollywood premiere for *The General*. But it was nothing more than a face-saver because his high-profile picture was not going to return a dime. Schenck was trying to stabilize financially. During the filming of *College* he began turning up the heat on Keaton about holding down expenses.

After a tenure of seven years as studio manager, Lou Anger was transferred to United Artists. Keaton was furious with Schenck. Occasionally his relationship with Anger had been bumpy, but with Anger he knew where he stood and regarded him as a friend he did not want to lose.

To placate his star, Schenck asked him to name a replacement. Keaton suggested another friend, Harry Brand, publicity director for the Keaton and Talmadge studios. In replacing Lou Anger with Brand, Keaton must have felt confident that his authority would never be undermined. But he was wrong. All too quickly the new position transformed Brand into a sobersides who was always bleating about costs. What may have hurt Keaton most was

Brand's eagerness to please Schenck, when formerly it had been Keaton he wanted to accommodate. While *College* was being completed, for example, Keaton decided to keep one of its leading actors, Snitz Edwards, on the payroll for a few extra days. Brand refused. To show him who was boss, Keaton took a three-day holiday to play baseball.

One night in Sacramento Keaton went to see the just-released *College* at the Senator Theatre. The credits began to roll: "Joseph M. Schenck Presents Buster Keaton in . . . " Then a separate title flashed on the screen: "Supervised by Harry Brand." Keaton recalled that "I all but jumped out of my seat. It had gone into the prints after I had okayed the sample." The credit had been added behind Keaton's back, and Schenck had approved it. Keaton decided the person to confront was Schenck, not Brand.

The title of supervisor would later be called producer. To Keaton the idea was laughable. Since when did bean counters deserve screen credits? Lou Anger had never asked for one. Henceforth, Keaton would fight Brand every chance he got. In later years he refused to acknowledge him as supervisor and insisted on calling him "the publicity man."

Schenck had already decided to clean house. He was having a bad year. The bulk of his time was spent in New York trying to salvage the fortunes of United Artists, but his own independent empire was also faltering. Nearly all of his productions, even those of the Talmadge sisters, had shown disappointing box office sales. Brand, he must have figured, would keep an eye on costs.

Before completing *College*, Keaton received an idea for an enchanting Mark Twain–type story from Charles Reisner, a comedy director known for his work with Chaplin on *The Kid* and *The Gold Rush*. A Mississippi steamboat captain has been separated for many years from his son, at school in Boston. Willie, now a college graduate, visits his father wearing a sissy beret and knickers and a silly little mustache and carrying a ukulele under his arm. The captain tries to whip his son into a proper man.

Schenck approved Reisner's story and permitted Keaton to bring him on as codirector. For leading lady, he hired an unknown fifteen-year-old who had appeared on the stage, four-foot eleven-inch Marion Byron.

At the end of June the crew traveled up to Sacramento. On

the bank of the Sacramento River opposite the city, they spent $100,000 to construct a cluster of piers and a three-block-long street.

It was Harry Brand who warned Schenck that Keaton's flood finale was going to spell needless trouble. Recent floods in the South had caused piteous loss of life. Not only would the picture be in poor taste, but the water sequences would be expensive to shoot. At the last minute Schenck told Keaton to cut the flood.

With no climax for his story, Keaton suggested substituting a modest cyclone. Schenck agreed. The replacement, however, required an extra $25,000 to rebuild sets and more to haul wind machines from Los Angeles to Sacramento. *Steamboat Bill Jr.* went one-third over its scheduled $300,000 budget with a negative cost of $404,282. Yet the cyclone is probably his most memorable finale.

That summer a revolution in motion picture technology approached: sound pictures. There was considerable sentiment that the public would find talking films more annoying than pleasing. The previous December, the rival studios had met secretly and, in effect, declared a boycott on sound for the time being.

During the spring of 1927, Al Jolson began working at a special stage up on the old Warner lot on Sunset Boulevard. On October 6, 1927, *The Jazz Singer* had its historic premiere featuring Jolson singing four songs and speaking a few lines of dialogue. Even though the picture now seems tedious, audiences responded enthusiastically.

Among those skeptical of talkies was Joe Schenck. "Talking pictures will never displace the silent drama from its supremacy. There will always be silent pictures." A few months later every studio in town was scrambling to build soundstages.

Joe Schenck's brother, Nick, was visiting from New York, and Keaton invited him to see his new house. Proudly conducting Schenck on a guided tour of the Italian Villa, Keaton watched his gray face and awaited a reaction.

The little man in horn-rimmed glasses seemed impressed. He whistled over the magnificent appointments and the elegant landscaping. As Keaton knew, Nick Schenck lived in a large, comfortable house in Great Neck, New York, but there was nothing elaborate about it.

Finally Schenck turned to Keaton. "I hope, Buster, you aren't going over your head on this place," he said in almost a whisper. There was an expression of apprehension on his face.

Keaton had a stock response. "It took a lot of pratfalls, my friend, to build this dump."

There was no reason to think that the money would ever stop. In any case, land values in Beverly Hills were continuing to soar, and his palazzo was a sound investment.

That year, despite his problems with Schenck, Keaton seemed not to have a care in the world. Just as he "lived in the camera" at the studio, as Arbuckle had once put it, and created worlds on film, now he lavished the same attention on his showplace. No detail was overlooked. The year before, when Wilshire Boulevard had been widened and scores of palm trees dug up, he arranged to buy forty-two trees to line his long driveway. Dissatisfied, he decided they were misplaced and spent $14,000 to have them moved to the rear of the house.

The Italian Villa was turning out to be a dream house for entertaining. In the halcyon weeks after they moved in, the whole Talmadge clan and their friends and lovers could be found curled up on chaise longues around the pool. Norma and Gilbert Roland were regular visitors. When Joe Schenck arrived one Sunday afternoon, people braced for fireworks, but Norma's two men greeted each other as warmly as father and son.

Until now the Keatons had never been stars on the Hollywood social scene. "Natalie was not sophisticated, and he was very, very uninteresting," said Irene Selznick. "I'm sure he must have had friends, but I never heard anyone say, 'my friend Buster Keaton.' Socially, he didn't give a damn about people. He was never what I would call popular."

Nevertheless, Italian Villa invitations became highly prized, especially to the Sunday barbecues held regularly from May to September. It struck some guests that the estate was less a home than a huge movie stage, and Keaton a lot like the celluloid Buster. "He went about each project with the same adorable conviction of a good little boy doing a good thing in the best possible way," Louise Brooks remembered. He took high-flying plunges into the pool, then at the barbecue pit he would grill your jumbo English lamb chop or steak or chicken to perfection. It occurred to Louise Brooks that his whole life had now become a motion picture. The Villa was "a magnificent playpen" for grown-ups.

There was a magical quality about the Italian Villa: a flock of quail, the trout in the brook, even pet raccoons for his sons. Cats and dogs wandered around outside. After his beloved police dog, Captain, was killed by a car, Keaton bought Trotsky, an Irish wolfhound who slept in a pond in hot weather, then a short-haired Saint Bernard, Barry, who had to be exiled after he broke his leash and wrecked a dog show at the Ambassador Hotel.

But the Italian Villa did not bring the Keatons any closer. In the months after they moved in, the house almost seemed like a Club Med with fabulous food and service and a variety of activities. People constantly coming and going would become a buffer that eventually drove them even farther apart.

In May *Photoplay* published a joke of Joe Keaton's: "Who is Hollywood's best dressed man?"

Answer: "Buster Keaton because he dresses Natalie."

All of Hollywood knew about Nate. In a town where high-maintenance wives were the norm, her extravagance had become a laughing matter. On her dressing-room shelves were more than 150 pairs of shoes, many never worn. On clothing alone, she spent $700 to $900 a week.

Apparently Keaton made no effort to restrain her. He himself spent so much on imported liquor, the most luxurious cars, the best hunting and fishing equipment, the finest clothing, not to mention a new yacht. Besides, there was the truckload of money he lost playing cards.

Although an ordinary family could have lived for a year on what he earned in one week, he was not among the top money earners in Hollywood. An article in *Motion Picture Classic* magazine said that richest by far was Harold Lloyd, whose earnings of $30,000 a week reflected the fact that he headed his own company. Other salaries combining salary guarantees and profit sharing were equally impressive: Douglas Fairbanks, $20,000; Lillian Gish $8,000–10,000; Gloria Swanson, $10,000; Keaton's cowboy-actor neighbor Tom Mix, $15,000.

Keaton earned more in a week than John Gilbert and Ramon Novarro ($2,000) but a lot less than Marion Davies ($10,000).

On his $200,000 a year, he was also taking care of Joe at the Continental Hotel and Myra and the kids on Victoria Avenue.

Filming on *Steamboat Bill Jr.* finally got under way on July 15 in Sacramento. Two weeks later production was held up briefly after Keaton broke his nose in a ball game—he had removed his catcher's mask in the eighth inning and got smashed by a fastball. When the company returned to Hollywood all Keaton had left to shoot was one stunt, in which Willie Canfield is standing in the middle of a street during the cyclone when the front wall of a two-story house crashes on him. He escapes unhurt because his body is framed in an open second-story window. While the wall was on a hinged base plate, it still weighed thousands of pounds; should Keaton be a few inches out of position, it could squash him like a bug.

He did not seem particularly worried. In 1919 he and Roscoe Arbuckle had staged a similar sight gag for *Back Stage,* and he had repeated it in *One Week*. This time the stunt was more elaborate and far more dangerous.

The wall stunt was scheduled for Labor Day weekend. That Saturday Keaton met with Schenck for a showdown about Harry Brand. He was out of patience, he told Schenck, and would not tolerate the presence of Brand or any so-called supervisor. Joe shrugged. All the studios were using supervisors.

Then, without warning, Schenck made an announcement that stunned Keaton. After *Steamboat Bill Jr.* Schenck was planning to dissolve Buster Keaton Productions and close the studio.

By Keaton's account, Schenck's words caught him completely unprepared. There had been no prior discussions of Joe's financial problems, no warning of approaching disaster, no attempt to cushion the blow in any way. It made no difference that the studio was Keaton's life, and it did not even matter that he was Joe's brother-in-law. In retrospect, it seems likely that warning signals were flashing for months and Keaton had not noticed them. He sat dumbfounded in Schenck's office that day. Later he would not even remember the explanations his brother-in-law had given. He left without saying another word.

On Sunday morning he showed up at the studio to do the wall scene. As he stood in the studio street waiting for a building to crash on him, he noticed that some of the electricians and extras were praying. The window was just big enough to give two inches clearance on either side. Keaton drove a nail in the ground to mark his position. When the moment came and the house front came down, he froze. The open window hit him exactly as planned. Afterward, he would call the stunt one of his greatest thrills. He said later that he did not care whether he lived or died. "I was mad at the time, or I would never have done the thing." But this was not the first time he had toyed with death.

As soon as production on *Steamboat Bill Jr.* was completed, he rushed to New York, the citadel of real power in the picture industry. He had never been in the habit of begging for favors; he waited for people to come to him. Now, however, he planned to fight for a studio of his own. Schenck had suggested that he would be better off at MGM as a salaried actor. Keaton wanted no part of that idea. Working for MGM sounded to him "just like the draft."

By now he must have realized that there was nobody he could depend on, not Schenck, who had withdrawn from the Talmadge clan after the unraveling of his marriage, certainly not his wife or his children or his parents. Only his work sustained him. He needed his own studio because without it he had nothing. So if Schenck would no longer bankroll him, then he must make a deal elsewhere. He dug in his heels for a fight.

Adolph Zukor, a small man behind a large desk, looked at Keaton.

Coming right to the point, Keaton said that he wanted to hook up his production unit with Paramount and bring his people with him.

Unfortunately, Zukor said, Paramount had just contracted to release Harold Lloyd's films. Keaton didn't expect him to cut the ground out from under a big star like Lloyd, did he?

That was the end of the conversation.

Keaton stormed back to his hotel and poured himself a whiskey. Zukor's excuses had been preposterous. Keaton and Chaplin both were releasing with United Artists. Besides, he had peeked at a letter from the Hays Office on Zukor's desk warning him to keep his hands off Keaton because he was the exclusive property of MGM. Or so he later said.

Before he had left the West Coast, news of his dismissal had traveled quickly. Chaplin called to warn him against going to MGM, using words like "ruin" and "warp your judgment." Harold Lloyd had agreed. "It's not your gang," he told him. But exactly who was his gang?

Keaton decided it might be a good idea to call on Nick Schenck, who on the death of Marcus Loew in September had become president of Loew's, Inc., and its subsidiary Metro-Goldwyn-Mayer Pictures. Keaton continued to believe that the Schencks were his friends.

Nick Schenck was just about to go to lunch when Keaton arrived at his office.

Why in the world, Nick demanded, did Keaton want to hold on to a dinky place like Lillian Way when he could make pictures at the Tiffany of studios? At MGM he would have access to the best writers, the most talented directors, the most brilliant cinematographers.

Keaton began laying out reasons why he needed his freedom. But Nick blitzed him with money. Three thousand a week and a percentage.

Nick smiled. "And now we go to lunch."

In later years, Keaton would think of the transaction as Joe and Nick transferring small change from one pocket to another.

"In 1928," Keaton said, "I made the worst mistake of my life. Against my better judgment I let Joe Schenck talk me into giving up my own studio to make pictures at the booming Metro-Goldwyn-Mayer lot in Culver City."

That was not exactly so. What he refused to acknowledge was that the industry changed, making independent studios as antiquated as the horse and carriage.

In 1927, reported *Variety*, there were nine major studios (MGM, Paramount, Warners, and so forth) and fifteen smaller outfits like Sennett and Universal, as well as minor comedy producers and independents such as Schenck. A number of these companies, especially the mom-and-pop studios, would soon fold or be swallowed up when they were unable to afford the expensive facilities needed to produce sound films.

The Buster Keaton Studio had been a mom-and-pop operation. A few guys with cameras could wander out on the streets of

Los Angeles and come back with a picture like *Seven Chances*. Soon making films on location would be much more difficult because the ambient sounds could not be controlled. For that matter, the cutting room that Keaton had built at the Italian Villa was already out of date.

Even had Schenck not decided to dissolve the Keaton Studio when he did, it would have been shut out within two years. The cost of converting to sound would have been too great. Harold Lloyd would have an increasingly hard time staying afloat, and Cecil B. De Mille would give up his studio and move to MGM.

It was no personal failing that ended Keaton's career as a film-maker.

Keaton had made three flops in a row. His favorite picture had failed; both *College* and *Steamboat Bill Jr.* sank at the box office. According to industry buzz, he had lost some of his edge.

F. Scott Fitzgerald put his finger on the problem when he wrote of Hollywood in 1928 that its great stars "were still young enough to believe that they would go on forever." Like the rest of the old crowd that thought of itself as unique, Keaton had not considered the possibility of becoming ancient history.

The reign of the twenties superstars was drawing to a close. Then, as now, Hollywood was not able to nurture its older stars. The exception was Greta Garbo. The Pickfords and Fairbankses and Talmadges would soon find themselves pushed aside by the Hepburns, Gables, and Grants, newcomers with greater box office value.

The same was true for the giants of silent comedy. With the advent of sound films, the Big Three (or Four if Harry Langdon is counted) gave way to clowns such as the Marx Brothers. An even greater threat were new comic stars and a new technology just about to burst on the picture business. Their names were Mickey Mouse, Bugs Bunny, and Donald Duck. Walt Disney was always quick to admit that he studied Keaton and Chaplin to learn how to base gags on personality. His first Mickey Mouse cartoon, released in November 1928, combined an animated rodent with a tightly synchronized soundtrack. It was titled *Steamboat Willie.*

Soon every theater screen in the country would be showing cartoon mice who could fall off buildings and reconstitute themselves in the next frame. That was something Keaton could not do.

16 KEATON'S KENNEL

On the corner of Fifth Avenue and Twenty-third Street, Keaton bounded across the trolley tracks with a heavy old-fashioned tintype camera slung over his shoulder. A trolley motorman stopped his car in the middle of the intersection.

"Hey, *Keaton!*" he yelled. Passengers on board the tram poked their heads out the windows and began whistling. Crosstown trolleys on Twenty-third screeched to a crawl. On Broadway, streetcars shut down their motors. And on Fifth Avenue, the double-decker buses herded together. A few minutes later, traffic was choked for blocks in all directions. Keaton had disappeared inside a crush of curious pedestrians. "People were enchanted," said Frank Dugas, the assistant cameraman. "They treated him as an angel from heaven, someone not really human."

Crowds terrified him. After being rescued by the police, the unit proceeded to the Battery in lower Manhattan, where director Eddie Sedgwick hoped to avoid curious passersby. While the crew was setting up, Keaton noticed a deserted park and played an inning of ball with his writers. Word of his presence got around. Just a few feet out of camera range, pressed back by the police, Keaton could see solid walls of spectators. His palms sweaty, he kept taking nips of 99-proof alcohol, until Sedgwick finally called it a wrap for Production No. 366, working title *Snap Shots*.

Keaton complained that Sedgwick was rushing him. Each morning Keaton liked to begin the workday with baseball, then a big pot of coffee and doughnuts. "They sat talking like they were around a campfire," recalled Dugas. "'Will this be funny?' 'Let's try this out.' Buster knew film from A to Z. He dug in like a flea on a dog, until he reached down to the skin, until he knew he had something terrific."

His work methods were painstaking and slow. A nervous Sedgwick reminded Keaton that the boys in Culver City wanted to see film. Keaton replied, "They can kiss my fanny. Besides, they don't know what I'm doing anyway."

Back at the Ambassador Hotel, Keaton talked about leaving New York immediately. He phoned Hollywood to complain: He had never used written continuities for any of his films. He suggested discarding the script. His arguments displeased his new employers, who were unable to prevent him from returning to the Coast a few days later. Nearly all the New York footage was discarded.

On January 26, 1928, after months of Faustian negotiations, Keaton signed a two-year contract and reported to Culver City. Metro-Goldwyn-Mayer was the biggest and richest of all the studios. Barely four years old, a merger of three smaller studios, MGM was a movie factory begun by two men who were determined to mass-produce one full-length feature every week: Louis B. Mayer, forty-two, a flamboyant onetime scrap-metal dealer, and his delicate protégé, Irving Thalberg, twenty-eight years old and hailed as the boy genius of Hollywood. Ultimate power at MGM lay with Nick Schenck, the new president of Loew's, and his East Coast gang. Keaton's family ties to Nick won him no points with L. B. Mayer, who loathed Schenck and called him "Nick Skunk."

By 1928 MGM dominated the picture industry. With Irving "The Boy Wonder" Thalberg at the helm, it had become the most profitable film company in the world, turning out quality entertainment featuring Greta Garbo, Norma Shearer, Marion Davies, and John Gilbert, among many others. Boasting that it had "More Stars Than There Are in Heaven," MGM took pride in offering top-of-the-line films, hence its trademark of a roaring lion emblazoned with the grandiose Latin motto *Ars Gratia Artis* (Art for Art's Sake). A vast plant covering some 180 acres, the studio was a collaborative enterprise that dumped into a single bubbling stew the talents of directors, writers, cinematographers, set designers, and technicians. Keaton, a loner accustomed to running his own show, had never been required to account for his time and whereabouts.

On paper he had cut a good deal. With a weekly salary of

$3,000 he became the third highest-paid actor on the lot. He would be making two pictures a year, and if he made three, he would receive an additional $50,000 per film. He had wheeled and dealt with uncharacteristic shrewdness to replicate the independent situation he had given up. He was promised jobs for two cameramen, his art director, Fred Gabourie, and a writer. (Another beneficiary was his father, who was to receive $100 a week.) He had the right to hand-pick his director, Ed Sedgwick, a veteran comedy director whom he knew from vaudeville. Keaton brought to his new employer a story idea about a New York tintype photographer who takes snapshots of people on the street but yearns to become a newsreel photographer. The studio purchased his idea for $250. It seemed a very good start.

The opening shot in his war of independence with the studio was fought over dressing rooms. Top stars at MGM were assigned elaborate accommodations. Instead, Keaton rented a house across the street from the main entrance of the studio and gathered his people there. Instead of lunching at the studio commissary, where the meals were both tasty and cheap, he had the devoted Willie Riddle make his food. Instead of behaving like an employee, he conducted himself as if he were separate but equal to Mayer and Thalberg.

Mayer was annoyed. Nothing like this had ever happened before. He wanted his uppity new star on the lot where he could keep an eye on him. At first, however, he did not make an issue of it. With his insatiable need to control, Mayer fancied MGM as a family, in which he of course was the daddy and the actors were children expected to obey for the sake of the common good. The studio replicated Mayer's real-life family in which, his daughter Irene said, "I learned to keep my mouth shut. He had a terrible temper and since there couldn't be two tempers in the family, the rest of us were allowed to have none."

Keaton did not worry about Mayer, because he believed the Schenck brothers were planning to force him out. He regarded Thalberg as a friend. They partied and played bridge together, and Irving had once been a suitor of Connie Talmadge's. It was Thalberg who had done the most to engineer Keaton's transfer to MGM.

Irving Grant Thalberg was Hollywood's royal prince. Born in Brooklyn to a lace importer, he was a small, frail, unimposing man with a slightly bluish complexion due to a deficit of oxygen in his blood from a congenitally defective heart. Doctors had warned that he might not live much beyond the age of thirty. The prince, before his marriage to Norma Shearer, was dominated by his protective mother, Henrietta. As a deal maker, however, he was ferocious, a practical, efficient man with an overpowering need to dominate.

Keaton's old friend Eddie Mannix, studio manager and third in command after Mayer and Thalberg, phrased it indelicately when he described Thalberg as a sweet guy who could "piss ice water." But Keaton continued to believe that Thalberg was gentle, despite all evidence to the contrary. Keaton had complained bitterly about the supervision of Harry Brand. To allay Keaton's fears, Thalberg promised to oversee his films, but practically before the ink had dried on the contract, he broke the promise. Keaton was handed off to an underling, Lawrence Weingarten, who was best known for his biblical pictures.

The son of a Chicago theater exhibitor, Weingarten joined MGM in 1927 as an assistant to producer Harry Rapf. Before long he married Thalberg's sister, Sylvia. "If he hadn't been Irving's brother-in-law, he never would have got to where he did," said Irene Mayer Selznick.

Weingarten had begun working his way up when Thalberg gave him the job of supervising MGM's slapstick comedies, mainly the films of Keaton and Marie Dressler. During his career at MGM Weingarten produced seventy-five films, some of them memorable: the Marx Brothers' *A Day at the Races* and two Tracy-Hepburn classics, *Adam's Rib* and *Pat and Mike*. But he was completely wrong for Keaton.

Director Alf Goulding once remarked about Keaton, "He never listens to anything you tell him. You just have to roll the cameras and hope for the best." Now Keaton found himself encumbered by an incurably humorless man who rushed around the set pulling everyone's strings. Even worse, Weingarten appeared to be patronizing him. Keaton was, Weingarten would say, "a child, with the mentality of a child. He had no other world as far as I know." At once Keaton swatted him aside, or simply ignored him by going over his head to Thalberg—until Thalberg put his foot down and started backing up Weingarten's decisions. Finally Keaton was forced to acquiesce, but he continued to battle Weingarten in what story editor Sam Marx would describe as "a holy war."

Released on September 22, the retitled *The Cameraman* would be 95 percent Keaton and 5 percent MGM, a model Buster Keaton vehicle with lovestruck playfulness and surely one of his most delightful pictures.

Thalberg loved *The Cameraman*. During production he was in stitches one day watching dailies of the bathhouse scene in which Keaton and Ed Brophy are trying to change clothes in the same cramped cubicle. Everybody at MGM admired the picture, which went on to become one of the most successful comedies of 1928, winning grand reviews and grossing $797,000, twice as much as *Steamboat Bill Jr.* For decades to come, the MGM writing department would use *The Cameraman* as a training film to demonstrate for newcomers a perfectly constructed comedy.

The message that Mayer and Thalberg extracted from the success of *The Cameraman* was that Keaton, for all his incessant griping about oversupervision, was able to work just as successfully with a script as anyone else. They also must have concluded that he no longer required special treatment. Before his next film, they quietly stripped him of his people by luring some of them away with plum promotions and firing others, leaving him with only Sedgwick. Too late, he realized the guarantees he had been given were worthless.

A sweet little comedy like *The Cameraman, Spite Marriage* is about a pants presser, Elmer Edgemont, who attends the theater every night wearing evening clothes his rich customers have left at the dry cleaner's where he works. He worships a glamorous actress from his front-row seat and visits her backstage. After being rejected by her fiancé, Trilby Drew marries Elmer out of spite. On their wedding night she gets drunk and passes out, and when she wakes she is horror-struck and promptly files for divorce. In a plot shift, Elmer gets tangled up with a gang of criminals and must embark on high-seas adventures to bring them to justice. Trilby has a change of heart about Elmer.

When Keaton urged shooting *Spite Marriage* in sound, the front office refused. His biggest battle with Weingarten erupted over a bedroom sequence in which Elmer is in a hotel room with his inebriated bride, who has passed out on the floor. Despite his efforts to pick her up and drag her into bed, she keeps slipping through his hands like a bar of soap that wants to go down the drain. The sequence, perhaps one of the funniest scenes ever seen on the screen, would become a famous Keaton routine repeated numerous times throughout his career. (In the fifties William Wyler borrowed it for Audrey Hepburn and Gregory Peck in *Roman Holiday.*) But Weingarten failed to grasp the humor. He decided the scene was blue and ordered it cut.

Keaton's typical response was to walk out. But now he hollered bloody murder. Against his best judgment, Weingarten capitulated. On opening day at the Capitol in New York, reported *Variety,* the scene in question got "a salvo from the Capitolites." If Keaton hoped this would teach Weingarten a lesson, it did not.

In years to come, Weingarten remembered Keaton as being notoriously difficult from the day he stepped on the lot—an actor whose popularity was already on the skids but who nonetheless had to be managed and coddled, a man who was depressed, unhappily married, and drinking heavily. That drunk scene, Weingarten insisted, was shot after Keaton had received treatment for alcohol abuse, "in a place called the Keeley cure down on Wilshire Boulevard that dried out drunks."

According to a friend of Keaton's, he was not a true drinker at this time. "He had cocktails," said actor Harold Goodwin. "He started drinking later when he was running into so much trouble with Larry Weingarten." J. J. Cohn, MGM's general manager throughout Keaton's years there, whose job it was to supervise the supervisors and keep every picture on schedule, did not remember Keaton as a problem. "I wasn't aware of his drinking problems. Occasionally Mr. Mayer would give parties and I'd see Keaton there, but he was always fine. He came to the studio with special advantages because he had worked with Joe Schenck. But he had no pretensions. He wasn't difficult." To Cohn, he was "a nice man who had a lot to say about his work."

Slowly, Keaton was being fitted with the new identity of actor. As a filmmaker, his entire oeuvre was being reduced to a few pratfalls dating back to the days of custard pies and two-reelers and relegated to ancient history. Nobody at MGM would be interested in silent pictures like *The Navigator* or *The General.*

With no outlets for his energy, Keaton remained in his illegal dressing room hosting bridge games while Willie took orders for drinks. The onetime workaholic struggled to find ways to amuse himself. In a spring-training game between the Chicago Cubs and the New York Giants, he arranged to play second base for the

Cubs. Comedian Joe E. Brown played second for the Giants. Keaton's first time up he faced the Giants' great screwball pitcher Carl Hubbell. "I swung my bat around three times and struck out while he was still winding up," Keaton joked.

At the studio, he was visiting Lew Cody on the set of *The Baby Cyclone* when he noticed that Cody's stunt double was having trouble falling down a flight of stairs. Keaton did it for him. The next morning L. B. Mayer called him in to his office. Never again did he want Keaton to take such chances. He might get hurt. Keaton did not seem to be listening. Apparently even though a studio stuntman was officially assigned to Keaton's pictures, he continued to do his own stunt work.

In New York in the early twenties, a select group of young women, handpicked for their beautiful faces and voluptuous bodies, were invited to attend private parties for visiting dignitaries, important politicians, and Wall Street deal makers. The women were usually high-quality chorus girls known to be well-bred, honest, and very discreet. Nobody forced them to go to bed with the great men. If they did, they could be confident of receiving cash, minks, or diamonds.

One of the showgirls who attracted attention in the 1924 *George White's Scandals* was Dorothy Sebastian. She had dark hair, an adorable smile, and a pronounced southern drawl that revealed her Alabama roots. Already married and divorced by the age of eighteen, she had set her heart on becoming a movie star.

At a party one night at the Ritz Hotel, in a suite bathed in soft lighting and shades of gray, Sebastian and Louise Brooks were sipping cocktails. A well-known British newspaper publisher, Lord Beaverbrook, engaged them in conversation. Small and ugly, the middle-aged Beaverbrook was unappetizing, but he had immense power and wealth. Not long afterward, Brooks remembered, he and Sebastian "disappeared into the little grey bedroom in the little grey suite in the Ritz, and then they came out a little while later and a few days later she told me she had a contract at MGM and she did do very well."

At MGM Sebastian proved herself a talented actress and performed as a featured player in seventeen pictures during her first three years. Her reputation as a famous New York showgirl followed her to Hollywood, where she continued to live in the fast lane, dancing and partying into the wee hours. She had difficulty holding her liquor, and her habit of easily passing out won her the nickname Slam Bang Sebastian.

By age twenty-two Dorothy Sebastian had risen to be Keaton's leading lady in *Spite Marriage*. He immediately fell for her with the intensity he had once felt for Viola Dana. It was no coincidence that soon afterward he vacated his off-campus accommodations.

MGM resembled a medieval walled city. Practically self-suffi-cient, it provided employment, temporary lodging, and food for close to 3,000—actors, secretaries, waitresses, executives, and more than 150 different types of craftspeople. It had a hospital, a dining hall (referred to as the commissary), a barbershop, even its own police force.

Irving Thalberg again reminded Keaton that he was the only top star to rent space off the lot, a totally unnecessary expense since the studio took pride in providing the most luxurious dress-ing rooms in Hollywood, and they were free. When William Randolph Hearst spent $75,000 on a fourteen-room Spanish-style stucco bungalow for Marion Davies, it was constructed inside the studio.

Keaton replied that he was not Marion Davies.

Thalberg selected his words carefully. Mr. Mayer wanted him to have a free dressing room. Keaton decided to take it.

Despite continuing battles with Weingarten, Keaton had plenty of reason to feel good. One was his affair with Dorothy Sebastian, with whom he also had developed a splendid working relationship. Part of *Spite Marriage* was shot on location aboard his yacht at the Long Beach marina. Away from the claustrophobic supervision in the studio, Keaton could relax and do the kind of stunt work he had always loved, swinging from the top of a ship's mast and leaping around boats—without the studio's knowledge, of course. A stunt double continued to appear on the set, even though he never worked.

On superstar row, Keaton was assigned a picture-postcard bun-galow nestled behind a tidy picket fence. His neighbors included John Gilbert and Marion Davies. The cottage was the size of a large hotel room, with a kitchen and a well-stocked bar. All four walls were lined with expensive glass-doored bookcases. It was centrally located, in the area where the Irving Thalberg Memorial

Building would later be built, and "all of the MGM stars, featured players, and Big Brass walked by daily," Keaton remembered. He continued to tweak management's noses. On the front porch he put up a painted sign, KEATON'S KENNEL, which he insisted was simply a reference to his new Saint Bernard. Elmer drove to the studio each morning and spent the day wandering around the lot as if he owned it. The Kennel, recalled Sam Marx, "became revolutionary headquarters, a center for employee dissent."

On Christmas Eve 1928 Keaton completed *Spite Marriage*, his last silent feature, released with a synchronized music track. It would be almost a year before he began his next picture.

During 1929 movie theaters began wiring for sound and the studios constructed huge soundstages. The days of shooting films outside were over. By the end of 1930, not a single major studio would be making silent features.

Fear swept through the industry. Who would survive the new technology? It was believed that her thick Swedish accent would kill Garbo's chances. The vocally inadequate Clara Bow told *Photoplay* that she was planning a year's trip abroad for her health. Chaplin's voice would not be heard until 1936.

Among the prominent victims of the revolution were the Talmadge sisters. Norma completed two movies that received poor reviews and then made a well-timed exit. She was rich. During her years as a star, she had earned more than $5 million, and now Joe Schenck continued to pay her a staggering $1,000-a-week maintenance. Connie was fearful of sound and bowed out before making a single talkie. She was now on her third marriage, to a wealthy Chicago department-store heir.

The most successful silent actresses would be Joan Crawford, Greta Garbo, and Norma Shearer, who understood that they had to alter their screen personalities to fit the new technology. Some people believed the Talmadges were lazy. "The Talmadge sisters epitomized an era when all a star had to do was appear in a feathered headdress and diamonds and emeralds," said Lina Basquette, star of Cecil B. De Mille's silent epic *The Godless Girl*. "Norma was such a snob. She took her stardom very seriously, even though much of her power came from being the wife of Joe Schenck. When she turned forty and found herself over the hill, she couldn't handle it."

In retirement the sisters made a career of being movie royalty—shopping in New York and Palm Beach, sunning themselves
in Palm Springs, traveling to Europe and Hawaii. Norma lived
with Gilbert Roland on the beach in Santa Monica.

Keaton could hardly wait for his first talkie. He and Norma
Shearer were the first MGM actors to take the hours-long sound
test in a specially built boxlike contraption. While he was inside the
claustrophobic chamber, a crowd gathered. Finally a technician
opened the door and yelled, "Keaton talks!" Unlike some actors,
Keaton had no trouble passing the test. His husky baritone proved
to have exactly the right timbre.

In the trades Keaton's sound debut was front-page news. In
private, some people at the studio found fault with Keaton's voice.
Lawrence Weingarten thought his flat drawl sounded hickish and
working-class. But his voice had a far more serious deficiency: It
failed to suit his screen personality. The whiskey-and-cigarette
growl might have been perfect for a western star, but not for
Keaton. Ed Bernds, Frank Capra's sound man at Columbia, said
"a lighter, more innocent voice would have suited him better. His
diction was too precise and his voice too strong for the victims he
usually played."

Keaton's first sound picture, *Hollywood Revue of 1929,* was a
promotional feature with an all-star cast that included most of the
big stars under contract. Produced by Harry Rapf in a vaudeville-
revue format to prove MGM talent could dance, sing, and crack
jokes, it is a long, tedious, embarrassing cinematic gumbo that
forces poor Joan Crawford to sing (off-key) and John Gilbert to
recite lines of Shakespeare in slang. Keaton does his Salome dance
but otherwise remains silent. In the finale he joins the chorus during a Technicolor number, "Singin' in the Rain," later to be
revived in the 1952 musical starring Gene Kelly.

Two months later Keaton began his first starring sound picture, a half-million-dollar musical that offered him a chance to use
his singing and dancing talents. *Free and Easy* relates the adventures of Elmer Butts, a timid garage mechanic from Gopher City,
Kansas, whose girlfriend, Elvira Plunkett (Anita Page), wins a
beauty contest and a trip to Hollywood. Determined to see that
she becomes a star, Elmer tags along, and somehow both of them
end up at MGM. A typical early MGM musical, it had high pro-

duction values and cameo appearances by Cecil B. De Mille, Lionel Barrymore, Jackie Coogan, and Dorothy Sebastian.

Free and Easy was an important turning point because it began the mutation of the screen personality Keaton had meticulously constructed a decade earlier. In *Spite Marriage* Elmer the pants presser was more or less the same character Keaton had been playing in all his films. Buster had intelligence, courage, and manly athleticism. Never had he presented himself as a bumbler. He was always resourceful in a crisis, a creative problem-solver. MGM viewed him as a loser, not sexy, not even all that masculine. In Keaton's own films Buster had a beautiful face and luscious body, and always got the girl. MGM castrated Buster. In *Free and Easy* Elmer from Gopher City is basically a twit. For the first time Keaton loses the girl to a rival suitor.

In every subsequent film he made for MGM, he would be typecast as a bonehead. Enticed to MGM by promises of creative freedom and first-rate scripts, he received only weaker and weaker properties. Thalberg reassured him by saying that everybody at the studio liked his pictures, which enjoyed big box office takes. It is not surprising that Keaton began questioning his own judgment.

At the end of October, a few weeks after Keaton's thirty-fourth birthday, the collapse of the stock market ushered in a decade of national suffering. For many months the picture business did not feel the effects because movie attendance, bolstered by the novelty of sound pictures, remained high. Nor did the Crash influence Hollywood social life. Keaton's Sunday barbecues only got showier, the liquor more expensive. At evening parties, Paul Whiteman and Leon "Bix" Beiderbecke provided music for dancing. Sometimes parties turned into all-night sessions with Keaton singing golden oldies from vaudeville, an imported English cigarette in one hand, a glass of whiskey in the other. His drinking did not worry him. Of course, he drank a bit too much. But everyone was on the bottle, and he was certainly not in the same class as John Barrymore or Marion Davies or any of Hollywood's famous drunks.

One night Buster Collier brought his girlfriend, Louise Brooks, to the Villa. After midnight Keaton suggested going for a drive with the couple, and they ended up in Culver City. At Keaton's Kennel they unwound with a nightcap. Keaton suddenly got up and grabbed a baseball bat. He swung at the glass-doored bookcases and made a shower of glass. Neither Collier nor Brooks tried to stop him. Keaton bludgeoned every pane in every bookcase.

In years to come Brooks's favorite subject would be "How Hollywood Destroys Talent." She would always pity Keaton because, she believed, he had been swindled by Joe Schenck. Not only had Schenck made sure Keaton didn't own his own films, but he also forced him into the producers' card games. "What did it matter to him or Sam Goldwyn if they lost two thousand to four thousand dollars a week in the big bridge games?" she said. But no actor could compete, certainly not Keaton. "Poor little Buster with his three thousand dollars a week, trying to live like a millionaire. It was impossible."

She approved of Keaton's symbolic violence against the studio. He was trying to "break out of his cage, escape to creation," she said. Possibly. And possibly he was dead drunk.

The German dirigible *Graf Zeppelin* was expected to land at Mines Field at sunrise on August 26, 1929, after a six-thousand-mile flight across the Pacific from Tokyo. That Monday morning all roads to the airport were jammed with spectators eager to get a look at the airship making a historic flight around the world. Keaton, among other dignitaries and celebrities, had been invited to visit the ship during its twenty-four-hour layover and decided to bring along his sons. Jimmy and Bobby would remember the occasion principally because their father seldom took them anywhere. Now seven and nine, the boys attended the local public grade school. Keaton's elder son remembered his father as a remote figure who was "not around. We barely ever saw him." Overnight absences at Dorothy Sebastian's house in Brentwood were becoming increasingly common. For that matter, their mother spent little time with them. Their lives revolved around their governess, Connie Castille, and a loyal maid, Eleanor White, who would remain with the household until they grew up.

Years later, Jimmy's son believed that his father "was not really aware of how families worked because there never was a family when he was growing up. It was always 'buy them what they want and get rid of them.' They grew up owning everything and having nothing." From everything he had heard, his grandmother Natalie concentrated on social obligations. "These people were young, with all the money they could possibly want, and their only ambition was to enjoy themselves. Having kids was a novel idea, until they got to screaming and misbehaving. My father's favorite person was his nanny."

Sometimes Keaton found his sons' behavior upsetting. Chided for refusing to wash their hands before meals, they turned off the water under every sink in the house, a prank not discovered until the Beverly Hills Water Department had dug up 150 feet of lawn. Another time they dumped plates full of unwanted dinner into the heating grates. The garbage began burning. At midnight the tutor, Oliver Lee, smelled smoke and found flames shooting from the nursery. The fire department evacuated the house.

"They said we threw liver down the furnace and caused the fire," Jimmy remembered. "We had to go over to Tom Mix's house for the night."

Before the blaze was extinguished, it destroyed the dining room and the children's nursery. Police estimated the damage at $10,000.

"Keaton was absent from home," reported the Associated Press.

Throughout most of the twenties, Keaton's sister and brother continued to flounder. Apparently Louise possessed some natural talent and could have become an accomplished comedienne. A family friend, Carol Arthur De Luise, described her as "a female version of Buster, but the way she was brought up never prepared her for life. She was always a dependent who took for granted that big daddy would take care of her."

During *Steamboat Bill Jr.,* Louise worked as a script supervisor and stunt woman doubling for Marion Byron. In *The Cameraman* both she and her brother appeared as extras in the Coney Island scene. But she did not have a productive life. Adorable as a child but homely as an adult, Louise at the age of twenty-four was unmarried. Having her stay home did not bother Keaton. On the contrary, her working would have been a reflection on his ability to take care of his family.

Jingles had not yet found his way either. Keaton was so eager for him to attend college that sometimes he told interviewers his brother was a student at the University of Southern California. He was not. Five years earlier, Jingles went to work for MGM as an office boy delivering mail. At the time he hoped to work his way up the ladder. After a few months, however, he fell off the bottom rung. Then, in 1930, Keaton thought Jingles could join a sound department, a perfect opportunity to get in on the ground floor of a brand-new field. Jingles enrolled in a course for sound-recording technicians but dropped out a few months later.

As Jingles grew older, his failure to support himself became a chronic disability. Invariably his promises turned out to be only talk. Buster was never heard complaining about any member of his family but to him, of all people, a compulsive worker, Jingles' employment phobia could hardly have made sense. Listening to his brother's cockeyed schemes and feeble excuses tried Keaton's patience and eventually could not help but sour their relations.

On May 13, 1930, Keaton began Production No. 497, working title *The Big Shot,* with Eddie Sedgwick as his director. It is 1918 and every able-bodied man is in uniform. Stylish, stuffy millionaire Elmer Stuyvesant only cares about dating a pretty clerk (Sally Eilers). When his chauffeur decides to enlist and Elmer must hire a new driver, he visits what he believes to be an employment agency. It is actually an army recruiting station. Before he knows it, he has been inducted into the military. Basically a standard war comedy, *The Big Shot* was a remake of a 1926 Wallace Beery comedy, *Behind the Front,* sprinkled with some of Keaton's own war experiences. Aside from a few funny sequences and some charming musical numbers, Keaton had nothing to do. Andy Nealis, third assistant director on the picture, said Keaton "and Sedgwick were as close as people could be who weren't related, but Eddie would wind up yelling at Buster because he couldn't remember his lines." Stuntman Gil Perkins recalls Keaton as a frustrated director who did a good deal of sulking on the set.

Retitled *Doughboys,* the picture was completed on June 9.

When the front office tried to keep Keaton busy by rolling him over to the production line of a picture called *Man O' War,* he walked off the lot. Irving Thalberg fired off a sharp telegram that ordered Keaton to show up at ten the next morning and reminded him of the "considerable loss" caused by his unprofessional behavior.

Thalberg could not complain too strongly because Keaton's

pictures consistently made money. Thalberg decided that the star needed a vacation. Calling him into his office, Thalberg took a positive approach. The studio was going to give him a $10,000 bonus and a three-month, all-expenses-paid vacation. He suggested that Keaton take Natalie to Europe for a second honeymoon.

The Keatons had not had a first honeymoon. In the ninth year of their marriage, they were barely on speaking terms. He had a mistress, and she may have had an occasional lover of her own. Spending three months alone with a woman with whom he had not had sex since 1923 was not his idea of a good time. On top of all this, Nate didn't play bridge.

Nevertheless, they went. With MGM footing the bill, they spent the better part of the summer making a grand tour of England, Germany, France, and Spain, where company representatives escorted them around and gave them celebrity treatment. Because his pictures were routinely released in French and Spanish, Keaton found himself a popular figure in Europe. After a few weeks Norma and Gilbert Roland joined them, arriving in France with Norma's Rolls-Royce. After four years, Norma and Gil were still a couple even though she remained married to Joe Schenck. Long ago Gil had proved that he couldn't act, but he continued to get work because he was handsome, sociable, and played a good game of tennis. Keaton liked having him around. In Barcelona Roland took them to a bullfight. The matador dedicated a bull to Keaton, and afterward crowds carried him back to his hotel on their shoulders. On the Riviera a French photographer caught him at the beach with his guard down. A cigarette is clamped between his teeth, and he is grinning. The picture was widely published because it was said to be the first ever to show him smiling. At the end of September he hurried back on the *Bremen* just in time to catch the World Series in Philadelphia, between Connie Mack's Athletics and St. Louis.

While Keaton was in Europe, Larry Weingarten saw the play *Parlor, Bedroom and Bath,* a revival of a 1917 farce, first filmed by Metro ten years earlier. He decided it would be a perfect vehicle for Keaton.

When Keaton returned in mid-October, he groaned at the news. He felt that farce comedy with its shrill pacing was completely wrong for him. But the front office had already made up its mind.

In *Parlor, Bedroom and Bath,* he once again plays a bumbling Elmer character, this time a wimp who is mistaken for a notorious Casanova and gets involved with several women at once. Though it was difficult material, Keaton found opportunities to slip in variations on his old Buster character. Contributing to the high production values was the decision to shoot exteriors on the grounds of the Italian Villa, a private movie set that was finally being revealed to the public as a studio movie set.

17 HIGH CRIMES AND MISDEMEANORS

On-screen Keaton played a harmless buffoon. Off-screen he played a buffoon whose behavior was becoming embarrassing and sometimes obnoxious. That winter he visited Tahoe City with Natalie and her sisters. To reach the ski-jumping trials on Olympic Hill, they hired a horse-drawn sleigh. Keaton slipped the driver a twenty-dollar bill and gave instructions to weave the sleigh around. It began spinning and tipping, while its occupants screamed in fear.

He was developing a compulsion for pranks that could make people suffer. Before a dinner at Tahoe City, he purchased chairs in the banquet room and had their back legs sawed halfway through so that every guest in his party would fall on his or her behind. As alcohol eroded his inhibitions, the escapades became accordingly worse. There is no way of knowing how much of this relentless hostility should be simply attributed to drinking. Probably a considerable amount. The creative energy that he had once thrown into building comic routines was now being channeled into playing practical jokes, getting extraordinarily drunk, and coping with raging hangovers, now a serious problem. No one made any effort to curb him. To his admirers, who basked in his reflected glory, Keaton would always be a great man who could do no wrong. "Well, he was brilliant," Gilbert Roland said. "One of the greatest, one of the most wonderful, altruistic men I've ever met in my life. Buster never depended on anything but himself."

The one person who had never been able to ignore his faults was Natalie. His drinking gave her more cause than ever for complaint. Her only choice was to put up with it. She was humiliated that he was making less and less effort to hide his relationships with other women. For two years Hollywood had been aware of his affair with Dorothy Sebastian. Even his children had met her. There was also a string of other affairs. One of the perks of being an MGM star was sex whenever and wherever he wanted it.

Keaton must have been surprised when Sebastian broke off with him. Now twenty-four, she had become increasingly unhappy with her life. She turned down the lead in *Free and Easy* and appeared only in a cameo. She announced to the papers that she was having a nervous breakdown. By this time she had tired of being a mistress and "wanted desperately to be married," said Anita Page. In 1926, while filming *The Last Frontier,* she had met a popular leading man, Bill Boyd, the future western star of *Hop-A-Long Cassidy,* but he had been married. While Keaton was vacationing in Europe, she renewed her relationship with Boyd, now divorced, and married him.

Keaton found other diversions, among them the comely Keystone actress Mae Busch. On the MGM lot he became chummy with a twenty-five-year-old stock contract player, Kathleen Key. This time he picked the wrong one for a meaningless romp; she jokingly described herself as "a little crazy. Not much, you understand, but just a little nutty in the head."

When Keaton first met her in the early twenties, she was a striking teenager from Buffalo: five feet six, 123 pounds, with dark hair, a saucy smile, and a pugnacious temperament. Hollywood insiders believed she had a good chance to make it. The great-granddaughter of Francis Scott Key, composer of "The Star Spangled Banner," she became a member of "Our Club," an exclusive sorority for screen actresses whose honorary president was Mary Pickford and whose notable members included Keaton's ex-leading lady Virginia Fox (Mrs. Darryl Zanuck) and Mildred Davis (Mrs. Harold Lloyd).

Like Keaton, Kitty Key had a passion for bridge. She too had a reputation for being her own worst enemy and offending the wrong people.

On Wednesday, February 4, 1931, she stormed into Keaton's Kennel and began to quarrel. Keaton shouted, "Flag your ass out of here quick." Key ripped his shirt and undershirt, then smacked his face. He punched her. She tried to skewer him with a knife. A few windows got broken. Studio police rushed in and hustled her off, struggling and yelling, to the Culver City Police Station. She was later released after Keaton declined to press charges.

EX FILM BEAUTY CLAWS KEATON, MOVIE CLOWN, the next-day headlines announced.

Mayer and Thalberg, along with Eddie Mannix, sat down with a bruised and scratched Keaton to hammer out a plausible explanation. Neither his relationship with Key nor the brawl was easily explained. Following instructions from MGM, Keaton explained to the press that he had teased the actress about being too plump—she weighed 139 pounds—and told her she might get more parts if she thinned down. He said they bet $500 (a huge sum for a mostly unemployed actress during the Depression) that she could lose twenty pounds in ten days. She shed only six, but he decided to pay her just the same, whereupon she demanded a loan of $4,000, which he also generously agreed to. In the end he wrote a whopping check to prevent a scandal, he would explain.

To his intense annoyance, the studio advised against locking horns with Key. Mayer and Thalberg suggested a check for $10,000, to come out of Keaton's pocket. To keep the payment a secret from Nate, it was not deducted from his weekly paycheck. His attorneys, Loeb, Walker and Loeb, advanced him $10,000 and settled with Key on his behalf. The entire amount was to be repaid in a lump sum within ten days. Then Keaton blew the whole thing by writing the check to Loeb, Walker and Loeb on his and Natalie's joint bank account.

Not for a second did he believe that MGM would fire him over such a trivial incident. L. B. Mayer was a powerful fixer whose influence extended to the district attorney's office. He did whatever was best for the studio, and was hard-nosed as always whenever money was involved. A comparable case to Keaton's would not occur until 1936. MGM managed to keep director George Cukor's homosexuality under wraps by covering up all evidence connected with an arrest. And in the 1940s Mayer would quash a morals charge against another top star, an adored idol of countless bobby-soxers, because his boyish, freckle-faced charm continued to sell movie tickets.

As for Keaton, he remained true royalty. Mayer was certainly not prepared to boot from the MGM heavens one of its brightest stars, no matter what private doubts he may have had about his future at the studio. Therefore, he held on to all of his options by defending Keaton but not spending a dime to do so.

It was only a matter of weeks before the release of *Parlor, Bedroom and Bath*. As *Variety* would comment in its review, "For farces, as clean as they come and okay for the kids, which all Keaton pictures should be—and to date have been."

Kitty Key was fired and quietly disappeared from Hollywood with Keaton's $10,000. According to tales on the MGM lot, actor William Bakewell recalled, "L. B. Mayer gave her a trip to Europe to get her out of the picture."

Never would Mayer grant Key amnesty for her participation in the Keaton's Kennel riot. Nor would any other studio, so enormous was his power. She never made another film and died young—only forty-eight—in the Motion Picture Hospital at Woodland Hills. Her fate elicited no tears from Keaton, who regarded her as a "floozy" and "tigress" who screamed like "some crazy old witch."

At Keaton's Kennel, broken windows were replaced for the second time in a year. On the door Keaton hung a sign, CLOSED FOR REPAIRS, which was replaced after a few days by a new sign, OPEN UNDER NEW MANAGEMENT. Then actors William Haines and Eddie Nugent came around with yet another sign—DANGER: WOMEN AT WORK! MGM publicized a wire to Keaton from New York *Daily News* columnist Sidney Skolsky—HEAR YOU ARE OFF KEY. As a gag, the publicity department asked women visiting the dressing room to sign a waiver agreement stating that they entered at their own risk and would hold Keaton harmless for anything that might happen.

One person not laughing was Natalie. She was threatening to divorce him over Kathleen Key and the $10,000 payoff.

Unlike previous flings, Keaton's trysts with Kathleen Key had breached an unwritten contract. Seven years earlier Keaton had assured the Talmadges that he would conduct his affairs discreetly. Kathleen Key managed to make Natalie—and by extension the whole Talmadge family—look bad in public.

On May 31 Keaton and Natalie observed their tenth wedding anniversary, a milestone noted by the fan magazines. Never had their marriage been so acrimonious.

Peg Talmadge was diagnosed with cancer and underwent surgery on July 14. Only this illness in the family prevented

Natalie from waging a full-scale war on her husband. Keaton did not believe she would ever leave him. He waited for the storm to pass and their relationship to settle back into its normal abnormality. No more was heard about Kathleen Key or divorce. Natalie told him she would forgive him "only for the sake of the children," he recalled. With Nate, nothing would really be forgiven, nothing forgotten.

Keaton pulled his most elaborate prank on Lew Cody, who collected antiques and whose house looked like a museum. Keaton arranged to substitute plaster of paris copies for several precious vases. Then, while visiting Cody's home, he picked up one of the antiques and dropped it, sending Cody into a state of shock. Pretending horror, Keaton stepped back and toppled another vase. After Cody recovered, he laughed. "Just jolly Hollywood pranking," *Photoplay* wrote.

At the studio Keaton devoted his spare time to annoying his neighbors. Next door to Keaton's modest bungalow was John Gilbert's pretentious stucco minimansion. To irritate Gilbert, Keaton strung a clothesline between the two buildings and hung up red flannel underwear. Another butt of his practical joking was Clark Gable. On an afternoon when Gable was scheduled to shoot a steamy love scene with Joan Crawford for *Possessed,* Keaton invited him to the Kennel for lunch and instructed Willie to serve corned beef and cabbage with lots of onions.

One weekend Keaton and a bunch of friends drove to the rustic estate of Marion Mack, his costar from *The General.* Though Mack and her husband, Louis Lewyn, had gone to Tijuana for the weekend, Keaton decided to stay and make himself at home.

The party guests soon had the run of the house. In Mack's bedroom closet Keaton found a very costly evening gown. Slipping into the dress, he marched down to the pool, vamped it up on the diving board, then dove in and performed a water ballet. Throughout the weekend, the frolic continued.

"They had the servants running for three days and they had all the booze they could drink," remembered Marion Mack, still outraged a half century later.

The Lewyns returned to a house that appeared to have been sacked. Mack was furious. Not only had her clothing been worn, but the expensive new gown was now completely ruined. To the

Lewyns, the invasion of their property was no laughing matter, though this was not the sort of incident that could be reported to the police. They felt so disgusted that they rented the estate to producer Arthur Hammerstein and moved back to town.

Keaton's struggle for high-quality scripts was losing steam. Usually the studio just slapped him into whatever junk was convenient. He worked one day in a one-reel short about swimming, *Splash!* In a musical revue, *March of Time,* also known as *Toast of the Town,* he had two days shooting as a caveman. Another bit cast him as a restaurant customer unable to laugh.

Keaton could not help seeing what his career had come to. Many reviews for *Parlor, Bedroom and Bath* had been good. But a 1931 book about current cinema dismissed it along with Harold Lloyd's *Feet First* as an assembly-line product that had been "mechanically constructed" by "a well-paid staff of 'gagmen.'" With such pictures, the author wrote, Keaton was forfeiting all chance of being considered a "serious creative" artist.

By then, Keaton worried less about being a serious creative artist than about simply getting a halfway decent script that would allow him to use his comic gifts. Despite Thalberg's original promises, he had gradually lost control. In January 1930, when his contract came up for extension, he was given a renewal for one picture only, *Doughboys.* At that time he could have quit and gone elsewhere. But by now quitting, even risking suspension, was out of the question. He had the Italian Villa to keep up, and he had a wife who shelled out hundreds of dollars a week on clothes. He had four Keatons depending on him. Besides, work was his emotional food; he could never stop working, even on mediocre films. In 1928 Harold Lloyd had warned him that MGM wasn't his gang. They weren't his gang, but they were his life.

In the spring of 1931 he was presented with another weak script, about another milksop millionaire. Homer Van Tine Harmon attempts to reform a gang of dead-end kids on New York's Lower East Side by building them an athletic club, all to win the affections of one tough's sister (Anita Page). It was a blatant but inept rip-off of his Rollo Treadway millionaire in *The Navigator.*

The script was not his only concern, however. His friend Eddie Sedgwick, who had been his director since *The Cameraman,* was assigned to another picture. In his place Keaton got a pair of young men in their late twenties, Jules White and Zion Myers, who had codirected *Splash!* and were now being given their first chance at a feature. White had been at the studio working on a canine series, the Dogville Comedies (*Dogway Melody, All Quiet on the Canine Front*), known around the lot as the Barkies.

During his three years at MGM, Jules White had not received so much as a hello from L. B. Mayer. "Nevertheless, the dog films were very successful," said Maurice Rapf, whose father, Harry Rapf, produced them. "White was being moved up from dogs to people, and they gave him Buster Keaton. You can't blame Keaton for being insulted."

On the set Keaton took a strong dislike to White, a six-foot, heavyset man whose style tended to be autocratic. Immediately White issued instructions on how to walk, talk, stand, and fall, an understandable carry-over from his work with canine actors and their trainers.

There was a baseball diamond on lot 2, and the afternoons were problem times. "After lunch Buster always wanted to play ball," said the assistant director, Willard Sheldon. "Half the crew went with him, and there were usually problems afterward getting everybody back on the set." Rumor had it that Mayer planned to insert a no-baseball clause in Keaton's next contract.

On location one day at the Wilmington harbor, Keaton disappeared altogether. During one scene he dove overboard. Instead of swimming to a waiting pick-up boat, he swam ashore, and he wasn't seen for a week.

Soon after completion of *Sidewalks of New York*, Mayer demoted White and Myers to Pete Smith shorts. After a poor start, *Sidewalks* fared much better than Keaton expected, grossing more than any of his independent features.

For his next film, Keaton demanded Ed Sedgwick back. This time the studio came up with a French farce, *Her Cardboard Lover*, which it had acquired in 1928 for a Marion Davies silent film (and would film again in 1942 with Norma Shearer). *Her Cardboard Lover* became *The Passionate Plumber*, in which Keaton plays the same doltish Elmer character, now an American plumber working in Paris. He is summoned to the home of a wealthy socialite (Irene Purcell) to repair a bathroom leak.

The ultimate indignity was being paired with a very popular

comedian whom MGM had signed to a five-year contract in June. Jimmy Durante had built his career as a piano player–comic (in the team of Clayton, Jackson & Durante) in speakeasies, on the Broadway stage, and on radio, and by the age of thirty-nine he had an immense number of fans. His physical trademark was a large nose, but what made people laugh was his croaky voice and Bowery accent, his stock exclamations ("What a revoltin' development," "Ev'rybody wants to get into the act") and high-decibel energy. He was not thrilled to play second fiddle to Buster Keaton, a star in obvious trouble.

By the late twenties, teaming had become standard practice at MGM. "Very seldom did they let a comic work alone," said Maurice Rapf, whose father also produced *The Passionate Plumber*. "Durante was a lovable guy whom they tried to do alone but it hadn't worked. Then they probably said, 'Buster is working alone too. The hell with that. Let's team him!' Actors had no voice in it."

Although Durante's role in *The Passionate Plumber,* a chauffeur, was more supporting than costarring, Keaton felt threatened. He believed that Mayer was grooming Durante to take his place.

MGM launched a publicity campaign for Durante, who would make all told some forty films during his career. His nose was insured for a million dollars with Lloyds of London. Although Keaton's anxiety about Durante triggered more drinking, he had nothing against the comedian personally and even became friends with him off-screen.

It was obvious to MGM that Keaton was coasting, professionally. Occasionally his former brilliance burst forth, like an unexpected bolt of lightning. One of his favorite routines, which he would repeat on stage, TV, and circus appearances for the rest of his life, was a pistol-dueling scene between him and Gilbert Roland in *The Passionate Plumber*. On-screen, Keaton and Durante lacked chemistry, and the film as a whole was a disappointment.

Just getting himself to Culver City some mornings was a battle for Keaton. When he woke up with trembling hands and scrambled thoughts, he would play hooky. Then telegrams would arrive at the Italian Villa demanding he report to work. Sometimes MGM employees hand-delivered the messages. AD Andy Nealis was one of them. "Buster was supposed to be home ill," he recalled. "But when I got to his house he wasn't there. His wife was so upset that I knew something was wrong. I figured Buster must be on a binge."

That fall Irving Thalberg's attention was focused on script development for *Grand Hotel,* which was to be an all-star picture that included every big star on the lot, among them Greta Garbo, Joan Crawford, John Barrymore, and Wallace Beery. One of the key roles still waiting to be cast was Kringelein, a fatally ill book-keeper who spends his life savings to enjoy his last days at the Grand Hotel. Director-writer Edmund Goulding thought the role was custom-made for Keaton, and Keaton agreed. He would have done anything to play Kringelein. Fresh in L. B. Mayer's mind were Keaton's absences, alibis, and lies. The role was assigned to Lionel Barrymore.

For Keaton, what followed next was *Speak Easily,* about a pince-nezzed absentminded professor who believes he inherits a fortune and so decides to back a Broadway show, then a post-Prohibition comedy about two would-be beer barons, *What! No Beer?,* which Keaton called "a 100 per cent turkey." In both films he played straight man to Jimmy Durante, who was just as dis-pleased as Keaton with the second-rate pictures. Durante also resented delays caused by Keaton's drinking and absences.

By Hollywood standards, the eleven-year-old Keaton-Talmadge marriage was extraordinarily stable. Unlike Natalie's high-profile sisters, whose marital and romantic escapades regu-larly made headlines, Natalie was the good sister who stayed at home and kept out of the papers. Ever since the Kathleen Key scandal, their relationship had been ugly as never before. He regu-larly stayed out all night and refused to tell Natalie where he had been. By now, his friends had learned not to express surprise when he arrived for engagements with a woman on his arm.

In early April Keaton decided to take his sons on a weekend airplane trip to Agua Caliente, Joe Schenck's gambling resort in Mexico, one of his favorite weekend getaways. His idea of taking them by plane sparked a serious quarrel with his plane-phobic wife. Keaton insisted that he had the right to take his children wherever he liked and had been promising them this treat for a long time. Furious, Natalie rushed out of the house.

Next morning Keaton bundled up Jimmy and Bobby, along

with governess Connie Castille, and took them up in a single-engine, four-place Curtiss Robin owned by western star Hoot Gibson. When they landed at San Diego Airport to get clearance for crossing the border, Connie Castille took the boys to the bathroom. Ten minutes went by and then Keaton went hunting for them, only to discover they had been taken away by the police. Buron Fitts, Los Angeles district attorney, had telephoned to order the boys be detained to thwart a kidnapping. It was clear to Keaton that the sisterhood was at work: Fitts was a close friend of Connie Talmadge's.

In San Diego, Keaton wondered how a father could kidnap his own children. He allowed himself to be strong-armed. The next day the fugitives flew back to Los Angeles.

To badgering reporters waiting for details back at Clover Field in Santa Monica, Keaton acknowledged that "it looks like I don't know where I stand matrimonially." He ridiculed rumors of serious marital troubles. "I just wanted to see who's boss. I didn't know I'd stir up a miniature war in doing it."

Myra Keaton told reporters that domestic battles were nothing new in her son's home, adding that "Natalie has not been home since Friday." Keaton posed with his sons on the lawn of the Italian Villa, "forlornly waiting for Mama to come home," as one photo caption read. He talked of putting a candle in the window for his prodigal wife. Shifting into his jokester mode, he sent her three phonograph records: "You Got Me in Between the Devil and the Deep Blue Sea," "All of Me," and "Can't We Talk It Over?" He did not believe Nate would ever leave him any more than he believed MGM would fire him.

He was right. She returned home the following day.

Photoplay pronounced the incident closed. "She's home. So is Buster. So are the kids. And all are forgiven."

Principal photography on Production No. 627 was due to begin shortly, and Keaton had not responded to L. B. Mayer's orders to get down to Culver City. It was not until April 14 that he returned to the studio. Three weeks into production of *Speak Easily,* he called in sick two days in a row. By the time the picture wrapped in mid-June, further absences had caused the studio to lose eleven shooting days. Memos traveling between the studio manager and Irving Thalberg recorded that Keaton's absences had cost the studio $33,000.

Speak Easily, his second picture with Jimmy Durante, is probably his best sound film, an amazing feat considering the turmoil in his personal life. He is a mousy college professor who is suddenly transformed into a swinger by winning a fake inheritance. An MGM press release stated that Keaton, "practically self-educated," prepared for his role by doing "considerable research in dictionaries and encyclopedias to make his portrayal authentic." In August *Speak Easily* opened strongly to good reviews. *Variety* thought the picture showed Keaton as "a much more satisfying comic than he has been in his last several films. Perhaps for the first time in talkers he really finds his old stride." In October, Mayer and Thalberg gave him a new one-year contract.

Once the film was completed, Keaton immediately decamped. With Natalie in Seattle he shelled out $25,000 for a ninety-eight-foot cruiser with five bedrooms and quarters for a crew of five. To reporters Keaton described the yacht as a "love gift" for his wife, though Keaton was passionate about boats while Natalie was not much interested in either boats or water. Nevertheless, it was christened the *Natalie* and registered in her name. After the yacht arrived in San Pedro Harbor, Keaton invited a large party of guests on a trip to Catalina Island, among them L. B. Mayer and the whole Talmadge clan. Natalie was upset by the rough weather and perhaps her husband's boozy behavior, and sufficiently overcame her dread of planes to fly home with her mother.

Emotions cooled down for a while. Then on July 5 another battle royal sent Natalie to her mother's house, dragging the boys with her. Late one afternoon Keaton drove over to the studio. Outside the casting office stood an attractive extra. In a matter of minutes, he had picked her up and was heading back to Beverly Hills.

At the Italian Villa he led the woman upstairs to Nate's room. Walking into her famous closet, he glanced around at the fur coats, evening gowns, leather pumps, and dozens of designer suits and dresses. Suddenly he began to rip clothing off the hangers.

"Take whatever you want," he said to the woman. He tossed the outfits into a pile—a mink coat, dresses, underwear, even Nate's pale silk stockings.

During the evening he drank heavily. Then he and the woman drove to San Pedro, where the *Natalie* was berthed. He had insisted that she help herself to as much of Nate's closet as she could carry. Keaton wanted to go for a cruise, but the captain refused—he needed the permission of its owner, Natalie.

On the verge of passing out, Keaton took the woman into one of the cabins. At 2:00 A.M. he woke up. Standing over them were Natalie and Connie, with two private detectives and a public official, whom Keaton never named but was very likely Buron Fitts. Keaton watched as the detectives made notes that could be used to establish adultery. Then Natalie and Connie scooped up Natalie's cocktail dresses and left.

After leaving the Italian Villa, Nate and the boys moved to a house that Connie bought her at 18904 Malibu Road in Las Tunas Beach.

Natalie wanted nothing more to do with Keaton. She did not bother to conceal the ferocity of her feelings about him from the boys. "My dad never uttered one bad word about my mother," Jimmy recalled. "He was not the kind to do that. He was the sweetest guy in the world. But my mother had nothing but the worst to say about him until the day she died."

18 DOWN AND OUT IN CHEVIOT HILLS

In 1932 Keaton increased his daily whiskey consumption to more than a fifth. He was no longer falling asleep and waking up; he was passing out and coming to.

Life was simple again. Soon he might own nothing but his clothes, one car, his dog, and a cottage he had hastily purchased after vacating the Villa. The new place in Cheviot Hills was used as little more than a walk-in closet for hanging his clothes, and he avoided staying there by himself. In August he noticed a newspaper article about a one-of-a-kind vehicle for sale, a powder-blue thirty-eight-foot house on wheels that the Pullman Company had custom built for the president of the Pennsylvania Railroad. It had double drawing rooms, a galley, and an observation deck, and slept six and a crew of two. In the middle of the Depression it was available for $10,000. Keaton borrowed the money to buy it.

In the fall after the divorce, he and Lew Cody left Hollywood and cruised the roads with Willie Riddle behind the wheel of his mobile home (which he called a land yacht). After posing for photos in costumes from the MGM costume department—admirals' uniforms and silly hats—they went to the mountains to hunt and fish. In San Francisco they parked in front of the St. Francis Hotel, which charged them fifty cents a day for the space and even strung them a telephone line from a second-story window.

After living in Harold Lloyd's Beverly Hills driveway for a while, Keaton decided to use the MGM studio as a free parking lot. "That trailer was the greatest party place I've ever known," Sam Marx recalled. "It rocked back and forth day and night with the drinking that was going on. It was like New Year's Eve every day. MGM was not happy about this."

Mayer decided to visit the renegade trailer himself. Strolling in unannounced one day, he was shocked to find the place full of his comedy writers and a number of unidentified women. Fuming, he let everyone know that this was no way to behave on studio property. Keaton told Mayer to jump in a lake. "You studio people warp my character," he said.

Three weeks after leaving her husband, Natalie filed for divorce. A court awarded her custody of Jimmy and Bobby and ordered Keaton to pay $300 a month in child support. But Natalie would sever him from his children by making it impossible for them to see him.

His reaction was typical of a lifelong aversion to dealing head-on with painful scenarios. He completely ignored the divorce. When served with papers, he could not bring himself to retain legal representation, indeed never even responded to Natalie's complaint. To represent her interests, Nate hired a young hotshot, Jerry Giesler, later nicknamed "lawyer of the stars" because of his success on behalf of clients like Charlie Chaplin and Errol Flynn. In the property settlement Giesler destroyed Keaton, who was lost in grief and said Nate could have everything. She made no demand for alimony. Instead, she received 90 percent of their joint property, including the Italian Villa and its furnishings, an estimated value of $425,000, the *Natalie,* $18,000 in cash, and other California property valued at $30,000. The first item she sold was the yacht, to Peg Talmadge for $25,000.

Abandoned in the Italian Villa were prints of Keaton's features plus many of his short comedies. In his cutting room, cans of film were dumped into the safe. Copies of other films that had been stored in the projection room were also left behind. Keaton never gave them a thought.

In 1932 the term *alcoholic* had not yet come into popular use; heavy drinkers were simply drunkards or lushes. In Hollywood there were a number of dry-out establishments offering treatment, even promising cures. One of them, the Keeley Institute on West Pico, offered "Liquor, Tobacco, and Drug Habit Treatment" that involved a three-day program in which the patient was forced to drink on a regular schedule: gin, brandy, rum, beer, wine, and whiskey, followed by vomiting to avoid alcohol poisoning. Since plenty of drunkards and lushes worked in the picture business, there was no shortage of customers for the Keeley quick cure, which is still in use today under the name aversion therapy. "Every studio had problems with drinking," said Irene Mayer Selznick. "If people weren't drinkers before they got to the studio, the tension helped make them drinkers. My father seldom drank himself. Maybe half a dozen times a year he would have a Dubonnet, but that was the most he ever drank."

MGM, recognizing Keaton's problem, intervened. "The studio was run on a tight rein," said Maurice Rapf. "If they wanted to save you, they tried to solve your problem. But for somebody they wanted to get rid of, they wouldn't bother." On several occasions MGM packed off Keaton to alcohol rehab clinics, but once released he got right back on the bottle at the first excuse.

In preparation for his next picture, he was obliged to dry out. A friend, Dr. Harry Watson Martin, arranged for Keaton to go to an Arrowhead Springs spa in the company of a doctor and a registered nurse who specialized in the private-duty care of alcoholics. One of her previous patients had been a friend of Keaton's, comedian Joe E. Brown.

Back from Arrowhead and sober, Keaton prepared for his next picture, *What! No Beer?*, a story that had been written for the screen. Keaton and Durante invest in an abandoned brewery after the repeal of Prohibition, hoping to get rich. In the role of Elmer, Keaton has some funny moments, but his physical condition is alarmingly apparent. For the first time, drinking was clearly affecting his performance. Lines were delivered with a distinct slur, and in some scenes he had to remain seated.

The registered nurse remained to provide further medical care at home and keep the patient sober enough to work. As the patient was far from ready to give up drinking, Mae Scriven earned every cent of her wages. At the studio, however, there was nobody to do her work. That Christmas at the company party, Keaton got out of control. Along with everyone else, he spent the afternoon drinking. He began doing pratfalls in one of the director's bungalows, but he stumbled and struck his head. When the party broke up, nobody remembered Keaton, who was left all night on a sofa. On Christmas morning he had no recollection of what had happened. Another casualty of the celebration was Irving Thalberg, who suffered a massive heart attack and had to take a leave of absence.

As Keaton was incapable of functioning on his own, having someone like Mae in the house was more or less necessary, and he quickly became attached to the attractive, gray-eyed, twenty-eight-year-old brunette. Inevitably, he slept with her.

On New Year's Day Louis B. Mayer hosted his annual party, a brunch at his Santa Monica beach house. Although appearances by MGM executives and stars were obligatory, Keaton planned to spend the holidays at Agua Caliente. Mae flew to Tijuana with him, and a week later they were married by a judge in Ensenada, Mexico—or so they claimed; the judge denied it. Buster, Mae reported, had swept her away one night with a serenade. The marriage was not legal, because his divorce from Natalie would not be final for another seven months.

Mae Elizabeth Scriven was born in Orange County, California, in 1905, to a forty-year-old poultry and truck farmer, Avert, and his twenty-year-old wife, Lucy. She had a twin brother, Rae, and a younger sister, Marie. Before World War I the family moved three hundred miles north to Merced County, a hay- and cotton-growing region.

Mae was serious and intelligent, a responsible girl who had always excelled in school. She wrote well, took an interest in philosophy and history, developed a social and political conscience, and grew up to become a liberal Democrat. She wrote poetry, songs, and plays, and looked to the theater for a road out of Merced County. In the Scriven family such ambitions were considered impractical, so Mae entered nurse's training at Methodist Hospital in Los Angeles.

By the time she met Keaton ten years later, she had married and divorced, worked as an office nurse for prominent physicians in Hollywood and Culver City, and also did private-duty nursing on the side. Mae clung to a romantic belief that "every girl finds the right man sooner or later." Keaton, she believed, was the right man for her.

Unlike Natalie, who had yearned to be a movie star, Mae knew that she lacked the talent; her ambition was to be the wife of a movie star. She was well aware that her husband suffered from bouts of depression and alcoholism. Caring for people in crisis was her business, and she certainly felt competent to handle the situation.

The wedding had delayed Keaton's return to Los Angeles and made it necessary for Production No. 655 to shoot around him. When he did show up, his voice sounded feeble and his face looked puffy. The makeup department colored his face light pink. At this point, the studio's legal department drafted a termination notice that used the word "intoxication," but the letter was never sent. Trade papers announced the next Keaton-Durante comedy, *Buddies,* featuring twelve-year-old Jackie Coogan. At studio previews of *What! No Beer?*, some MGM executives came away glum. But the picture opened strongly on February 11 at New York's Capitol and broke attendance records. *Variety* thought that Durante "dominates nearly every scene, Keaton's quiet, deadpanned being about eclipsed as a result."

With Irving Thalberg still recuperating from his heart attack, Mayer decided to get rid of Keaton as soon as *Beer* finished shooting at the end of January. At noon on Tuesday, February 2, two men from his staff hand-delivered a letter to Keaton's Kennel: "You are hereby notified that for good and sufficient cause we hereby terminate the contract with you dated October 5, 1932."

Keaton was utterly astounded. He could not help interpreting it as persecution on the part of Mayer. Although the reason for his dismissal would remain a mystery to him, he would finally decide it had to do with a football game. In later years he said that Mayer ordered his appearance on the lot on Saturday afternoon, to greet touring visitors. He had promised to attend a football game between the undefeated UCLA Bruins and a Northern California team, the St. Mary's Gaels. UCLA invited him to sit on their bench as a mascot. (They lost anyway.) In fact, the game had taken place three months earlier, on Armistice Day, a legal holiday when the studio was closed. Nonetheless, in his mind, the dismissal was a direct result of this game.

Returning to the studio after a three-month rest, Irving Thalberg learned of Keaton's ouster with some annoyance. When he suggested to Mayer that they reinstate Keaton, Mayer said, "Go ahead, argue with me. Show me where I'm wrong." And Thalberg did exactly that, no doubt arguing that Keaton had just gone through a messy divorce on top of severe health problems. Mayer backed down and Thalberg enlisted Eddie Sedgwick to visit Keaton and talk about a reconciliation.

To the amazement of all, Keaton refused. He vowed never to step foot on the MGM lot again until Mayer apologized.

When the smoke cleared, Keaton was history at MGM.

Keaton married Mae again once his divorce became final. Later he would treat the marriage as some terrible accident that had occurred during an extended blackout. Nevertheless, he and Mae and Keaton's Saint Bernard, Elmer, set up housekeeping at 3151 Queensbury Drive in Cheviot Hills, in the cozy Spanish-style cottage he had purchased for $5,000 before his departure from MGM. It was a sturdy six-room house with two bedrooms and two baths, and a backyard full of lemon and orange trees and flowers that bloomed year-round. The rear porch of the house faced the greens of a country club golf course. Barker Brothers, a classy Los Angeles furniture store, did the tasteful interior in Spanish-style furnishings, probably under Mae's supervision.

Keaton may not have felt deep love for his wife, but he certainly needed her, which probably seemed like love at the time. Although he was unemployed, he felt confident there would be job offers from Paramount, Warners, or one of the other big studios. Mae contented herself with running the home and looking after him, assuming the personal valet-type duties that had been the responsibility of Willie Riddle, now with the Southern Pacific Railroad. In due course she took charge of bookkeeping and paying bills. Mae was not crazy about Elmer; she bought herself a puppy. The newlyweds appeared in public for the first time in April at the premiere of *King Kong*. Arriving at Grauman's Chinese Theatre in the sidecar of a motorcycle, Keaton looked natty in tux, top hat, and cane, and Mae dressed in a slinky evening gown with matching shawl and beret.

Her presence did nothing to curb his drinking. Long stretches of restraint were interspersed with periods of desperation and high bingeing. He suffered regular bouts of delirium tremens.

Most of the time Keaton and Mae were alone together. The celebrities who had flocked to the Italian Villa for Sunday barbecues had vanished, along with Joe Schenck, Sam Marx, Sam Goldwyn, and the rest of the high-stakes bridge players. Buster

Buster Keaton as a toddler in Kansas, the state of his birth. His parents were struggling medicine-show actors. *(Harry Ransom Humanities Research Center, the University of Texas at Austin)*

At age five Buster became the star of a successful family act in which his father threw him around the stage. The Three Keatons were known as the roughest act in vaudeville. *(Eleanor Keaton)*

The Keaton children and an aunt on a rare family visit to Myra Keaton's home, in Modale, Iowa, in 1908. *(Eleanor Keaton)*

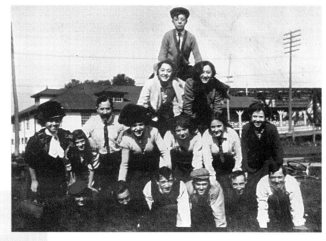

At the Actors' Colony near Muskegon, Michigan, the Keatons' summer home from 1909 to 1920. Buster, Jingles, and Louise would remember those summers as the best times of their lives. *(Eleanor Keaton)*

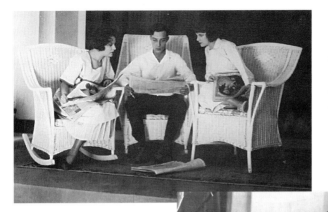

Bachelor Buster relaxing between two of his fun-loving girlfriends, Alice Lake and Viola Dana, 1919. *(Sheila Lanfield Kaufman)*

Harry Houdini *(far right)* visiting the Comique Company in 1919. *Front row:* Roscoe "Fatty" Arbuckle, unidentified woman, Bess Houdini with her husband. *Back row:* Buster and Al St. John. *(Author collection)*

On the Comique set in Long Beach, California, 1918: playful Charlie Chaplin behind camera, company manager Lou Anger with hammer, studio owner Herbert M. Horkheimer, and Buster. *(Author collection)*

More clowning by Chaplin and Keaton in front of the studio. *(From the collection of Joel Goss)*

Buster and Natalie's wedding, May 31, 1921, at Joseph Schenck's home in Bayside, New York. *(From the collection of Marty Davis)*

The newlyweds in a romantic moment, but arguments erupted soon after they returned to Los Angeles. *(From the collection of Marty Davis)*

Ball-and-chain gag photo taken a few weeks after the wedding proved prophetic. Both had trouble adjusting to married life. *(Author collection)*

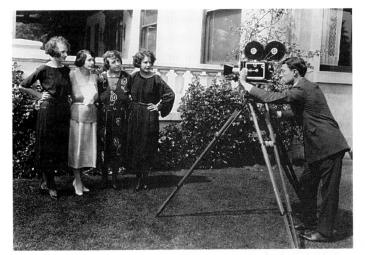

The famous Talmadge sisters: Constance, Natalie, and Norma, with matriarch Peg Talmadge, on the lawn of Keaton's Westmoreland Place home, 1922. *(Author collection)*

Buster holding Joseph Talmadge Keaton, called Jimmy by the Talmadges. *(Melissa Talmadge Cox)*

Buster's newborn son, Joseph, with his Aunt Connie and his parents in 1922. A second son, Robert, would arrive in 1924. Keaton felt increasingly shut out of his children's lives. *(From the collection of Marty Davis)*

Buster the dandy, without his pancake hat and baggy pants. His elegant good looks attracted plenty of women. *(Melissa Talmadge Cox)*

Peg Talmadge and Joseph Schenck flanked by Constance, Natalie, Norma Talmadge Schenck, and family friend Annie Brophy. *(Melissa Talmadge Cox)*

Dinner party at the Roosevelt Hotel attended by silver-screen aristocrats of 1925: the Talmadge sisters, William S. Hart, Douglas Fairbanks and Mary Pickford, Charlie Chaplin, Rudolph Valentino, Joe Schenck, and Buster Keaton. This framed photograph hung on the wall of Keaton's den in Woodland Hills. *(From the collection of Joel Goss)*

With Joe Roberts
and Virginia Fox in
The Blacksmith.

In *Our Hospitality*.

In *Sherlock, Jr.*

Smoking off-camera,
*The Navigator. (From
the collection of Joel
Goss)*

Train wreck, *The General*, 1926—the most expensive shot in silent films.

In *The General*.

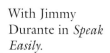

With Jimmy Durante in *Speak Easily*.

In *The Cameraman*.

The Italian Villa, Keaton's ornate Beverly Hills mansion, was a model of movie-star style in the twenties. "It took a lot of pratfalls, my friend, to build this dump," Buster said. *(Museum of Modern Art Film Stills Archive)*

Sailing party at Newport Beach, 1927. *Front row:* Louise Keaton, Myra Keaton, Constance Talmadge, Natalie, Annie Brophy. *Back row:* unidentified, Eddie Brophy, Buster, William Collier, Jr. *(Melissa Talmadge Cox)*

At the Keaton studio in Hollywood with Joe Keaton, unidentified character actor, and Roscoe "Fatty" Arbuckle during filming of Buster's masterpiece, *The General*, 1926. *(From the collection of Joel Goss)*

Edward Sedgwick (in hat and overcoat), MGM comedy director and Buster's dear friend, on the set of *The Cameraman*, 1928. Keaton's first picture for MGM was a hit. *(Edward T. Hutson)*

Clowning with Dorothy Sebastian, his costar in *Spite Marriage* and off-and-on girlfriend for nearly ten years. *(Author collection)*

Jimmy and Bobby Keaton tooling around the grounds of the Italian Villa in one of their father's favorite cars. The yellow and black American Austin Bantam roadster was wrecked in 1931 for a scene in *Parlor, Bedroom and Bath*. *(Melissa Talmadge Cox)*

At MGM, Keaton brought his St. Bernard, Elmer, to work every day and named his dressing room Keaton's Kennel. *(Melissa Talmadge Cox)*

Gag photo of Keaton and his boys waiting forlornly for Natalie to return home in 1932. Alcoholism and infidelity drove her away. *(Author collection)*

Buster with his second wife, Mae Scriven, a nurse he hired in 1932 to help him get sober. She did not succeed. *(Author collection)*

Keaton's famous $10,000 "land yacht," bought after the divorce from Natalie and parked illegally on the MGM lot. *(From the Marty Davis Collection)*

Jimmy and Bobby Keaton with their mother and aunts Norma and Constance. In 1934, Natalie changed the boys' name to Talmadge. *(From the collection of Joel Goss)*

At Columbia, Harry, Louise, and Myra Keaton joined Buster for *Love Nest on Wheels,* a 1937 comedy short. *(From the collection of Joel Goss)*

With Jules White, the head of Columbia's shorts department and one of Buster's least favorite directors. *(Author collection)*

Eleanor Norris, the dancer with beauty-queen good looks who became Buster's third wife in 1940. It was a perfect match. *(Eleanor Keaton)*

Buster and Charlie Chaplin in *Limelight,* 1953, their only screen appearance together. *(From the collection of Joel Goss)*

Youthful Raymond Rohauer in front of the Coronet Theater in Hollywood around the time he first met Buster. *(From the collection of Joel Goss)*

Eleanor and Buster on the set of *Route 66* in 1962. He made hundreds of television appearances in the fifties and sixties. *(Eleanor Keaton)*

Buster in front of the train station in Piqua, Kansas, in the summer of 1964. This unplanned visit to his birthplace lasted about ten minutes. *(Eleanor Keaton)*

On the streets of New York in 1964, Buster with Samuel Beckett and director Alan Schneider for the shooting of *Film,* Beckett's only screenplay. *(From the collection of Joel Goss)*

In Madrid with Jack Gilford and Zero Mostel for the filming of *A Funny Thing Happened on the Way to the Forum* in September 1965. Undiagnosed lung cancer was draining Keaton's vitality. *(Madeline Lee Gilford)*

On location for *The Railrodder,* a 1964 travelogue that followed Buster riding a railway handcar across Canada. *(Courtesy of the National Film Board of Canada)*

With Raymond Rohauer at the 1965 Venice Film Festival, where Keaton, the living legend, received a standing ovation. *(Chris K. Economakis)*

Collier was married. For some time Keaton had been out of touch with Roscoe Arbuckle, who died of a heart attack that June in New York City. Another loss would be Keaton's old friend Lew Cody, who died shortly at the age of fifty. No friends turned up for Keaton's second wedding to Mae.

Never for a moment did Keaton doubt he would find a new job. His last picture, *What! No Beer?*, was a box office smash. Too proud to ask for work, he sat back and waited to be courted. To his shock, people suddenly didn't want to know him.

Not until spring did Keaton receive a piece of good news. Kennedy Productions, a new independent film company that was building a production center in St. Petersburg, Florida, approached him, and by May Keaton had contracted to star in six features at his MGM rate of $3,000 a week. The director was to be Marshall Neilan, who had been a top silent-film director before he succumbed to alcohol, and the script would be written by Lew Lipton, an old friend of Keaton's who had worked on *The Cameraman* and *Spite Marriage*. With a 21,000-square-foot soundstage, the studio would be one of the largest in the country.

The six-picture deal promised steady income, and he would be working with accomplished people whom he knew and trusted. As it happened, both Lipton and Neilan were ex-MGM employees who had gotten on the wrong side of L. B. Mayer. Neilan was famous for the crack: "An empty taxicab drove up and Louis B. Mayer got out."

At the end of May Keaton arrived in Hollywood East by air to begin *The Fisherman*. He held a press conference to announce he was through with Hollywood. In the future, or at least for the next five years, he intended to make his home in Florida. A few days later, Mae and Jingles arrived by car with the dogs. They leased a five-bedroom Spanish-style stucco house facing Tampa Bay. Keaton also set up his own production company, Flamingo Films, with himself as president.

From the outset there were plenty of reasons to feel apprehensive about his new studio. Producer Aubrey Kennedy seemed hopelessly disorganized. Owing to heavy rains, construction of the Weedon's Island soundstage (now down to 10,000 square feet) had fallen a month behind schedule; two other films were being shot either out of doors or in private homes. To top if off, no attempt had been made to find a first-rate technical crew. Keaton also discovered that he did not especially enjoy living in St. Petersburg with its heat, humidity, and mosquitoes. For a month he killed time: He accepted the key to the city; he drew record crowds when he played third base with the Coca-Cola Bottlers; he was guest of honor at a boxing match; he went fishing. In early July he accompanied Neilan and Lipton to Havana to scout locations, but political unrest scared them off. By the end of July construction had completely stopped due to the rain. Keaton was totally disgusted. Since there were ample opportunities for quickies back in Hollywood, he dissolved his production company and kissed St. Petersburg good-bye. All he had to show for nine wasted weeks was $27,000 and some giant mosquito bites. That fall the Internal Revenue Service foreclosed on Kennedy Studio for back taxes and confiscated the soundstage and three completed pictures.

St. Petersburg had turned out to be a mirage on the unemployment desert. Keaton made a halfhearted attempt at a vaudeville comeback before returning to the Coast. At the Hippodrome Theater in Baltimore, he earned $8,000 for a week of appearances. But vaudeville, a dying branch of show business, was not the solution.

Back in Cheviot Hills, he found no job offers. He continued to wait.

Sam Goldwyn's secretary called him one day. Goldwyn was considering a picture about fighter John L. Sullivan and wanted to see Keaton. When he walked into the office of his onetime bridge-playing buddy, Goldwyn stared at him, then shook his head. It was true that a role might be available, but now that he saw Keaton he realized his mistake. "You'd never be able to do it," he said. The scene was so insane that Keaton could not help laughing as he walked out.

Louis B. Mayer's power was so great that a person he blacklisted would never work in the business again. Whether Mayer exercised this power in Keaton's case is impossible to know, but Keaton himself came to believe it. "Mayer gave me such a black eye when he tore up my contract," he recalled bitterly. "He said I was unreliable and drinking. No producer would make me an offer after that."

To prove that there is more than one way to black an eye, in 1933 MGM released a picture about a popular turn-of-the-century vaudeville act, the Three Hacketts, one of whose members winds up in Hollywood as a huge star but comes to ruin. In *Broadway to Hollywood,* Ted Hackett 3rd, a debauched, womanizing drunk, lives in a palatial Beverly Hills mansion not unlike the Italian Villa and causes his studio to lose thousands of dollars by his habitual disappearances. Story editor Sam Marx remembered that the film was nothing more than a bunch of unused footage left over from Harry Rapf's 1931 bomb *March of Time*—"it had nothing to do with Buster." Still, it was a blow to Keaton's career.

In January 1934 he signed a six-picture, $105,000 contract with another fringe independent, only to discover that the company had no money. By now he was terrified. His income had plummeted from $147,300 in his final year at MGM to $47,400 the following year, over half of which had been his payment from the St. Petersburg disaster. In 1934 his income was down to $42,500. Joe Schenck arranged through his brother, Nick, for Joe Keaton to receive an MGM stock contract. This did not mean he actually worked, but in effect it gave him a generous pension of $150 a week, which made him self-supporting. Once a week Joe Keaton appeared at the studio in person to pick up his check.

The Keaton who returned from Florida was a scared, severely depressed man suffering from delirium tremens. Twice he returned to the Keeley Institute for aversion treatments. Each time he would start drinking again shortly after his release. In between trips to Keeley, he knocked off two quickies at Educational Pictures, a Poverty Row studio that could turn out a comedy short in less than a week. Educational was an unofficial burial ground for comedians, including Harry Langdon, Al St. John, Lupino Lane, and Lloyd Hamilton. Arbuckle, too, had once found directing assignments on their low-budget Mermaid and Tuxedo comedies. By now Keaton could not afford to be picky. Ernest Pagano, a former MGM colleague and a writer on *Spite Marriage,* now wrote for Educational and kept telling him that he could probably make a lucrative deal. Keaton sobered himself up and cranked out *The Gold Ghost* and *Allez Oop,* even arranging work for Dorothy Sebastian, who had left MGM and was having a hard time. But there is no comparison between Educational's two-reelers and the ones he had made for Joe Schenck only fifteen years earlier.

*   *   *

In the thirties bankable stars with international followings headed for Europe. In the spring of 1934 Keaton set off for Paris to star in a French comedy. Nero Films was an independent company whose producer, Seymour Nebenzal, was a refugee from Nazi Germany. He offered Keaton a princely $15,000 for two weeks' work, though the deal did not include traveling expenses to Paris. By this point, Keaton was dead broke.

During the divorce settlement, Keaton had managed to conceal precious few assets. He remembered a hidden safe deposit box containing several Liberty bonds he had purchased during his Army service. The cash value was just enough to take Buster and Mae to Paris. In June they boarded a freighter traveling from Los Angeles to Scotland by way of the Panama Canal. Three weeks later they arrived in Glasgow and immediately headed for London, where they stopped for a few days of luxury at the Grand Palace Hotel before continuing on to Paris.

In *The King of the Champs-Élysées* (*Le Roi des Champs-Élysées*), Keaton plays a dual role: an escaped American gangster and an employee in the publicity department of a large Parisian company who rides down the Champs-Elysees in a limousine distributing advertising fliers in the shape of banknotes (and who is fired for giving away real notes). Shot in only twelve days, the picture is fast-paced, and Keaton seems to be in good physical shape. As the gangster, he is energetic and wonderfully acrobatic.

Jean Delannoy, the film's editor, recalled that the biggest problem was Keaton's drinking. Local bars were instructed not to serve him. There is no sign that drinking affected his performance. He was miscast though. In long shots Keaton, thirty-eight, comes across as a lively, physically agile young man, but in some of the close-ups he looks like a middle-aged man masquerading as an adolescent. For the fade-out, director Max Nosseck persuaded Keaton to do something he had fought almost his entire career: smile. It was not a good idea.

Le Roi, dubbed into French and released in limited distribution, did nothing for Keaton's career or Nero Films' bottom line. Not until 1992 would it have its American theatrical premiere.

After completing *Le Roi,* Keaton and Mae stayed on in Paris. According to an affidavit filed by Natalie in Los Angeles Superior Court in September 1935, they were squandering Keaton's earnings by "indulging in extravagant living and expenditures." The delay paid off, because Seymour Nebenzal passed him along to his former office clerk, a thirty-year-old Polish Jew, another fugitive from Hitler, who had formed British and Continental Productions Corporation. In the fifties and sixties Sam Spiegel would produce three Academy Award–winning pictures: *On the Waterfront, The Bridge on the River Kwai,* and *Lawrence of Arabia.* But in 1934 he had never made a film and was grossly underfinanced. He lured Keaton to London with a promise of $12,000, which he did not have. Keaton moved into the Dorchester Hotel and killed time until filming began in early October.

Although Keaton does not receive writing credit, the story was his and so were the gags, recycled from *The Cameraman* and *The Passionate Plumber.* Keaton is Leander Proudfoot, a wealthy American simpleton who sails his yacht, the *Invader,* to a village on the Spanish coast. In a local cantina Leander meets trouble in the shape of a fiery cabaret dancer, played by twenty-three-year-old Mexican actress Lupita Tovar.

Keaton complained about the amateur production, and Spiegel complained about the insobriety of his leading actor. A potentially serious accident took place while they were filming the water scenes in a studio tank. Lupita Tovar fell off a boat and was supposed to be rescued by Keaton. Tovar said that "they didn't tell me that he'd been drinking and his reflexes were not so quick. He tried to get me out of the tank by pulling my legs instead of my head. By the time the crew jumped in to pull us out I had swallowed a great deal of water and my costume was in shreds. Afterward I didn't say a word. I was so grateful to be alive. Except for that one incident, I had a lovely time. Buster was such a sweet, gentle person." Keaton had to have his stomach pumped.

The picture ran a mere sixty-one minutes. Five years later Keaton would compress the story into an eighteen-minute two-reeler, *Pest from the West.* One of Keaton's least successful pictures, *The Invader* failed both in England and in the United States, where it would be released as *An Old Spanish Custom.* Shortly after Keaton and Mae set sail for New York, Sam Spiegel was arrested for forging checks, sentenced to three months' imprisonment, and deported to Mexico. Soon he drifted north to Hollywood. Keaton had been lucky to bring home his $12,000.

After three months abroad, eating well and living in nice

hotels, the return to Cheviot Hills was not cheerful. Keaton has-tened to sign a contract to make a series of two-reelers at Educational Pictures for $5,000 each. He also persuaded Educational to put his family to work. *Palooka from Paducah* would feature Joe, Myra, and Louise, while *Love Nest on Wheels* brought back Keaton's brother as well.

Between 1933 and 1937 Keaton filmed a total of sixteen comedies for Educational. The most perfectly oiled is *Grand Slam Opera* (1936), about a hick who journeys to New York to become a contestant on a radio show based on *Major Bowes Amateur Hour. Variety* called the picture "pretty near good enough to be sold as a baby feature." He continued to play Elmer. Charles Lamont, his director at Educational, was struck by the gulf between Keaton and his character. "Despite that dumb look he was a very smart guy, who had made himself into one of the sensa-tions of the motion picture business."

At this period Keaton seemed confused about what kind of character he ought to be playing. There was no going back to the old Buster, the darling boy who had projected innocence. On the other hand, he had no idea how to be a middle-aged man with a lined brow and thinning hair.

Natalie began dating a number of men, among them Howard Hughes. Her steadiest boyfriend was Larry Kent, an extremely good-looking actor with minimal screen talent. Once her boys were enrolled in boarding school, Nate and Kent lived together at her beach house. Sometimes they took cruises to the Caribbean or vacationed with Connie and her husband, Townsend Netcher, in Palm Springs.

Keaton, returning from England in the fall of 1934, discov-ered that Natalie had not been content to return to using her maiden name. She had obtained a court order that changed Jimmy and Bobby's surnames from Keaton to Talmadge.

Keaton felt crushed. He was confident that the order would be revoked should he appeal. Then he reminded himself that the Talmadges had a great deal of money and someday his boys would be heirs to a fortune. In the end he chose to drop the matter.

By this time the paternal bond had withered. Natalie and her family had never hesitated to express their great anger toward Keaton, which was transferred to Jimmy and Bobby, now ages twelve and ten. Made to reject their father as an act of loyalty to the Talmadges, they found the name change natural. "Maybe it shouldn't have been done," Jimmy said. "But my mother was such a vindictive person. You've got to realize that we weren't close to my father. It was a lot easier to get along in life with the name Talmadge. Everybody knew who Buster Keaton was, but very few knew Talmadge."

In the fall of 1932 Natalie had enrolled the boys in a military school known for its strict discipline and high academic standards. Black-Foxe was a preparatory school for athletes heading for important college teams. The Keaton boys were not athletic though, and Jimmy could never understand why his mother uprooted them from the El Rodeo school and shipped them to military school. Earl Foxe, cofounder of the school, was an old friend of the Talmadges. As a tall, blond, and handsome actor, he had been Norma's leading man in *Panthea,* her first starring vehicle for Joe Schenck. Black-Foxe was popular among prominent movie parents. "In those days it was a posh Hollywood school," said Samuel Goldwyn, Jr., who attended Black-Foxe with Keaton's sons and lived in the same wing of the dorm. "It was a miserable place but very Hollywood. Everybody there was somebody's kid." Among the Talmadges' classmates were Charles Chaplin, Jr., who recalled crying for weeks, and his brother Sydney, Shirley Temple's brother George, and Paul Whiteman, Jr.

To the Keaton boys, who had seldom been required to obey rules, discipline came as a rude shock. Jimmy still regards the school as "a prison. I escaped from there five times, until they finally took us out. The happiest day of my life was when I began public school at Lincoln Junior High in Santa Monica."

Soon after the divorce Keaton had appeared at the school one weekend to take his sons on a camping trip, only to be informed that Natalie had left orders forbidding him any overnight visits. He soon stopped visiting altogether. At school the Talmadge boys never mentioned being the sons of Buster Keaton. "But everyone knew who they were," said a classmate, John Jennings.

While working in France, Keaton had been forced to declare personal bankruptcy, listing liabilities of $303,832 and assets of $12,000. Bankruptcy did not, however, wipe out the $28,000 in back taxes he owed the government, nor did it affect a separation agreement to pay $300 a month child support. Thanks to a kindly

Cheviot Hills Cadillac dealer, his only remaining personal luxury was a new-model car every year.

In the first four years after the divorce, Natalie filed a flood of petitions with superior court: nonpayment of child support, attempts to conceal income, insurance premiums unpaid. The Italian Villa had turned out to be a proverbial white elephant. During the Depression there were no customers for an estate of that size. She was forced to hold on to it until the spring of 1933, when she unloaded it to the dance team of Fanchon and Marco; most of the profit went to clear debts. Her Las Tunas beach house had been attached as security for the unpaid taxes Keaton had promised but failed to pay in 1932 and 1933.

As his income spiraled ever downward, he attempted to have support payments lowered to $100 a month. At the time of the original property agreement, he pointed out, he was earning $150,000 a year under contract, but now he had no regular income. He asked for custody of the boys because his ex-wife, he charged, had never provided a proper home for them but rather stashed them in an expensive boarding school. Should he be granted custody, he said, his sons would go to public schools "for the best interest of said boys."

Natalie took the position that his downfall at MGM had been caused "by the conduct of the defendant." To back up her demand for unpaid child support, she submitted a remarkably accurate rundown of his 1932–1935 earnings, which never dropped below $42,000. Her only income, she claimed, was a $200-a-month trust fund provided by Connie. She drove a 1934 Packard coupe, employed only one maid, and had a small savings account earmarked for her sons' education.

So far as she was concerned, Black-Foxe was the best boys' school in Hollywood and she the better parent. In no sense did she neglect the boys, with whom she spent weekends, holidays, and summer vacations "in the northern part of the state where they can enjoy country life." She neglected to mention that Jimmy and Bobby had been packed off to live for almost a year in Florida with Norma. After finally divorcing Joe Schenck and then breaking up with Gilbert Roland (he later married Constance Bennett), Norma was now living in Palm Beach with her second husband, comedian George Jessel. "We were very close to our aunts," said

Jimmy Talmadge, "closer than to our mother." It seemed to the boys that they were always being sent away.

Eventually, when Keaton had fallen some $4,500 behind in the payments, Natalie attempted to attach his income from Educational Pictures. Keaton screamed to reporters that his ex-wife was a wealthy woman while he had only $2,100 in the bank. Actually, he had earned $42,500 in 1935 while Natalie's income from her trust funds and rental of the beach house totaled only $23,000. "I don't see why that woman has to hound me," Keaton said. "She knows I'm broke. She knows I'm trying to get back in the money again and if I do she knows I'll square everything with her."

In the end, he lost the battle for custody of his boys. He agreed to pay part of his debt to Nate, and he also got his monthly payments reduced to $100, though it is doubtful that he paid even the lesser amount.

After two years of marriage, Mae's charms had petered out and she bored Keaton senseless. Mae had married with golden expectations, but economic realities were getting her down, and now she considered going back to work. Rather than return to nursing, she decided to become a hairstylist and persuaded her husband to stake her the $5,000 for her own business, the Buster Keaton Beauty Parlor, at the Hollywood Knickerbocker Hotel. When he balked at having his name on a beauty shop, she changed it to Mrs. Buster Keaton Beauty Parlor.

Over the Fourth of July, while the couple spent a few days in Santa Barbara, Keaton began to behave with special friendliness toward another guest at the hotel, Leah Clampitt Sewell, a wealthy Los Angeles socialite who had recently made spicy headlines over some kinky sexual adventures. Mrs. Sewell and her husband, millionaire yachtsman Barton Sewell, had been involved in an extremely messy wife-swapping divorce suit. At a Malibu beach party Leah, handcuffed to a bed, had copulated with actor Walter Emerson while her husband bedded Emerson's wife. In Santa Barbara, Leah and Keaton became chummy. On the afternoon of July 4 Mae paid an unannounced visit to Leah Sewell's room and found her and Keaton naked in bed together. Shocked, she sped back to Cheviot Hills, where she waited for Keaton to come home and say he was sorry, so that she could forgive him. Instead, he remained with Sewell at the Santa Barbara Hotel until the end of the week.

He continued to see Sewell. In a reprise of his earlier behavior with Nate, he responded to Mae's questions over his whereabouts by becoming "very abusive and quarrelsome and threatened to use force and violence," she said. After he stayed out all night several times, she moved out and filed suit for divorce on the grounds of adultery. Leah Sewell was named corespondent. Mae slapped Sewell with a $200,000 alienation-of-affections action; Sewell countersued.

This time Keaton responded to the suit. He denied "each and every allegation." Leah Sewell also denied Mae's charges. She was asleep, with her clothes on and other people in the room, she said, when "Buster—just kidding—had made a running jump and landed on the bed by me just as his wife walked in the room. It was just a gag." Besides, Keaton had told her that Mae was in the habit of keeping him sedated with whiskey, or arranging bridge games for him, so that she could sneak out with other men.

Mae was out for blood. Before her departure from Cheviot Hills, she cleaned out the $4,000 in their bank account, divided the silver and china, and as a final spiteful gesture sold Elmer. Keaton hired a private detective, but he could never locate his pet.

Mae became obsessed with divorce. By August she had turned the proceedings into a full-time profession. Her attorney resigned after she drove him nuts with daily visits and phone calls. By the time the case came to court on October 4, Keaton's fortieth birthday, she had to drop Sewell as corespondent and settle for grounds of cruelty. Mae testified to Judge Dudley Valentine that her husband was ice-cold and crabby. "He criticized everything I did and everything that happened, including keeping the car away too long when he wanted to use it." Since he did not appear at the hearing, the decree was granted by default. Afterward Keaton fell into a depression. Bills kept mounting, and now two ex-wives were waiting in line: Mae asking $750 a month alimony and Natalie demanding $3,300 in delinquent child support.

Although Keaton knew that he was well rid of Mae, he had come to depend on her presence. Drinking heavily, he sleepwalked his way through his birthday. His mental state so alarmed Myra that she sent Jingles to watch him. On the afternoon of October 20, Keaton's doctor, John Shuman, decided that he should be hospitalized. Keaton became violent. Restrained in a straitjacket, he was transported to the Veteran's Hospital on Sawtelle Boulevard and admitted to the locked psychiatric ward. His condition was reported to the press as a nervous breakdown following a case of influenza, complicated by domestic and financial problems.

One of his first visitors was Mae. Full of remorse, she sent in a mushy note with the nurse: "Darling, Please tell the nurse when you feel like seeing me. Elmer and I are waiting. Oodles of love, Mae." He refused to see her.

She seemed determined to get her husband back. "I nursed him through a similar collapse three years ago and I can do it again," she said in interviews.

Released from Sawtelle on Halloween, with ten days of sobriety under his belt, Keaton returned home to Cheviot Hills. The first thing he did was to down two double Manhattans. He wanted to prove to himself that he could control his drinking.

Two months later he quit drinking entirely. On Christmas Day, after a round of celebratory drinks, he stared into an empty glass and decided that was the last one.

19 THE LEMON-MERINGUE BLONDE

His life revolved entirely around bridge. On weekends, holidays, days he had no work, he would start playing at 11:00 A.M. and continue until 2:00 in the morning, or whenever people ran out of steam. Then everyone would go home to get a little sleep before starting again.

Once he was abstinent, there was finally time to stop and figure out who he was. He found out that he tended to be a homebody. Occasionally he went out to watch wrestling or for a restaurant meal, but increasingly he preferred the serenity of his home and the company of his new Saint Bernard. His social life centered on his bridge and friends: Clyde and Gladys Bruckman, Harold Goodwin, Lex Neal, his doctor, Jack Shuman, and a few others. Except for Goodwin, most of his companions still drank, some of them heavily, but he managed to maintain his sobriety. As in childhood, his main supports were his family, who had rented out the Victoria Avenue bungalow and moved in with him. Suddenly the house was extremely cramped. Myra and Louise squeezed into the small back bedroom, Buster slept in the front bedroom, and Harry took the living room couch. Harry wrote checks for his brother's bills and shopped for groceries, the same things he had done for his mother.

By 1938, a new regular around the bridge table was Eleanor Ruth Norris, a dancer who worked at MGM and lived with her mother and sister. She was a lemon-meringue beauty, blond and blue-eyed. Buster was immediately enthralled with her.

She was a mere baby, eighteen, looking even younger. The main reason he pretended to disregard her was that he was otherwise engaged. Right after separating from Mae, he had taken up with a Ziegfeld Follies showgirl, Marlyn Stuart, for whom he had obtained parts in several of his Educational shorts. After Marlyn, he had resumed his relationship with Dorothy Sebastian, now divorced. At this point, she had been the only woman in Keaton's life for nearly two years and practically lived at his house.

Movie stars did not impress Eleanor Norris, who was born in Hollywood and raised in show business. Her father was an electrician at Warner Bros. In December 1929, the Christmas before her tenth birthday, he was killed at the studio, in a freak accident while stringing lights for the studio Christmas party.

From an early age, Eleanor showed a talent for dance. She got lessons from her cousin Donna, who once had studied with Pavlova and now operated a dance studio in Palos Verdes.

The Norris family was typical of female-headed Depression households, in which everyone took hard work for granted. An accomplished dancer by the age of fourteen, Eleanor got a chance to visit Mexico City with a dance troupe. Then she joined another dance company, the Six Hollywood Debutantes, and spent twenty-two months in the Far East. She got a chorus job back home at MGM, dancing with the prestigious Albertina Rasch company, and appeared in numerous musicals, including *Rosalie* and *Born to Dance*. By the time she met Keaton in 1938, she had been self-supporting for four years.

From the first day, Keaton impressed her as "quiet, well-mannered, steady, a nice person." She was too young to remember him as a member of the Hollywood aristocracy. The only reason he looked familiar to her was because she used to see him around the studio commissary at lunchtime.

Keaton's house tended to be silent and smoky. What conversation there was generally took place at the bridge table. One day he realized that Eleanor Norris was not the timid young thing he imagined. After somebody criticized her for screwing up a hand, she erupted. Keaton looked up from his hand in amazement. "Lord, there's a person behind the cards," he said.

Suddenly Dorothy Sebastian was gone. Keaton invited Eleanor to a show, and soon he was teaching her how to throw a baseball. One day at MGM he arranged a screening of *Battling Butler*. She left the room understanding how "beautiful" he had once been. "He just bowled her over," said an observer.

Why he should have fallen in love with Eleanor Norris is no mystery. Physically, she resembled his ideal woman, one of those voluptuous, leggy, street-smart chorus girls on whose laps he had snuggled as a little boy in vaudeville. She made it her chief business to accommodate him, catering to his moods and supplying the mothering he had never received from Myra. Above all, they simply got along perfectly.

Although Eleanor was exactly what Keaton needed, his friends seemed reluctant to accept her. Said one of them, "She was a toughie, a pretty sophisticated little lady who had been all over the world and had played the field." She was not like a Talmadge princess, not even a ladylike girl next door. She was working-class, a little too common in her speech and manners for their taste. By the time they realized the relationship was growing serious, they were appalled. Jack Shuman and Pops Freuh, a friend of Keaton's, took her aside and lectured her about marrying Keaton. She was twenty-one, he was forty-four, old enough to be her father. They would never be happy together. Unsaid was the suspicion that she might be another Mae, who they believed had married Buster for his name and money.

In all the world, the person who Keaton would have most liked to forget completely was his second ex-wife. Publicly he said little about Mae, just as he said little about Natalie, but he detested the woman. In his autobiography he refused to mention her name and instead referred to her as "the nurse," as if the relationship had been some hospital romance. The second of his marriages would be written off in less space than he devoted to a 1907 train wreck.

In private, however, he vilified Mae. He contended that she was a prostitute who had masqueraded first as a nurse and then as a hairstylist. Refusing to admit that he had ever loved or even liked her, he insisted that the marriage had been brief and meaningless.

To both the Keaton and the Talmadge families, Mae was never a real wife. Natalie's grandson Jim, who thinks that Mae would today be described as a groupie, remembers that "my grandmother hated my grandfather until her dying day. She could have easily said something about Mae or used something against him. But she never did. Never even acknowledged the woman's existence."

After the divorce Mae never returned to nursing. Throughout the thirties she sought stability in matrimony. First there was Sam

Fuller, a Hollywood publicist, whom she bigamously wed in Tijuana in January 1936, ten months before her divorce became final. By October, when she was finally free to marry Fuller, she had met William Walter Gassert, a Reno man, whom she married in 1937. After that relationship ended in divorce less than two years later, she went back to central California, where she had grown up. In Fresno she soon met a forty-year-old recently divorced butcher, Albert C. Zengel, with whom she eloped to Reno. The Los Angeles *Examiner* announcement gives her name as Jewel Mae Keaton, a first reference to the new first name she would use for the rest of her life. Her marriage to Albert Zengel broke up in less than a year.

All Mae's marriages were reported in the newspapers, since she continued to use Keaton's name and to identify herself as his ex-wife.

Eleanor Norris wanted to be married. Polite to her elders, she hid her indignation when Shuman and Freuh suggested she get lost. "I sat there and agreed," she said. "Then I went and did as I pleased. I had a pretty good idea of what I was getting into." Her sister believed that it was a perfect fit of needs: "She liked to have someone dependent on her, and of course Buster was very dependent. He let her do everything."

Among the last of Keaton's friends to take Eleanor Norris seriously was Dorothy Sebastian. Although still youthful and attractive at thirty-seven, she could not compete physically with a girl almost seventeen years her junior. Keaton wanted to avoid hurting Sebastian, not only because of their long involvement but because he hated emotional scenes of any kind. Perhaps he was hoping that she would be the one to end the affair. He felt reluctant about dating Eleanor until he had "organized Dorothy Sebastian," Eleanor recalls.

In his memoirs, he told how he dug up a new boyfriend for her, a muscular, curly-haired wrestler they had seen at Olympic Stadium. According to Keaton's account, his plotting had a classic screen fade-out, with the couple falling in love and eloping, leaving him free to marry Eleanor with a clear conscience. This story sounds unlikely. Their parting was probably as messy as he had anticipated.

After the war Sebastian married an aircraft technician and died in 1957 at the Motion Picture Hospital in Woodland Hills, only a mile away from where Keaton was then living. By that time she had ceased to exist for him. In 1962, when Louise Brooks mentioned Sebastian's name to him, Keaton stared at her as if she were talking about a complete stranger.

Buster and Eleanor were married downtown on May 29, 1940, in the chambers of Superior Court Judge Edward Brand. They were accompanied by the immediate families—Myra, Joe, Louise, and Harry, and Dot and Jane Norris. The judge at first assumed Keaton was marrying Dot Norris, who was four years his senior. The word *obey* had been omitted from the ceremony, but, he jokingly told the press, his wife's word would be law around the house just the same. The newlyweds departed for a fishing trip at June Lake in the High Sierras.

At first Eleanor's family seemed skeptical of the marriage. "I don't know how madly in love she was," her sister Jane said, "because Eleanor is not the type of person who talks about that sort of thing." Eleanor had been on her own for a half dozen years and would not have appreciated interference. "But none of us thought it would work. Both Mother and I said it wouldn't last six months because Buster had been a drunk and he didn't work that much."

To all outward appearances, Keaton's career during this period had disintegrated. For two years his main source of income had been Educational Pictures, where he got $5,000 for each two-reel comedy short. But in 1937, after filming sixteen comedies, the studio went bankrupt. Keaton suddenly found himself without work. Just a year earlier, his agent, Leo Morrison, had been quietly negotiating with Irving Thalberg so that Keaton might return to MGM. But before they could reach an agreement, Thalberg died. In June 1937, Morrison managed to get Keaton on the MGM payroll, not as an actor but as a comedy consultant troubleshooting for writers or directors. His salary: $100 a week, eventually raised to $350.

The year he met Eleanor, the studio's short-subject department finally put him to work directing three one-reelers: *Life in Sometown, U.S.A.; Hollywood Handicap;* and *Streamlined Swing.* The producer of all three was Louis Lewyn, the husband of Marion Mack and the man whose house Keaton had almost wrecked in 1931.

Another producer who took advantage of his presence on the MGM lot was his old nemesis, Lawrence Weingarten, who asked him to work out routines for *Too Hot to Handle,* a Clark Gable–Myrna Loy comedy about newsreel cameramen. Keaton obliged. He turned out gags from his little office, whiling away his time between assignments by tinkering with erector sets. It would have been impossible to guess that once he had been the comedy king of the lot. Nobody ever heard him weep over his fate. When asked how it felt to be making $300 a week after being as big as almost any star in the business, he replied, "Well, if I'm worth more, they'll pay me more."

The work was not steady. When his contract expired in September 1938, it would be nine months before the studio rehired him as one of eighteen writers working with the Marx Brothers on *At the Circus.*

Some people who knew Keaton in the twenties now thought that his personality had changed. Always basically moody and laconic, he seemed to have fallen into a state of limbo, a kind of soul-sickness. Charles Lamont, his director at Educational Pictures, said that offscreen "he was a pretty dull man. There was no conversation with Buster. And moody. Tremendously moody." By the end of the thirties, however, he lightened up. "By the time I met him in 1939," said a friend, Janet Humble, "he was neither silent nor depressed. He was always laughing, showing those beautiful teeth. I thought it was too bad he had never laughed on-screen, because his laughter was very infectious."

"I think that he thought of himself as a failure," said Trudi Cowlan Maizel, another longtime friend. "All his earlier life, even as a child, he had been a success. Now he was fifty, and what did he have to show for it? Very little. I used to wonder which was the real Buster, the star or the failure."

Having never known the star, Eleanor accepted him completely as he was now. "That happy-boy personality had a lot to do with being a big star and having all the money in the world to play with," she said. "When he divorced and lost all his money, he became more introverted." That she accepted as natural. She thought of her husband as an ordinary man who worked for a living and did the best he could, just like everybody else.

In 1939, after he was seemingly forever cast as a stumblebum drunk in a rumpled suit, his agent managed to secure his first acting role at a major studio in six years. It was at 20th Century-Fox, the studio created in 1935 after Fox Films merged with Twentieth Century. The new shop was controlled by Joe Schenck and Darryl F. Zanuck, but it was not Schenck who brought him in. Keaton's old friend Mal St. Clair, who had once worked for him as codirector on *The Goat* and *The Blacksmith*, asked both Keaton and Mack Sennett to be technical advisers on a feature about silent-comedy days in Hollywood. *Hollywood Cavalcade*, a glossy Technicolor production starring Alice Faye and Don Ameche, put Keaton back in front of the camera, in a nice supporting role as himself. However, the Buster in the script was a Buster who had never appeared on-screen. The man who claimed never to have thrown a custard pie in his career was being portrayed as one of Mack Sennett's protégés, a combination Keystone Kop and Arbuckle pie-slinger. Keaton never utters a word throughout the picture.

Meanwhile his old friend Clyde Bruckman had been writing comedy shorts for Columbia Pictures. In December 1938 he asked his boss to sign Buster Keaton. The head of Columbia's comedy shorts department was one of Keaton's least favorite directors, Jules White, who with Zion Myers had been responsible for *Sidewalks of New York*. White had no hard feelings about Keaton; *Sidewalks* was, after all, his only feature. It was also true that no one of Keaton's caliber had ever appeared in a Columbia short. But the contract was disappointing: only $2,500 for each two-reeler, half of what Keaton had been getting at Educational.

Pest from the West was completed in four days, including location shots of Keaton diving into icy Balboa Bay. Once a Poverty Row studio, Columbia had become a major player that allotted its shorts operation fairly generous budgets. But the quality of these enterprises was slapdash. There was no reason to spend time developing original material since the shorts were freebies given to theaters that happened to be running Columbia features. As a result, only Harry Langdon and Charlie Chase had sunk so low as to labor on the shorts assembly line at Columbia.

Despite flashes of the old Keaton brilliance, the Columbia two-reelers are among the worst of his pictures. Jules White recalled that his stars had no say in choice of material. All they had to do was be on time, learn their lines, and play their scenes. Keaton saw no reason to expend energy or do risky stunts, which is why some of the acrobatics involved back projection and use of a double. Columbia chief Harry Cohn "would give them X number of dollars, and if it wasn't done on Friday, everybody was in trouble," Eleanor Keaton recalled. "Cohn didn't care what got on the screen."

Special effort went into the making of the first picture, *Pest from the West,* in which Keaton remade his 1934 feature *The Invader,* playing a dopey millionaire in pursuit of a fiery señorita. Directed by Del Lord, *Pest from the West* is generally rated as Keaton's best Columbia short. After that, he phoned in his performances. "He was good when he had a chance to be good," said Ed Bernds, Columbia's top sound mixer during the thirties, who worked on *Pest.* "But he was done in by poor story construction and improper use of his talents. White's pace was frantic, but Buster's comedy required a more deliberate pace. Many actors disliked working with Jules because he had a habit of showing actors how to work. It's not surprising that Buster disliked Jules White, who may have tried to show Buster how to be Buster Keaton. Possibly because he was so disenchanted with White, Buster adopted a take-the-money-and-run attitude." Keaton never considered coming up with fresh concepts but merely recycled routines from his silent pictures: *Spite Marriage, Doughboys,* even *The General.* There was nothing extraordinary about the recycling because all film comics did so. It was the key to survival in early Hollywood. The challenge was to do it well.

Even though the Columbia comedies ranged from merely annoying to embarrassing, they proved to be hits with both exhibitors and audiences. In the long run, they benefited Keaton's career by helping him to get acting jobs in features again.

Jimmy Talmadge decided to look up his father. "A friend of mine pushed me, that's all," he said. Fifteen years old, a student at Santa Monica High School, he was not yet old enough to drive. His friend offered to take him to the house and wait while he knocked on the door. By now he had few memories of living at the Italian Villa, even fewer memories of his Keaton relatives. During those years, he recalled, "we didn't see Myra or Joe or Louise. My mother wouldn't have allowed it."

After Jimmy turned sixteen in the summer of 1938 and earned his driver's license, he drove to Cheviot Hills with his younger brother. For Keaton, who had not seen his sons for five years, it was one of "the thrills of my lifetime."

"I didn't tell Mother," Jimmy said. "Hell no." She strictly forbade any contact.

As they became more independent of their mother, their relations with her grew poor. Natalie found it tough to manage two adolescents. Among their classmates at Santa Monica High, Jimmy was said to be the quiet brother, always tinkering with automobiles, while Bobby Talmadge had a reputation as a wild type who rode motorcycles and teased girls. They were known as hard-to-handle kids who were running a little wild.

Keaton's life began falling into orderly routines. Eleanor took over running the house. When they went out he paid for dinners and cabs, but otherwise he let her handle the money.

He had no tolerance for bickering. "We never argued," Eleanor said. "We agreed on practically everything." Which did not mean that there were no storms. As Myra Keaton once remarked, "Eleanor is the sweetest little thing, but when she gets mad we all hunt our corners."

Neither one of them was interested in having children. "I never missed kids," she said. "I figure I'd raised him and that was enough."

"It was a queer household," recalled a friend. "They played cards all night and got up at four in the afternoon."

So many good things happened to Keaton in 1940 that he would always think that was when his luck changed. Having his boys back and a new marriage to a beautiful woman half his age were part of his happiness. At the same time, all this good luck must have made him a bit anxious. After five years of sobriety he began drinking again. In the summer of 1941 he drove East to appear in a summer-stock revival of *The Gorilla,* a comedy written by his old friend Ralph Spence. On the way home in August, Buster and Eleanor detoured up to Muskegon because Keaton wanted to taste Bullhead Pascoe's fried perch again. Driving back to the Coast, he was depressed and started drinking practically the minute they got home. In no time at all, he found himself in heavy weather. The episode surprised Eleanor, who had never seen him drunk.

This time, it was not as noticeable as the suicidal drinking that he had done in the early thirties. His sister-in-law remembered no loss of self-control, no arguments, only nostalgia for the simpler times of vaudeville. He often wanted to sing his favorite songs, over and over again.

It didn't help that he was surrounded by hard drinkers, including his mother (a steady nipper who took her bourbon straight) and Louise (a Saturday-night binger).

Always promising Keaton work was his old boss, Joe Schenck, now president of 20th Century-Fox. Stringing him along, Joe would tell Keaton to call Fox production chief Darryl Zanuck. The Ritz Brothers were going to make a picture; Eddie Cantor's new picture needed a director and Buster's name had come up; he should call Darryl. Keaton was not very good at this sort of thing, but each time he dutifully telephoned Darryl Zanuck. Zanuck never returned his calls. It took a while for him to realize that he would never hear from Zanuck.

Keaton continued to feel affection for his former brother-in-law. He treasured the platinum-and-diamond Cartier pocket watch that Joe had given him in the twenties.

Meanwhile, Schenck was having troubles of his own. In 1941 he was indicted on perjury charges involving 1937 payoffs of $100,000 to Willie Bioff, a West Coast labor racketeer who had been extorting money from the studios. It was an industry-wide scandal, but Schenck willingly took the rap for everyone. He was also facing four counts of income tax evasion. His trial offered the public a rarely opened window into the private life of a Hollywood studio tycoon: the $50,000 pin money kept in a steel box at his office, the hedonistic cruises on his two yachts, the payments to various mistresses, as well as $1,000 a week to Norma Talmadge, and above all the gambling losses. Despite such character witnesses as Irving Berlin, Harpo Marx, and Charlie Chaplin, Schenck was convicted on two counts of income tax evasion and sentenced to serve three years in the Federal Correctional Institute at Danbury, Connecticut.

After furious plea bargaining, the sixty-two-year-old Schenck's sentence was reduced to one year and a day. Only four months later he was paroled and returned to Hollywood.

After the Japanese bombed Pearl Harbor, the studios geared up to produce patriotic films. Both artistically and financially, the forties were to be the least productive decade of Keaton's career.

Throughout most of 1942 he was unemployed. In October Leo Morrison got him rehired by MGM's gag department, but the week-to-week contract offered $100 a week (upped to $250 in 1944) and no job security. A memo in the MGM files described Keaton as being almost destitute, which was not accurate because Eleanor was employed. With only one car and Keaton going to MGM every day, she had to confine her dancing to the studio. Even though his hours did not begin until ten, he drove her to work before seven and then went to the commissary for a leisurely breakfast. She would continue to work until 1953, when television changed the picture business and studios gradually stopped making big musicals. For thirteen years she was a breadwinner in the Keaton household.

After high school Jimmy and Bobby passed up college and went into the service. They joined the Coast Guard and saw action: Bobby lost the lobe of an ear to a sniper. Eleanor's sister Jane enlisted in the Marine Corps and went off to boot camp. Jingles was now married and his wife, Ernestine, a tall, dark young woman, had become another permanent guest at Victoria Avenue. Their son, born on Christmas Day 1941, was named after his father.

In the spring of 1942, Harry and his family and Louise moved to Las Vegas, where they found well-paying work in a magnesium plant. It had taken President Roosevelt *and* Congress *and* a world war to pull Harry loose of Myra's steel apron strings. The war plant was Harry's first real job.

Hollywood was worried about an attack by the Japanese. Keaton was concerned about his mother. When all attempts at persuading her to move to Cheviot Hills failed, Keaton decided to sell his place. For the next fifteen years he and Eleanor lived in Myra's house on Victoria Avenue.

During the war years, Joe Keaton grew senile and had to be moved to a nursing home. He died on January 13, 1946, at the age of seventy-eight, and was buried at Inglewood Park Cemetery in Culver City. His death certificate reports the cause of death as pneumonia due to senile psychosis, a common enough affliction in the elderly but one that made Keaton very uncomfortable. Joe's obituaries said that he had died at home after a long illness. Later, Keaton would tell biographer Rudi Blesh that Joe had been struck by a car and killed.

*   *   *

After the war Harry and Louise returned from Las Vegas. Counting Ernestine and little Jingles, there were now seven people living in the house, and it was getting crowded. Louise took a clerical job, but the rest of the family relied on Eleanor and Buster to bring home the meat and potatoes.

Keaton was still working at MGM as a technical adviser on such Red Skelton pictures as *Merton of the Movies* and *A Southern Yankee,* a retooling of *The General* directed by Keaton's old friend Ed Sedgwick. On the *Southern Yankee* set, Keaton could not help dozing off. Arlene Dahl, who played opposite Red Skelton, said, "Whatever ideas Buster had were given sotto voce, so as not to hurt Red's feelings. He was a quiet presence who always knew what worked and what didn't." Dahl said that "you never would have imagined he was one of the great comedians of all time."

With the end of the war, tired of the whole picture business, Keaton decided to drop out of Hollywood and turn to other sources of income. He would spend part of his time doing live performances in the circus, Broadway musical road shows, summer stock, and later at nightclubs.

In 1947 he made his first appearance at the Cirque Medrano in Paris. Keaton's popularity abroad remained strong, and his Medrano appearances drew fans from all over Europe. One of his skits was a revamped version of the duel scene from *The Passionate Plumber,* another the strenuous drunk-bride routine from *Spite Marriage,* with Eleanor as his partner. An American clown employed at Medrano said, "He was in fantastic physical shape. Every performance the Medrano clowns would hang out in the entrances watching him work. His comedy was completely different from the French clowns. Everyone was in awe of the man."

The Keatons loved working in the circus. His European engagements were also highly lucrative for Keaton, who was paid $1,500 a week at the Medrano, then he sometimes went on to tour Italy or England. Life on the road for four or five months at a time, however, could get boring. When people remarked to Eleanor about how fortunate she was to have a chance to travel, she said, "What difference does it make if you sit in one hotel room and play bridge or you sit in another one?"

Keaton loved fine food and wine. This turned out to be a double-edged sword since Parisians consumed wine like water. He soon developed a taste for ice-cold Calvados. "Buster had elegant tastes in food," recalled family friend Bert Cowlan, "and he was also a gourmet cook."

In Paris, where French law restricted the earnings that foreigners could take out of the country, he and Eleanor lived in regal style at the George V. They discovered a small restaurant, Chez Joseph, which served mouthwatering seafood dishes. Keaton became hooked on Lobster Joseph, a rich concoction floating in butter, cream, brandy, and sherry. When making friends with the owner did not help him learn the recipe, "Buster stole it," Eleanor said. "Every time we'd go there, he would come back to the hotel and write down two or three ingredients, until finally he had the whole thing." Back in the States, he would prepare Lobster Joseph for special guests, even presenting containers to friends traveling to New York on the red-eye, with instructions to "have it for breakfast."

In 1948 Jimmy Talmadge and his wife, Barbara, received a new household toy called a television from his Aunt Norma. "It was the first TV set on our block," he said, "a ten-inch GE that weighed a ton. My dad came over the first weekend we had it. All afternoon he sat mesmerized in front of this thing. Maybe it wasn't the first time he'd seen TV, but it was the first time he'd sat down and actually watched it. At dinner, I remember him saying, 'This is the coming thing in entertainment.' Now this was at the time when Zanuck and many others were saying TV was a fad that would soon disappear."

The first important show to originate on the West Coast was *The Ed Wynn Show,* a live revue mixing variety and comedy. Keaton made his debut on December 8, 1949. He did his so-called Butcher Boy routine, in which he at one point suspends himself in midair after throwing both legs up on a grocery store counter. Hal Kanter, Wynn's head writer, thought that "it was remarkable physical comedy." Wynn's director, Ralph Levy, said, "He did things that would have to be done with trick photography today."

Two weeks later Buster's own show, a half-hour program sponsored by Studebaker, premiered on the CBS local affiliate KTTV. *The Buster Keaton Show* received superb reviews, including coverage in *Life* that marveled at his pratfalls. A regular on the show was Shirley Tegge, a blond beauty queen who had won the Miss USA contest that year. She said, "Buster just winged it. He would be in front of the camera and behind the camera. Twice I remember him arriving tipsy, but he was such a pro that it didn't affect his timing." Unlike other vaudeville greats who had difficulty adjusting to TV and felt terrified about working live, Keaton wasn't concerned about forgetting his lines because most of his comedy routines were silent. But after four months, the pressure of producing a weekly show was excruciating. Never had he imagined the new medium's voracious appetite for material. He was forced to raid his old movies for routines. Eventually he was reduced to repeating routines and varying the backgrounds.

CBS was considering him for a network series, but one night when top decision makers were in the audience he collapsed. "He had a little too much to drink, cut his head, and there was blood," Harold Goodwin reported.

In 1951 he attempted a syndicated weekly series, working on film without a studio audience, but it was canceled after thirteen weeks.

Keaton was then content to do guest shots. During the next seventeen years he would appear on hundreds of shows: dramas (*Playhouse 90, The Twilight Zone*); variety (*Ed Sullivan, Colgate Comedy Hour*), late-night talk shows (Johnny Carson, Steve Allen), and quiz shows (*What's My Line?, I've Got a Secret*), earning an estimated $1.5 million. In 1956 he made his first television commercial for Colgate toothpaste, and after that he continued to work regularly for the biggest advertisers, among them Ford Motor Company, U.S. Steel, Alka Seltzer, and Budweiser beer.

By 1952, bolstered by television guest shots, his income began to climb and eventually hit $90,000. A good deal of his success was due to a new agent, Ben Pearson, to whom he transferred after Leo Morrison retired. The thirty-four-year-old Pearson specialized in representing veteran performers such as Harold Lloyd and Joe E. Brown. There was very little that Pearson offered that Keaton turned down.

By now he looked perhaps a decade older than his actual age. As he advanced into his fifties, the effects of twenty years of drinking caught up with him. The famous face had been described as frozen, stony, and masklike, with a beauty as cool and ethereal as Garbo's. Keaton, unlike Garbo, could never have tolerated the life of a recluse. That meant a continuing struggle with physical deterioration in a medium that insisted on youth and beauty. He accepted screen roles that would have humiliated other stars of his stature, films like *El Moderno Barba Azul,* which film historian Kevin Brownlow would select as probably the worst film ever made. While still physically athletic, his hairline had continued to recede and he had a bald spot, so he took to wearing a hat. Eleanor remembered touching up the bald patch with black shoe polish, then combing his hair over it.

In the summer of 1949 Pearson booked him at $1,000 a week for a summer-stock production of *Three Men on a Horse.* The John Cecil Holm–George Abbott comedy clearly showed that Keaton was far too old to play the Runyonesque character of Erwin Trowbridge.

The Keatons drove to the Berkshire Playhouse in Stockbridge, Massachusetts. At the outset, Keaton had difficulty remembering his lines. But his energy level was high. He played to full houses and glowing reviews. In early July he moved on to Hoboken, New Jersey, where the situation was much different.

In its glory days, the gilt-painted, thousand-seat Rialto theater had been home to some of the greatest acts in vaudeville, among them the Three Keatons. But now the theater looked sad and shabby. Producer Bill Hunt was confident that Hoboken was an ideal spot for a summer theater. New Yorkers, he decided, would love to ride the ferry across the Hudson, dine in the town's great seafood restaurants, and see a show. Opening his season with stripper Margery Hart in *Rain,* Hunt did good business, despite the theater's lack of air-conditioning. He followed Hart with Keaton. "I thought he was the kind of star people would go for," Hunt said. "But in eight performances I grossed $1,100. People thought it was a Keaton movie. There was this huge cavern of a theater with sometimes only twelve people in the audience. Buster was marvelous because he never complained, just gave his all. I followed him with Jackie Coogan in *Room Service,* which grossed $700, and then I folded."

For an athletic man who had always been vain about his body and who regarded his face as his trademark, the loss of his looks must have been difficult. When somebody would recall his youthful elegance, he gobbled up the compliment.

His favorite critic was *Life*'s James Agee, who would write an article about Keaton that September that was instrumental in establishing his place in film history. Agee adored Keaton's films, "the most wonderful comedies ever made." Agee described Keaton's face as ranking with Abraham Lincoln's "as an early American archetype. It was haunting, handsome, almost beautiful." Keaton used these words as the opening lines of his autobiography.

20 KEATON'S ANGELS

In 1948 director Robert Leonard bounded into Keaton's office at MGM brandishing a script. His picture was a musical adaptation of a 1940 Ernst Lubitsch comedy, *The Shop Around the Corner.* Judy Garland and Van Johnson were set to play the embattled lovers. At the climax, Leonard needed an actor to smash a Stradivarius, but it had to look like an accident. Keaton spent the weekend mulling over the problem. On Monday morning he laid out a solution for Leonard.

These days Keaton spent most of his time playing with his erector set, strumming his ukulele, or kibitzing with Ed Sedgwick and Lucille Ball. Along with Pan Berman, Dore Schary, and Gene Kelly, he was a member of the MGM softball team, the Wolves. "Buster usually played third base for us," Kelly recalled. "Even at his age, he was an all-round terrific player." Still, Keaton felt bored. In recent years the studio had changed. It was reeling from competition from television and a number of box office flops that had slashed its production output from fifty-two pictures a year to half that number. So Keaton passed the day socializing with friends. As Gene Kelly remembered, "he would hang around the area circumscribed by the commissary, shoeshine parlor, and barbershop. I used to see him almost every day for a chat."

A few days after his conversation with Bob Leonard about the Stradivarius, the director called to say, "You're gonna be in this picture. So you can break it and I'll know it'll be done right."

The character was an important supporting role. Keaton, who had not rated a credited screen appearance in an MGM picture since 1933, was flabbergasted. In *In the Good Old Summertime* he was to play Hickey, a clumsy, slow-witted clerk in a music store owned by his uncle. At fifty-three, Keaton looked too old to be the boss's nephew. The studio made him up in a wavy strawberry-blond wig and sideburns that succeeded in making him look more silly than youthful. Nonetheless Keaton was overjoyed. He was to get fifth billing after Garland and Johnson, S. Z. Sakall, and Spring Byington. Better yet, he got to write and direct the first meeting of the lovers, the delightful Keatonesque scene when Johnson knocks Garland down with his bicycle, ruins her hat and parasol, then pedals away with her skirt caught in the spokes.

At the end of October, Keaton went on the payroll for this two-week assignment, but as a result of Judy Garland's personal problems, the two weeks became three months. Some actors liked working on Garland films because they could be sure of steady employment, but Keaton hated idleness.

In the Good Old Summertime, released in the summer of 1949, was a hit for MGM, and it put Keaton back into the public eye. It also brought him to the attention of various filmmakers. Billy Wilder was "looking for faces" for a satiric screenplay about Hollywood. Wilder had already cast *Sunset Boulevard* with Gloria Swanson as the aging film legend Norma Desmond and Erich von Stroheim as her adoring butler. Wilder decided to stud his supporting cast with some of those great faces whose disappearance Norma Desmond is heard to lament. In one scene Norma invites friends to her baroque mansion for bridge, a group that the down-on-his-luck screenwriter Joe Willis (William Holden) describes as Norma's waxworks. Anna Q. Nilsson and H. B. Warner were two of the card players. Wilder, a bridge addict himself, asked Keaton to be the fourth.

"When I was a student in Vienna I adored Buster Keaton and had seen every Keaton film," Wilder said. "The beauty was not only that I finally encountered him but that he was also one of the great amateur bridge players. Look, I would have taken him even if he never had played cards. I wanted his face."

When the four old-timers were assembled on the set, Keaton looked at the others, especially Swanson, whom he had not seen since he was married to Natalie, and said, deadpan, "Waxworks is right." Swanson recalled that "we all howled with laughter." In her memoirs, she wrote that Keaton "looked ravaged, as indeed he had been, by alcohol." The bridge game took two days to shoot.

"Just watch what Buster does with the cards," Wilder told the others. "See how he picks them up and holds them, how he takes the tricks." Wilder found Keaton "an absolute delight to work with."

Working with old friends was a lark for Keaton. For his one line—"Pass, pass"—he earned a bundle of money.

At the end of 1951 Keaton received one of his most unusual job offers, a small supporting role in Charlie Chaplin's newest film.

Of Hollywood's Big Three silent comics, only Keaton continued to work steadily. Harold Lloyd, nearing fifty, lived a life of luxurious retirement at his Beverly Hills mansion. Chaplin was so rich that he had made only two films during the previous decade. According to Jerry Epstein, Chaplin's assistant on the film, Chaplin had not thought of Keaton because the part was too small. "But when our production manager told Charlie Buster was hard up, Charlie immediately hired him." Keaton in fact was not hard up—and if he had been the $1,000 salary for three weeks' work would not have been especially helpful. But he jumped at the chance to work with Chaplin for the first—and only—time.

Limelight tells the story of Calvero, once a great music-hall star, now an unemployed drunk who rescues and rehabilitates a young dancer (Claire Bloom) who is thinking of ending her life. Keaton plays Calvero's onetime partner and accompanist. At the climax of the film they perform a musical duet in which Chaplin plays a comic violin solo, accompanied by Keaton as a nearsighted, bespectacled pianist whose sheet music keeps falling onto the stage.

The shooting script delivered to Keaton supplied little information about his character. The pantomime sketch was described as follows: "Then Calvero and his Partner enter and proceed with their musical act. As a climax, Calvero falls into the orchestra pit, playing the violin. His partner frantically beckons to the wings for help." Keaton arrived at the Selznick studios wearing his trademark Buster hat, which prompted a few smiles from the company. "But the moment Charlie explained that neither of them were playing their old characters," Jerry Epstein said, "he completely understood, went to the wardrobe department and emerged wearing the outfit he has on in the film."

Chaplin supplied Keaton a few gags, and Keaton brilliantly improvised the rest. His opening line in the scene is "I never thought we'd come to this."

The *Limelight* company tiptoed around Keaton in awe. He preferred keeping to himself, sitting quietly with Eleanor on camp chairs and waiting until he was called. Actor Norman Lloyd thought his deportment "reticent. It was Chaplin's show." Claire Bloom tried to make friends. One day he showed her a color picture postcard of the Italian Villa, which struck Bloom as "the sort of postcard that tourists pick up in Hollywood drugstores. In the friendliest, most intimate way, he explained to me that it had once been his home. That was it. He retreated back into his silence and never addressed a word to me again."

Among the visitors on the set was James Agee, the *Life* critic. Another visitor, Hollywood syndicated columnist James Bacon, asked why he had done dangerous stunts in his silent comedies when he might have used a stuntman. "Stunt men don't get laughs," Keaton said.

Life photographer Berni Schoenfield recalled that the two comics were "acutely aware of each other. In their conversation with each other, there was strength and honesty." There was also an undercurrent of tension. While the two men avoided reminiscing about the old days, they did converse, sometimes passionately. Evidently Keaton got the impression that Chaplin was regarding him condescendingly, as a man who had let his career go to hell. He had been expecting "a physical and mental wreck," Keaton guessed. "But I was in fine fettle."

Keaton decided to goad Chaplin. "Do you look at television, Charlie?" he asked.

"Good heavens, no," Chaplin replied. He hated the "stinking little screen" so violently that his children were not permitted to watch.

Keaton defended the instrument that revived his career overnight, even going so far as to claim that it was the secret of his good health and boundless energy. The clash over TV was metaphorical: Chaplin the elitist, elegantly scornful of what he considered a mindless medium, opposed by Keaton the populist's infatuation with a new machine. The poet and the mechanic.

Deep in his heart, Keaton felt intense envy of Chaplin. The debate over which one of them was the more gifted only arose after Keaton's death; during his lifetime Chaplin was a genius, Keaton just a comic. Unlike W. C. Fields, who hated Chaplin and ridiculed him as a goddamned ballet dancer, Keaton was careful not to criticize anyone. In an interview he made a show of enthusiasm about working with "the greatest of all comedy directors." On the set, Norman Lloyd said, "they were like two masters who keep a respectful distance; one, rich and flourishing, the other in the shadow of his life, but still a master. Chaplin respected that, and I think he was aware of the historic importance of their teaming together."

After *Limelight,* Keaton sometimes would spout off for reporters with barbed comments labeling Chaplin as an ostentatious phony, sniping at him for being self-indulgent. "Following *The Dictator* was when he got good and lazy," he said. "By the time he'd decide on a subject and make it, it would be three years later."

In both *Sunset Boulevard* and *Limelight* Keaton basically played himself. The now-classic story of Norma Desmond, still looking for her close-ups, could have been a page straight out of his own life. Even though *Sunset Boulevard* was perhaps the best movie about Hollywood ever made, Keaton, who dealt with the pain of looking back by ignoring it, never bothered to see either *Sunset Boulevard* or *Limelight.*

In *Limelight,* Keaton's ravishing performance in a supporting part gave a clue to what he could do with a juicy screen role. Ironically, none were forthcoming. Although he continued to act in television dramas, it would be almost five years before he was offered another feature film.

In the summer of 1954, a theater on La Cienega Boulevard in Hollywood was showing *The General.* Ordinarily Keaton disliked watching himself in silent films because it was "like watching my grandson," he said. But a chance to see a favorite picture on a large screen in a real movie theater did not come along every day. One evening he and Eleanor drove over.

Formerly the home of an experimental acting group founded by Charles Laughton and John Houseman, the Coronet Theater had been taken over by the Society of Cinema Arts in 1950. It showed the work of Sergei Eisenstein, Fritz Lang, and Kenneth Anger, and occasionally the filmmakers themselves would give impromptu talks there.

At the conclusion of *The General,* the Keatons were leaving when a slender young man hurried down from the projection booth. He caught up to them and introduced himself as Raymond Rohauer. He was the Coronet's manager.

Rohauer began talking about the importance of preserving classics from the golden age of cinema. Keaton, who always tended to squirm in such situations, listened politely and looked for the closest avenue of escape.

"I understand you save a lot of old junk," Keaton said, in reference to Rohauer's silent films. "I've got a lot of stuff in my garage if you want to take a look at it."

The very next day Rohauer arrived at Victoria Avenue and began rummaging through cobweb-shrouded cans of film. There were only a few prints—*The Three Ages, College, Sherlock Jr.,* and *The Navigator*—and those had reached an advanced state of deterioration. Until the forties all films had been shot on thirty-five-millimeter stock manufactured with silver nitrate. Nitrate, highly combustible, also decomposed and shrank under the influence of heat, moisture, acids, and time. In 1951 nitrate had been superseded by acetate-based stock, or safety film. Though a movement was under way to rescue some of the old nitrate negatives and prints by transferring them to modern safety stock, the majority of silents, perhaps 80 percent, were crumbling to powder.

Rohauer was racing with excitement. He knew that a few prints of *The General* were still floating around, because they were constantly being pirated (he himself doubtless being one of the pirates), sometimes cut from eight reels to four and released under fake titles. He also recalled having seen clips from a few other Keaton films but never the entire film. Now he had a chance to obtain what nobody else possessed.

"Look," he said to Keaton, "if I save these films, if I transfer them to safety stock and this and that, do we have a deal?" He did not elaborate what he meant by "a deal."

Keaton said, "Sure." But, he added, "I don't own them."

Rohauer let that last remark pass. For the moment, he spoke only of preserving the films.

Rohauer knew surprisingly little about Keaton's work. Very likely the only feature he had seen from start to finish was *The General*. He knew none of the two-reelers. Almost entirely, his familiarity with Keaton came from having seen him as a comedian in lesser movies.

While Rohauer was inspecting the cans, Keaton chain-smoked

and talked about clearing out the garage so that he could set up an electric train set. After nearly sixty years, he was still obsessed with railroads. Opening a can to uncork a foul odor, Rohauer noticed that rust had formed inside the container and the film had hypo, a condition in which the emulsion has eroded. There was danger of explosion. Glancing nervously at Keaton's cigarette, he begged him to put it out before he blew them up.

"No danger, no danger," Keaton rasped.

Of all the films, *The Three Ages* appeared to be in the worst shape. "We've got to do this one immediately," Rohauer said. "This won't last." He suggested taking the film to a lab that very afternoon.

"Okay," Keaton said amiably, taking another drag on his Camel. "If you want to waste your money on it."

Probably Rohauer feared that Keaton might change his mind, because he loaded six cans of film into the trunk of Keaton's Cadillac and took them to the Deluxe General Film Laboratory. Rohauer announced that he wanted to get a dupe negative. When the lab personnel opened up the first can and saw the print was nitrate, Keaton and Rohauer were ordered to leave the premises immediately. What were they trying to do, blow up the place?

"This is Buster Keaton standing there," Rohauer informed the lab manager. "You can't refuse to take the films." The lab manager finally agreed to accept the endangered film.

For several days, Deluxe General worked on *The Three Ages,* which was stuck together and had to be carefully peeled apart and respliced. When it came time to run the film through the printer, the emulsion began to dissolve. The lab claimed its printer had been ruined and presented Rohauer with a bill amounting to $15,000 over and above the processing costs. Rohauer flatly refused to pay. Eventually this dispute was cleared up, but the lab refused to touch any more Buster Keaton nitrates. After that, Rohauer had to go to some lengths to find other labs to do the work.

"He wasn't particularly interested in saving anything," Rohauer said in 1986. "He didn't care." Keaton dispensed a single piece of advice to Rohauer: Stop throwing away money. "But it didn't make any difference what he said," Rohauer said. "I had to do it. It's a compulsion."

Raymond Rohauer and his compulsions were crucial to

Keaton's transformation from a paunchy, weather-beaten comic and a relic from silent films into an icon in screen history. Stan Brakhage, the independent filmmaker, had an opportunity to see Rohauer at close range in the fifties. "You have to give the devil his due," said Brakhage. "With his wild and sometimes vicious love of film, Rohauer did more to preserve meaningful work than any museum in the world." Had it not been for Rohauer and his boundless energy, Keaton would have been lost to a mass audience.

Rohauer could never be called a scholar or a gentleman. Brilliant, greedy, arrogant, spiteful, and devious, he truly had no life beyond business. He boasted about having bribed government officials when unmarked vaults of Chaplin negatives were auctioned for back taxes, which allowed him to bid on and win Chaplin home movies, some of which were pornographic. At the Coronet Theater he rigged the house with concealed microphones, then eavesdropped on his audience, his primary interest being sexual conversation, not film commentary. His fascination with the sadomasochistic was fed by a collection of horror literature and police manuals, including a favorite photograph of what happens to a man with a lit stick of dynamite in his mouth. Stan Brakhage said, "He was a strange man with very kinky habits, one of the weirdest people I've ever met." Larry Austin, owner of the Silent Film Theater in Los Angeles, first met Rohauer in the late forties. "Even then there were people who wanted to kill him." At a Keaton film festival, when the first title to flash on-screen was "Raymond Rohauer Presents," practically the entire audience booed. To the festival director, Rohauer said proudly, "You see, everyone knows who I am."

In a Buffalo winter, on a cold, gray morning when he was nine, maybe ten, he raced about playfully in the snow. A news photographer looking for an interesting storm shot posed him crouched on a bench while the snow blew in milky spirals all around him. On Sunday he was thrilled to find the photo in the rotogravure and his name even mentioned. RAYMOND ROHAUER. It was a first taste of celebrity, his first credit, really, and he was delighted.

Thirty years old at the time he met Keaton, Raymond Rohauer was the son of a seamstress. In the twenties Buffalo was an important transportation center and the Fiebelkorns were a railroad family, German immigrants who repaired railway cars. In 1922 Rose Fiebelkorn met a man—whose name she never revealed—and became pregnant as a result. As was customary in such circumstances, she delivered in a foundling hospital and arranged for the child to be placed in an orphanage. Four months later she changed her mind and fetched Kenneth home to be brought up as a Fiebelkorn. By this time Rose was pregnant again by another man. A second child was born on March 17, 1924, and this time there could be no doubt about the paternity because she named her son after his father—Raymond Rohauer. "There was no marriage either time," said Kenneth Fiebelkorn. "She had both of us out of wedlock."

Rose never married. Her sons grew up in their grandparents' home and never met their fathers. As a teenager, Raymond collected throwaways that film exchanges and exhibitors had consigned to their garbage cans. At theaters, he would beg projectionists for snippets of film they had cut out. Never mind that he could never actually watch the films, since he didn't own a projector. *Watching* was not the point—the pleasure was in the *collecting* and *owning*.

After his brother enlisted in 1942, Raymond dropped out of high school and persuaded his mother to leave Buffalo for palm-fringed Southern California. In Hollywood Rose found a sewing job with a film costume company, while Raymond finished school and worked weekends digging graves at a cemetery.

In 1947 he established a film society in a rented room at the former USO in Hollywood and began screening silent pictures once a week.

Business had always bored Keaton. Leaving his business decisions entirely to Joe Schenck contributed to his downfall, and Keaton now seemed to be turning ostrichlike again. Raymond Rohauer was bright and enthusiastic, but Keaton understood no more about him than he had about Schenck. A few phone calls would have set him straight, but Keaton chose to take Rohauer on faith.

At this point, Keaton's brilliant directing had been virtually forgotten and his masterworks had wound up in garages, sheds, and museums. His grandchildren had only seen him on television. "He was the postman who gets an upset stomach, takes Alka Seltzer, and delivers mail on a motorcycle to a mobile home," said his grandson Jim Talmadge, who was in high school at the time.

Prints of *The General*, *Cops*, and *The Balloonatic* could be rented from or seen at the Museum of Modern Art Film Library in New York. (Also in the MOMA archives, but not for rent, were prints of *Our Hospitality*, *Sherlock Jr.*, *The Navigator*, and *What! No Beer?*) George Eastman House in Rochester had *The General*, *Go West*, and *The Cameraman*, none of them available for rental. In Hollywood a distributor was offering *The Haunted House* and *Roaring Rails*, a four-reel abridgment of *The General*. And that was it.

It took Keaton four years to tie the business knot with Rohauer. In September 1958 they re-formed Buster Keaton Productions. In the twenties, the company's major stockholder had been Joe Schenck; this time the directors would be Keaton, Rohauer, and Rohauer's friend Kristian Chester. According to their agreement, all legal work involved in reviving the company, renewing old copyrights, and establishing clear title to the films would be undertaken by Rohauer at his own expense. In addition, Rohauer agreed to search for negatives and prints so that they could be transferred from nitrate to safety film. In exchange for these services, Keaton agreed to give Rohauer half ownership of the films, plus 50 percent of the profits.

There was another bonus. Whenever and wherever a Buster Keaton picture would be screened, in perpetuity, it would be preceded by the opening credit: "Raymond Rohauer Presents." At last, Rohauer would achieve top billing, with his name plastered on every advertisement, poster, and lobby card, in type equal or larger in size than Keaton's. Not only would he be hailed as Keaton's savior, but their names would be linked forever.

For all practical purposes, Rohauer ran Buster Keaton Productions single-handedly throughout the next ten years. He scoured the entire world for Keaton's films. In France he chased down a print of *The Butcher Boy*, Keaton's very first film with Arbuckle. He found *Good Night, Nurse!* in Denmark and *Daydreams* and *The Frozen North* in Czechoslovakia. Keaton could not even begin to imagine the complicated process of legal clearances. Rohauer claimed that his legal costs alone exceeded $200,000, a figure challenged by his enemies as a gross exaggeration.

Over the years, Rohauer's legal brawls were the subject of fierce gossip among collectors and archivists, who claimed to be horrified by his rip-and-slash tactics. He became increasingly abrasive and paranoid about his rights to films. Even a simple matter like renting a Keaton film from him could turn into a delicate transaction. "He distrusted people but often had grounds for suspicion," said a friend, Jack Dragga. Said Joel Goss, who worked as a writer and researcher for Rohauer during the last years of his life, "Raymond had a clearly defined set of rules. Those who transgressed them found themselves in trouble. His reputation preceded him, and most people now approached him aggressively. He responded in kind." Keaton, aware of Rohauer's reputation, chose to ignore it.

Rohauer was not above bullying Keaton. Stan Brakhage remembers him being deferent but firm. According to Eleanor Keaton, "Raymond knew where to draw the line because Buster would walk out on him if he didn't." Buster often argued, but he never walked away. In the case of *Seven Chances,* for example, complications arose because it had been based on a Broadway play and there were five different copyright holders. Rohauer decided he would pay everyone, but Keaton began to balk. He considered it an extravagant waste of money. Besides, he declared, *Seven Chances* was his worst film. That remark simply floored Rohauer. "It must be done," he sputtered. "It was one of your main features." Keaton was perfectly willing to forget he had ever made *Seven Chances.* In the end, Rohauer got his way and the money was spent. Afterward Keaton refused to look at the picture.

Keaton's rights to his pictures were challenged on all sides. MGM, for example, claimed to own seven of his ten features, including those originally released by Metro. Not true, Rohauer countered, because the films had been produced by Buster Keaton Productions, a company owned by Joe Schenck and other stockholders, and Metro/MGM had only been the distributor. Rohauer decided to go ahead and screen *The Navigator.* MGM promptly sued.

A far more formidable opponent was Leopold Friedman, who argued that it was he who officially controlled the rights to Keaton's films. In the twenties Friedman had been one of Joe Schenck's minions. With the dissolution of Buster Keaton Productions, a years-long process that began around 1939, Friedman had been named one of the two trustees for the purpose of dissolving the company and liquidating its assets. To prevent Rohauer and Keaton from showing *The Navigator* and several other comedies, Friedman got an injunction. It was not until 1970, after years of negotiation and litigation, that Rohauer was able to work out a licensing deal with Friedman. A Keaton film rented from the Rohauer Collection is preceded by the words: "The films of Buster Keaton are shown with the special permission of Leopold Friedman, trustee, and Raymond Rohauer."

In time, all ten features and nineteen shorts would be legally cleared and transferred to safety stock. For the first time in nearly three decades, Keaton began to realize profits from his work.

Through the Italian Villa over the years had come and gone a number of celebrities: the dance team of Fanchon and Marco, Barbara Hutton and Cary Grant, Marlene Dietrich and Jean Gabin, members of the Libby glass family. Just a few yards from the main entrance stood Keaton's tiny cutting room, where work prints had been forgotten during his hasty exodus in 1932 and whose original use remained unknown. Subsequent tenants and their gardeners used it to store wheelbarrows and lawnmowers.

In 1949 the Italian Villa was purchased by James Mason, one of England's best-known movie stars. Seven years passed before Mason and his wife got to poking around in their dirt-floored toolshed and examining a rusting safe. It turned out to be crammed with film. "We were horrified to find Keaton's old films rotting away in there," said Pamela Mason. James Mason began running his favorite Keatons until some of the sprocket holes started snapping. At that point, he decided he must do something about preservation, and he donated some of the Keaton films to the Academy of Motion Picture Arts and Sciences.

Word of Mason's treasure soon got back to Rohauer, who urged Keaton to demand the return of the films. In fact, Keaton did apparently turn up unannounced one day in spring 1956, his first return to the Italian Villa in twenty-four years. The Masons had changed the name of the street from Hartford Way to Pamela Drive. They had also sold most of the land out of economic necessity, and the property had been subdivided. The house that had once overlooked a sweeping emerald lawn and robin's egg-blue swimming pool now looked over a row of ordinary backyards belonging to ordinary Beverly Hills houses. When he rang the bell, a maid informed him that Mason was not at home. Keaton believed that he refused to show his face. "Mason wouldn't come to the door and the maid said I couldn't get the film," he told *New York Post* reporter Jim Cook a few months later. He felt humiliated and called his treatment "a crowning indignity."

For James Mason, Keaton's demand presented a dilemma. Should he return the work or preserve it? Eventually he decided that Keaton did not possess the facilities for preservation and could never derive any financial advantage from having his films anyway. He chose the Academy, but Rohauer subsequently persuaded AMPAS to return the films to Keaton.

Accompanied by Rudi Blesh, Keaton returned to the Villa for films not given to AMPAS. Inside the house he found alterations even more striking than those made to the grounds. Exquisite chandeliers had been replaced. For the Mason children, the original Oriental carpets had been removed and the marble and oakwood floors covered with cork. There was also acoustical tile lining the ceiling of the drawing room, which Pamela Mason used to broadcast a radio show. Dozens of cats roamed freely through the house.

At home, Keaton carried the film cans into the kitchen and unpacked the nitrates as nonchalantly as a bag of groceries. There was a cutting copy of *The General*, as well as a number of Keaton's earlier shorts, including the only print of *The Boat* that would ever be found. As it turned out, *The Boat* was almost beyond redemption. Once he had screened the pictures, he turned them over to Raymond for transfer to safety stock.

Shortly afterward Keaton phoned the Masons to ask if he might bring his wife around to visit. Pamela Mason, embarrassed about the alterations she had made, refused. "I ruined his beautiful house," she said. "But I was young and didn't understand that the place was historical. I was afraid—what if he had told his wife about his grand house and then she walked in and saw the cork. It would have broken his heart." Keaton did not ask a second time.

21 SCHENCK REDUX

Raymond Rohauer kept nagging Keaton to visit Joe Schenck. If the old man knew about the legal fight his executors were waging against Keaton, perhaps he might call off Leopold Friedman.

Schenck's reign had spanned motion picture history from Norma Talmadge and Roscoe Arbuckle to Gregory Peck and Jennifer Jones. Despite his conviction for income tax evasion and the subsequent perjury indictment, Schenck was released from prison and returned to 20th Century-Fox, no longer as chairman of the board but as an executive producer. If anything, imprisonment had enhanced his mythic position in the industry. Now, in his late seventies, Schenck was revered as a pioneer and elder statesman. In 1952 he had received a special Academy Award "for long and distinguished service to the motion picture industry." "All brain and iron," Frank Capra wrote admiringly in his autobiography.

Schenck lived like a Lotus Land Dalai Lama in a showy estate situated on six acres in Holmby Hills. In the living room of his Spanish stucco mansion hung a larger-than-life oil painting of Norma Talmadge. As one of Hollywood's most clubbable hosts, Schenck continued to hold court with his fabled high-stakes poker games, in which the pot sometimes contained $100,000 for a single hand.

As a younger man, paunchy but redolent with the sexy aroma of power, he had gotten along without physical appeal. He had since become impotent. Seeking a miracle cure, he discovered a doctor who had developed an injection designed to restore potency, but the effects lasted no more than a minute or two. Still, a stable of gorgeous women were eager to barter artful fellatio for professional favors. The cream of the movie-starlet crop gathered like deer to a salt lick.

The most memorable of Schenck's women was a plumpish, custard-faced brunette named Norma Jean Baker, whose mother had worked as a film cutter on several Norma Talmadge pictures and named her illegitimate daughter after the actress she considered the most beautiful woman in the world. In 1946, prior to getting a contract at Fox and the new name Marilyn Monroe, Norma Jean lived in Schenck's luxurious guest house, in order to be right there should the miracle shot work. Norma Jean and the impotence doctor synchronized schedules because "this stuff can't wait for a studio limousine to drive me across town," she said. She also entertained attractive young men, whom she regaled with stories of Schenck's condition and the special services required.

In 1957 Schenck had a stroke and lost the power of speech. Confined to bed, his mind eventually unraveled into senility. Throughout this period, Keaton was a frequent visitor at the royal bedside. Sometimes his calls resulted in a handout of few hundred dollars, with Schenck claiming he just happened to sell some long-forgotten asset of Buster Keaton Productions. At such times, Keaton pocketed the money, though he never liked to take anything that didn't belong to him.

Louise Keaton, speaking about her brother's relationship with their father, once remarked that "Buster always thought he owed him a lot." Likewise, Keaton believed he owed Schenck a lot, even though his initial handout back in 1918—sending Joe and Myra $25 a week while Keaton was in the army—had amounted to only some $800, a spit in the wind for a man of his wealth. "He would never say a rotten word about Schenck," recalled James Karen. "Once I blew up and said what was on my mind: 'Look, he made a fortune off you and then he destroyed you!' Buster got up and walked away from me."

By the late fifties, discussion of Keaton's films—or of practically anything—with Joe had become out of the question. Schenck died in his sleep, at the age of eighty-one, in October 1961. At the funeral *Variety* counted four hundred mourners at the Wilshire Boulevard Temple waiting to pay their respects. Among the early arrivals was Keaton. (Although Schenck's will contained numerous bequests, nothing was left to Buster.) To the end, Keaton followed the script he had first written for Schenck in 1917. His ego never permitted him to acknowledge that he had written the wrong character into the wrong movie.

In the years that followed, Keaton was closely involved with Rohauer, who had insinuated himself into his professional life. Even so, Keaton showed little personal interest in him and denied him entree, except as a business flunky, into his life. He did not like his angel very much. Since Rohauer understood this, he was forever trying to ingratiate himself and always failing.

Under the right circumstances, Keaton enjoyed being fussed over. He was delighted when he was recognized by Las Vegas maître d's and escorted to a ringside table. What he did not find comfortable was the adulation of overwrought fans. He mistrusted compliments, which he dismissed as "that genius bullshit." Carol De Luise, a friend of the Keatons, said, "He believed he was an average man." He preferred to simplify events: Filmmaking had been a job. He had done his work and collected his wages, like everybody else. Whenever aficionados began aggrandizing his past life, he was desperate to escape.

"Christ!" he once growled to Jim Karen, "Why do people want to see pictures that were made fifty years ago?"

Like it or not, he found it necessary to meet those people. He would vent his complaints to Rohauer, whom he held responsible for his new fame.

Sensitive to Keaton's feelings, Rohauer was careful never to gush. Inwardly, he remained the world's foremost Keaton fan, and this was obvious to almost everyone. "He got crazy on the subject of Buster," said Eleanor Keaton. "Raymond was a fighter, but he was greedy and grabbed every still and poster he could find. Some of it was trash. But he didn't want anyone else to have it."

Rohauer took pride, understandably, in his efforts to resurrect Keaton's reputation and rescue the films. Long before it became a matter of urgency for the film industry, Rohauer understood the importance of film preservation—and not only because preservation went hand-in-hand with making money. "Raymond's reputation didn't bother me," said Joel Goss. "Because despite all the talk, he was the guy who had worked with Buster to save the films and win his rights back. Others profited but didn't do a thing for Buster."

"It was his one good deed," said Stan Brakhage, "and it was so huge and so offsetting" that Rohauer could be forgiven a great deal.

The more Keaton tried to reduce Raymond to a prop in his life, the more Raymond hungered for his idol's approval, or at least gratitude. "Buster tolerated him," said Jane Kelly. "But as far as liking him, forget it. For one thing, Buster didn't have much use for anyone who didn't play cards."

Rohauer liked to point out that even those closest to Keaton never received verbal thanks. "Eleanor Keaton told me several times that in all the years they'd been married she doesn't remember his ever saying 'I love you' once," Rohauer told Kevin Brownlow and David Gill in a 1986 interview for a documentary on Keaton's life.

Just as meeting Roscoe Arbuckle in 1917 was the pivotal moment in Keaton's artistic life, so encountering Rohauer at the Coronet Theater was the second luckiest. As critic Walter Kerr put it, "Before Rohauer there were no standing ovations at film festivals for Buster Keaton." But Keaton would never give Rohauer credit. Keaton's autobiography does not mention the fact that some of his films could be seen again for the first time in nearly forty years—and that he had one person to thank.

Shortly after the Christmas holidays in 1954, Clyde Bruckman stopped by. He was planning a motor trip to Montana and wanted Buster to loan him one of his guns for protection. Keaton gave him a .45 Colt automatic.

Bruckman then visited Columbia Pictures in the hope that Jules White would give him work on a Three Stooges picture, but the only writing assignment that White had available was promised to another writer.

Bruckman had been sliding downhill professionally for years. It had been more than a year since his last job, an Abbott and Costello picture for which he supplied gags, mostly recalled from Keaton's old films. Though in his glory days he directed two W. C. Fields classics, *The Fatal Glass of Beer* and *The Man on the Flying Trapeze*, now he had a reputation for borrowing freely from earlier films, usually without artistic or legal right. He was sixty, and nobody would hire him.

After borrowing Keaton's Colt automatic, Bruckman returned

home to Santa Monica and dragged through New Year's weekend. On January 4, after typing a note for his wife, he drove to Bess Eiler's Cafe on Wilshire and ordered a meal. When he finished, he went into the men's room and shot himself through the head.

That evening, Santa Monica police called Keaton and described the gun, which appeared to be his. In this way Keaton received word of his friend's death.

Keaton had seen Bruckman regularly. He was in a better position than most to notice ominous signs, so thought Bruckman's family. They believed Buster should not have handed over his pistol; Bruckman's father had also shot and killed himself. Keaton knew this, just as he knew that Bruckman was depressed and drank heavily. Unfortunately, there was nothing unusual about desperate people in Hollywood, where unemployment and alcoholism were facts of life.

Keaton and Bruckman went back thirty-four years. The moon-faced writer-director, the last remaining link to Keaton's old gang at the Keaton Studio, had first joined him in 1923 as "outfielder and writer." In the twenties Bruckman visited his house four or five nights a week to think up gags. At midnight he would troop into the kitchen and sit on the sink while Buster fried hamburgers. In the 1950s Gladys and Clyde Bruckman still came to the house to play cards.

Although Keaton shrank from expressing grief, Bruckman's suicide rattled him.

Keaton had moved into the Victoria Avenue house to ensure the safety of his mother in case of a Japanese invasion. Thirteen years later he remained there, and so did all his relatives. Although Myra was hardly an ideal mother, especially during Keaton's childhood, he always felt close to her and accepted her idiosyncracies as simply part of her personality. After the breakup of his first two marriages, their emotional bond became stronger than ever. His worries about her welfare transcended any family obligations. There was never any question that Myra, seventy-seven, was entitled to his support. It was a different story with Louise and Harry, who were, in the eyes of one family member, "pure parasite," whose attitude basically amounted to "'You're rich. We're not. Take care of us.'"

Louise, in her midforties, had ventured out into the business world. Long ago she had given up hoping for a shining knight. Once she had taken a holiday in Hawaii and met a man in a bar, but the romance, which may have been platonic, lasted only a short time. In the 1930s, while attending Monday-night wrestling matches with Buster and Dorothy Sebastian, she developed a crush on one of the wrestlers, and one evening her brother arranged for the man to fall accidentally into her lap. She had put up with endless teasing about the wrestler, just as she continued to be a good sport when people referred to her as "Buster's spinster sister, Louise."

Louise did clerical work—filing and rudimentary bookkeep-ing—for an insurance company. Harry, who finally managed to shed his unlikely nickname, continued to dream. "He always had some crack-brained scheme, until Buster put his foot down and said no more schemes," said Jimmy Talmadge. The only time he had worked for any extended period was during the war. Since his return from Las Vegas he had been lying around, and now he was fifty and overweight. Perhaps the only one who understood him was Louise. "He always held Buster's coat," she said. In 1948 his wife had left him and taken their seven-year-old son with her. When she remarried, Ernestine, like Natalie Talmadge, changed her son's name. Baby Jingles was growing up as Harry Moore.

Once a week Harry Keaton did the marketing. Eleanor Keaton wrote a blank check to cover the cost of groceries, and Harry would tack on an extra fifteen or twenty dollars for his pocket money.

That summer Buster was itching to hit the road. Since 1947 he spent several months each year in Europe, where his popularity continued strong and the money proved substantial. "He never flew over, but always took the boat," his grandson Jim Talmadge recalled. "It wasn't a fear of flying. Usually he found someone like Charles Goren with whom he could play bridge. He could pay for his whole trip on the crossing."

Keaton refused to return to the Cirque Medrano. In a money dispute the previous year, the owner had impounded the Keatons' luggage. Instead in June he and Eleanor sailed for England, where he was to begin work on a pilot for a television series called *The Adventures of Mr. Pastry,* with Richard Hearne, a popular music-hall comedian. Keaton had agreed to be technical adviser for a series of thirty-nine half-hour shows, in addition to directing and acting in the pilot. Hearne, forty-seven, played a character called Mr. Pastry, an old man who keeps falling down. In contrast, Keaton, at sixty, was to portray a much younger man, the owner of a drama school. As it turned out, he stole nearly every scene in which the two of them appeared, which may have irritated Hearne. Whenever Keaton took a fall, he would respond with a double somersault. To Keaton's keen disappointment the pilot turned out to be a banal, low-budget effort. It was never sold.

All day long Myra Keaton sipped straight bourbon out of a shot glass. Her only real meal was breakfast. Each morning she had a bowl of oatmeal, then ate snacks for lunch and dinner.

By the middle of July, Myra was virtually on a permanent fast. After contracting an infection, her strength began to decline. On Wednesday, July 20, 1955, Harry drove her to Midway Hospital on West San Vicente Boulevard, where the doctors diagnosed pneumonia and malnutrition. The next morning at eight o'clock she died.

Harry took charge of funeral arrangements. Some years earlier, while working as a bartender in San Fernando, he had gotten a bargain deal at a newly opened cemetery. Keaton returned to California to find his mother buried up in Harry's cut-rate plot in the hills above San Fernando. Later he purchased a lovely stone marker adorned with a rose. Eventually both Harry and Louise would be interred in the same grave with their mother.

Myra's sudden departure was not completely unexpected. To Harry, who had not been separated from his mother except briefly during his marriage, the loss was overwhelming. Keaton also was unprepared.

After Myra's death, Keaton decided to liberate himself from the Three Keatons. As year had followed year, he stopped trying to make himself believe that his brother might actually get a steady job. He thought of him as a leech. Mostly for their mother's sake, he had continued to offer his support but now he quickly cut Harry off.

"Either Buster said it or I said it," Eleanor Keaton remembered. "Now we can go out on our own." Never again would they live with Buster's relatives. After fifteen years of marriage, it was time to look after themselves.

*   *   *

Keaton appeared to take his mother's death in stride, but he quietly eased the pain of loss by drinking too much. "A lot of people never knew he was drunk," said his sister-in-law. "He never lost control of himself or his tongue." Nor did his work suffer, but the shadow of alcohol began to hover over his life once more.

That summer of 1955 Ben Pearson had been unusually busy scheduling guest shots for Keaton. Ahead lay a busy fall television season that included appearances on Arthur Murray, Ed Sullivan, and many other top-rated variety shows. He also was offered a number of amusing dramatic parts. One was the *Eddie Cantor Theater*, on which he played a travel agent who never has traveled.

His most important dramatic role that fall was a forgotten star who watches the Academy Awards ceremony on a barroom television set and sees his former partner being honored for all of his achievements. In *The Silent Partner*, produced by Hal Roach, Keaton re-created some of his two-reeler slapstick routines by playing both the elderly and the youthful star. Keaton's acting was fine. However, in long shot he looks like a kid doing acrobatic falls and somersaults, while the close-ups reveal an old man's head on the agile body. The overall effect is quite alarming.

In midautumn he left for a three-week job in the fresh mountain air and wooded tranquillity of Durango, Colorado. *Around the World in 80 Days*, a film version of the Jules Verne novel, is a splashy, star-cluttered $6 million travelogue about a Victorian adventurer who wagers £20,000 that he can circle the globe in eighty days. First-time movie producer Michael Todd showed off Hollywood's latest technological miracle, a glittering sixty-five-millimeter wide-screen process that he had developed in partnership with Joe Schenck.

In Phileas Fogg's sprint across America, Keaton would be a frontier train conductor. His scenes were to be filmed in the Rockies aboard a historic, narrow-gauge railroad running between Durango and Silverton. Keaton said, "I must have been on the screen a minute and a half, and I was three weeks in Colorado on location to do it."

The wily Todd financed *80 Days* as he went along and kept just a step ahead of his creditors. Some people were forced to plead and threaten to extract their salaries, while others had to be

satisfied with barter gifts. Noel Coward got a small Bonnard painting and £100, but Keaton insisted on being paid in cash.

Arriving in Durango, he was pleasantly surprised to learn that he
had been assigned a private trailer, an amenity normally provided for
the expensive talent. Even more remarkable, it looked to Keaton as
if his dressing-room accommodations were every bit as elaborate as
David Niven's and Shirley MacLaine's. Perhaps even more so.
Surely, a mistake had been made and he would be asked to switch.
He decided to seek out Todd and report the mix-up right away.

Todd was as squat, ugly, and bull-necked as a middle-aged
fighter. Frequently hysterical, he hopped around screaming like a
five-year-old. One of his writers on the film, humorist S. J.
Perelman, called him a "psychopathic little bastard" and a "sinister
dwarf."

When Keaton brought the trailer situation to Todd's attention, Todd waved his words away with the Flor de Magnifico cigar
that always protruded from his mouth. "There's no mistake," he
declared. "You're the biggest star in the picture."

Nothing could have been further from the truth, of course.
Twenty-four hours earlier Keaton had rated so low with Todd's
production people that giving him a trailer of any kind had never
even occurred to them and they assigned him an ordinary dressing
room. When Todd heard about it, he raised hell. Like everyone in
a Todd picture, Buster Keaton was entitled to first-class treatment.

The weekend before Thanksgiving, Keaton traveled to Rochester, New York. George Eastman House, an important research
center that owned valuable archives relating to the history of film,
had asked three hundred silent-film actors, directors, and cameramen to choose those who had made the most distinctive contributions to American cinema between 1915 and 1925. Keaton was
selected as one of the ten most distinguished living actors, along
with his former sister-in-law Norma, Charlie Chaplin, Richard
Barthelmess, Ronald Colman, Harold Lloyd, Mary Pickford,
Gloria Swanson, Lillian Gish, and Mae Marsh.

Not every winner planned to attend the awards ceremony.
Chaplin was unable to reenter the U.S., and Norma, practically an
invalid now, sent regrets from Las Vegas. Keaton was determined
to enjoy his sudden elevation to celebrity status and collect his
Eastman Award in person. He considered it more prestigious than
an Oscar, because it was a onetime award.

Mary Pickford, who was to deliver the keynote address, had a well-known drinking problem and was notorious for falling on her face in public. As it turned out, she gave a charming speech and spent the weekend completely sober. The same could not be said for Keaton, though Eleanor was doing her best to keep him in line, and in addition he was suffering from a bad chest cold.

By the time the Rochester weekend ended and Keaton got home to the balmy weather of Los Angeles, it was Thanksgiving. His cold continued to linger, accompanied by painful coughing spasms. One afternoon he began coughing up blood, and Eleanor called his doctor, John Fahey, who prescribed medication and instructed Keaton to go to the hospital if his condition had not improved by 8:00 P.M. The hospital Fahey selected was the Veterans Administration Hospital on Sawtelle Boulevard, which was not particularly convenient to their home but provided excellent free care for veterans.

That evening veins in his esophagus ruptured and he began to hemorrhage. Eleanor drove him to the emergency room at the Veterans Hospital, where he was rushed into surgery. The next morning she was advised to summon Keaton's sons and Harry and Louise, because the doctors could not be sure how much longer he would live—not more than a few days, they estimated. It would be twenty-seven hours before the bleeding could be stopped. On the fifth day he finally showed signs of significant improvement.

22 WOODLAND HILLS

Keaton remained at the VA hospital three weeks. While his hospitalization was widely reported in the press, the details of his illness—particularly any part played by alcohol dependence—were not publicized. *Life* blamed the problem on his recent television appearance in *The Silent Partner,* where Keaton "hurt himself in a re-enactment of an old 2 reeler."

Once he began to rally, "he regained his strength pretty fast," Eleanor Keaton remembered. When Ben Pearson paid a visit, he found his client sitting up in bed listening to a transistor radio, the latest gadget in electronics technology, a gift from Mike Todd. Listening to the radio was a good deal less nerve-racking than listening to Todd, who phoned at all hours. Not even Keaton's brush with death could subdue Todd's habit of juggling three phones at once.

The most important visitor at Keaton's bedside was Robert Smith, a producer at Paramount Pictures. Before Keaton took ill, he had sold Smith the screen rights to his life story. If peddling his life seemed a good idea at the time, he was not the first person to make this mistake.

"Yeah, I made a deal," Keaton admitted to Raymond Rohauer. "I need the money." Rohauer rolled his eyes. "And don't queer it for me," Keaton snapped at him. Rohauer was shocked to learn that Keaton had not obtained script approval.

When Robert Smith and another producer, Sidney Sheldon, had first approached Keaton, he had shrugged. Others before them had shown an interest in his life in recent years. The deals always fell through, which was a fact of life in the picture business.

He didn't expect it would be any different with Smith and Sheldon, who were not major players. As it turned out, Paramount was serious and Pearson was able to negotiate $50,000 from the studio. As rights for biopics went, this figure was not large. Only four years later, Jimmy Durante would be offered $250,000 for his life story, for a Columbia feature to be directed by Frank Capra, but the deal collapsed.

Keaton had always been the hero of his own pictures, and many of his features had been somewhat autobiographical. Paramount didn't love Keaton's real-life story. The real world, even the real world of Hollywood, simply wasn't commercial enough for the screen. That was not a problem because it could be fixed by studio writers. Unbeknownst to Keaton, Paramount already was cooking up a fresh story line for his life.

During his weeks of recuperation at the hospital, staff doctors kept complimenting Keaton on his constitution. This was good news. The bad news was he had to refrain from chili and the other highly seasoned dishes that he loved. And there was a far more alarming prohibition: If he wanted to have a normal life expectancy, he had to stop drinking.

Exactly twenty years earlier, when he could no longer function, he had willed himself to give up alcohol, and remained stone-cold sober for five years. Even though he had resumed drinking during the forties, the problem was under control and now he could go for months without a drink. He understood there was no choice now. He assured the doctor that of course he was going to quit.

Yet Keaton refused to believe everything the doctor had told him. He devised a compromise interpretation of the ban. He placed himself on a strict regimen that allowed him to consume a fixed amount of beer each day, usually a glass or two before dinner.

When Keaton emerged from the hospital after Christmas, he was in good spirits. He felt grateful to be alive. Yet by the end of January, neither working nor drinking, he began to fret. One day Arthur Friedman, a professor from the UCLA Department of Theater Arts, telephoned to request an interview for the university's oral-history program. The purpose of the interview, the professor emphasized, would be "historical, not commercial." Keaton, generally uninterested in both history and academics, seemed reluctant at first. But when he learned that other silent-film figures—Mack Sennett, Harold Lloyd, and Mary Pickford—had already participated in the series, he consented.

Friedman arrived at the house and began setting up his two-track, forty-pound Echotape recorder. Eleanor hovered nervously, worrying that Buster would overtire himself. Keaton happened to be in a talkative mood that day and proceeded to offer a blow-by-blow description of how he made *The Navigator.* To hear him talk, it might have been last week.

Every morning that winter and spring, Keaton turned down tiny Marathon Street and pulled up his dark blue Cadillac at the Paramount gate, the famous wrought-iron gate that Billy Wilder had used in *Sunset Boulevard.* Wherever Keaton went on the lot he was greeted by smiling people, old-time employees who remembered and admired his work.

In addition to selling his story, Keaton had also agreed to serve as technical adviser for *The Buster Keaton Story,* and then to tour after the film's release. As Keaton had guessed, the credit of "technical adviser" was purely honorary. He was prepared to offer advice but soon found it was seldom wanted. At preproduction meetings, a familiar face was Francisco "Chico" Day, assistant director and younger brother of Keaton's old friend Gilbert Roland. Otherwise, the conference room was filled with bright young executives with expensive suits and deep tans, who sat around a walnut table while they deconstructed, and then reconstructed, his life.

The director was Sidney Sheldon, thirty-nine years old, who had been in the business since the early forties—and who would later become rich writing a string of best-selling novels, as well as a hit TV show, *I Dream of Jeannie.* In Hollywood, in the fifties, he was known as a competent writer of routine, moderately successful screenplays, including *The Bachelor and the Bobby Soxer,* for which he won an Oscar in 1947. His initial attempt at direction, *Dream Wife,* in 1953, had turned out poorly, but now the studio had decided to give him another chance.

First Sheldon and his crew tossed around motifs from earlier pictures and attempted to manufacture a workable story structure. Brash kid, desperate to crash movies, tries to sneak by the studio gate, but the guard throws him out. Was there a second act? What's the love story? What turns Buster into a lush? Is there a happy ending? Was it a funny *Lost Weekend* with heart? *A Star Is Born* meets *I'll Cry Tomorrow*, with the spirit of *The Jolson Story? Yankee Doodle Dandy* as a lonely drunk in Bel-Air? How about *The Bachelor and the Bobby Soxer II?* Wouldn't it be better if Buster had been born into a family of circus clowns?

What *was* the hook?

For the female lead, who corresponded to nobody in Keaton's real life, Sheldon wanted to hire one of MGM's biggest contract properties, petite, dark-haired Ann Blyth. The twenty-seven-year-old actress with an operatically trained voice had starred in a string of filmed operettas (*The Student Prince, Kismet, Rose Marie*). In 1945 she had been nominated for an Academy Award as best supporting actress for her role as Joan Crawford's daughter in *Mildred Pierce*. She was tied up with a Van Johnson picture but would be available shortly.

The role of Buster proved harder to cast. The first actor proposed was George Gobel, who was very big in television. An obscure Chicago nightclub comic only a few years earlier, he had become an overnight TV sensation and now had his own network show on NBC. His television character was a charming half-wit named Lonesome George.

It was decided that George Gobel was too old for the part. Others considered were Bob Hope, Danny Kaye, Jerry Lewis, and Red Skelton.

Finally, it came down to Donald O'Connor, a musical star who had danced to teenage prominence in the forties but whose glory days were behind him. His last hit had been *Singin' in the Rain,* released four years earlier. The acrobatic O'Connor did not really fit the role any better than Gobel did. Keaton had been neither dancer nor singer, so O'Connor's abilities in those areas didn't count for much. Physically he was completely wrong for the part of Keaton. In the end, O'Connor would get the part, but he came across like Spam trying to pass for filet mignon, however amiably.

For several months Keaton dutifully attended preproduction meetings. Cowriters Smith and Sheldon talked about making one or two changes in the main character, because the material had to fit the structure—it was a matter of simplifying. In the end, they decided that Keaton's true story wasn't about a man so obsessed with making films that he puts his faith in the wrong people, nor a case of a man walking the Hollywood high wire without a net. It was about a lush and his battle with the bottle, a cliche that Hollywood had been recycling for almost fifty years.

Later Keaton claimed never to have read the script, which was probably true, but he certainly knew what it contained. He had been in the business a long time. By now his knowledge about the corruption of the Hollywood system was encyclopedic. After Sheldon had approved a shooting script for *The Buster Keaton Story*, Keaton could not help noticing that it was a big lie. He decided to play the game, perhaps hoping that, for once, he might beat the system.

All his life Keaton had dreamed of owning a home in the country. His most vivid memory was of visiting his grandparents in Oklahoma. He could remember little about the old people or the town of Perry, only the pleasurable feeling of the land and how he had hated to leave. In later years, after settling in Southern California, his attention turned to the wild, undeveloped country in the San Fernando Valley. Once more he imagined the simplicity of ranch life: a sprawling farmhouse, orange groves, horses and poultry. Marriage had forced him to abandon his fantasy. Natalie, fresh from a Manhattan hotel, would not have been caught dead pioneering in such an isolated place.

Within weeks of receiving the $25,000 payment from Paramount—the first serious money he had seen in a long while—Keaton went shopping with his old friend Harold Goodwin, who had become a realtor. They drove up to the San Fernando Valley, rural and wild in the twenties, now dominated by discount furniture stores and used-car lots. That winter of 1956, Keaton was thrilled to put a down payment on a six-room ranch house, set on one and a half acres in Woodland Hills. Ranch homes, with their low-pitched roofs and airy, open floor plans, were a staple of the production housing boom that followed World War II.

Out back Keaton installed a swimming pool and later built a bunkhouse so that his grandchildren and Eleanor's nephews could spend the night. Behind the house, he would tuck a chicken coop, shaped like a miniature schoolhouse, with a working flagpole. In

the mornings he raised the American flag, then at night he lowered it. "The chickens seem to like it," he explained.

On Easter Sunday 1956, he drove to a section of Beverly Hills
not far from where he had once lived. The road wound past
Chaplin's old estate and Harold Lloyd's Greenacres, all the glittery
showplaces built for, in the words of F. Scott Fitzgerald, "great
emotional moments." At the top of the hill stood Pickfair, "a sad,
overfurnished, and melancholy place," thought David Niven when
he first saw it in 1935, a house of "memories and closed doors."
Twenty years later, Pickfair had drifted even farther from the real
world. After the royal marriage of Douglas Fairbanks and Mary
Pickford ended in 1936, the giddy parties that had symbolized the
twenties receded into memory. Pickford married a curly-haired
actor ten years her junior, Charles "Buddy" Rogers.

America's Sweetheart was now sixty-three. To honor Old
Hollywood, she had decided to host a party, not a classic Pickfair
party of the twenties with its exclusive guest list, but instead a
democratic function to which she invited obscure supporting players and unsung prop people and makeup artists, along with
renowned actors and directors.

Some two hundred guests made their way up Summit Road.
Outside the main gate of the walled estate had congregated a
sprinkling of fans, who were hoping for a glimpse of silent-movie
celebrities. *Life* photographers arrived to cover the historic social
event, "a wistful reunion."

The prospect of seeing old friends excited Keaton. Six months
earlier, at the Eastman Awards debacle, he had been in no condition to talk, but now he was feeling fit and looking forward to a
reunion with people like Harold Lloyd and Francis X. Bushman.
Many of the crowd mingling on the Pickfair lawn seemed to be in
reasonably good health. On an ornate sofa, whispering and giggling, Marion Davies sat with her arms around Hedda Hopper.
Ramon Navarro hammed it up for the *Life* photographers, elaborately kissing Mary Pickford. Some of the guests believed Keaton
to be a pauper. He got his role in *Limelight,* they thought, because
Chaplin took pity on him. Other gossip said that Chaplin had
given him cash handouts, even though Chaplin was the Ebenezer
Scrooge of movie producers. Another person rumored to have
helped Keaton financially was Harold Lloyd, one of the richest

actors in the world and also one of the tightest with a buck. Lloyd continued to think of Keaton as squatting just above the poverty line. "Poor Buster!" he remarked to *New Yorker* writer Brendan Gill. "He was never very good at managing his affairs."

If Keaton always ignored reports of his penury, Ben Pearson took them as a personal affront and wrote a letter to *Variety* stating that since 1947 Keaton had never failed to make less than $25,000 to $90,000 a year. Citing details of his client's income, he announced that Keaton had made more than a hundred television guest shots at an average of $2,000 per show (an exaggeration), hosted his own TV series, and commanded top dollar at Las Vegas. He could afford cash payments for his new Cadillac every year and trips to Europe, where he stayed at such plush hotels as the George V in Paris and the Savoy in London. The tales he heard about his client "made me cry myself to sleep," he wrote.

Instead of the family reunion he had been expecting at Pickfair, Keaton found himself bored and increasingly uncomfortable. He nonetheless circulated and said hello to everyone. "I tried to have fun," he confessed later to Rex Reed, "but I discovered we had nothing to talk about." After the party broke up around eight, he drove home feeling disappointed.

Afterward he would recall that some of the guests had never heard an Elvis Presley record—in fact, he had to explain who Presley was. It was remarkable, he thought, that they made no attempt to keep up with the times.

He felt ready for change. Instead of his usual navy blue Cadillac, his next was a rich tan. In June 1956, he moved into the new house. It had only two bedrooms, one for Buster and Eleanor, the other for guests. The era of the family parasites had drawn to a close at last.

Louise rented a small apartment in a residential hotel on Berendo Street. She would become a frequent visitor to Woodland Hills, where the white chenille-covered bed in the guest room would be heaped with her favorite ceramic dolls.

Harry made no plans. The day before Buster and Eleanor were scheduled to leave Victoria Avenue, he had no place to go. "He stayed there hanging on to the bedpost by his fingernails," said Eleanor Keaton. After the convoy of packers and movers had gone, he hurried to find a furnished room. It must have been a terrible blow to realize that his brother had cut him off. (In his will, Keaton didn't leave him one cent.)

A few months later, Harry left Los Angeles. He wound up on the Mexican border, some twenty miles south of San Diego in San Ysidro, opposite the seedy frontier town of Tijuana. He moved into a motel where he picked up a few dollars tending bar. His son, Harry Moore, recalled, "He had quite a reputation as a fisherman in the area, and he played the horses and dog races." Louise worried about her brother. Whenever people asked for news she gave a stock answer: "He lives in a hotel down there and when you try to call him a Mexican answers who can't speak English." The idea of Harry fending for himself was not reassuring to her.

Production of *The Buster Keaton Story* began on June 12, 1956. Sidney Sheldon said, "I had him there all the time. We got hold of his old films and I had him explain all the routines. Then he helped me set them up so I could shoot them."

Initially, the production generated a good deal of enthusiasm. Some of the crew who remembered Keaton's films felt thrilled to be working with him. There was a stream of visitors, many of them veterans exhilarated by the prospect of a nostalgic look at the old days. Sheldon sometimes burst out laughing during a scene. So did the crew. But not Keaton. Like a statue, he sat on a canvas chair only a few feet away from Sheldon and observed. Whenever Sheldon asked his opinion or brought him some technical problem, he rose respectfully to his feet. "Buster's face looked numb," said Chico Day. "There was always the same expression. Nothing."

On the set, Keaton was aloof. Away from the set, he and Donald O'Connor spent hours in a gym where Keaton tried to teach him routines. Keaton's unique neck-roll tumble was a pratfall that O'Connor could never do. A few of Keaton's trickier falls were not even attempted because O'Connor found them "scary."

Keaton did not watch the dailies. Chico Day sympathized. "By the way a scene was shot he knew what they had and didn't have to look at the footage. That he was not particularly eager to see dailies was obvious."

With Keaton on the set every day, Paramount's publicity department set up interviews for him. United Press International's

Aline Mosby, taking a survey on breasts, asked Keaton to name the five most beautiful sweater girls of all time in the movies. Keaton gritted his teeth and finally selected Billie Dove, Betty Blythe, Olive Thomas, and Barbara La Marr, all of whom had been hot stuff in the twenties, along with Jean Harlow. Mosby kept pressing for an opinion on the bosoms of contemporary beauties such as Gina Lollobrigida ("too big") and Marilyn Monroe ("all right").

Finally, Keaton decided that if Mosby wanted size, he would give her size. He nominated Marie Dressler, a large, matronly character actress with a great shelflike bosom and the proportions of a bookcase. Dressler, he grunted, "had such a veranda she looked like an old Pierce Arrow coming down the street."

During the filming of *The Buster Keaton Story*, Keaton was invited to attend a dinner party at Sidney Sheldon's home. The guest list included studio heads, producers, agents, and a few stars. "There were maybe sixteen people for dinner," said Sheldon. "Buster sat in the corner reading a magazine. He may have been a genius at what he did, but he had absolutely no social graces at all." Despite having just written his "life story," Sheldon did not know Keaton in the slightest and failed to realize that he had always been terribly inadequate in groups, and his deafness didn't help. Talking one-on-one was not a problem, and he also did fine with several people if the spotlight was on himself. But having to make chitchat with a bunch of strangers terrified him.

Sheldon felt certain Keaton did not intend to be rude. "But he had no education. He just didn't know any better. It was shyness more than anything."

If someone spoke to Keaton at parties, or asked him a question, he became chirpy and animated. Otherwise he tended to disconnect from his surroundings. "During other people's conversations he would drift away," said painter Arthur Josephson, who met Keaton at the home of Rudi Blesh during this period. "His wife would lean over and repeat conversation, raising her voice. But if you asked him a question about his work, his memory was astounding. He was like an old prizefighter who remembered what he did in every round."

"It wasn't that he was incapable of socializing," said Chico Day. "He just *didn't care to*. He was never, never awkward, but simply himself, always watching everything that was going on."

*   *   *

In Woodland Hills, the biggest attraction was the Motion Picture Country House and Hospital, a forty-seven-acre institution where the industry took care of its elderly and ill. For quite a few stars a bungalow at Woodland Hills turned out to be their last address. Several of Keaton's former girlfriends—Kathleen Key, Dorothy Sebastian, and later on Viola Dana—would die there. Even though the home was only a mile and half from Keaton's new house, he always dreaded having to visit old acquaintances in decline. As Keaton was probably the only celebrity in Woodland Hills *not* living at the home, the community decided to elect him honorary mayor.

During the years on Victoria Avenue, Keaton had never been a big party-giver. There was no need because the house was always full of people playing cards. Now, due to his move to the valley, death, or resentment, many of his former drinking and card-playing companions stopped coming and were replaced by new and younger people. It was the friends who made the journey to Woodland Hills. Seldom did Keaton travel to see them.

In his den were a pool table and an old black stove. When visitors arrived, Eleanor escorted them to her husband. The TV was always blaring. With age, Keaton's hearing loss had worsened. He tried a hearing aid but could never get used to wearing it. Watching television, however, was no problem. All he had to do was turn up the volume.

Parked at a card table in front of the set, Keaton played solitaire. The arrival of guests failed to move him out of his chair. He kept right on playing. "The man never left his den," laughed his grandson Jim. "He *loved* television. And he watched everything." The appearance of friends never spurred him to turn the set off or lower the volume. They would be simply added to the action. It was not unusual for him to stay up all night when he had no work the next day. As he watched the screen, he would become a director again. When scenes were sloppily edited or actors badly directed, he could barely control his irritation.

"*Cut!*" Jimmy Karen overheard him shouting one evening. "Now move that camera!"

From time to time Ben Pearson stopped in with his new wife, Jean. "What Buster called his den had once been the garage and was a very primitive room," Jean Pearson said. "He'd sit there and the dog'd sit and we'd sit. He would keep one eye on a little black-and-white TV set, the tiniest little thing that just killed your eyes. Once in a while we would ask a question and Buster would answer."

"Buster, who is the best comedian?" she asked one day, tempting him with a tasty subject.

"Lucille Ball," rasped Keaton in his cigarette-and-whiskey voice. He never moved his eyes from the screen. "Her timing is impeccable." That was the end of the conversation.

One way to get close to him, his grandchildren discovered, was at the bridge table. If they played well, he said nothing, but if they were terrible, he told them so in no uncertain terms. Remembered Jim Talmadge, "One time he looked at me after I'd screwed up a hand and said, 'You played that like a fish.'"

He could show an entirely different face. In 1959, while filming *The Adventures of Huckleberry Finn* with twelve-year-old Eddie Hodges, he won over the boy in seconds. "I had had my fill of I-hate-kids types and could smell 'em a mile away," recalled Hodges. "Mr. Keaton treated me as an equal. He was kind and very gentle with this young and thirsty skill of mine."

Keaton had become a commercial spokesperson for Smirnoff vodka. All afternoon he had been posing for an ad at a photographer's studio. Afterward, he joined Eleanor and Ben Pearson at the Picwood Theatre in Westwood to attend a 7:00 P.M. preview of *The Buster Keaton Story.*

The opening title announced, "This is the sad, happy, loving story of one of the immortals of the silent screen." For almost two hours he sat in the film-house dark watching "Buster" drink his way through a bacchanal covering some twenty years of show business. Finally, the lights came up. Ben Pearson said later, "By sheer osmosis, the fumes emanating from the screen as a result of this thorough saturation sent the audience reeling into the night."

Pearson cringed over the mythologization of Keaton's alcoholism, which suggested that he still might have a drinking problem. To Pearson's thinking, this could affect his client getting work. For Keaton, the real trouble did not begin until after *The Buster Keaton Story* was released.

23 FAMILY GHOSTS

To promote the forthcoming biopic, Keaton's appearance was arranged on Ralph Edwards's *This Is Your Life,* a popular television show on which celebrities were "surprised" by relatives and neighbors from their distant past, many of whom they had never much liked in the first place. Keaton's life, scheduled for April 3, 1957, followed "six months of hell" for Eleanor, who had helped Edwards dredge up guests: Louise Dresser, vaudevillian Will "Mush" Rawls from Muskegon, Red Skelton, even Harry Keaton was dragged back from San Ysidro. By the day of the show she was frazzled.

At the NBC studio in Burbank, the camera caught Keaton emerging from an elevator for what he had been led to believe was a business appointment. At the sight of Ralph Edwards, "Buster was dumbfounded," Eleanor Keaton recalled, and clutched his head in panic. His initial embarrassment turned to clear agony. "The little man who never smiled has found a lot to smile about," intoned Ralph Edwards. "Millions of people around the globe to whom you gave blessings, fun, and happy laughter join me in saying, 'Thank you.' This is your life, gifted comedian Buster Keaton." Keaton kept sinking deeper into silence. In the lineup of misty-eyed guests, two appeared even more miserable than Keaton. His sons Jimmy and Bobby, despite their stage fright, had been induced to deliver rehearsed tributes extolling him as "a great guy to us always," as Bobby said grimly. Not once did Keaton's eyes meet those of his brother Harry's.

For a show that didn't pay guests, *This Is Your Life* turned out to be fairly lucrative. Keaton received a keepsake sixteen-millimeter kinescope of the show along with a projector and camera. Other merchandise included a miniature tractor for his yard and a Magnavox color television (color sets were still rare then), which he asked to have delivered with his compliments to the Elks Lodge in Muskegon. For Eleanor, who had been using Green Stamps to furnish her new house in colonial style, the ordeal paid off with "a lot of presents. I furnished my whole damned house in Woodland Hills out of Ralph Edwards. We got a refrigerator, a dishwasher, sets of dishes and crystal, everything imaginable. The gal who was in charge of procuring all that stuff just turned over her list to me, so that I could pick whatever I wanted." And it was only the very best: "real gorgeous, made-to-order china with platinum trim. Those dishes didn't even sell in stores."

Two weeks later, Keaton departed on a coast-to-coast promotional tour that even included a stopover in Perry, Oklahoma. He skirted the subject of the picture's gross inaccuracies whenever possible. In point of fact, *The Buster Keaton Story* embarrassed him. Reviewers roasted the picture. "Apparently pure fiction," decided the *New York Herald Tribune*.

Ironically, for a picture that was so badly received, it still made money. With a production cost of $800,000, Keaton's biopic has earned double, maybe even triple that amount over the years and continues to be aired on television.

Aside from collecting $50,000 for the rights, and thus being able to provide for Eleanor, Keaton's principal interest was saying something about his life without mentioning the name of his first wife. At all costs, he wanted to avoid stirring up the wrath of Natalie Talmadge, who was, said her son Jimmy, "very, very vindictive."

Despite tensions and unspoken resentment on both sides, Keaton and his sons had finally established a semblance of a father-son relationship. Years of hearing their father painted as a monster who had publicly disgraced the Talmadges would live in them like a low-grade infection. As adults, neither son chose to ply the family trade, although given the Talmadge money and the Keaton name they might have launched formidable careers. Shunning the limelight, they looked down their noses at Hollywood and pleaded stage fright and a general distaste for public life. More anti-

Hollywood children would be hard to find. In later years they claimed not to understand why the world made such a fuss about their father.

By this time both Talmadge boys were married. Jimmy had wed his high school sweetheart, Barbara Tichenor, and they had four children: Jim, Michael, Melissa (Missy), and Mark. Bobby and his wife, Patricia, had two boys named Bobby and Tommy. Keaton enjoyed their company. "When they were living on Victoria Avenue," Jimmy said, "we were over there every Sunday afternoon for dinner and bridge."

Jimmy's eldest son, Jim, remembers being baby-sat by Myra, who had a tree with round silver leaves in her room and convinced him it grew silver dollars. "When Grandpa played bridge, he had no use for kids at all, which was fine with me because he always smelled like cigarette smoke," he said.

For family visits, Keaton expected his children to travel to him. Jim Talmadge recalls only a few times in his life when his grandfather visited their house. "On Christmas we would go to their house the day before, or day after, and Eleanor would have gifts from both of them," he said. Whenever he received a silver dollar in his stocking, he knew it came from Myra. Keaton never indulged them with costly toys. "On Christmas Grandpa Buster sent us kids ten pounds of walnuts from his trees," remembered Jimmy's daughter, Melissa. "When we visited him in Woodland Hills we played in the barn and collected eggs from the chicken coop. But I don't remember toys, or hugging or sitting on his lap."

By the fifties, Jimmy was working at 20th Century-Fox as manager of the publicity-stills department. Later he operated a resort on Lake Tahoe. Bobby wanted no part of the movie business. Both sons acquired some of their father's enthusiasms, Bobby for boats and Jimmy as a collector of Duesenbergs—at one time he owned eight—and other classic cars.

From his sons, Keaton could not help hearing snippets of news about the Talmadges. Accordingly, he knew that Natalie's hatred for him continued to burn like an eternal flame. A Roman Catholic, forbidden to divorce and remarry, she apparently considered herself still married to Buster, at least when it suited her purposes. In her view, another union would have constituted bigamy, despite the fact that her sisters had a total of seven marriages between them. She had grown out of the habit of being in the company of the male sex and eventually entered into a virtual self-imposed exile. After her Las Tunas beach house was gutted by fire in 1943, she moved to another beachfront home in Santa Monica, this one owned by Connie.

Now sixty-one, she was bound to Keaton more closely than she had ever been during the marriage. Twenty-five years after the divorce, she would not permit his name to be spoken in her house. Within the family it had become a joke. The grandchildren delighted in deliberately mentioning Buster's name. Natalie would glare and fly into a rage. "She just hated the man to death," said her grandson Jim.

"She never went out or did anything," said Melissa Talmadge Cox. "Her hobby was painting, but she had no social life at all. We thought of her as a little old lady who had never done anything with her life—and who drank." Nate's infrequent outings were usually to see her sisters. The Talmadge Girls had sunk into oblivion. Norma, divorced from George Jessel in 1939, lived in Las Vegas with her third husband, a gynecologist named Carvel James, and a parrot. Afflicted by severe arthritis, she stuffed herself with massive doses of drugs, and walked with a cane. In New York, Connie lived at the Drake Hotel with her fourth husband, Walter Giblin, a Wall Street broker. According to Anita Loos, Connie often seemed to be in an alcoholic fog.

When the sisters visited the Coast, Natalie dressed up and emerged to dine at an upscale restaurant. Otherwise, she tended to drift through the days, gazing at the ocean, chain-smoking, and drinking a quart of whiskey a day.

And so Keaton was not quite sure what to expect of Natalie in the movie about his life. Like God, Sidney Sheldon and Robert Smith had handmade for him a new wife. Her name was Gloria Brent, and "there was not an ounce of truth about her or about anything in the picture," Eleanor Keaton said. "The character played by Ann Blyth was supposed to be half Natalie and half me."

There was one person who disagreed: Mae Keaton.

In the spring of 1941, Mae Scriven Hawley Keaton Gassert Zengel came East to begin a new life. At the age of thirty-six she was a combat veteran of four failed marriages, five if the bigamous alliance with Sam Fuller is counted. She arrived in New York as an aspiring playwright. She changed her name to the more theatrical Jewel Elizabeth Steven and finally to just Jewel Steven. She bleached her hair blond and described herself as "actress, producer, lyric writer, and inventor."

The five plays she wrote reflect Mae's worldview of men and women: her heroes are tall, handsome, and suave; her heroines invariably smartly dressed; the themes are patriotic. While the dramas would certainly never have won any writing prizes, they are unquestionably imaginative and literate. Insofar as is known, her dramas were never published or performed.

One of the leitmotivs of her writing was fear of persecution by malevolent forces. Believing that she had uncovered a narcotics ring peddling dope-filled candy to schoolchildren, she staked out a Queens apartment building, spending the night in the lobby. The next morning tenants called the police. She was picked up—abducted and kidnaped, she insisted—by two cops, who threw her screaming and fighting into a police car and delivered her to Kings County Hospital for observation. The psychiatrists decided she was delusional. After two weeks she was committed to Creedmoor Psychiatric Center, an overcrowded state mental hospital in Queens.

Mae was released into the custody of friends, but in December 1953 she was sent back to Creedmoor, where she would spend the next twenty-two months. There she received more than two dozen shock treatments and later described how she "prepared for death 28 times, as I full expected to be electrocuted each time I went to the shock table. It was a city of the living dead, a Siberia, where I was afraid to speak." To win her freedom, she wrote pleading letters to everyone she knew, including Buster Keaton. He did not answer. Keaton made several trips abroad during the period she was locked up. Even so, it is inconceivable that he would have replied under any circumstances. "Buster told me that he could hardly remember what Mae looked like," remembered Susan Reed.

Leaving Creedmoor in October 1955, Mae was a tired-looking middle-aged woman in desperate need of dental work. She owned scarcely more than the clothes on her back.

In the midfifties, the shadowy side streets of Times Square were honeycombed with cheap theatrical hotels. Their clientele tended to be ex-vaudevillians with their hot plates and scrapbooks full of curling clippings, living cheek by jowl with hookers and assorted transients and eccentrics. One of the grimiest and most picturesque was the Hotel America, where a suite rented for $36 a month and a single room for practically nothing, but toilets were scarce and maid service nonexistent. Mae, grateful to live there cheaply, sometimes defrayed costs by helping out at the front desk.

Mae dreamed of breaking into the film business as an independent producer and set about trying to attract investors for a picture called *Four Guns in Armijo*. It was announced that she would costar in the film with Brian Donlevy, and the enterprise did have some basis in reality. Working with composer-arranger Harold Potter, a man of sixty-seven who had done little since the war, Mae wrote the lyrics for a theme song called "Arms in Armijo" and another song, "No News Is Good News." She tried to conceal her hospitalizations, which she would always treat as bureaucratic mistakes, but word eventually got out and jeopardized her business projects. Later she claimed that she had succumbed to blackmail and paid unnamed extortionists $5,000 to keep her medical history quiet.

For a while she worked at a telephone-answering service, but even the most menial jobs were hard for her to obtain. Because of the missing years in the institution, employment agencies refused to accept her applications. So when *The Buster Keaton Story* opened in the spring of 1957, Mae took it as a personal attack, the last straw of many last straws, and all the more bitter for being completely unexpected. Paramount had included the intimate details of her marriage to Buster, she said, because they figured her to be *non compos mentis* and not likely to complain.

That summer, after release of his biopic, Keaton joined a touring stock company of *Merton of the Movies*, an old George S. Kaufman–Marc Connelly comedy about a country boy who goes to Hollywood in the twenties. It was a play he had always liked. His phone was ringing off the hook because of *The Buster Keaton Story* and *Around the World in 80 Days*, a film that had won the Oscar for best picture of 1956. Those who tracked him down in the Los Angeles telephone directory and dialed his number got a surprise, because it would usually be Keaton himself who picked up the phone. Without saying hello, he would start, "Go ahead." After the caller had explained why he or she was phoning, Keaton would reply "yep," "nope," and then "good-bye"—as efficient as a phone machine that takes thirty-second messages.

Three years later, Keaton would take to the road for seven months with the national company of the hit musical *Once Upon a Mattress* in the role of the king. Eleanor was cast as a member of the chorus. During the first days of rehearsals in New York in August 1960, their relationship caused a few lifted eyebrows. To the dismay of some company members, Keaton and his wife were practically joined at the hip. "She took over," recalled Willy Switkes, Keaton's understudy. "Communicating with Buster directly was difficult because anytime a question was directed to him, he was silent and Eleanor would speak for him."

The first days Keaton kept to himself, but it didn't take long for him to warm up. When director Jack Sydow once addressed him as "Mr. Keaton," he chirped, "Call me Buster. Mr. Keaton is my father."

Keaton soon cast a spell over the youngsters. "The man had an utterly delicious sense of humor," said Fritzi Burr, who played the queen. Those who were expecting a big star with a big ego got a surprise. Keaton's costar, Dody Goodman, said, "Buster was always in the best of humor, always considerate, even-tempered, and sweet. There was never a word of complaint out of his mouth." With a company so much his junior, Keaton tended to be paternal. His dressing-room door always remained open. "There was a big box of chocolates sitting there, and he loved you to come in and help yourself," recalled actor Richard Lyle Thomas.

Moving from city to city by train, Keaton was very much in his element. A hotel suite was just like home—kitchen, bedroom, television, and card table. He would return to his hotel after the show, order beer and sandwiches, then play bridge with John Baylis and other regulars until two or three in the morning. Other nights he prepared meals. His favorite quick entree was gourmet canned chili accompanied by a salad that he ordered from room service. After testing a number of chili brands, he finally settled on Gebhard's, which he ate so frequently that it had to be ordered by the case. When the *Mattress* tour finally reached Los Angeles, he invited the entire company to Woodland Hills for a spaghetti party and wound up entertaining with a glorious medley of vaudeville songs. Another evening he commandeered Raymond Rohauer's Coronet Theater for a movie party and screened *The General*.

Long after the road tours were over, they continued to enrich his life with new friendships. When he moved to Woodland Hills, he lost the regular company of longtime friends. But now for the first time in years he began forming strong connections with actors young enough to be his children, from *Merton* and *Mattress* and other shows. Over the next few years, a tight circle of these young friends would serve as a support network. Unlike Jimmy and Bobby, the newcomers shared his love of performing and generally spoke his language. Keaton's show business friends expressed a ferocious love and admiration for him. "He was like a step-dad to us," said Ruth Earl Silva. Keaton met Ruth and Jane Earl in a Las Vegas nightclub revue and developed a close relationship with the pair of twenty-year-old twin dancers from Iowa. "When we visited we would just do normal family things together," said Ruth. "He'd take us around to the meat market and the hardware store. One Christmas he made bunk beds with little ladders for my cats, Bussie and Ellie."

During the *Merton* tour, he got acquainted with Jane Dulo, a television actress who commuted between the coasts. She would become a family confidante and a frequent visitor. On Sunday afternoons she and her dog would drive up to Woodland Hills. "We'd play bridge all afternoon, then eat dinner and Buster would drink one beer, then we'd play until midnight." He also came to dote on, and treat like a son, young Jim Karen, an actor who lived in New York with his wife, Susan Reed, a well-known singer, and their infant son, Reed. Keaton was crazy about Susie and Jimmy, and their child got the same rough affection his own grandchildren received.

Keaton's new friends were angered by what they perceived as his sons' neglect. "I knew Buster pretty well for ten years," said one of them. "And in all that time I never met Jimmy or Bobby. They had no place in his life. They showed up when he got sick. I think they were a constant disappointment to him. But he never showed any emotion about it, and if anyone said anything about his boys being disloyal, forget it!"

In October 1957, *Merton of the Movies* opened at the Huntington Hartford Theatre in Hollywood. On opening night, many of Keaton's old friends were on hand. "He was hoping his sons would come," recalled Jane Dulo. "It was the only time I ever saw him show concern about who was out front. But they didn't. So when I later met Jimmy I asked when they were coming to the show. 'Oh,' he said, 'I can't afford tickets for all my kids, and if I came without them they'd never speak to me again.' I thought that was a very peculiar thing for a grown man to say. God knows what his mother had said to him about his father. It was very sad."

In the judgment of Keaton's new friends, the boys' chief disloyalty was hanging on to the Talmadge name. "They could have changed their names back to Keaton," one said. "There was nothing to prevent them from going to court and saying that 'we were children who were robbed of a great name.'" They were "pedestrian children who had no get up and go. All of Norma Talmadge's enormous estate went to them, but they piddled the money away. They had no inspiration for living."

On August 28, 1957, while Keaton was on the road with *Merton of the Movies*, Mae Keaton filed a $5 million libel lawsuit against Paramount. *The Buster Keaton Story*, she contended, held her up to ridicule by portraying her as a woman who married Keaton while he was drunk "and that she married him for his name . . . and that Keaton was also of the foregoing opinion." Keaton ignored Mae and her lawsuit.

In the Paramount legal department attorneys were curious to meet the second Mrs. Keaton. When she dropped by their New York office in the fall of 1957, she impressed Marvin Ginksy, a junior attorney working on the case, as a "decent-looking, neatly dressed woman." He had no inkling of Mae's medical history. Then "somebody called us out of the blue," Ginsky recalled. "A person who operated a cigar and news stand in a hotel offered to give us information. Evidently she had worked at the hotel. He began to tell us all about her." From that moment, Ginsky could not help regarding Mae as "disturbed."

Mae's case was ill-advised, and the film company, as so often happens, held all the winning cards. By giving Keaton only one wife, a character who bore no resemblance to anyone, Sidney Sheldon and Robert Smith had erased all semblance of truth. Mae had trouble pinpointing precisely what material constituted the libel.

In 1958 she sold her story to *Confidential*, a scandal magazine. In "I Am Being Blackmailed!" Mae agreed to identify herself as "Ex Mrs. Buster Keaton," instead of Jewel Steven, undoubtedly because the blackmailing of Jewel Steven did not sell magazines. Otherwise, however, she was careful to avoid the subject of her marriage to Keaton, aside from a reference to her lawsuit against Paramount. She revealed in *Confidential* circumstances of her illness, hospitalization, and reentry into society, spelled out in gruesome detail.

The following year, still without a job or prospects, she came forward with a $50 million lawsuit. This time, she sued the state and city of New York for gross negligence on the part of its mental-hospital employees, citing both physical and mental injuries sustained during involuntary incarceration in Creedmoor. It proved no more successful than her case against Paramount Pictures.

Keaton's oldest grandson, Jim, a teenager now, would visit and bring along eight-millimeter home movies with titles like *Gangs, Guns, Gore, and Girls*, which he and his friends had filmed. "We'd go to his house and he'd tell us what we were doing right and wrong. I had no idea Grandpa knew what he was talking about. Nobody said he had been a movie star."

Keaton had a hard time establishing closeness with his grandchildren. "Grandpa was a brilliant, very self-centered man," Jim Talmadge said. "He was concerned with himself. The rest of us didn't really matter that much as long as he could play bridge or solitaire."

Keaton reveled in the attention he was finally getting. Working steadily meant appearances in teenage necking movies, state fairs in Minnesota and Michigan, club dates in Las Vegas, commercials in which he stripped practically to the buff for a bubble bath, and consultant for the Ice Capades. Stanley Kramer cast him as Jimmy the Crook, Spencer Tracy's pal, in *It's a Mad, Mad, Mad, Mad World*. "I wanted Buster for that small role," said producer-director Kramer. "I thought I could work out a special piece of business for him. Well, I never did work it out. But he did. I was delighted, because it was *so* Buster." A longer scene with Tracy was eliminated during the final cut. Keaton didn't care. "He had no artistic ego whatsoever," Eleanor Keaton said. "I would say his personality and ego might be the equivalent of a house painter's."

House painters aren't known for worrying about posterity. Keaton continued to feel exceptionally unhappy about the picture of his life as a sot presented by Paramount. To be sure, he had the studio's money. But now he wanted to set his life story straight with a memoir. He hooked up with Charles Samuels, a veteran writer who had ghosted Ethel Waters's memoir, *My Eye Is on the Sparrow*. Samuels caught up with Keaton in Las Vegas, where he was appearing at the Desert Inn in *Newcomers of 1928*, a musical revue with Paul Whiteman and Rudy Vallee. Taking an apartment in the same building, Samuels interviewed him for weeks on end, not tape-recording but typing very fast as Keaton talked. Generally Keaton put the best face on every story and skated over some of the more unpleasant memories he had confided to a previous writer, Rudi Blesh. Samuels was a professional doing his job, and this "as told to" version of the story would turn out to be far less emotional. *My Wonderful World of Slapstick* was published in January 1960. Keaton seemed pleased with the result, though he never read the book.

Three months later, he was canonized by the picture industry with a special Academy Award for "having made pictures that will play as long as pictures are shown." As Keaton trudged up to receive his Oscar from master of ceremonies Bob Hope, many in the audience rose to their feet. Keaton, who had no idea he was to get an award, was "all choked up," Eleanor recalled. He accepted the statue, murmured "Thank you," and walked slowly back to his seat, without a shadow of a smile.

Modern-day critics knew very little about Keaton's career as an MGM movie star, or how he had managed to survive in the thirties and forties. For these writers, Keaton seemed to be an Old Master intent on demeaning himself, as if he had descended into porn movies.

Since 1928 he had been doing jobs that were offered to him. It wasn't as if he had turned down any great roles. Dumb pictures were just a natural trade-off for a sixty-five-year-old actor determined to keep on working in the Hollywood marketplace. The rest of his silent contemporaries had no third acts in their careers. Most of them did not even achieve second acts.

In the winter of 1962, Keaton traveled to Europe with Raymond Rohauer. In West Germany, Rohauer had planned a gala revival of *The General* and *Cops* and talked Keaton into making personal appearances. Since he disliked conversing with strangers, the trip proved to be an ordeal. Rohauer expected that his star would graciously accept homage. Keaton tried to oblige. At the Cinémathèque Française in Paris, which had put together as complete a retrospective of his work as was possible at the time, Keaton rose to take a bow. At once people began crowding around him. "He had to duck into an alley and throw up," Eleanor said. "He couldn't take the pressure."

In Munich, he stood in front of the theater looking up at the marquee: BUSTER KEATON IN DER GENERAL. Suddenly he heard screams of laughter and turned to Rohauer. "What are they laughing at?"

"Your picture," Rohauer said. "Let's go in and see it."

"Oh no," Keaton said. "I never go and see my own films with an audience. Never." Eleanor accompanied Raymond inside while Keaton went back to the hotel.

Leni Riefenstahl lived with her mother in the Schwabing district of Munich, on the top floor of a five-story postwar building of beige stucco. Her career as Hitler's most prestigious filmmaker had been brilliant but brief, and by 1962, not having worked for many years, she was obliged to live in reduced circumstances.

One day Rohauer visited her and took Keaton along. He wanted to talk business involving the rights to her epic documentaries *Triumph of the Will,* a record of the 1934 Nazi rally at Nuremberg, and *Olympia,* her masterpiece on the 1936 Olympic Games in Berlin and in the opinion of some the best sports film ever made. Bringing Keaton was probably calculated to soften up Riefenstahl, who was furious at Rohauer for renewing the copyright on *Olympia* in his name. It turned out to be a shrewd move. Seeing Keaton at her door was "a complete and delightful surprise for me," Riefenstahl recalled. "I had especially admired him in his film *The General.*"

Riefenstahl, a tall, vigorous, handsome woman of sixty who looked forty-five, invited them to the basement of a neighboring house where she had her cutting room. Unlike Keaton's film archive in his garage among old paint cans and lawnmowers, Riefenstahl kept her work nicely organized. She had thirty-five-millimeter prints of all her films arranged on shelves, and boxes contained her voluminous correspondence and press clippings. The need to talk about her work remained strong, and her memory for details seemed phenomenal: She could rattle off brands of film and color filters and how she had achieved various shots, a tunnel vision similar to Keaton's own. Riefenstahl had not made a film in nearly twenty years, not since the end of the war when she had been incarcerated for three years in various detention centers and prisons. Now Riefenstahl was excited about a forthcoming expedition to the Sudan, where she planned to photograph the Nuba tribespeople.

Afterward, in her apartment for coffee and cake, Riefenstahl passed around scrapbooks containing snapshots of herself with Adolf Hitler and Heinrich Himmler. Rohauer, riveted, began asking questions. What kind of man *was* Hitler anyway? Charismatic, she told him, a very unusual person, a wonderful man. Keaton grunted.

But, Rohauer prompted, what about Joseph Goebbels? She loathed the propaganda minister, Riefenstahl replied. As her indignation swelled, so did her voice. She pounded the pillows on the sofa so hard that Keaton bounced.

Keaton, who had been keeping a straight face as he jiggled up and down, finally glanced at his watch. It was getting late and he wanted to return to the hotel. Rohauer followed him out.

Did Buster catch Riefenstahl's remarks? he asked.

Not a word, Keaton told him and stepped into the lift.

"We only managed to exchange a few words during the stay," Riefenstahl recalled. But she had liked Keaton because he was "a very modest, unassuming, wholly sympathetic man. He spoke very little, and really remained in the background as Rohauer discussed his business matters."

When the customs inspector came through the train at the Canadian border, Bert Lahr turned to Keaton. "Did you bring the cocaine?" The inspector failed to find them amusing, not even after he recognized Keaton, Lahr, and Eddie Foy, Jr.

The three veterans were headed for Toronto to shoot *Ten Girls Ago,* a rock and roll comedy spoofing television. The story was about an ex-vaudeville headliner (Lahr) turned TV variety host who is topped in the ratings by a sitcom starring a basset hound.

The three on the train knew that the screenplay stank. But the money was good, and none of them had been offered a starring picture role in a long while. "They seemed ancient to me," said pop idol Dion DiMucci. "They struck me as three enormously insecure guys. Only Keaton was friendly. We used to shoot a little pool, but the others paid no attention to me. Foy was in another world, and once I saw him duck behind the set and throw up. Lahr was always trying to upstage everyone. But Buster was sweet and quiet."

Although the crew did include a few first-rate people—cinematographer Lee Garmes had worked on *Gone With the Wind*—there was no getting around the insipid script and incompetent direction. In no time Keaton was directing his own scenes. Bert Lahr, recalled cowriter-lyricist Diane Lampert, "would knock at my door at three in the morning and say, 'Do you think Buster should have so many lines?' Your budget-breaker was Eddie Foy, a horrendous problem because he couldn't remember a line." What is more, the three old-timers constantly bickered among themselves.

After a month, *Ten Girls Ago* ran out of money. Shooting stopped several times. Finally, the stars left Toronto without their final week's pay, and *Ten Girls Ago* was abandoned.

Keaton's next job was on the television show *Candid Camera*. Disguised in a toupee, he is eating breakfast at a diner counter. He spills coffee on a sandwich and wrings it out, then drops a pepper shaker into his soup. He sneezes, and his toupee also flies into the bowl. Keaton retrieves the toupee. After wringing it out, he slaps it back on his head. In one take he did gag after gag, recalled producer Allen Funt. It was Keaton's most hilarious TV guest shot.

At home again, Keaton found bliss in his rituals of cards, television, and cold draft Michelob from the keg he kept in his den. He never bothered to dress up but wore chinos and comfortable knit sport shirts. His daily routine was to sleep until nine, then go out back to his garden and chicken coop. At around eleven, Eleanor would prepare him brunch: bacon and eggs, scrapple, or sometimes chipped beef on toast. His only other meal would be dinner, and afterward he usually lay down for a half-hour nap. "Then he would be good until midnight," she recalled.

In recent years Keaton had developed a wheezy smoker's cough that left him gasping for breath. His doctors diagnosed bronchitis and suggested that he stop smoking. He promised to try. Once Donald O'Connor came to visit. He said Keaton "had a little train that went around inside the garage. So when I walked in he had just taken a puff of his cigarette and he put it on the train." Each time the train completed a circuit, Keaton would bring it to a stop and take another puff on his Camel. "That was his idea of giving up smoking." Chatting with Keaton in the spring of 1963, Brendan Gill found the sound of his racking cough "terrifying. He was just a wreck."

By fall, Keaton's card table was littered with bottles of cough medicine and bags of hard candy. Sometimes the coughing spells were an inconvenience. He was eager to go to the Hollywood premiere of *It's a Mad, Mad, Mad, Mad World,* but Eleanor took a dim view. What if he began coughing? What if they had to leave in the middle?

"We have aisle seats," he said. They attended the premiere and the party afterward, with no problems.

24 BOTTOM OF THE NINTH

He was at his favorite New York hotel, the St. Moritz—on the twentieth floor facing the park—trying to watch a ball game on WPIX television and sip a can of beer. Now that the Giants and the Dodgers, his pet New York clubs, had abandoned the city, he mostly watched the Yankees, or whomever. He was not particular.

But now he was distracted because visitors wanted to talk. One of them was a fifty-eight-year-old Irish playwright with a leathery face, the other a Broadway director who had made a special trip to Woodland Hills a few months earlier to meet him. The director was a high-strung man who had not impressed him, at least not after he wondered aloud why Keaton was playing four-handed poker by himself. When Keaton answered tongue in cheek that it was an imaginary game with the likes of Irving Thalberg and Nick Schenck and had been going on since 1927, Alan Schneider failed to laugh. Keaton explained that Thalberg owed him over $2 million. Schneider still didn't crack a smile.

At the St. Moritz, Schneider recalled asking Keaton, "Did you have any questions about anything in the script, Buster?"

"No." He wanted the money: $5,000 for three weeks' work. As for the picture, its market would be limited to art houses in Albania and Bulgaria, as Ben Pearson had once wisecracked about *Limelight*. Keaton did not imagine this pretentious film would do well even in those countries. Privately, he and Eleanor referred to it as "the art picture."

Schneider said, "What did you think about the film when you first read it?"

"Well . . . " He paused, as if searching for the right words. In his opinion, the twenty-one-page script that the Irishman had cooked up was hopeless. And despite his forty-seven years in the business, he hadn't the slightest idea how to fix it. He kept his eyes glued to the television screen.

Then Samuel Beckett tried talking to him but concluded that Keaton wasn't listening, which may have been in part true because his hearing loss had grown worse. "It was no good," recalled the author of *Waiting for Godot, Endgame,* and *Krapp's Last Tape* in a 1986 interview with Kevin Brownlow. "He was absent. He didn't even offer us a drink, not because he was being unfriendly but because it never occurred to him."

Initially Keaton was flattered when he was approached by the legendary Irish writer. Not only would it be Beckett's first and only work for the screen, but it was to be directed by prominent Broadway director Alan Schneider, whose hits had included Edward Albee's *Who's Afraid of Virginia Woolf?* Samuel Beckett had given his movie a generic title, *Film.* A twenty-two-minute black-and-white virtually silent picture (except for one character who whispers "Shhhh") without music, its main character is an old man, O, who never utters a word. What's more, his back is to the camera and his face hidden until the closing frames, when there is a quick shot revealing a patch over one eye. The other eyeball reflects horror.

A decade earlier Keaton had been approached about the role of Lucky in Beckett's *Waiting for Godot.* As always, he handed the script to Eleanor, and it made no sense to her. Relying on her judgment, he turned it down. But months later when *Godot* turned out to be one of the most successful plays of the 1956 season, he blamed her for steering him wrong. So when he was contacted about doing a Beckett film, Eleanor kept her mouth shut, even though the film made no more sense to her than the play had.

Neither Beckett nor Schneider was familiar with Keaton's silent films, though they pretended to be. They knew he was an actor but did not know his work as a director and had no inkling of the profoundly absurdist vision of such sophisticated films as *The Paleface.* In fact, nothing that Beckett dreamed up in the sixties would have mystified Keaton. All they wanted from him was a performance, and as an actor he had been their fourth choice after Charlie Chaplin, Zero Mostel, and Irish actor Jack MacGowran.

On Monday, July 20, 1964, location filming began on Gold Street in the shadow of the Brooklyn Bridge. By afternoon the temperature was 90 degrees. Throughout the entire filming temperatures regularly soared into the nineties with typical midsummer New York humidity. Keaton was decked out in a smocklike overcoat, pancake hat, baggy black trousers, eye patch, and red suspenders. In the bridge scene, he was supposed to run along Gold Street, whose sidewalk had been strewn with broken glass and rocks.

In addition to a flotilla of reporters, celebrities stood around squinting in the simmering heat: French director Alain Resnais, actress Delphine Seyrig, poet Kenneth Koch. Sitting on a construction beam, legs dangling, were the Beat poet Allen Ginsberg and his roommate, Peter Orlovsky. Ginsberg, inspired by Keaton in his red suspenders, went home that afternoon and wrote "Today," a poem about seeing Buster Keaton under the Brooklyn Bridge and about the hairy bum who asked Keaton for—but did not get—drink money.

Roberta Hodes, the script supervisor, thought the project "was ass backwards, written by a great poet who knew nothing about film, directed by a man of the theater who knew nothing about film, starring a man who knew everything about film. They were just using Keaton's name. Anybody could have played the part."

To Beckett's surprise, Keaton never inquired what the film was about—"he wasn't interested"—and so Beckett didn't tell him. Keaton was prepared to improvise, but when he suggested comedy bits for O, Beckett and Schneider ignored them. Soon communication ceased altogether.

When reporters from the *New Yorker* and the *Saturday Evening Post* came up to Keaton on the set and asked what the picture was about, he talked articulately about O and how "a man may keep away from everybody but he can't get away from himself." His explanation wasn't too different from Beckett's: "It's about a man trying to escape from perception of all kinds—from all perceivers—even divine perceivers."

It was only to be expected that *Film* drew widespread attention from the creative community. It was Beckett's first visit to the United States; Schneider came trailing clouds of glory from his Broadway hits; cinematographer Boris Kaufman had won an Oscar for photographing *On the Waterfront*, and Sidney Meyers was a gifted film editor who had collected awards at Venice and Edinburgh. Accordingly, flurries of hype surrounded the experimental film.

In his autobiography, Schneider would repeatedly suggest that Keaton was a lowbrow who did not get Beckett's symbolism. "What Buster didn't get," said James Karen, "was their goddamned amateurism. These were people who didn't know how to make a movie, who had given him a script that didn't make sense. It was anti-film. He saved their asses, shot after shot." Even though Schneider insisted on handling Keaton as if he were an amateur, afterward he would admit that his star had been patient, imperturbable, and "magnificent."

That summer Keaton returned, accidentally, to the place of his birth. During the cross-country drive to New York City, he and Eleanor were speeding along the highway through Kansas. Looking out the window of the Cadillac, they noticed a road sign for Piqua.

At the Piqua railway depot, the Keatons pulled up. The place appeared deserted, not a car or truck parked outside the creaky station, not a single soul in sight, not even a stray dog. Eleanor snapped a picture of him tramping along the railway tracks in straw hat, white T-shirt, and rumpled pants, beneath the Piqua sign dangling from the depot's sloped roof. The snapshot, still in the family photo album, shows an uncomfortable and hot Keaton, his shirt stuck to his stomach. His face wears the expression of an unhappy old poker player.

Keaton stepped into the station and introduced himself to the agent on duty. Then he hopped into the Cadillac and they left.

When Piquans learned that their most famous native son had actually returned and then silently departed, all in less than ten minutes, they were hurt and insulted. Keaton, according to the Piqua centennial book, "in a chauffeur-driven car, came through the town of his birth, but he evidently did not want to see much of the town or talk to anyone. He stopped at the depot and talked to the agent, Dick Miller, and drove off."

Now close to seventy, Keaton had become the Willy Loman of movies, slogging year after year through international departure lounges: Rome, Venice, Toronto, New York, Paris. No question, he worked on some of the cheapest films of the decade, but he never stopped moving. As he got older, his obsession with work became more pronounced. Some of his friends believed he flogged himself with the zeal of a twenty-year-old in order to leave Eleanor a nest egg.

The following year *Film* had its world premiere at the New York Film Festival. One critic described it as twenty minutes of chic boredom; others thought it a depressing waste of Keaton. Critic Andrew Sarris described Schneider's direction of Keaton as "nothing short of catastrophic" and correctly supposed that the only reason Keaton could have agreed to play O was a very tasty salary.

After nine days among the New York literati, Keaton gratefully returned to Woodland Hills for a break. But being a man who didn't know the meaning of the words *time off,* he soon found easy ways to rustle up a buck or two. Between his return from New York in August and the following January, he appeared in four films for James Nicholson and Samuel Z. Arkoff's American International Pictures. Arkoff, best known for inventing a new genre of such teenage monster movies as *I Was a Teenage Werewolf,* was now pioneering another genre, beach-party movies. Keaton stumbled into the cast of *Pajama Party,* costarring Annette Funicello and Tommy Kirk, in which Keaton plays an Indian chief who chases a bosomy blonde in a bikini. "Somehow he had dignity even though they had him rigged up in a ridiculous Indian outfit," said Tom Kirk, who played a Martian in the picture.

Keaton undertook three more Arkoffian epics: *Beach Blanket Bingo, How to Stuff a Wild Bikini,* and *Sergeant Deadhead.* Shot on location at Malibu or on a soundstage filled with tons of sand, the beach pictures took fifteen days to make and all of them had cookie-cutter plots. Peter Lorre, Boris Karloff, and Mickey Rooney were also hired for cameos. Annette Funicello waxed rhapsodic about the chance to work with "older, established actors." Not that the youngsters had ever seen this older actor in anything, except maybe *Mad, Mad World.* "We all knew who he was," said Irene Tsu, who first met Keaton dressed as a tropical-island witch doctor in *How to Stuff a Wild Bikini.* "But off-camera we didn't talk much to him. He was old and sick, and when he wasn't working he would be resting or sitting with his wife. Nobody wanted to bother him." Tom Kirk figured that Keaton's reasons for being there were similar to his own. "It was work. But I still felt sorry for him."

Keaton connoisseurs watched in dismay. By this time, nothing could destroy Keaton's reputation, but the beach-party movies were pushing it. The *New York Times* reviled *Wild Bikini* as the worst film of the last two years, and maybe the next two. Jim Kline writes in *The Complete Films of Buster Keaton* that the AIP pictures feature "some of the worst acting, writing, directing, camera work, choreography, and music ever recorded on film."

Keaton had already lined up his next film, the eighty-seventh by his own calculation, and was preparing to rough it in the Canadian wilderness. In July, while he had been staying at the St. Moritz, he had a visit from a young British animator, Gerald Potterton, who had been pursuing him for months about making a travelogue for the Canadian National Railways. He wanted Keaton to go from the Atlantic Ocean to the Pacific on one of the tiny motorized railway handcars used by track crews.

Keaton looked at the kid director and rolled his eyes. "Sounds crazy," he said. Suddenly a racket down on Central Park South sent him clomping to the window. He pulled it up and stuck his head out. "Quiet!" he bawled at Manhattan. Then he closed the window and turned back to Potterton. "I'll do it. When do we start?" He never could resist trains.

It was September by the time that *The Railrodder* began shooting. Already the weather was getting chilly, and nobody wanted to think about what conditions might be like once they hit the Rockies. Gathered in Montreal to meet him were Gerry Potterton and his crew of five, plus a second, smaller crew led by director John Spotton, who would be traveling along with them and filming a backstage documentary about Keaton. For the next five weeks the group would trundle across Canada from Halifax, Nova Scotia, to White Rock, British Columbia, on a private railroad car with sleeping compartments, a lounge for relaxing, and their own chef and steward. Keaton could not have felt more at home.

The Railrodder is a one-joke commercial for Canada. In England, Keaton, costumed in his Buster coat and hat, reads a newspaper ad—"See Canada Now"—and jumps into the Atlantic.

Wading ashore in Canada, he notices a sign that says "Pacific Ocean, West 3,982½ miles" and starts down some railroad tracks, then climbs on an abandoned handcar. Suddenly the handcar takes off down the track. Whizzing through the Canadian countryside, Buster is pleased to find in the car's storage trunk all of life's necessities—including a formal tea set.

At the beach on the opening day of shooting a low-flying sea gull made a bombing run on Keaton. Potterton, delighted with the bird poop, proposed to use this unrehearsed business. "No, no," Keaton told him, "you leave those kinds of jokes to Peter Sellers."

John Spotton's documentary on the making of *The Railrodder* captures a little-seen side of Keaton. One of the most revealing scenes is a clash between Potterton and Keaton over a gag, the kind of fight that must have erupted countless times in Keaton's earlier career. *The Railrodder* was Potterton's film, but Keaton figured he knew what was best. On a windy day, he wanted to cross a two-hundred-foot-high trestle bridge enveloped by a map (his newspaper gag from *The High Sign*). When Potterton had other ideas, Keaton gave his director a lesson in filmmaking. "The bridge is *not* your gag. The bridge is only suspense." The argument grew heated. When Potterton insisted, Keaton did the scene Potterton's way before stomping off to his compartment. Later Spotton's camera caught him looking for consolation from Eleanor, who agreed with Potterton. The shot was too dangerous.

"I generally know what I'm doing," Keaton barked. "That's not dangerous. It's child's play, for the love of Mike."

The next day the scene was reshot.

"Let's face it," Potterton said. "He was Buster Keaton, and who the hell was I to tell him what to do. The bridge didn't worry him at all. He thought it was sissy stuff. We ended shooting the gag his way, with the map wrapped all around his head."

At his sixty-ninth birthday party, the company presented him with a toy locomotive and a cake. Urged to make a speech, he said, in an Irish accent, "I'm not very good at public speaking, but to show you my heart's in the right place, I'll fight any man in the house."

By the middle of October, the Canadian weather was getting "bloody cold," Spotton recalled, and Keaton's coughing provided an ever-present soundtrack. "But he was a tough son of a bitch. If there was anything wrong with him, he kept it to himself."

A few months later, when Potterton visited his star in Woodland Hills, Keaton marched him around to the corner hardware store and spent an hour showing him screws and chisels. Then, having promised to introduce his young director to Stan Laurel, they drove to Santa Monica. Laurel, jolly and smiling in his wheelchair, seemed enormously pleased to see Keaton, who began describing how he had just crossed Canada from coast to coast in *The Railrodder.*

"And guess who directed it?"

"Who?" said Laurel.

Keaton pointed a finger at the kid sitting on the couch. "That," he said.

"That" held a 7-Up in his hand as he listened to the two masters talking shop. "It was terrific," Potterton recalled. "There was no sadness in either of them."

On May 29, 1965, the Keatons celebrated their twenty-fifth wedding anniversary, though the marriage had been given only a few months. To columnist Hedda Hopper, Keaton joked that "there's a night club here in Woodland Hills, with a bowling alley connected. Maybe I'll take her there."

That summer he had commitments to shoot two films in Europe and another in Canada, requiring an extended stay away from home. He was having coughing spells that left him out of breath, so before leaving home he got a complete physical. Once again, the report came back: bronchitis.

He spent most of the summer shooting *War Italian Style,* a low-budget Italian film in which he played a wacky German general. It was the sixth film he had made in the last twelve months. As soon as the picture was finished, he was scheduled to join Zero Mostel and Phil Silvers in Spain for the movie version of *A Funny Thing Happened on the Way to the Forum,* receiving third billing after the two stars. But in August Raymond Rohauer called him from Italy where the Venice Film Festival had just gotten under way. At the last minute Rohauer had fast-talked the festival director into screening Samuel Beckett's *Film* and inviting its star. Within hours Rohauer had turned the showing of the twenty-two-minute film into a special tribute to Buster Keaton. Now his star was refusing to cooperate.

Keaton resisted appearing at a film festival. "You know how much I hate them."

Rohauer began pleading. He reeled off names of film luminaries who were attending the festival: Federico Fellini, Jean-Luc Godard, Michelangelo Antonioni, Luchino Visconti, all the important film critics, press from all over the world.

Keaton finally said that he would show up on one condition: He would not do more than two or three interviews.

Rohauer met the Keatons at the Venice airport. Instead of going to their hotel, he guided them to the main entrance of the film festival.

"Just go through those doors," he told Keaton.

Keaton was suspicious. "What for?"

When Rohauer swung open the door of the grand salon people were cheering. Keaton refused to enter. Rohauer pushed him.

As Rohauer would recall, "Eleanor looked at me. She was furious."

It was a twenty-minute standing ovation. *Films in Review* reported that "even the most sedate journalists stood on their chairs to cheer." In the end, Keaton had no choice but to walk inside. Poker-faced, he slowly went down the aisle, climbed onto the stage, and seated himself at a table. But as the pandemonium continued, with people shouting *"Caro Buster!"* and paparazzi clambering over the stage, Keaton softened and his face betrayed emotion. "Glad to see you," he said with a smile. Then he began answering questions from the audience.

A few days later he arrived in Madrid and checked into the Hilton, where he met Richard Lester, director of *A Funny Thing Happened on the Way to the Forum*. Lester was a flashy young American expatriate who had won international fame in England, primarily as the director of two Beatles films, *A Hard Day's Night* and *Help!* He had a reputation for creativity and bold technical innovations. Lester regarded Keaton's silent films "with true envy and respect. He had an extraordinary ability to make the space around objects seem funny. And there was never anything wasted, not a shot that you could take out of a Keaton film. He was a bit like Mozart, effortless."

A successful Broadway musical comedy set in ancient Rome, *Forum* was being transferred to the screen with its original star, Zero Mostel. A blacklisted actor, Mostel had been absent from the screen for some fifteen years. The other principal repeating his Broadway role was comedian Jack Gilford. Lester jumped at the chance to hire Keaton for the character of Erronius, a man who searches for his children, who were stolen in infancy by pirates. Unlike Alan Schneider and Samuel Beckett, Lester honored him as a master. He had seen all of Keaton's features and could remember individual frames—the cow and the bucket from *Go West,* for example—that he considered perfection.

Despite his top billing, Keaton's role was tiny. He runs through the film as a moving sight gag. "I wasn't aware of his health problems until he got to Madrid," said Lester. "He still had a marvelous physique and the legs of an athlete. But any movement produced a shortness of breath." Erronius is supposed to race around the Seven Hills of Rome seven times, but it was clear that Keaton was incapable of running. Jockey and stuntman Mick Dillon was hired to double Keaton in the long shots. The most startling scene, showing Erronius smashing into a tree, is Keaton himself. "It took everyone's breath away," Dillon recalled. "He ran straight into the tree with his head. Bang. We thought he hadn't seen it."

In Madrid the weather was cold and rainy. "It was terrible for healthy people," said Madeline Gilford. "The outdoor shooting involved many different locations, which was very strenuous. And it was also a long day because the company operated on Spanish time schedules." Each morning a car arrived at the Hilton before 6:00 A.M. Midafternoon, shooting would stop for siesta, then resume for several more hours. "They would shoot quite late, and then by the time you ate it would be ten o'clock," said Madeline Gilford. Although Keaton's stamina impressed his coworkers, he would be utterly exhausted by bedtime. On Sundays, when Mostel and Gilford were out tramping through the Prado Museum, he rested. His health, Eleanor Keaton recalled, "wasn't good, but he was coping." In fact, he was coping well enough to shoot a Pepsi commercial in his spare time.

Keaton ignored the disharmony on the set. Lester refused to hear arguments from his actors. Mostel, who had a reputation for rubbing people the wrong way, was submissive while at the same time complaining that Lester was ruining the film. Keaton found the shoot a welcoming environment. Everyone treated him like royalty, including fifty-eight-year-old Jack Gilford, who had begun his career in vaudeville doing imitations of Keaton and Chaplin.

With Dick Lester, Keaton felt comfortable offering directorial sympathy. When Lester one day expressed dissatisfaction with a certain scene, Keaton remarked, "You'll know better when you preview it."

"I don't think so," Lester replied, a gentle reminder that film-making had changed since Keaton's day.

"We previewed everything," Keaton told him.

At the Venice Film Festival, Keaton had told columnist Rex Reed that "I have so many projects coming up I don't have time to think about kicking the bucket." Nevertheless, by the end of September the coughing spells sometimes left him blue in the face. Keaton then flew to Canada. In May, when his health had been better, he had promised to do a film for $10,000. He could not back out now.

In Toronto in 1965, he began filming *The Reporter* (released as *The Scribe*), a thirty-minute industrial film for the Construction Safety Association of Ontario. He plays a janitor who wants to be a newspaper reporter and visits a construction site to get a story on unsafe conditions. Director John Sebert was surprised to see Keaton smoking three or four packs of Winstons a day. "He always had a cigarette in his hand," he remembered. "He used to smoke like a stove. Then he'd go into these coughing seizures that lasted four or five minutes. The racking that poor guy went through was terrible. But he looked fine and physically seemed quite agile."

Since the entire film was a chase, a local actor had been hired to double Keaton in several scenes that required strenuous run-ning. The fact that almost the whole shoot took place out of doors did not help Keaton's coughing. The weather was cold and wet.

John Sebert was completely in awe of Keaton, who advised the novice on how every scene should be played. "You didn't direct Buster too much," he said. "*The Scribe* is not much of a film. It's a young guy's first film." The young guy's first would be the old guy's last.

On October 18 he boarded a plane for home.

FADE OUT

On the flight to Los Angeles, oxygen had to be administered to Keaton. When the plane landed he was so weak that he made no objection to being pushed in a wheelchair to his car. The next day he saw his doctor. After the examination and X rays, the physician took Eleanor aside. "When he gets dressed, take him to the hospital. Go now." At West Hills Hospital in Canoga Park, Keaton underwent a biopsy of the lymph nodes in his neck.

He had inoperable lung cancer, with a prognosis of one week to three months. Keaton left West Hills with medication to make him comfortable. Unaware of the diagnosis, he continued to believe that he was suffering from severe chronic bronchitis.

Word of his condition traveled quickly. A Van Nuys informant passed a tip to Hedda Hopper: "You might like to know that he came home from the hospital last week and is very ill with a chest complication. He probably won't recover."

For a while he seemed to bounce back. He joined Lucille Ball and Dick Van Dyke on a CBS television tribute to Stan Laurel. In December, he posed for a Levy's Rye Bread advertisement. "This medication is working," he assured Eleanor. Since he enjoyed seeing visitors, Ruth and Henry Silva brought over a new comedian whom he had seen on television and found quite amusing. They took him into the den where Keaton was seated at his card table. "He was playing double-handed solitaire," Bill Cosby remembered. "I went over to him and asked how he was doing, and he said, 'How are you, young fellow?' That was all he said to me, period. I could have sat at his feet, but he was playing that solitaire."

Bill Cosby was one of Keaton's last guests at Woodland Hills. Soon enough the cancer metastasized to his brain, and then he began losing ground rapidly.

At the end of January, Raymond Rohauer described his plans for a Keaton film festival in London in the spring. He wanted Buster to be there.

"Okay," Keaton agreed. "Well, you know you can count on me."

On Sunday, January 30, Jane Dulo stopped by for brunch and cards, as she often did. They were in the middle of a game when Keaton suddenly seemed to lose interest and went into his den to finish a game of solitaire. Half an hour later, he began choking and lost consciousness. That night he spent at West Hills Hospital, but the hospital released him the following day.

Arrangements were made to set up a hospital bed in his den and to obtain the services of a nurse. By this time Keaton's mood had turned rebellious. He refused to lie down on the hospital bed. He refused to get into his own bed. He refused to sit down on chairs.

"He became more and more irrational," Eleanor Keaton said. "He wanted to fight, and he didn't care about what or who. He wouldn't let anybody touch him." He paced the floor, dragging one foot a little. Out poured long rambling stories. Never before had she heard him talk quite so much.

At 7:00 P.M. the nurse gave him an injection that knocked him out. Eleanor Keaton recalled, "We finally got him into bed and he went out like a light. That was it. He never came back."

At 6:15 A.M. on Tuesday, February 1, 1966, Joseph Frank Keaton made his exit in his sleep at the age of seventy.

Eleanor and Ruth Silva arranged for the funeral service. The funeral director was prepared to sell them a burial befitting one of the great names in the film industry. Eleanor remembered her husband's clucking when Gracie Allen had died and George Burns spent something like $25,000. She said to the mortician, "We're not going to spend one penny over $3,500. I don't care how you do it, that's the top."

The startled undertaker nodded. "What do you think would be Mr. Keaton's favorite music?" he asked.

Eleanor did not hesitate for a second. "'Hello, Dolly!'"

He was buried at Forest Lawn Hollywood Hills in Burbank. Eleanor placed a rosary in one pocket—and a deck of cards in the other. Come what may, he would be ready for his close-up.

END TITLE ROLLS

ELEANOR KEATON sold the Woodland Hills house after her husband's death. Since 1966 she has worked in a pet shop, as a bail bondsman with her sister, Jane Kelly, and as a volunteer at the Los Angeles Zoo. Still active, beautiful, and healthy at the age of seventy-six, she lives in a one-bedroom condo in North Hollywood. Eleanor never remarried.

JIMMY TALMADGE, seventy-three, and his wife, Barbara, live in Santa Ynez, California. He continues to take an active interest in the restoration of antique cars, especially Duesenbergs.

BOBBY TALMADGE, seventy-one, is a retired businessman living in Solana Beach, California. His wife, Patricia, died a few years ago.

LOUISE KEATON spent her last years in a Van Nuys, California, retirement home. One evening family friend Bob Borgen screened several Keaton two-reelers for residents of the home. Apparently Louise failed to make clear that the films starred her brother. The next morning at breakfast she asked her friends if they had liked the show. "Oh, yes," said one, "but the movies were so awfully old." Louise asked what she meant. "Well," said the woman, "it was before Charlie Chaplin even had his mustache." Louise died of lung cancer on February 18, 1981, at the age of seventy-four.

HARRY KEATON died in San Ysidro, California, at the age of eighty-three. In May 1988—twenty-two years after his brother died—he was crossing the street to his motel after dinner when he fell, hit his head on the curb, and fractured his skull. Postmortem X rays revealed previous head fractures, suggesting this was not his first serious fall. He was not penniless. His son, Harry Moore, said, "He left a small amount of money, $3,200, buried in the bottom drawer of his dresser in a carton from a bottle of Crown Royal whiskey." He was buried next to his mother and sister in Sunland.

NATALIE TALMADGE spent her last years in frail health, living in a Santa Monica nursing home. She died on June 19, 1969, of cardiovascular disease.

MAE KEATON was a character in a 1969 film inspired by Keaton's life, *The Comic*. Billy Bright (Dick Van Dyke) is a silent comic whose career is ended by talkies and alcohol. His wife leaves him over his infidelities, one of which resembles Keaton's affair with Kathleen Key, and he also becomes estranged from his son. Billy's second wife marries him for his name and money while both of them are drunk—unmistakably suggesting Mae. After 1959 Mae sank completely out of sight. Reports that she died in a mental institution could not be verified. Creedmoor Psychiatric Center in Queens, New York, refuses to disclose information about patients, past or present. There is no official death certificate under any of her known aliases.

KEATON'S KITCHEN

An aficionado of great food, Buster Keaton was known to tuck into a plate of just about anything so long as it was well prepared. The dishes he liked least were stews and macaronis, probably because he associated them with the boardinghouse fare of his early years in vaudeville.

Cooking became one of his pastimes. In Beverly Hills, where meals were prepared by cooks, not amateurs, Keaton became famous for barbecues at his Italian Villa. His specialty was English-cut lamb chops, which he personally grilled to order for each guest. Thirty years later, friends invited to his home in Woodland Hills could expect superb T-bone steaks. "He knew exactly what he wanted," said Ruth Silva, one of the regulars, "and he knew exactly how to do it." At Thanksgiving he roasted a turkey to perfection.

Keaton used every utensil whenever possible. If a recipe called for two bowls, he would dirty seven. Afterward the place looked as if the Red Army had passed through. Washing up was an entirely different matter. He regarded a sinkful of messy dishes as in no way the cook's responsibility.

LOBSTER JOSEPH

This is Keaton's recipe for his all-time favorite dish, purloined over a period of years from a Parisian restaurant. Serve with bite-size boiled potatoes, green salad, and sourdough bread. Bread and potatoes are dunked in the sauce.

1 pint sour cream
1 square butter, ¼ pound
2 30-ounce cans solid pack tomatoes (unseasoned)
1 teaspoon salt
¼ teaspoon pepper
4 medium lobsters (cooked)
1 ounce brandy
2 ounces sweet sherry

Melt butter. Blend in sour cream, add tomatoes (putting aside tomato juice). Combine sherry and brandy in separate pan. Burn out most of the alcohol and add to sauce. Add tomato juice as needed to desired consistency. Cut lobster into bite size and heat in sauce.

Fish fillets can be substituted for the lobster. Melt butter and quickly saute 1 pound fillets (sole is good). Remove to warm dish. Do not overcook. Add well-drained tomatoes to remaining butter, mixing and chopping with spoon. Add salt and pepper. When tomato-butter mixture is hot (but not boiling) mix in sour cream, a bit at a time. Add brandy and sherry, or white port. Mix well.

BULLHEAD PASCOE'S FRIED PERCH

The best fish Buster ever ate were the platters of fried perch served at Bullhead Pascoe's restaurant in Bluffton, Michigan, before World War I. "Most people don't know how to cook perch," he once said.

This is how:

> *"You have to skin 'em, roll 'em in half corn meal and half flour, and fry 'em in half butter and half lard."*

And that's it. Serve with rye bread and wash down with cold beer.

DRIED CHIPPED BEEF SANDWICH

One of Keaton's favorite sandwiches—salty but delicious—used dried chipped beef.

Dried beef (the kind sold in glass jars)
White bread
Raw onion slices
Mustard

Spread bread with lots of mustard. Pile on dried beef and slices of onion.

CHOP SUEY

Keaton adored Chinese food. This recipe was first cooked in the twenties and included chopped salted almonds and a whole roasted chicken. Over the years he changed the ingredients slightly.

1 quart beef stock
1 quart chicken stock (clear)
1 full cup onions (small-green or white)

Grease pan with peanut oil all around. Cook onions. Add 2 cups chopped celery; 2 cups Chinese greens (don't use leaf part); 2 cups diced water chestnuts; 1½ cups bamboo shoots (canned—stripped like string beans). Put lid on for about 5 minutes.

Now take 1 lb. pork shoulder. Trim & dice. Fry separately, make sure *no* fat. Slice pork thin. Add 2 cups beef stock to one of chicken, almost up to level of ingredients. Add 1 large can mushrooms; 1 cup of dried black mushrooms (soak and break up first by hand—do not use much water); 1 lb. bean shoots (washed, put in dry cloth in ice box for about five minutes).

Mix in bowl four heaping tablespoons of cornstarch, add just enough chicken stock to dissolve it; turn dish over till well circulated. Add 1 cup soya sauce; turn over Chinese molasses (3 tablespoons). Do not cover again. Cook 3 minutes. Add soya sauce to taste. If cornstarch thickens too much use same proportions stock to thin.

Add to Chinese noodles.

CUSTARD PIES

In his very first film, The Butcher Boy, *Keaton can be seen heaving a pie. Never, ever did pies, custard or otherwise, fly in any of his own films, but he knew exactly how to make them and how to throw them.*

1: You get the baker to make two pie crusts, baking them until they're nice and brown, not brittle.
2: Then you paste them together with flour and water, so you have a solid foundation that your fingers won't go through.
3: Once that's done, you fill the pie with about an inch of flour and water so that it's good and sticky.
4: If you're going to throw it at a blonde, or someone in a light suit, garnish the top liberally with chocolate or strawberry. If you're aiming for a dark suit or complexion, better use lots of whipped cream.

THROWING TECHNIQUES

- Shot-put (if target is within 5 ft.)
- Catcher throwing to second base
- Discus-throwing (sometimes called the Roman)

Warning for beginners: "Don't try it in the house."

PORKPIE HAT

Keaton's trademark hats were homemade. The first was created in 1917 for The Butcher Boy.

1 Stetson hat, which has been cut down to size
3 heaping teaspoons granulated sugar
1 teacup warm water

Mix sugar and water. Wet the top and bottom of the brim. Smooth it out on a clean, hard surface. Allow to dry until stiff.

"I did the early ones myself, always—and then I trained my wife," Keaton said.

FILMOGRAPHY

COMPILED BY JACK DRAGGA

As with any filmography, many thanks must go to those who have tread this ground before, as their efforts provide a starting point from which to base my own research. They are: Samuel A. Gill (Arbuckle films), Leonard Maltin, J. P. Lebel, Maryann Chach, Rudi Blesh, David Robinson, George Wead, George Ellis, and Jim Kline. Also many thanks to Eleanor Keaton and Raymond Rohauer, who checked what few records Buster had kept. This was very helpful in listing Keaton's work for television. Thanks to Joel Goss for his input and to my wife, Gail, for her support and typing ability.

Film credits were checked from original title footage when available. Running times listed are approximated. Alternate titles are listed in parentheses after the most commonly used title.

ARBUCKLE-KEATON SHORTS

The Butcher Boy (1917)
Released: April 23, 1917. Copyright: April 12, 1917. Length: 2 reels. Distributed by: Paramount Pictures. Produced by: Comique Film Corporation.

Technical Credits:
Director: Roscoe Arbuckle. Writer: Roscoe Arbuckle. Story: Joe Roach. Scenario Editor: Herbert Warren. Photography: Frank D. Williams.

Cast:
Roscoe Arbuckle (butcher boy), Buster Keaton (customer), Al St. John (rival), Josephine Stevens (daughter of proprietor and pupil at girls' boarding school), Arthur Earle (store proprietor), Agnes Neilson (principal), Joe Bordeau (accomplice), Luke the Dog.

A Reckless Romeo (1917)
Released: May 21, 1917. Copyright: Unknown. Length: 2 reels. Distributed by: Paramount Pictures. Produced by: Comique Film Corporation.

Technical Credits:
Director: Roscoe Arbuckle. Writer: Roscoe Arbuckle. Story: Joe Roach. Scenario Editor: Herbert Warren. Photography: Frank D. Williams.

Cast:
Roscoe Arbuckle (husband), Buster Keaton (rival), Al St. John (rival), Alice Lake, Corinne Parquet, Agnes Neilson (husband's mother-in-law).

Note: Considered a lost film.

The Rough House (1917)
Released: June 25, 1917. Copyright: June 20, 1917. Length: 2 reels. Distributed by: Paramount Pictures. Produced by: Comique Film Corporation.

Technical Credits:
Director: Roscoe Arbuckle. Writer: Roscoe Arbuckle. Story: Joe Roach. Scenario Editor: Herbert Warren. Photography: Frank D. Williams.

Cast:
Roscoe Arbuckle (Mr. Rough), Buster Keaton, Al St. John, Alice Lake, Agnes Neilson, Glen Cavender.

His Wedding Night (1917)
Released: August 20, 1917. Copyright: August 20, 1917. Length: 2 reels. Distributed by: Paramount Pictures. Produced by: Comique Film Corporation.

Technical Credits:

Director: Roscoe Arbuckle. Writer: Roscoe Arbuckle. Story: Joe Roach. Scenario Editor: Herbert Warren. Photography: George Peters.

Cast:

Roscoe Arbuckle, Buster Keaton, Al St. John, Alice Mann, Arthur Earle, Jimmy Bryant, Josephine Stevens.

Oh, Doctor! (1917)

Released: September 30, 1917. Copyright: September 19, 1917. Length: 2 reels. Distributed by: Paramount Pictures. Produced by: Comique Film Corporation.

Technical Credits:

Director: Roscoe Arbuckle. Writer: Roscoe Arbuckle. Scenario: Jean Havez. Scenario Editor: Herbert Warren. Photography: George Peters.

Cast:

Roscoe Arbuckle (doctor), Buster Keaton, Al St. John, Alice Mann.

Note: Considered a lost film.

Fatty at Coney Island (1917) *(Coney Island)*

Released: October 29, 1917. Copyright: October 11, 1917. Length: 2 reels. Distributed by: Paramount Pictures. Produced by: Comique Film Corporation.

Technical Credits:

Director: Roscoe Arbuckle. Writer: Roscoe Arbuckle. Scenario Editor: Herbert Warren. Photography: George Peters.

Cast:

Roscoe Arbuckle, Buster Keaton, Al St. John, Alice Mann, Agnes Neilson, James Bryant, Joe Bordeau.

A Country Hero (1917)

Released: December 10, 1917. Copyright: December 13, 1917. Length: 2 reels. Distributed by: Paramount Pictures. Produced by: Comique Film Corporation.

Technical Credits:

Director: Roscoe Arbuckle. Writer: Roscoe Arbuckle. Scenario Editor: Herbert Warren. Photography: George Peters.

Cast:

Roscoe Arbuckle, Buster Keaton, Al St. John, Alice Lake, Joe Keaton, Stanley Pembroke.

Note: Considered a lost film.

Out West (1918)

Released: January 20, 1918. Copyright: February 20, 1918. Length: 2 reels. Distributed by: Paramount Pictures. Produced by: Comique Film Corporation.

Technical Credits:

Director: Roscoe Arbuckle. Writer: Roscoe Arbuckle. Scenario: Natalie Talmadge. Scenario Editor: Herbert Warren. Photography: George Peters.

Cast:

Roscoe Arbuckle (bartender), Buster Keaton (saloon owner), Al St. John (outlaw), Alice Lake (Salvation Army worker), Joe Keaton.

The Bell Boy (1918)

Released: March 18, 1918. Copyright: March 7, 1918. Length: 2 reels. Distributed by: Paramount Pictures. Produced by: Comique Film Corporation.

Technical Credits:

Director: Roscoe Arbuckle. Writer: Roscoe Arbuckle. Scenario Editor: Herbert Warren. Photography: George Peters.

Cast:

Roscoe Arbuckle (bellboy and barber), Buster Keaton (bellboy), Al St. John (desk clerk), Alice Lake (Cutie Cuticle, manicurist), Joe Keaton (guest), Charles Dudley (guest).

Moonshine (1918)

Released: May 13, 1918. Copyright: May 6, 1918. Length: 2 reels. Distributed by: Paramount Pictures. Produced by: Comique Film Corporation.

Technical Credits:

Director: Roscoe Arbuckle. Writer: Roscoe Arbuckle. Scenario Editor: Herbert Warren. Photography: George Peters.

Cast:

Roscoe Arbuckle (revenue officer), Buster Keaton (his assistant), Al St. John (madman), Charles Dudley (moonshiner), Alice Lake (his daughter), Joe Bordeau.

Good Night, Nurse! (1918)

Released: July 8, 1918. Copyright: June 22, 1918. Length: 2 reels. Distributed by: Paramount Pictures. Produced by: Comique Film Corporation.

Technical Credits:

Director: Roscoe Arbuckle. Writer: Roscoe Arbuckle. Scenario Editor: Herbert Warren. Photography: George Peters.

Cast:

Roscoe Arbuckle (resort guest/"nurse"), Buster Keaton (visitor/doctor), Al St. John (assistant), Alice Lake (patient), Kate Price (nurse), Joe Keaton.

The Cook (1918)

Released: September 15, 1918. Copyright: August 20, 1918. Length: 2 reels. Distributed by: Paramount Pictures. Produced by: Comique Film Corporation.

Technical Credits:

Director: Roscoe Arbuckle. Writer: Roscoe Arbuckle. Scenario Editor: Herbert Warren. Photography: George Peters.

Cast:

Roscoe Arbuckle (cook), Buster Keaton (waiter), Al St. John (rival), Alice Lake (cashier), Glen Cavender, Luke the Dog.

Note: Considered a lost film. Once thought to be found but turned out to be The Rough House. *Also, Buster's last film before going into the Army.*

A Desert Hero (1919)

Note: Many filmographies list this film as having Keaton in it. However, the film has been found and without a doubt does not contain him in the cast. Most of the Keaton stills that are credited to this film are actually from Out West, *made in 1918.*

Back Stage (1919)

Released: September 7, 1919. Copyright: August 20, 1919. Length: 2 reels. Distributed by: Paramount Pictures. Produced by: Comique Film Corporation.

Technical Credits:

Director: Roscoe Arbuckle. Writer: Roscoe Arbuckle. Scenario: Jean Havez. Photography: Elgin Lessley.

Cast:

Roscoe Arbuckle (stage manager), Buster Keaton (stagehand), Al St. John (stagehand), Molly Malone (strongman's assistant), John Coogan (dancer).

Note: Buster's first film after returning from the Army. Cast member John Coogan is the father of child star Jackie Coogan.

The Hayseed (1919)

Released: October 26, 1919. Copyright: October 13, 1919. Length: 2 reels. Distributed by: Paramount Pictures. Produced by: Comique Film Corporation.

Technical Credits:

Director: Roscoe Arbuckle. Writer: Roscoe Arbuckle. Scenario: Jean Havez. Photography: Elgin Lessley.

Cast:

Roscoe Arbuckle (rural mail carrier), Buster Keaton (general helper), John Coogan (sheriff; some filmographies erroneously list Al St. John as the sheriff), Molly Malone (the girl), Luke the Dog.

The Garage (1920) (Fire Chief)

Released: January 11, 1920. Copyright: December 15, 1919. Length: 2 reels. Distributed by: Paramount Pictures. Produced by: Comique Film Corporation.

Technical Credits:

Director: Roscoe Arbuckle. Writer: Roscoe Arbuckle. Scenario: Jean Havez. Photography: Elgin Lessley.

Cast:

Roscoe Arbuckle (garage owner and fire chief), Buster Keaton (his assistant), Molly Malone (the girl), Harry McCoy (spurned lover), Daniel Crimmins, Luke the Dog.

KEATON SILENT SHORTS

Note: Some filmographies list all the Keaton silent shorts as having been produced or presented by Buster Keaton Productions. However, Buster was under contract with Comique. Joe Schenck didn't form Buster Keaton Productions until March 2, 1922, as Arbuckle neared the end of his third trial for manslaughter. Perhaps this change was to remove the Comique name that had so strongly been associated with Arbuckle.

One Week (1920)

Released: September 1, 1920. Copyright: September 3, 1920. Length: 2 reels. Distributed by: Metro Pictures. Presented by: Comique Film Corporation. Producer: Joseph M. Schenck.

Technical Credits:

Director: Buster Keaton and Eddie Cline. Script: Buster Keaton and Eddie Cline. Photography: Elgin Lessley.

Cast:

Buster Keaton and Sybil Seely (newlyweds), Joe Roberts (piano mover).

Convict 13 (1920)

Released: October 27, 1920. Copyright: October 4, 1920. Length: 2 reels. Distributed by: Metro Pictures. Presented by: Comique Film Corporation.

Technical Credits:

Director: Buster Keaton and Eddie Cline. Script: Buster Keaton and Eddie Cline. Photography: Elgin Lessley.

Cast:

Buster Keaton (golfer/convict), Sybil Seely (warden's daughter), Joe Roberts (convict), Eddie Cline (hangman), Joe Keaton (convict).

The Scarecrow (1920)

Released: December 22, 1920 (some list November 17, 1920). Copyright: November 12, 1920. Length: 2 reels. Distributed by: Metro Pictures. Presented by: Comique Film Corporation. Producer: Joseph M. Schenck.

Technical Credits:

Director: Buster Keaton and Eddie Cline. Script: Buster Keaton and Eddie Cline. Photography: Elgin Lessley.

Cast:

Buster Keaton, Sybil Seely, Joe Keaton (her father), Joe Roberts (rival), Eddie Cline, Luke the Dog.

Note: Some filmographies list Al St. John in the cast, but it is hard to distinguish him in the film. He may be the minister who ends up on the motorcycle at the end. One filmography lists St. John as "the truck driver," but that is Eddie Cline.

Neighbors (1921)

Released: January 3, 1921 (some list December 22, 1920). Copyright: December 20, 1920. Length: 2 reels. Distributed by: Metro Pictures. Presented by: Comique Film Corporation.

Technical Credits:

Director: Buster Keaton and Eddie Cline. Script: Buster Keaton and Eddie Cline. Photography: Elgin Lessley.

Cast:

Buster Keaton (the boy), Joe Keaton (his father), Virginia Fox (the girl), Joe Roberts (her father), Eddie Cline (cop), James (Jack?) Duffy (judge), The Flying Escalantes.

Note: Original working titles: Mailbox *and* Backyard.

The Haunted House (1921)

Released: February 10, 1921. Copyright: February 7, 1921. Length: 2 reels. Distributed by: Metro Pictures. Presented by: Comique Film Corporation.

Technical Credits:

Director: Buster Keaton and Eddie Cline. Script: Buster Keaton and Eddie Cline. Photography: Elgin Lessley.

Cast:

Buster Keaton (bank teller), Virginia Fox (banker's daughter), Joe Roberts (cashier), Eddie Cline (man who gets glue on his pants).

Hard Luck (1921)

Released: March 16, 1921. Copyright: March 14, 1921. Length: 2 reels. Distributed by: Metro Pictures. Presented by: Comique Film Corporation.

Technical Credits:

Director: Buster Keaton and Eddie Cline. Script: Buster Keaton and Eddie Cline. Photography: Elgin Lessley.

Cast:

Buster Keaton, Virginia Fox, Joe Roberts, Bull Montana.

The High Sign (1921)

Released: April 12, 1921. Copyright: April 11, 1921. Length: 2 reels. Distributed by: Metro Pictures. Presented by: Comique Film Corporation. Producer: Joseph M. Schenck.

Technical Credits:

Director: Buster Keaton and Eddie Cline. Script: Buster Keaton and Eddie Cline. Photography: Elgin Lessley.

Cast:

Buster Keaton, Bartine Burkett, Al St. John (cameo).

Note: This was actually Keaton's first independent two-reeler, but he wasn't satisfied with it and had it shelved. It was only released after Keaton broke his leg while shooting The Electric House.

The Goat (1921)

Released: May 18, 1921. Copyright: May 17, 1921. Length: 2 reels. Distributed by: Metro Pictures. Presented by: Comique Film Corporation. Producer: Joseph M. Schenck.

Technical Credits:

Director: Buster Keaton and Mal St. Clair. Script: Buster Keaton and Mal St. Clair. Photography: Elgin Lessley.

Cast:

Buster Keaton, Virginia Fox (girl), Joe Roberts (her father, a detective), Mal St. Clair ("Dead Shot" Dan), Eddie Cline (cop), Jean Havez (man cleaning gun).

The Playhouse (1921)

Released: October 6, 1921. Copyright: October 6, 1921. Length: 2 reels. Distributed by: First National. Produced by: First National. Claimant: Joseph M. Schenck.

Technical Credits:

Director: Buster Keaton and Eddie Cline. Script: Buster Keaton and Eddie Cline. Photography: Elgin Lessley. Technical Director: Fred Gabourie.

Cast:

Buster Keaton (assistant stage manager), Joe Roberts (stage manager/Zouve guard), Virginia Fox (one of the twins).

Note: Some filmographies list Fred Gabourie as technical director starting with the first independent Keaton short. According to the biography by Rudi Blesh (page 154), Gabourie wasn't hired until after Buster broke his leg during his first attempt to film The Electric House. *Going by this,* The Playhouse *would be the first film he could have worked on. Some list his first film as* The Boat, *which is actually the one after* The Playhouse.

I have never found a listing as to who played the other twin in this film. In Blesh's biography of Keaton (pages 159–60), there is an excerpt from a Times *article on Keaton's marriage to Natalie Talmadge. At the end of the article it states, ". . . the bride is to appear with the bridegroom in his next picture play." Buster's next picture was* The Playhouse, *and there is a similarity between Natalie and Virginia Fox. Maybe the other twin was Natalie Talmadge.*

The Boat (1921)

Released: November 1921. Copyright: November 10, 1921. Length: 2 reels. Distributed by: First National. Produced by: Comique Film Corporation. Claimant: Comique Film Corporation. Presented by: Joseph M. Schenck.

Technical Credits:

Director: Buster Keaton and Eddie Cline. Script: Buster Keaton and Eddie Cline. Photography: Elgin Lessley. Technical Director: Fred Gabourie.

Cast:

Buster Keaton (husband), Sybil Seely (wife), Eddie Cline (telegrapher).

The Paleface (1922)

Released: January 1922. Copyright: December 17, 1921. Length: 2 reels. Distributed by: First National. Produced by: Comique Film Corporation. Claimant: Comique Film Corporation. Presented by: Joseph M. Schenck.

Technical Credits:

Director: Buster Keaton and Eddie Cline. Script: Buster Keaton and Eddie Cline. Photography: Elgin Lessley. Technical Director: Fred Gabourie.

Cast:

Buster Keaton, Joe Roberts (Indian chief), Virginia Fox (Indian maid).

Cops (1922)

Released: March 1922. Copyright: February 15, 1922. Length: 2 reels. Distributed by: First National. Produced by: Comique Film Corporation. Claimant: Comique Film Corporation.

Technical Credits:
Director: Buster Keaton and Eddie Cline. Script: Buster Keaton and Eddie Cline.
Photography: Elgin Lessley. Technical Director: Fred Gabourie.

Cast:
Buster Keaton, Virginia Fox (mayor's daughter), Joe Roberts (plainclothes cop),
Eddie Cline.

My Wife's Relations (1922)
Released: May 1922. Copyright: June 12, 1922. Length: 2 reels. Distributed by:
First National. Produced by: Comique Film Corporation. Claimant: Comique
Film Corporation. Presented by: Joseph M. Schenck.

Technical Credits:
Director: Buster Keaton and Eddie Cline. Script: Buster Keaton and Eddie Cline.
Photography: Elgin Lessley. Technical Director: Fred Gabourie.

Cast:
Buster Keaton, Kate Price (wife), Monte Collins (her father), her brothers: Joe
Roberts, Tom Wilson, Harry Madison, Wheezer Dell.

The Blacksmith (1922)
Released: July 21, 1922. Copyright: July 21, 1922. Length: 2 reels. Distributed
by: First National. Produced by: Comique Film Corporation. Claimant: Comique
Film Corporation. Presented by: Joseph M. Schenck.

Technical Credits:
Director: Buster Keaton and Mal St. Clair. Script: Buster Keaton and Mal St.
Clair. Photography: Elgin Lessley. Technical Director: Fred Gabourie.

Cast:
Buster Keaton (blacksmith's assistant), Joe Roberts (blacksmith), Virginia Fox
(girl with white horse).

*Note: The beautiful white horse in this film is the same broken-down nag
from* Cops. *The horse, which they had named Onyx, was pregnant when they
bought her. This caused her swayback condition. One day the crew showed up
to work and there was the foal. Buster named the offspring Onyx-pected.*

The Frozen North (1922)
Released: August 1922. Copyright: August 3, 1922. Length: 2 reels. Distributed
by: First National. Produced by: Buster Keaton Productions. Claimant: Buster
Keaton Productions. Presented by: Joseph M. Schenck.

Technical Credits:
Director: Buster Keaton and Eddie Cline. Script: Buster Keaton and Eddie Cline.
Photography: Elgin Lessley. Technical Director: Fred Gabourie.

Cast:

Buster Keaton, Bonnie Hill, Freeman Wood, Joe Roberts, Sybil Seely, Eddie Cline, Robert Parker.

Daydreams (1922)

Released: September 1922 (some list November 1922). Copyright: September 28, 1922. Length: 3 reels. Distributed by: First National. Produced by: Buster Keaton Productions. Claimant: Buster Keaton Productions. Presented by: Joseph M. Schenck.

Technical Credits:

Director: Buster Keaton and Eddie Cline. Script: Buster Keaton and Eddie Cline. Photography: Elgin Lessley. Technical Director: Fred Gabourie.

Cast:

Buster Keaton, Renée Adorée (the girl), Joe Keaton (her father), Joe Roberts (O'Grady, politician), Eddie Cline (stage manager).

The Electric House (1922)

Released: October 1922. Copyright: October 19, 1922. Length: 2 reels. Distributed by: Associated First National. Produced by: Buster Keaton Productions. Claimant: Buster Keaton Productions. Producer: Joseph M. Schenck.

Technical Credits:

Director: Buster Keaton and Eddie Cline. Script: Buster Keaton and Eddie Cline. Photography: Elgin Lessley. Technical Director: Fred Gabourie.

Cast:

Buster Keaton, Joe Roberts, Virginia Fox.

Note: There was an attempt to make this film after The Goat, *but when Keaton broke his leg, shooting stopped and the footage was destroyed. Some stills from this first version still survive.*

Joe and Myra Keaton are sometimes listed as being in this film, but if they are, they are unrecognizable. Perhaps they were to have been in the first version.

The Balloonatic (1923)

Released: January 22, 1923. Copyright: January 22, 1923. Length: 2 reels. Distributed by: Associated First National. Produced by: Buster Keaton Productions. Claimant: Buster Keaton Productions.

Technical Credits:

Director: Buster Keaton and Eddie Cline. Script: Buster Keaton and Eddie Cline. Photography: Elgin Lessley. Technical Director: Fred Gabourie.

Cast:
Buster Keaton, Phyllis Haver.

The Love Nest (1923)

Released: March 1923. Copyright: March 1923. Length: 2 reels. Distributed by: Associated First National. Produced by: Buster Keaton Productions. Claimant: Buster Keaton Productions.

Technical Credits:
Director: Buster Keaton and Eddie Cline. Script: Buster Keaton and Eddie Cline. Photography: Elgin Lessley. Technical Director: Fred Gabourie.

Cast:
Buster Keaton, Joe Roberts (ship captain), Virginia Fox (Buster's girlfriend).

KEATON SILENT FEATURES

The Saphead (1920)

Released: October 11, 1920. Copyright: October 18, 1920. Length: 7 reels. Distributed by: Metro Pictures. Presented by: John L. Golden and Winchell Smith, in conjunction with Marcus Loew.

Technical Credits:
Director: Herbert Blache. Scenario: June Mathis, based on *The New Henrietta* by Winchell Smith and Victor Mapes, adapted from *The Henrietta,* a play by Bronson Howard. Photography: Harold Wenstrom.

Cast:
Buster Keaton (Bertie Van Alstyne), William Crane (Nicholas Van Alstyne), Irving Cummings (Mark Turner), Carol Holloway (Rose Turner), Beulah Booker (Agnes Gates), Jeffery Williams (Hutchins), Edward Jobson (Rev. Murray Hilton), Edward Alexander (Watson Flint), Jack Livingston (Dr. George Wainwright), Edward Connelly (Musgrave), Odette Tyler (Mrs. Cornelia Opdyke), Katherine Albert (Hattie), Helen Holte (Henrietta Reynolds), Alfred Hollingsworth (Hathaway), Henry Clauss (Valet).

Note: The Saphead, *Keaton's first feature, was made concurrently with the start of the production of his own two-reel comedies. He was loaned out for this film, and not much of his genius can be seen here, as he had no creative control over the project.*

The Three Ages (1923)

Released: September 24, 1923. Copyright: July 25, 1923. Length: 6 reels or 5,251 feet. Distributed by: Metro Pictures. Claimant: Joseph M. Schenck Productions. Produced by: Buster Keaton Productions.

Technical Credits:
Director: Buster Keaton and Eddie Cline. Script/Titles: Clyde Bruckman, Joseph A. Mitchell, Jean C. Havez. Technical Director: Fred Gabourie. Photography: William McGann, Elgin Lessley.

Cast:
Buster Keaton (the hero), Margaret Leahy (the girl), Joe Roberts (her father), Lillian Lawrence (her mother), Wallace Beery (rival), Oliver Hardy (rival's Roman helper), Horace "Cupid" Morgan (the emperor), Blanche Payson (amazon cavewoman), Lionel Belmore.

Our Hospitality (1923)
Released: November 3, 1923 (Los Angeles premiere); November 19, 1923 (general release). Copyright: November 20, 1923. Length: 7 reels or 6,220 feet. Distributed by: Metro Pictures. Produced by: Buster Keaton Productions. Claimant: Joseph M. Schenck Productions.

Technical Credits:
Director: Buster Keaton and Jack C. Blystone. Script/Titles: Clyde Bruckman, Jean C. Havez, Joseph A. Mitchell. Art Director: Fred Gabourie. Electrician/Lighting: Denver Harmon. Costumes: Walter Israel. Photography: Elgin Lessley and Gordon Jennings.

Cast:
Prologue: Edward Coxen (John McKay), Jean Dumas (his wife), Buster Keaton, Jr. (Willie McKay, age one), Leonard Clapham [later called Tom London] (James Canfield), Joe Roberts (his brother, Joseph Canfield). Main story: Buster Keaton (Willie McKay, age twenty-one), Kitty Bradbury (his Aunt Mary), Joe Keaton (Lem Doolittle, train engineer), James [Jack?] Duffy (Sam Gardner, train guard), Natalie Talmadge (Joseph Canfield's daughter, Virginia), Ralph Bushman [later called Francis X. Bushman, Jr.] and Craig Ward (her brothers, Clayton and Lee), Erwin Connelly (husband quarreling with wife), Monte Collins (Rev. Benjamin Dorsey).

Note: The Rocket, *the train used in this film, was also used by Al St. John in his two-reel short* The Iron Mule *(1925). This film exists today only in a one-reel Kodascope abridgment but contains many inventive gags with the train. It is also suspected to have been directed by Roscoe Arbuckle.*

Sherlock Jr. (1924)
Released: April 21, 1924. Copyright: April 22, 1924. Length: 5 reels or 4,065 feet. Distributed by: Metro Pictures. Claimant: Joseph M. Schenck. Produced by: Buster Keaton Productions.

Technical Credits:
Director: Roscoe Arbuckle (early sequences) and Buster Keaton. Script/Titles: Clyde Bruckman, Jean C. Havez, and Joseph A. Mitchell. Technical Director:

Fred Gabourie. Costumes: Clare West. Photography: Elgin Lessley, Byron Houck.

Cast:

Buster Keaton (the projectionist), Kathryn McGuire (his fiancée), Joe Keaton (her father), Ward Crane (the rival), Erwin Connelly (handyman/butler), Jane Connelly, Ford West, George Davis, Horace Morgan, John Patrick, Ruth Holley.

Note: In Keaton's autobiography, he states that Arbuckle was difficult to work with and that it was arranged for him to direct The Red Mill, *causing him to drop out of* Sherlock Jr. *so Keaton could finish directing. Yet according to Arbuckle's third wife, Doris Deane, Arbuckle finished directing* Sherlock Jr. *as well as having supplied the story idea. One fact that supports this claim is that* The Red Mill *wasn't filmed until three years later, so there would be no need for Arbuckle to drop out as director of* Sherlock Jr.

The Navigator (1924)

Released: October 13, 1924. Copyright: October 14, 1924. Length: 6 reels or 5,600 feet. Distributed by: Metro-Goldwyn Pictures Corp. Produced by: Buster Keaton Productions. Claimant: Metro-Goldwyn Pictures Corp. Presented by: Joseph M. Schenck.

Technical Credits:

Director: Buster Keaton and Donald Crisp. Script/Titles: Clyde Bruckman, Joseph A. Mitchell, Jean C. Havez. Technical Director: Fred Gabourie. Electrical Effects: Denver Harmon. Photography: Elgin Lessley and Byron Houck.

Cast:

Buster Keaton (Rollo Treadway), Kathryn McGuire (Betsy O'Brien), Frederick Vroom (John O'Brien, her father), Clarence Burton and H. M. Clugston (spies), Donald Crisp (face on picture at porthole), Noble Johnson (cannibal chief), the liner *Buford* (*Navigator*).

Seven Chances (1925)

Released: March 16, 1925 (some list March 11, 1925). Copyright: April 22, 1925. Length: 6 reels or 5,113 feet. Distributed by: Metro-Goldwyn Pictures. Produced by: Buster Keaton Productions. Claimant: Buster Keaton Productions. Presented by: Joseph M. Schenck.

Technical Credits:

Director: Buster Keaton. Script/Titles: Clyde Bruckman, Jean C. Havez, and Joseph A. Mitchell, based on Roi Cooper Megrue's play originally produced by David Belasco. Art Director: Fred Gabourie. Electrical Effects: Denver Harmon. Photography: Elgin Lessley and Byron Houck (black and white, with Technicolor prologue sequence).

Cast:

Buster Keaton (Jimmie Shannon), Ruth Dwyer (Mary Jones), T. Roy Barnes (Jimmie's partner, Billy Meekin), Snitz Edwards (the lawyer), Frankie Raymond (Mary's mother), Jules Cowles (the hired hand), Jean Arthur (Miss Jones, switchboard operator at country club), Erwin Connelly (clergyman), Jean Havez (man on the stair landing); and Loro Bara, Alma Bramley, Bartine Burkett, Doris Deane, Hazel Deane, Connie Evans, Eugenia Gilbert, Edna Hammon, Marion Harlan, Judy King, Rosalind Mooney, Peggy Pearce, Barbara Pierce, Kate Price, and Pauline Toler (women sought in marriage).

Note: According to Moving Picture News, *Jack McDermott was announced as a codirector.*

Go West (1925)

Released: October 25, 1925 (New York premiere); November 1, 1925 (general release). Copyright: November 23, 1925. Length: 7 reels or 6,293 feet. Distributed by: Metro-Goldwyn-Mayer. Produced by: Buster Keaton Productions. Claimant: Buster Keaton Productions. Producer: Joseph M. Schenck.

Technical Credits:

Director: Buster Keaton, assisted by Lex Neal. Script/Titles: Raymond Cannon, from Keaton's original idea. Art Director: Fred Gabourie. Electrical Effects: Denver Harmon. Photography: Elgin Lessley and Bert Haines.

Cast:

Buster Keaton (Friendless, Homer Holiday), Howard Truesdale (Thompson, owner of the Diamond Bar Ranch), Kathleen Myers (Gloria, his daughter), Ray Thompson (foreman), Brown Eyes (cow), Joe Keaton (man in barber chair), Roscoe Arbuckle and Babe London (fat woman and daughter in store), Erwin Connelly (stockyard owner).

Note: Working titles were Mr. Nobody *and* Tramp! Tramp! Tramp!

Battling Butler (1926)

Released: August 22, 1926 (New York premiere); September 4 or 19, 1926 (general release). Copyright: August 30, 1926. Length: 7 reels or 6,970 feet. Distributed by: Metro-Goldwyn-Mayer. Produced by: Buster Keaton Productions, Inc. Claimant: Metro-Goldwyn-Mayer.

Technical Credits:

Director: Buster Keaton. Script/Titles: Paul Gerard Smith, Albert Boasberg, Charles Smith, and Lex Neal, from the play *Battling Buttler* by Stanley Brightman, Austin Melford, Philip Brabham, Walter L. Rosemont, and Douglas Furber, adapted by Ballard McDonald. Technical Director: Fred Gabourie. Electrical Effects: Ed Levy. Photography: J. Devereaux Jennings and Bert Haines.

Cast:

Buster Keaton (Alfred Butler), Snitz Edwards (his valet), Sally O'Neil (mountain girl), Walter James (her father), Bud Fine (her brother), Francis McDonald (Alfred "Battling" Butler), Mary O'Brien (his wife), Tom Wilson (his trainer), Eddie Borden (his manager).

Note: Lex Neal started directing but was taken off the picture and Buster took over.

The General (1926)

Released: December 31, 1926 (Tokyo); February 5, 1927 (New York). Copyright: December 22, 1926. Length: 8 reels or 7,500 feet. Distributed by: United Artists Corporation. Produced by: Buster Keaton Productions. Claimant: Joseph M. Schenck.

Technical Credits:

Director: Buster Keaton and Clyde Bruckman. Script/Titles: Buster Keaton and Clyde Bruckman from William Pittinger's book *The Great Locomotive Chase*. Adaptation: Al Boasberg and Charles Smith. Technical Director: Frank Barnes. Lighting Effects: Denver Harmon. Production Manager: Fred Gabourie. Editors: J. Sherman Kell, Harry Barnes, and Buster Keaton. Wardrobe and Makeup: J. K. Pitcairn, Fred C. Ryle, and Bennie Hubbel. Chief Mechanic: Fred Wright. Special Effects: Jack Little. Location Manager: Bert Jackson. Still Photography: Byron S. Houck. Photography: J. Devereaux Jennings and Bert Haines; Elmer Ellsworth, asst.

Cast:

Buster Keaton (Johnnie Gray), Jackie Lowe and Jackie Hanlon (boys who follow Johnnie), Marion Mack (Annabelle Lee), Charles Smith (her father), Frank Barnes (her brother), Frank Agney (recruiter), Frederick Vroom (Confederate general), Glen Cavender (Captain Anderson, chief spy), Ross McCutcheon, Charles Phillips, Jack Dempster, Red Thompson, Anthony Harvey, Ray Hanford, Tom Moran, Bud Fine, Jimmie Bryant, and Al Hanson (raiders), Jim Farley (Union General Thatcher), and Joe Keaton, Mike Donlin, and Tom Nawn (Union officers).

College (1927)

Released: September 10, 1927 (New York premiere); November 1927 (general release). Copyright: September 10, 1927. Length: 6 reels or 5,916 feet (originally 7,000 feet).* Distributed by: United Artists. Produced by: Buster Keaton Productions. Claimant: Joseph M. Schenck.

---

*The difference in film length may be due to the elimination of a football sequence. Though not supported by documentation, this hypothesis is based on the fact that in the beginning of the film, when Buster gets to college, he looks through a series of "How To" books on sports, one of which is football. Sequences appear in the film for each "How To" sport except football. Also, in

Technical Credits:

Director: James W. Horne. Supervisor: Harry Brand. Script/Titles: Carl Harbaugh and Bryan Foy. Technical Director: Fred Gabourie. Lighting Effects: Jack Lewis. Editor: J. Sherman Kell. Photography: J. Devereaux Jennings and Bert Haines.

Cast:

Buster Keaton (Ronald), Florence Turner (his mother), Ann Cornwall (Mary Haines), Harold Goodwin (Jeff Brown), Snitz Edwards (Dean Edwards), Flora Bramley (Mary's friend), Buddy Mason and Grant Withers (Jeff's friends), Carl Harbaugh (boat crew coach), Sam Crawford (baseball coach), Lee Barnes (USC athlete doubling for Keaton in pole vault into a window), and the following USC athletes: Paul Goldsmith, Morton Kaer, Bud Houser, Kenneth Grumbles, Charles Borah, Leighton Dye, "Shorty" Worden, Robert Boling, and Eric Mack.

Steamboat Bill, Jr. (1928)

Released: May 12, 1928. Copyright: June 2, 1928. Length: 7 reels or 6,400 feet. Distributed by: United Artists. Produced by: Buster Keaton Productions. Claimant: Joseph M. Schenck (Carl Harbaugh, author). Presented by: Joseph M. Schenck.

Technical Credits:

Director: Charles F. Reisner. Supervisor: Harry Brand. Script/Titles: Carl Harbaugh. Editor: J. Sherman Kell. Technical Director: Fred Gabourie, assisted by Sandy Roth. Photography: J. Devereaux Jennings and Bert Haines.

Cast:

Buster Keaton (William Canfield, Jr., "Willie"), Ernest Torrence (William Canfield, Sr., "Steamboat Bill"), Tom Lewis (his first mate), Tom McGuire (John James King), Marion Byron (his daughter, Kitty), Louise Keaton (stunt double).

Note: Some filmographies list Joe Keaton as the barber, but it is someone else.

The Cameraman (1928)

Released: September 22, 1928. Copyright: September 15, 1928. Length: 8 reels or 6,995 feet. Distributed by: Metro-Goldwyn-Mayer. Produced by: Metro-Goldwyn-Mayer. Claimant: Metro-Goldwyn-Mayer Distributing Corp. Producer: Lawrence Weingarten (uncredited).

Technical Credits:

Director: Edward M. Sedgwick, Jr. Script: Clyde Bruckman and Lew Lipton.

---

the climax of the film, when Buster races to save Mary from Jeff, he uses actions needed in all the sports he had failed at. His zigzag down the field would be football. Some stills from this film exist with Keaton holding a football. If these sequences did exist, they were probably removed so as not to be compared with Harold Lloyd's *The Freshman*.

Continuity: E. Richard Schayer. Titles: Joe W. Farnham. Technical Director: Fred Gabourie. Wardrobe: David Cox. Editor: Hugh Wynn. Photography: Elgin Lessley and Reggie Lanning.

Cast:

Buster Keaton (Luke Shannon, called Buster), Marceline Day (Sally Richards), Harold Goodwin (Harold Stagg), Sidney Bracy (Edward J. Blake, boss of film office), Harry Gribbon (Hennessey the cop), Edward Brophy (man in the bathhouse), Josephine (monkey), William Irving (photographer), Vernon Dent (man in tight bathing suit), Dick Alexander (The Big Sea Lion), Ray Cooke (office worker).

Spite Marriage (1929)

Released: April 6, 1929. Copyright: April 22, 1929. Length: 9 reels or 6,500 feet in original silent version; later 7,050 feet with synchronized music track added April 5, 1929. Distributed by: Metro-Goldwyn-Mayer Distributing Corp. Produced by: Metro-Goldwyn-Mayer. Claimant: Metro-Goldwyn-Mayer Distributing Corp.

Technical Credits:

Director: Edward M. Sedgwick, Jr. Supervisor: Larry Weingarten. Producer: Edward M. Sedgwick, Jr. Story: Lew Lipton. Adaptation: Ernest S. Pagano. Continuity: E. Richard Schayer. Titles: Robert Hopkins. Art Director: Cedric Gibbons. Wardrobe: David Cox. Editor: Frank Sullivan. Photography: Reggie Lanning.

Cast:

Buster Keaton (Elmer Edgemont), Dorothy Sebastian (Trilby Drew), Edward Earle (Lionel Benmore), Leila Hyams (Ethyle Norcrosse), William Bechtel (Frederick Nussbaum), John Bryon (Giovanni Scarzi), Hank Mann (stage manager), Pat Harmon (ship captain).

MGM SOUND FEATURES

The Hollywood Revue of 1929 (1929)

Released: November 23, 1929. Copyright: September 23, 1929. Length: 11,669 feet (130 minutes; current prints 113 minutes); black and white with color sequences. Distributed by: Metro-Goldwyn-Mayer. Produced by: Harry Rapf.

Technical Credits:

Director: Charles Reisner. Dialogue: Al Boasberg, Robert E. Hopkins. Costumes: David Cox. Photography: John Arnold, Irving G. Ries, Maximilian Fabian. Editor: William S. Gray, Cameron K. Wood. Art Director: Cedric Gibbons, Richard Day. Recording Engineer: Douglas Shearer. Sound Technician: Russell Franks. Dances and Ensembles: Sammy Lee, George

Cunningham. Orchestra and Musical Arrangements: Arthur Lange. Music: Gus Edwards. Lyrics: Joe Goodwin. Interpolations by: Nacio Herb Brown, Arthur Freed, Dave Snell, Jesse Greer, Ray Klages, Martin Broones, Fred Fisher, Andy Rice.

Cast:
Conrad Nagel and Jack Benny (emcees), Marion Davies, John Gilbert, Norma Shearer, William Haines, Joan Crawford, Buster Keaton, Bessie Love, Charles King, Marie Dressler, Gus Edwards, Dane and Arthur, Laurel and Hardy, Ukulele Ike, Anita Page, Polly Moran, Gwen Lee, Brox Sisters, Albertina Rasch Ballet, Natacha Nattova and Company, and The Rounders.

Note: Keaton, as Salome, performs "The Dance of the Sea" and joins the cast in the finale, "Singin' in the Rain," which is missing in most prints released for television.

Wir Schalten Un Auf Hollywood *(German version of The Hollywood Revue)*
Director: Frank Reicher. Adaptation: Paul Morgan.

Free and Easy *(1930)* *(Working title: On the Set; TV title: Easy Go)*
Released: March 22, 1930. Copyright: April 2, 1930. Length: 93 minutes or 8,413 feet; silent version 5,240 feet. Distributed by: Metro-Goldwyn-Mayer. Produced by: Edward Sedgwick.

Technical Credits:
Director: Edward Sedgwick. Scenario: Richard Schayer. Dialogue: Al Boasberg. Adaptation: Paul Dickey. Photography: Leonard Smith. Editor: William Le Vanway, George Todd (uncredited). Art Director: Cedric Gibbons. Recording Engineer: Douglas Shearer. Songs: Roy Turk, Fred E. Ahlert. Dances staged by: Sammy Lee.

Cast:
Buster Keaton (Elmer Butts), Anita Page (Elvira Plunkett), Trixie Friganza (Ma Plunkett), Robert Montgomery (Larry Mitchell), Fred Niblo (director), Edgar Dearing (officer), David Burton (director), Edward Brophy (stage manager), and as themselves: Gwen Lee, John Miljan, Lionel Barrymore, William Collier Sr., William Haines, Dorothy Sebastian, Karl Dane, Jackie Coogan, Cecil B. De Mille, Arthur Lange, and Joe Farnham.

Note: Judy Garland recorded a version of the song "Free and Easy" that had different lyrics and a slowed-down tempo.

Le Metteur en Scene *(French version of Free and Easy)*
Titles: Alexander Stein, Allen Byre.

Estrellados (Spanish version of *Free and Easy*)

Cast:
Buster Keaton, Raquel Torres, Don Alvarado, Maria Calvo, Emile Chautard.

Doughboys (1930) (Working title: *The Big Shot*; British title: *Forward March*)

Released: August 30, 1930. Copyright: September 8, 1930. Length: 81 minutes or 7,325 feet. Distributed by: Metro-Goldwyn-Mayer. Produced by: Buster Keaton.

Technical Credits:
Director: Edward Sedgwick. Scenario: Richard Schayer. Dialogue: Al Boasberg, Richard Schayer. Story: Al Boasberg, Sidney Lazarus. Photography: Leonard Smith. Editor: William Le Vanway. Art Director: Cedric Gibbons. Recording Engineer: Douglas Shearer. Songs: Edward Sedgwick, Joseph Meyer, Howard Johnson. Dances staged by: Sammy Lee. Wardrobe: Vivian Baer.

Cast:
Buster Keaton (Elmer Stuyvesant), Sally Eilers (Mary Rogers), Cliff Edwards (Cliff Nescopeck), Edward Brophy (Sergeant Brophy), Victor Potel (Svendenburg), Arnold Korff (Gustave), Frank Mayo (Captain Scott), Pitzy Katz (Abie Cohn), William Steele (Lieutenant Randolph), Ann Sothern (WAC), Edward Sedgwick (Guggelheimer, camp cook), John Carroll (soldier/singer).

De Fronte, Marchen (German version of *Doughboys*)

De Frante Marchen! (Spanish version of *Doughboys*)

Cast:
Buster Keaton, Conchita Montenegro, Juan de Landa, Romualdo Tirado.

Parlor, Bedroom and Bath (1931) (British title: *Romeo in Pyjamas*)

Released: February 28, 1931. Copyright: May 1, 1939. Length: 73 minutes or 6,563 feet. Distributed by: Metro-Goldwyn-Mayer. Produced by: Buster Keaton.

Technical Credits:
Director: Edward Sedgwick. Adaptation: Richard Schayer, Robert E. Hopkins, from the play by Charles W. Bell and Mark Swan. Editor: William Le Vanway. Recording Engineer: Karl Zint. Art Director: Cedric Gibbons. Recording Engineer: Douglas Shearer. Photography: Leonard Smith. Wardrobe: Rene Hubert.

Cast:
Buster Keaton (Reginald Irving), Charlotte Greenwood (Polly Hathaway), Reginald Denny (Jeffery Haywood), Cliff Edwards (bellhop), Dorothy Christy

(Angelica Embrey), Joan Peers (Nita Leslie), Sally Eilers (Virginia Embrey), Natalie Moorhead (Leila Crofton), Edward Brophy (detective), Walter Merrill (Frederick Leslie), Sidney Bracy (butler).

Note: Filmed at Keaton's home, the Italian Villa.

Buster Se Marie (French version of *Parlor, Bedroom and Bath*)
Length: 80 minutes. Director: Edward Brophy, Claude Autant-Lara. French Dialogue: Yves Mirande. Dialogue Director: Andre Luguet.

Cast:
Buster Keaton (Reggie), Andre Luguet (Jef), Jeanne Helbling (Virginia), Françoise Rosay (Angelique), Andre Berley (police commissioner), Mona Goya, Mireille, Georgette Rhodes, Lya Lys, Rolla Norman, George Davis, Paul Morgan.

Casanova Wider Willen (German version of *Parlor, Bedroom and Bath*)
Director: Edward Brophy.

Cast:
Buster Keaton, Paul Morgan, Marion Lessing, Egon von Jordan, Françoise Rosay, Leni Stengel, Gerda Mann, George Davis, Wolfgang Zilzer.

Sidewalks of New York (1931)
Released: September 26, 1931. Copyright: September 21, 1931. Length: 70 minutes. Distributed by: Metro-Goldwyn-Mayer. Produced by: Lawrence Weingarten (uncredited).

Technical Credits:
Directors: Jules White, Zion Myers. Scenario: George Landy, Paul Gerard Smith. Dialogue: Robert E. Hopkins, Eric Hatch. Photography: Leonard Smith. Editor: Charles Hochberg. Art Director: Cedric Gibbons. Recording Engineer: Douglas Shearer.

Cast:
Buster Keaton (Homer Van Dine Harmon), Anita Page (Margie), Cliff Edwards (Poggle), Frank Rowan (Butch), Norman Phillips, Jr. (Clipper), Frank La Rue (police sergeant), Oscar Apfel (judge), Syd Saylor (Mulvaney), Clark Marshall (Lefty).

Buster Millionaire (French version of *Sidewalks of New York*)

The Passionate Plumber (1932)
Released: February 6, 1932. Copyright: February 8, 1932. Length: 73 minutes. Distributed by: Metro-Goldwyn-Mayer. Produced by: Harry Rapf (uncredited).

Technical Credits:
Director: Edward Sedgwick. Dialogue: Ralph Spence. Adaptation: Laurence E. Johnson from the play *Her Cardboard Lover* by Jacques Deval. Photography: Norbert Brodine. Editor: William S. Gray. Art Director: Cedric Gibbons. Recording Engineer: Douglas Shearer.

Cast:
Buster Keaton (Elmer Tuttle), Jimmy Durante (McCracken), Irene Purcell (Patricia Alden), Polly Moran (Albine), Gilbert Roland (Tony Lagorce), Mona Maris (Nina), Maude Eburne (Aunt Charlotte), Henry Armetta (bouncer), Paul Porcasi (Paul Le Maire), Jean Del Val (chauffeur), August Tollaire (General Bouschay), Edward Brophy (unbilled bit outside of beauty parlor).

Note: This film has a shot of the ocean as seen from a balcony in Paris. Paris has no ocean views. This is Hollywood, after all.

Le Plombier Amoureux (French version of *The Passionate Plumber*)
Director: Claude Autant-Lara.

Cast:
Buster Keaton, Irene Purcell, Jimmy Durante, Mona Maris, Polly Moran, Jeanette Ferney, Barbara Leonard, Maude Eburne, Jean Del Val, George Davis, Fred Perry.

Speak Easily (1932)
Released: August 13, 1932. Length: 80 minutes. Distributed by: Metro-Goldwyn-Mayer. Produced by: Lawrence Weingarten (uncredited).

Technical Credits:
Director: Edward Sedgwick. Adaptation: Ralph Spence, Laurence E. Johnson, from the story *Footlights* by Clarence Budington Kelland. Photography: Harold Wenstrom. Editor: William Le Vanway. Art Director: Cedric Gibbons. Recording Engineer: Douglas Shearer. Costumes: Arthur Appell.

Cast:
Buster Keaton (Professor Timoleon Zanders Post), Jimmy Durante (James), Ruth Selwyn (Pansy Peets), Thelma Todd (Eleanor Espere), Hedda Hopper (Mrs. Peets), William Pawley (Griffo), Sidney Toler (stage director), Lawrence Grant (Dr. Bolton), Henry Armetta (Tony), Edward Brophy (Reno).

What! No Beer? (1933)
Released: February 10, 1933. Copyright: March 13, 1933. Length: 70 minutes. Distributed by: Metro-Goldwyn-Mayer. Producer: Lawrence Weingarten (uncredited).

Technical Credits:
Director: Edward Sedgwick. Story: Robert E. Hopkins. Additional Dialogue:

Jack Cluett. Script: Carey Wilson. Photography: Harold Wenstrom. Editor: Frank Sullivan. Art Director: Cedric Gibbons. Recording Engineer: Douglas Shearer.

Cast:

Buster Keaton (Elmer J. Butts), Jimmy Durante (Jimmy Potts), Roscoe Ates (Schultz), Phyllis Barry (Hortense), John Miljan (Butch Lorado), Henry Armetta (Tony), Edward Brophy (Spike Moran), Charles Dunbar (Mulligan), Charles Giblyn (chief).

OTHER SOUND FEATURES

Le Roi des Champs-Élysées (1934) *(The Champ of the Champs-Élysées/The King of the Champs-Élysées)*

Released: December 1934 (not released in the U.S.). Length: 70 minutes. Distributed by: France-Paramount. Produced by: Nero Film Productions. Producer: Seymour Nebenzal.

Technical Credits:

Director: Max Nosseck. Supervisor: Robert Siodmak. Script: Arnold Lipp. Dialogue: Yves Mirande. Photography: Robert Le Febvre. Art Director: Hugues Laurent, Jacques-Laurent Atthalin. Music: Joe Hajos.

Cast:

Buster Keaton (Buster Garner/Jim Le Balafre), Paulette Dubost (Germaine), Colette Darfeuil (Simone), Madeline Guitty (Mme. Garnier), Jacques Dumesnil, Pierre Pierade, Gaston Dupray, Paul Clerget, Frank Maurice, Pitouto, Lucien Callamand.

An Old Spanish Custom (1935) *(The Invader/The Intruder)*

Released: January 2, 1935. Length: 61 minutes. Distributed by: British & Continental Films (MGM). Released in U.S. by: J. H. Hoffberg. Producer: Sam Spiegel, Harold Richman.

Technical Credits:

Director: Adrian Brunel. Assistant Director: Pelham Leigh Aman. Script: Edwin Greenwood. Photography: Eugene Schuefftan, Eric L. Gross. Editor: Dan Birt. Music: John Greenwood, George Rubens. Recording Engineer: Denis Scanlan.

Cast:

Buster Keaton (Leander Proudfoot), Lupita Tovar (Lupita Malez), Esme Percy (Jose), Lyn Harding (Gonzalo Gonzalez), Webster Booth (serenader), Andrea Malandrinos (Carlos), Hilda Moreno (Carmita), Clifford Heatherley (David Cheeseman).

Note: J. P. Lebel's Keaton filmography lists a film titled The Serenade *for 1935. This is the only such listing that I have found, and it probably refers to*

An Old Spanish Custom *despite the fact that* The Invader *is listed for 1934, which was when the filming was completed.*

Keaton remade this film as a two-reel short for Columbia Pictures in 1939 called Pest from the West.

Hollywood Cavalcade (1939)
Released: October 13, 1939. Copyright: October 13, 1939. Length 96 minutes; color. Distributed by: 20th Century-Fox. Produced by: Darryl F. Zanuck.

Technical Credits:
Director: Irving Cummings. Script: Ernest Pascal. Story: Hilary Lynn, Brown Holmes, based on an idea by Lou Breslow. Photography: Allen M. Davey, Ernest Palmer. Editor: Walter Thompson. Keystone Kops sequences directed by: Mal St. Clair. Technical Adviser: Mack Sennett and Buster Keaton (uncredited).

Cast:
Don Ameche, Alice Faye, Buster Keaton, Al Jolson, Stuart Erwin, Mary Forbes, Chester Conklin, Rin-Tin-Tin Jr., Harold Goodwin, Willie Fung.

The Villain Still Pursued Her (1940)
Released: October 11, 1940. Copyright: October 4, 1940. Length: 67 minutes. Distributed by: RKO. Produced by: Franklin-Blank Productions. Producer: Harold B. Franklin.

Technical Credits:
Director: Edward Cline. Script: Elbert Franklin, based on the play *The Fallen Saved,* also known as *The Drunkard.* Additional Dialogue: Ethel La Blanche. Photography: Lucien Ballard. Editor: Arthur Hilton. Music: Frank Tours.

Cast:
Alan Mowbray (Silas Cribbs), Richard Cromwell (Edward Middleton), Anita Louise (Mary Wilson-Middleton), Hugh Herbert (Frederick Healy), Buster Keaton (William Dalton), Joyce Compton (Hazel Dalton), Margaret Hamilton (Widow Wilson), Billy Gilbert (announcer), Diane Fisher (Julia Middleton), Charles Judels (pie vendor), Jack Norton (customer), Vernon Dent (police officer), Carlotta Monti (woman who drops handkerchief).

Li'l Abner (1940)
Released: November 1, 1940. Copyright: November 1, 1940. Length: 78 minutes. Distributed by: RKO (Astor Pictures). Produced by: Vogue Pictures. Associate Producer: Herman Schlom.

Technical Credits:
Director: Albert S. Rogell. Screenplay: Charles Kerr and Tyler Johnson, based on comic strip by Al Capp. Musical Director: Lud Gluskin. Art Director: Ralph

Berger. Photography: Harry Jackson. Edited by: Otto Ludwig, Donn Hayes. Song: "Li'l Abner" by Ben Oakland, Milton Drake, Milton Berle.

Cast:

Granville Owen (Li'l Abner), Martha O'Driscoll (Daisy Mae), Mona Ray (Mammy Yokum), Johnnie Morris (Pappy Yokum), Buster Keaton (Lonesome Polecat), Bud Jamison (Hairless Joe), Edgar Kennedy (Cornelius Cornpone), Al St. John (Joe Smithpan), Kay Sutton (Wendy Wildcat), Billie Seward (Cousin Delightful), Maude Eburne (Granny Scraggs), Charles A. Post (Earthquake McGoon), Dick Elliot (Marryin' Sam), Johnny Arthur (Montague, the bank clerk), Walter Catlett (barber), Chester Conklin (Mayor Gurgle), Doodles Weaver (Hannibal Hoops), Hank Mann (a bachelor), Lucien Littlefield (sheriff), Mickey Daniels (Cicero Grunts), Frank Wilder (Abuah Gooch), Eddie Gribbon (Barney Bargrease), Blanche Payson (large bachelorette), Louise Keaton (small bachelorette).

Forever and a Day (1943)

Released: March 26, 1943. Copyright: March 19, 1943. Length: 104 minutes. Distributed by: RKO. Produced by: Anglo-American Productions. Production Supervisor: Lloyd Richards.

Technical Credits:

Directors: René Clair, Edmund Goulding, Cedric Hardwicke, Frank Lloyd, Victor Saville, Robert Stevenson, Herbert Wilcox. Script: Charles Bennett, C. S. Forester, Lawrence Hazard, Michael Hogan, W. P. Lipscomb, Alice Duer Miller, John Van Druten, Alan Campbell, Peter Godfrey, S. M. Herzig, Christopher Isherwood, Gene Lockhart, R. C. Sherriff, Claudine West, Norman Corwin, Jack Hatfield, James Hilton, Emmett Lavery, Frederick Lonsdale, Donald Ogden Stewart, Keith Winter. Photography: Robert DeGrasse, Lee Garmes, Russell Metty, Nicholas Musuraca. Editor: Elmo J. Williams, George Crone. Music Director: Anthony Collins.

Cast:

Buster Keaton (plumber), Brian Aherne, Robert Cummings, Ida Lupino, Charles Laughton, Herbert Marshall, Ray Milland, Anna Neagle, Merle Oberon, Claude Rains, Victor McLaglen, Roland Young, C. Aubrey Smith, Edward Everett Horton, Elsa Lanchester, Edmund Gwen, Cedric Hardwicke, and many more cameo appearances, mostly by British stars.

San Diego, I Love You (1944)

Released: September 29, 1944. Copyright: September 15, 1944. Length: 85 minutes. Distributed by: Universal Pictures. Produced by: Michael Fessier, Ernest Pagano.

Technical Credits:

Director: Reginald Le Borg. Script: Michael Fessier, Ernest Pagano. Story: Ruth McKenney, Richard Bransten. Photography: Hal Mohr, John P. Fulton. Editor: Charles Maynard.

Cast:
Louise Allbritton, Jon Hall, Buster Keaton (bus driver), Edward Everett Horton, Eric Blore, Irene Ryan, Rudy Wissler, Chester Clute, Hobart Cavanaugh.

That's the Spirit (1945)
Released: June 1, 1945. Copyright: April 24, 1945. Length: 93 minutes. Distributed by: Universal Pictures. Produced by: Michael Fessier, Ernest Pagano.

Technical Credits:
Director: Charles Lamont. Script: Michael Fessier, Ernest Pagano. Photography: Charles Van Enger, John P. Fulton. Editor: Fred R. Feitshans, Jr. Songs: Inez James, Sidney Miller, Jack Brooks, Richard Wagner, Hans J. Salter.

Cast:
Jack Oakie, Peggy Ryan, June Vincent, Gene Lockhart, Johnny Coy, Andy Devine, Arthur Treacher, Irene Ryan, Buster Keaton (as L.M., head of complaint department in heaven).

That Night with You (1945)
Released: September 28, 1945. Copyright: September 21, 1945. Length: 84 minutes. Distributed by Universal Pictures. Produced by: Michael Fessier, Ernest Pagano. Executive Producer: Howard Benedict.

Technical Credits:
Director: William A. Seiter. Script: Michael Fessier, Ernest Pagano. Story: Arnold Belgard. Photography: Charles Van Enger. Editor: Fred R. Feitshans, Jr. Songs: Jack Brooks, Hans J. Salter. Choreography: Leslie Horton, George Moro, Louis Dapron.

Cast:
Franchot Tone, Susanna Foster, Buster Keaton (Sam, who works at Johnny's Diner), David Bruce, Louise Allbritton, Jacqueline de Wit, Irene Ryan.

God's Country (1946)
Released: April 1946. Copyright: May 18, 1946. Length: 62 minutes; Cinecolor. Distributed by: Screen Guild Productions. Produced by: Action Pictures. Producer: William B. David.

Technical Credits:
Director/Screenplay: Robert Tansey. Photography: Carl Webster.

Cast:
Robert Lowery, Helen Gilbert, Buster Keaton (Mr. Boone), William Farnum, Stanley Andrews, Trevor Bardette, Si Jenks, Estelle Zarco, Juan Reyes, Al Ferguson.

El Moderno Barba Azul (1946) (The Modern Bluebeard/Boom in the Moon)

Released: August 2, 1946. Length: 90 minutes. Produced by: Alsa Films-Mexico. Producer: Alexander Salkind.

Technical Credits:

Director: Jaime Salvador. Script: Victor Trivas, Jaime Salvador. Photography: Agustin Jiminez.

Cast:

Buster Keaton, Angel Garasa, Virginia Serret, Luis Barreiro, Fernando Sotto, Jorge Mondragon, Luis Mondragon.

Note: Not released in U.S. until released on video under the title Boom in the Moon. New version (dubbed) copyright © 1983 by Cantharus Productions N.V.

The Loveable Cheat (1949)

Released: May 11, 1949. Copyright: May 11, 1949. Length: 74 minutes. Distributed by: Film Classics. Produced by: Skyline Pictures. Producers: Richard Oswald, Edward Lewis. Associate Producer: Rosario Castagna.

Technical Credits:

Director: Richard Oswald. Script: Edward Lewis, Richard Oswald, based on the play Mercadet le Falseur by Honoré de Balzac. Editor: Douglas Bagier.

Cast:

Charlie Ruggles, Peggy Ann Garner, Buster Keaton, Richard Ney, Alan Mowbray, Iris Adrian, Ludwig Donath, Fritz Feld, John Wengraf, Otto Waldis, Curt Bois, Edna Holland, Minerva Urecal, Helen Servis, Jody Gilbert, Judith Trafford.

In the Good Old Summertime (1949)

Released: July 29, 1949. Copyright: June 23, 1949. Length: 102 minutes; color. Distributed by: Metro-Goldwyn-Mayer. Producer: Joe Pasternak.

Technical Credits:

Director: Robert Z. Leonard. Screenplay: Samson Raphaelson. Adaptation: Albert Hackett, Frances Goodrich, Ivan Tors, based on the play Parfumerie by Miklos Laszlo. Photography: Harry Stradling. Editor: Adrienne Fazan. Gags: Buster Keaton (uncredited).

Cast:

Judy Garland, Van Johnson, S. Z. "Cuddles" Sakall, Spring Byington, Buster Keaton (Hickey), Clinton Sundberg, Marcia Van Dyke, Lillian Bronson, Liza Minnelli.

Sunset Boulevard (1950)

Released: August 1950. Copyright: August 4, 1950. Length: 110 minutes. Distributed by: Paramount Pictures. Producer: Charles Brackett.

Technical Credits:

Director: Billy Wilder. Script: Charles Brackett, Billy Wilder, D. M. Marshman, Jr., based on the story "A Can of Beans." Photography: John F. Seitz. Editor: Doane Harrison, Arthur Schmidt. Music: Franz Waxman.

Cast:

Gloria Swanson, William Holden, Erich von Stroheim, Fred Clark, Jack Webb, Hedda Hopper, Buster Keaton, Cecil B. De Mille, Anna Q. Nilsson, H. B. Warner, Nancy Olson.

Note: Keaton appears as himself, playing bridge with Swanson, Nilsson, and Warner.

Un Duel à Mort (1950)

Released: 1950 (not released in U.S.). Length: 3 reels. Produced by: Films Azur, Paris.

Technical Credits:

Director: Pierre Blondy. Script: Pierre Blondy, Buster Keaton.

Cast:

Buster Keaton, Antonin Berval

Note: Dueling scene from The Passionate Plumber *is re-created in this film. Shot in Paris while Keaton was appearing at Cirque Medrano.*

The Misadventures of Buster Keaton (1950)

Released: 1950. Copyright: 1950. Length: 70 minutes. Distributed by: British Lion Films. Producer: Carl K. Hittleman.

Technical Credits:

Director: Arthur Hilton. Script: Harold Goodwin. Photography: Jackson Rose.

Cast:

Buster Keaton, Marcia Mae Jones, Eleanor Keaton.

Note: Three episodes ("The Billboard Story," "The Little Theater Story," and "The Shakespeare Story") of the TV series Life with Buster Keaton *strung together to make a feature-length film.*

Limelight (1952)

Released: October 23, 1952 (in England); February 6, 1953 (U.S.). Copyright: October 23, 1952. Length: 143 minutes. Distributed by: United Artists. Producer: Charles Chaplin.

Technical Credits:
Director: Charles Chaplin. Script: Charles Chaplin. Assistant Director: Robert Aldrich. Photography: Karl Struss. Editor: Joe Inge. Musical Score: Charles Chaplin.

Cast:
Charles Chaplin, Claire Bloom, Sydney Chaplin, Buster Keaton (piano accompianist in finale), Nigel Bruce, Norman Lloyd, Marjorie Bennett, Wheeler Dryden, Barry Bernard, Stapleton Kent, Mollie Blessing, Leonard Mudi, Julian Ludwig, Snub Pollard, Loyal Underwood, Andre Eglevsky, Melissa Hayden, Charles Chaplin, Jr., Edna Purviance (in audience during ballet), and the children outside Calvero's boardinghouse are Michael, Josephine, and Geraldine Chaplin.

L'Incantevole Nemica (1952)
Released: 1952 (not released in U.S.). Length: 86 minutes. Distributed by: Orso Films (Rome), Lambar Films (Paris). Executive Producer: Ferruccio Biancini. Director: Claudio Gora.

Cast:
Robert Lamoureux, Buster Keaton, Carlo Campanini, Raymond Bussiers, Silvana Pampanini, Ugo Tognazzi, Pina Renzi, Nyta Dover.

Note: Keaton appears onstage at Milan theater.

Around the World in 80 Days (1956)
Released: October 17, 1956. Copyright: October 17, l956. Length: 148 minutes (some list 168 minutes); color. Distributed by: United Artists. Produced by: Michael Todd.

Technical Credits:
Director: Michael Anderson. Script: S. J. Perelman, James Poe, John Farrow, adapted from the novel by Jules Verne. Photography: Lionel Lindon. Editors: Gene Ruggiero, Howard Epstein, Paul Weatherwax. Music: Victor Young.

Cast:
David Niven, Cantinflas, Shirley MacLaine, Robert Newton, and cameo appearances by many stars, including Buster Keaton (train conductor).

The Adventures of Huckleberry Finn (1960)
Released: June 17, 1960. Copyright: March 7, 1960. Length: 107 minutes; color. Distributed by: Metro-Goldwyn-Mayer. Producer: Samuel Goldwyn, Jr.

Technical Credits:
Director: Michael Curtiz. Script: James Lee, based on novel by Mark Twain. Photography: Ted McCord. Editor: Frederic Steinkamp. Music: Jerome Moross. Art Director: George W. Davis, McClure Capps.

Cast:

Eddie Hodges, Archie Moore, Tony Randall, Patty McCormack, Neville Brand, Buster Keaton (lion tamer), Judy Canova, Mickey Shaughnessy, Andy Devine, Josephine Hutchinson, Finlay Currie, Royal Dano, John Carradine, Sterling Holloway, Sherry Jackson.

Ten Girls Ago (1962)

Unfinished, never released (it has been reported that it was 98 percent completed and would have run approximately 92 minutes). Produced by: Am-Cam Productions. Producer: Edward A. Gollin.

Technical Credits:

Director: Harold Daniels. Script: Peter Farrow, Diane Lampert. Photography: Lee Garmes, Jackson M. Samuels. Music director: Joseph Harnell. Music/Lyrics: Diane Lampert, Sammy Fain. Choreography: Bill Foster.

Cast:

Buster Keaton, Bert Lahr, Eddie Foy, Jr., Dion DiMucci, Austin Willis, Risella Bain, Jennifer Billingsly, Jan Miner.

It's a Mad, Mad, Mad, Mad World (1963)

Released: November 7, 1963. Copyright: November 7, 1963. Length: 192 minutes (cut to 154 minutes; some footage was recently restored for video release); color. Distributed by: United Artists. Producer: Stanley Kramer.

Technical Credits:

Director: Stanley Kramer. Assistant Director: Ivan Volkman. Script/Story: William Rose, Tania Rose. Photography: Ernest Lazlo. Editor: Fred Knudtson. Music: Ernest Gold. Production Design: Rudolph Sternad.

Cast:

Spencer Tracy, Milton Berle, Sid Caesar, Buddy Hackett, Ethel Merman, Mickey Rooney, Jimmy Durante, Jonathan Winters, Dick Shawn, Buster Keaton (Jimmy the Crook), and many, many others.

Pajama Party (1964)

Released: November 11, 1964. Copyright: November 11, 1964. Length: 85 minutes; color. Distributed by: American International. Produced by: James H. Nicholson, Samuel Z. Arkoff.

Technical Credits:

Director: Don Weis. Script: Louis M. Heyward. Photography: Floyd Crosby. Editor: Fred Feitshans, Eve Newman. Music: Les Baxter.

Cast:

Tommy Kirk, Annette Funicello, Elsa Lanchester, Jesse White, Jody McCrea,

Buster Keaton (Chief Rotten Eagle), Dorothy Lamour, Harvey Lembeck, Susan Hart, Bobbi Shaw, Don Rickles, Frankie Avalon.

*Note: One of the background dancers is Teri Garr (*Young Frankenstein*). A sequel,* Pajama Party in a Haunted House, *was planned but never filmed. There was even talk of starring Keaton and Elsa Lanchester in a silent film to be called* The Chase *and then changed to* The Big Chase. *This also was never filmed.*

Beach Blanket Bingo (1965)
Released: April 15, 1965. Copyright: April 14, 1965. Length: 98 minutes; color. Distributed by: American International. Produced by: James H. Nicholson, Samuel Z. Arkoff.

Technical Credits:
Director: William Asher. Script: William Asher, Leo Townsend. Photography: Floyd Crosby. Editor: Fred Feitshans, Eve Newman. Music: Les Baxter.

Cast:
Frankie Avalon, Annette Funicello, Deborah Walley, Harvey Lembeck, Linda Evans, Don Rickles, Buster Keaton, Bobbi Shaw, Timothy Carey, Paul Lynde, Earl Wilson, John Ashley.

How to Stuff a Wild Bikini (1965)
Released: July 14, 1965. Copyright: July 14, 1965. Length: 90 minutes; color. Distributed by: American International. Produced by: James H. Nicholson, Samuel Z. Arkoff.

Technical Credits:
Director: William Asher. Script: William Asher, Leo Townsend. Photography: Floyd Crosby. Editor: Fred Feitshans, Eve Newman. Music: Les Baxter.

Cast:
Frankie Avalon, Annette Funicello, Dwayne Hickman, Harvey Lembeck, Mickey Rooney, Brian Donlevy, Buster Keaton (Bwana the witch doctor), Beverly Adams, John Ashley, Jody McCrea, Marianne Gaba, Irene Tsu, Bobbi Shaw, Elizabeth Montgomery (cameo).

Sergeant Deadhead (1965)
Released: August 18, 1965. Copyright: August 11, 1965. Length: 90 minutes; color. Distributed by: American International. Produced by: James H. Nicholson, Samuel Z. Arkoff.

Technical Credits:
Director: Norman Taurog. Script: Louis M. Heyward. Photography: Floyd Crosby. Editor: Ronald Sinclair, Fred Feitshans, Eve Newman. Music: Les Baxter. Songs: Guy Hemric, Jerry Styner.

Cast:

Frankie Avalon, Deborah Walley, Fred Clark, Eve Arden, Buster Keaton (Private Blinken), Cesar Romero, Gale Gordon, Reginald Gardiner, Harvey Lembeck, John Ashley, Donna Loren, Norman Grabowski, Pat Buttram, Patti Chandler, Bobbi Shaw.

A Funny Thing Happened on the Way to the Forum (1966)

Released: October 16, 1966. Copyright: October 15, 1966. Length: 99 minutes; color. Distributed by: United Artists. Producer: Melvin Frank.

Technical Credits:

Director: Richard Lester. Script: Melvin Frank, Michael Pertwee, based on stage play produced by Harold S. Prince. Music/Lyrics: Stephen Sondheim. Book: Burt Shevelove, Larry Gelbart. Photography: Nicolas Roeg. Editor: John Victor Smith.

Cast:

Zero Mostel, Phil Silvers, Jack Gilford, Buster Keaton (Erronius), Michael Crawford, Michael Hordern, Annette Andre, Patricia Jessel, Inga Neilsen, Leon Greene, Myrna White, Pamela Brown, Roy Kinnear.

War Italian Style (1967) (Due Marines e un Generale/Two Marines and a General)

Released: January 18, 1967. Copyright: January 11, 1967. Length: 84 minutes; color (film ran 100 minutes at premiere in Rome). Distributed by: American International. Produced by: Fulvio Lucisano.

Technical Credits:

Director: Luigi Scattini. Script: Franco Castellano, Pipolo, Fulvio Lucisano. Photography: Fausto Zuccoli. Music: Piero Umiliani.

Cast:

Buster Keaton (General Von Kassler), Franco Franchi, Ciccio Ingrassia, Fred Clark, Martha Hyer.

EDUCATIONAL PICTURES: "THE SPICE OF THE PROGRAM"

The Gold Ghost (1934)

Released: March 16, 1934. Copyright: March 16, 1934. Length: 2 reels. Distributed by: 20th Century-Fox. Presented by: E. W. Hammons. Produced by: Educational Pictures. Producer: E. H. Allen.

Technical Credits:

Director: Charles Lamont. Story: Ewart Adamson, Nick Barrows. Adaptation/ Continuity: Ernest Pagano, Charles Lamont.

Cast:

Buster Keaton, Dorothy Dix, William Worthington, Lloyd Ingraham, Warren Hymer, Joe Young, Billy Engle, Al Thompson, Leo Willis.

Allez Oop (1934)

Released: May 25, 1934. Copyright: May 31, 1934. Length: 2 reels. Distributed by: 20th Century-Fox. Presented by: E. W. Hammons. Produced by: Educational Pictures. Producer: E. H. Allen.

Technical Credits:

Director: Charles Lamont. Story: Ernest Pagano, Ewart Adamson. Photography: Dwight Warren.

Cast:

Buster Keaton, Dorothy Sebastian, George Lewis, Harry Myers, the Flying Escalantes.

Palooka from Paducah (1935)

Released: January 11, 1935. Copyright: January 10, 1935. Length: 2 reels. Distributed by: 20th Century-Fox. Presented by: E. W. Hammons. Produced by: Educational Pictures. Producer: E. H. Allen.

Technical Credits:

Director: Charles Lamont. Story: Glen Lambert. Photography: Dwight Warren.

Cast:

Buster Keaton, Joe Keaton, Myra Keaton, Louise Keaton, Dewey Robinson, Bull Montana.

One Run Elmer (1935)

Released: February 22, 1935. Copyright: February 22, 1935. Length: 2 reels. Distributed by: 20th Century-Fox. Presented by: E. W. Hammons. Produced by: Educational Pictures. Producer: E. H. Allen.

Technical Credits:

Director: Charles Lamont. Story: Glen Lambert. Photography: Dwight Warren.

Cast:

Buster Keaton, Harold Goodwin, Dewey Robinson, Lon Andre, Jim Thorpe.

Hayseed Romance (1935)

Released: March 15, 1935. Copyright: March 15, 1935. Length: 2 reels. Distributed by: 20th Century-Fox. Presented by: E. W. Hammons. Produced by: Educational Pictures. Producer: E. H. Allen.

Technical Credits:

Director: Charles Lamont. Story: Charles Lamont. Dialogue/Continuity: Glen Lambert. Photography: Gus Peterson.

Cast:

Buster Keaton, Jane Jones, Dorothea Kent.

Tars and Stripes (1935)

Released: May 3, 1935. Copyright: May 3, 1935. Length: 2 reels. Distributed by: 20th Century-Fox. Presented by: E. W. Hammons. Produced by: Educational Pictures. Producer: E. H. Allen.

Technical Credits:

Director: Charles Lamont. Story: Charles Lamont. Adaptation: Ewart Adamson. Photography: Dwight Warren.

Cast:

Buster Keaton, Vernon Dent, Dorothea Kent, Jack Shutta.

The E-Flat Man (1935)

Released: August 9, 1935. Copyright: August 9, 1935. Length: 2 reels. Distributed by: 20th Century-Fox. Presented by: E. W. Hammons. Produced by: Educational Pictures. Producer: E. H. Allen.

Technical Credits:

Director: Charles Lamont. Story: Charles Lamont, Glen Lambert. Photography: Dwight Warren. Sound: Karl Zint.

Cast:

Buster Keaton, Dorothea Kent, Si Jenks, Fern Emmett, Broderick O'Farrell, Charles McAvoy, Jack Shutta.

The Timid Young Man (1935)

Released: October 25, 1935. Copyright: October 25, 1935. Length: 2 reels. Distributed by: 20th Century-Fox. Presented by: E. W. Hammons. Produced by: Educational Pictures. Producer: Mack Sennett.

Technical Credits:

Director: Mack Sennett. Photography: Dwight Warren. Sound: Karl Zint.

Cast:

Buster Keaton, Lona Andre, Kitty McHugh, Tiny Sandford, Harry Bowen.

Three on a Limb (1936)

Released: January 3, 1936. Copyright: January 3, 1936. Length: 2 reels. Distributed by: 20th Century-Fox. Presented by: E. W. Hammons. Produced by: Educational Pictures. Producer: E. H. Allen.

Technical Credits:
Director: Charles Lamont. Story: Vernon Smith. Photography: Gus Peterson.

Cast:
Buster Keaton, Lona Andre, Harold Goodwin, Grant Withers, Barbara Bedford, John Ince, Fern Emmett, Phyllis Crane.

Grand Slam Opera (1936)
Released: February 21, 1936. Copyright: February 21, 1936. Length: 2 reels. Distributed by: 20th Century-Fox. Presented by: E. W. Hammons. Produced by: Educational Pictures. Producer: E. H. Allen.

Technical Credits:
Director: Charles Lamont. Story: Buster Keaton, Charles Lamont. Photography: Gus Peterson.

Cast:
Buster Keaton, Harold Goodwin, Diana Lewis, John Ince, Bud Jamison, Eddie Fetherstone, Melrose Coakley.

Blue Blazes (1936)
Released: August 21, 1936. Copyright: August 21, 1936. Length: 2 reels. Distributed by: 20th Century-Fox. Presented by: E. W. Hammons. Produced by: Educational Pictures. Producer: E. H. Allen.

Technical Credits:
Director: Raymond Kane. Story: David Freedman. Photography: George Webber.

Cast:
Buster Keaton, Arthur Jarrett, Patty Wilson, Marlyn Stuart, Rose Kessner.

The Chemist (1936)
Released: October 9, 1936. Copyright: October 9, 1936. Length: 2 reels. Distributed by: 20th Century-Fox. Presented by: E. W. Hammons. Produced by: Educational Pictures. Producer: Al Christie.

Technical Credits:
Director: Al Christie. Story: David Freedman. Photography: George Webber.

Cast:
Buster Keaton, Marlyn Stuart, Donald McBride, Earl Gilbert, Herman Lieb.

Mixed Magic (1936)
Released: November 20, 1936. Copyright: November 20, 1936. Length: 2 reels. Distributed by: 20th Century-Fox. Presented by: E. W. Hammons. Produced by: Educational Pictures. Producer: E. H. Allen.

Technical Credits:
Director: Raymond Kane. Story: Arthur Jarrett, Marcy Klauber. Photography: George Webber.

Cast:
Buster Keaton, Eddie Lambert, Marlyn Stuart, Jimmy Fox, Eddie Hall, Harry Myers, Pass Le Noir, Walter Fenner.

Jail Bait (1937)

Released: January 8, 1937. Copyright: January 8, 1937. Length: 2 reels. Distributed by: 20th Century-Fox. Presented by: E. W. Hammons. Produced by: Educational Pictures. Producer: E. H. Allen.

Technical Credits:
Director: Charles Lamont. Story: Paul Gerard Smith. Photography: Dwight Warren.

Cast:
Buster Keaton, Harold Goodwin, Mathew Betz, Bud Jamison, Betty Andre.

Ditto (1937)

Released: February 12, 1937. Copyright: February 12, 1937. Length: 2 reels. Distributed by: 20th Century-Fox. Presented by: E. W. Hammons. Produced by: Educational Pictures. Producer: E. H. Allen.

Technical Credits:
Director: Charles Lamont. Story: Paul Gerard Smith. Photography: Dwight Warren.

Cast:
Buster Keaton, Harold Goodwin, Barbara and Gloria Brewster, Al Thompson, Bob Ellsworth, Lynton Brent.

Love Nest on Wheels (1937)

Released: March 26, 1937. Copyright: March 24, 1937. Length: 2 reels. Distributed by: 20th Century-Fox. Presented by: E. W. Hammons. Produced by: Educational Pictures. Producer: E. H. Allen.

Technical Credits:
Director: Charles Lamont. Story: William Hazlett Upson. Adaptation: Paul Gerard Smith.

Cast:
Buster Keaton, Myra Keaton, Louise Keaton, Harry Keaton, Al St. John, Diana Lewis, Bud Jamison, Lynton Brent.

Note: Remake of The Bell Boy.

COLUMBIA SHORTS

Pest from the West (1939)
Released: June 16, 1939. Copyright: June 7, 1939. Length: 2 reels. Distributed by: Columbia Pictures. Produced by: Columbia Pictures. Producer: Jules White.

Technical Credits:
Director: Del Lord. Script: Clyde Bruckman.

Cast:
Buster Keaton, Lorna Gray (later called Adrian Booth), Richard Fiske, Gino Corrado, Bud Jamison, Eddie Laughton, Ned Glass, Forbes Murray.

Note: Remake of An Old Spanish Custom.

Mooching Through Georgia (1939)
Released: August 11, 1939. Copyright: August 14, 1939. Length: 2 reels. Distributed by: Columbia Pictures. Produced by: Columbia Pictures. Producer: Jules White.

Technical Credits:
Director: Jules White. Script: Clyde Bruckman.

Cast:
Buster Keaton, Monty Collins, Bud Jamison, Ned Glass, Jill Martin, Lynton Brent, Jack Hill, Stanley Mack.

Nothing but Pleasure (1940)
Released: January 19, 1940. Copyright: December 18, 1939. Length: 2 reels. Distributed by: Columbia Pictures. Produced by: Columbia Pictures. Producer: Jules White.

Technical Credits:
Director: Jules White. Script: Clyde Bruckman. Photography: Henry Freulich.

Cast:
Buster Keaton, Dorothy Appleby, Beatrice Blinn, Bud Jamison, Richard Fiske, Robert Sterling, Jack Randall, Johnny Tyrell, Eddie Laughton, Victor Tremers, Lynton Brent.

Pardon My Berth Marks (1940)
Released: March 22, 1940. Copyright: March 18, 1940. Length: 2 reels. Distributed by: Columbia Pictures. Produced by: Columbia Pictures. Producer: Jules White.

Technical Credits:
Director: Jules White. Script: Clyde Bruckman. Photography: Benjamin Kline.

Cast:
Buster Keaton, Dorothy Appleby, Vernon Dent, Richard Fiske, Dick Curtis, Eva McKenzie, Billy Gilbert, Bud Jamison, Clarice the parrot.

The Taming of the Snood (1940) (Four-Thirds Off)
Released: June 28, 1940. Copyright: May 28, 1940. Length: 2 reels. Distributed by: Columbia Pictures. Produced by: Columbia Pictures. Producer: Jules White.

Technical Credits:
Director: Jules White. Script: Clyde Bruckman, Ewart Adamson. Photography: Henry Freulich.

Cast:
Buster Keaton, Dorothy Appleby, Elsie Ames, Richard Fiske, Bruce Bennett.

The Spook Speaks (1940)
Released: September 20, 1940. Copyright: August 31, 1940. Length: 2 reels. Distributed by: Columbia Pictures. Produced by: Columbia Pictures. Producer: Jules White.

Technical Credits:
Director: Jules White. Script: Clyde Bruckman, Ewart Adamson. Photography: Henry Freulich.

Cast:
Buster Keaton, Dorothy Appleby, Elsie Ames, Don Beddoe, Bruce Bennett, Lynton Brent, Orson the penguin.

His Ex Marks the Spot (1940)
Released: December 13, 1940. Copyright: February 3, 1941. Length: 2 reels. Distributed by: Columbia Pictures. Produced by: Columbia Pictures. Producer: Jules White.

Technical Credits:
Director: Jules White. Script: Felix Adler. Photography: Benjamin Kline.

Cast:
Buster Keaton, Elsie Ames, Dorothy Appleby, Matt McHugh.

So You Won't Squawk (1941)
Released: February 21, 1941. Copyright: February 21, 1941. Length: 2 reels. Distributed by: Columbia Pictures. Produced by: Columbia Pictures. Producer: Del Lord, Hugh McCollum.

Technical Credits:
Director: Del Lord. Script: Elwood Ullman. Photography: Benjamin Kline.

Cast:

Buster Keaton, Matt McHugh, Eddie Fetherstone, Hank Mann, Bud Jamison, Edmond Cobb, Vernon Dent.

General Nuisance (1941) *(The Private General)*

Released: September 18, 1941. Copyright: September 18, 1941. Length: 2 reels. Distributed by: Columbia Pictures. Produced by: Columbia Pictures. Producer: Jules White.

Technical Credits:

Director: Jules White. Script: Felix Adler, Clyde Bruckman.

Cast:

Buster Keaton, Elsie Ames, Monty Collins, Dorothy Appleby, Bud Jamison, Lynton Brent, Harry Semels, Nick Arno.

She's Oil Mine (1941)

Released: November 20, 1941. Copyright: November 20, 1941. Length: 2 reels. Distributed by: Columbia Pictures. Produced by: Columbia Pictures. Producer: Jules White.

Technical Credits:

Director: Jules White. Script: Felix Adler.

Cast:

Buster Keaton, Monty Collins, Elsie Ames, Eddie Laughton, Bud Jamison, Jacqueline Dayle.

Note: Remake of The Passionate Plumber.

MISCELLANEOUS AND UNCREDITED APPEARANCES

The Round Up (1920)

Released: October 10, 1920. Copyright: August 26, 1920. Length: 7 reels. Distributed by: Paramount Pictures. Produced by: Famous Players–Lasky Corp. Producer: George Melford.

Technical Credits:

Director: George Melford. Script: Edmund Day, Tom Forman. Photography: Paul Perry.

Cast:

Roscoe Arbuckle (Slim Hoover), Tom Forman (Jack Payson), Irving Cummings (Dick Lane), Mabel Julienne Scott (Echo Allen), Jean Acker (Polly Hope), Lucien Littlefield (Parentheses), Wallace Beery (Buck McKee), Edward Sutherland (Cowboy), Buster Keaton (Indian who gets shot by Arbuckle).

Screen Snapshots #3 (1922)

Released: June 2, 1922. Copyright: June 26, 1922. Length: 1 reel. Distributed by: Pathé Exchange. Produced by: Jack Cohen, Louis Lewyn.

Note: Hollywood newsreel in which several Hollywood stars are shown.

Life in Hollywood #1 (1927)

Released: 1927. Length: 1 reel. Distributed by: Goodwill Production. Presented by: L. M. BeDell.

Note: Hollywood newsreel in which the exterior of the Buster Keaton studio is shown. Buster himself does not appear.

The Baby Cyclone (1928)

Released: 1928. Distributed by: Metro-Goldwyn-Mayer.

Technical Credits:

Director: Edward Sutherland. Script: F. Hugh Herbert, based on a play by George M. Cohan.

Cast:

Lew Cody, Aileen Pringle, Robert Armstrong, Gwen Lee, Buster Keaton (stand-in for Lew Cody for a stunt where he falls down a flight of stairs).

Tide of Empire (1929)

Note: This film started showing up in Keaton filmographies after Allan Dwan stated in Peter Bogdanovich's book Allan Dwan: The Last Pioneer *that Keaton did a bit as a drunk being thrown out of a saloon in order to show off to the Talmadge sisters, who where visiting the set. Allan Dwan said he liked it so much he left it in. However, there is no such scene in the picture. If it did happen, perhaps it was cut or is in a different film.*

The Voice of Hollywood (1929–1930)

Length: 1 reel. Produced by: Tiffany Pictures. Director: Lewis Lewyn.

Note: Keaton appeared in two installments of Voice of Hollywood. *In one he is at a nightclub and does a bit with flipping a spoon into a glass, then he picks up a salt shaker and acts as if the salt is pouring out of his nose. In the other, he appears with Raquel Torres in front of Leo the Lion's cage. The two exchange banter on how tame Leo is, but when Leo growls, they both take off.*

The Stolen Jools (1931) (The Slippery Pearls)

Released: April 1931. Length: 2 reels. Distributed by: Paramount Pictures and National Screen Service. Producer: Pat Casey.

Technical Credits:
Director: William McGann. Supervisor: E. K. Nadel.

Cast:
Buster Keaton, Wallace Beery, Allen Jenkins, J. Farrel MacDonald, Edward G. Robinson, George E. Stone, Eddie Kane, Laurel & Hardy, Our Gang, Norma Shearer, Hedda Hopper, Wheeler & Woolsey, Richard Dix, Joe E. Brown and many more.

Note: Keaton appears as a policeman in a Keystone Kop–style bit in this charity film.

Hollywood on Parade #A-6 (1933)
Released: January 1933. Length: 1 reel. Distributed by: Paramount Pictures. Produced and Directed by: Louis Lewyn.

Cast:
Richard Arlen (Emcee), Frances Dee, Clark Gable, Tallulah Bankhead, Lew Cody, Buster Keaton.

Note: Keaton and Cody appear in a sequence with Buster's "dry land cruiser."

La Fiesta de Santa Barbara (1935)
Released: December 7, 1935. Copyright: April 2, 1936. Length: 2 reels; color. Distributed by: Metro-Goldwyn-Mayer. Producer: Louis Lewyn.

Technical Credits:
Director: Louis Lewyn. Script: Alexander Van Dorn. Photography: Ray Rennahan.

Cast:
Gary Cooper, Harpo Marx, Maria Gambarelli, Warner Baxter, Leo Carrillo, Adrienne Ames, Robert Taylor, Mary Carlisle, Edmund Lowe, Buster Keaton, Andy Devine, Ted Healy, the Garland Sisters (with Judy Garland), Ida Lupino.

Note: Keaton appears as a referee in comic bullfight between Andy Devine and two people in a bull suit.

The Garland Sisters used to be known as the Gumm Sisters.

Much of this film was shot in producer Lewyn's backyard.

Sunkist Stars at Palm Springs (1936)
Released: 1936. Length: 2 reels; color. Distributed by: Metro-Goldwyn-Mayer. Producer: Louis Lewyn.

Technical Credits:
Director: Roy Rowland. Dialogue: John Kraft. Photography: Allen Davey, Aldo Ermini.

Cast:
Buster Keaton, Jackie Coogan, Betty Grable, Johnny Weissmuller, Claire Trevor, Betty Furness, Walter Huston, Frances Langford, Robert Benchley, Edmund Lowe, the Downey Sisters, the Fanchonettes.

Note: Keaton appears relaxing by a swimming pool and gets set adrift on an air mattress.

New Moon (1940)
Released: 1940. Distributed by: Metro-Goldwyn-Mayer. Produced and Directed by: Robert Z. Leonard.

Cast:
Jeanette MacDonald, Nelson Eddy, Mary Boland, George Zucco, H. B. Warner, Nat Pendleton, Stanley Fields, Grant Mitchell, (Buster Keaton).

Note: Though not officially in the cast of the released film, Keaton did have a role. However, the film ran too long and Buster stole too many scenes. His part was then edited out, but he can still be glimpsed in the background in some scenes. It is not known if the excised footage still exists. Keaton also supplied gags for this film.

Two Girls and a Sailor (1944)
Note: This film, starring Van Johnson, June Allyson, and Gloria DeHaven, has appeared in a couple of Keaton filmographies. One even lists Keaton as playing Jimmy Durante's son. While such a role does exist in the film, the part is played by Ben Blue. Buster does not appear in this film.

She Went to the Races (1945)
Released: 1945. Length: 86 minutes. Distributed by: Metro-Goldwyn-Mayer. Producer: Frederick Stephani.

Technical Credits:
Director: Willis Goldbeck. Script: Lawrence Hazard, based on a story by Alan Friedman and DeVallon Scott.

Cast:
James Craig, Ava Gardner, Edmund Gwenn, Francis Gifford, Sig Ruman, Reginald Owen, J. M. Kerrigan, Chester Clute, Frank Orth, Charles Halton, Buster Keaton (uncredited bit as a bellboy; also supplied gags).

You're My Everything (1949)

Released: August 1949. Copyright: July 16, 1949. Length: 94 minutes; color. Distributed by: 20th Century-Fox. Producer: Lamar Trotti.

Technical Credits:

Director: Walter Lang. Script: Lamar Trotti, Will H. Hays, Jr. Original Story: George Jessel. Photography: Arthur E. Arling. Editor: J. Watson Webb, Jr.

Cast:

Dan Dailey, Anne Baxter, Anne Revere, Buster Keaton, Stanley Ridges, Alan Mowbray, Selena Royle.

Note: In a black-and-white segment that re-creates a silent film, Keaton appears as a butler.

Screen Snapshots: Hollywood Pie Throwers (1951)

Released: 1951. Length: 1 reel. Distributed by: Columbia Pictures.

Cast:

Ken Murray, the Brewster Twins, Milton Berle, Ella Logan, Buster Keaton, Joan Davies, Billy Gilbert.

Note: Keaton appears with Joan Davies and Billy Gilbert as they demonstrate the art of pie throwing.

Screen Snapshots: Memories of Famous Hollywood Comedians (1951)

Note: This film has been listed in some Keaton filmographies, but he does not appear. The confusion most likely arose when Columbia released this film to the home market (Super 8 film) and combined it with Hollywood Pie Throwers *under the title* Memories of Famous Hollywood Comedians.

INDUSTRIAL SHORTS AND OTHER SHORT FILM WORK

Paradise for Buster (1952)

Released: for private showings only. Copyright: October 15, 1952. Length: 39 minutes; 16 millimeter. Produced by: Wilding Picture Productions. Made for the John Deere Co.

Technical Credits:

Director: Del Lord. Script: J. P. Prindle, John Grey, Harold Goodwin. Music: Albert Glasser. Editor: William Minnerly. Supervisors: H. M. Railsback, G. M. Rohrbach. Photography: J. J. La Fleur, Robert Sable.

Cast:
Buster Keaton, Harold Goodwin.

The Devil to Pay (1960)
Released: not released commercially. Length: 28 minutes; 16 millimeter. Produced by: Education Research Films for the National Association of Wholesalers. Production Company: Rodel Productions.

Technical Credits:
Director: Herb Skoble. Script/Editor: Cummins-Betts. Photography: Del Ankers, Fritz Roland. Sound: Nelson Funk. Art Director: Peter Masters, Joseph W. Swanson.

Cast:
Buster Keaton (Diablos), Ralph Dunne (furnace man), Ruth Gillette (Minnie), Marion Morris (Esther), John Rodney (druggist).

The Triumph of Lester Snapwell (1963)
Released: not released commercially. Copyright: March 25, 1963. Length: 22 minutes; color. Produced by: Eastman Kodak Co.

Technical Credits:
Director: James Cahoun.

Cast:
Buster Keaton (Lester Snapwell), Sigrid Nelsson (Clementine), Nina Varela (Mama).

Note: Promotional film for the Kodak Instamatic camera.

There's No Business Like No Business (1963)
Made for Maremont Exhaust and Gabriel Shocks Division/Arvin Corp.

Note: Keaton plays a gas station attendant in this one-reel short promoting the company's products.

The Fall Guy (1965)
Made by U.S. Steel. Director: Darrel Bateman.

Cast:
Buster Keaton (Mr. Goodfarmer/Mr. Badfarmer).

Film (1965)
Released: September 1965. Length: 22 minutes. Distributed by: Grove Press. Produced by: Evergreen Theatre. Producer: Barney Rosset.

Technical Credits:
Director: Alan Schneider. Script: Samuel Beckett. Photography: Boris Kaufman. Editor: Sidney Meyers. Art Director: Burr Smidt. Camera Operator: Joe Coffey.

Cast:
Buster Keaton (Object/Eye), James Karen, Nell Harrison, Susan Reed.

The Railrodder (1965)
Released: October 1965. Length: 21 minutes; color. Distributed by: National Film Board of Canada. Producer: Julian Biggs.

Technical Credits:
Director: Gerald Potterton. Script: Gerald Potterton. Photography: Robert Humble. Editor: Jo Kirkpatrick, Gerald Potterton. Music: Eldon Rathburn. Assistant Director: Jo Kirkpatrick. Sound Effects: Karl du Plessis. Sound Recording: George Croll, Ted Haley.

Cast:
Buster Keaton.

The Scribe (1966)
Released: May 1966. Length: 30 minutes; color. Produced by: Film-Tele Productions for the Construction Safety Association of Ontario. Producer: Ann and Kenneth Heely-Ray. Executive Producer: Raymond Walters, James Collier.

Technical Credits:
Director: John Sebert. Script: Paul Sutherland, Clifford Braggins. Photography: Mike Lente. Music: Quartet Productions. Editor: Kenneth Heely-Ray.

Cast:
Buster Keaton, Larry Reynolds (stunt double).

Note: Filmed in October 1965.

CREDITED NONAPPEARANCE FILMS

Life in Sometown, U.S.A. (1938)
Released: February 26, 1938. Copyright: February 18, 1938. Length: 1 reel. Distributed by: Metro-Goldwyn-Mayer.

Technical Credits:
Director: Buster Keaton. Script: Carl Dudley, Richard Murphy. Narrator: Carey Wilson.

Hollywood Handicap (1938)
Released: May 28, 1938. Copyright: June 2, 1938. Length: 1 reel. Distributed by: Metro-Goldwyn-Mayer. Producer: Louis Lewyn. Director: Buster Keaton.

Cast:
The Original Sing Band.

Streamlined Swing (1938)

Released: September 10, 1938. Copyright: September 7, 1938. Length: 1 reel. Distributed by: Metro-Goldwyn-Mayer. Producer: Louis Lewyn.

Technical Credits:

Director: Buster Keaton. Script: Marion Mack (Keaton's leading lady from *The General* and wife of producer Louis Lewyn). Dialogue: John Kraft.

Cast:

The Original Sing Band.

The Jones Family in Hollywood (1939)

Released: June 2, 1939. Copyright: June 2, 1939. Distributed by: Metro-Goldwyn-Mayer.

Technical Credits:

Director: Mal St. Clair. Original Story: Joseph Hoffman, Buster Keaton, based on characters by Katherine Kavanaugh. Script: Harold Tarshis.

Cast:

Jed Prouty, Spring Byington, Ken Howell, June Carlson, Florence Roberts.

The Jones Family in Quick Millions (1939)

Released: August 25, 1939. Copyright: August 25, 1939. Distributed by: Metro-Goldwyn-Mayer.

Technical Credits:

Director: Mal St. Clair. Original Story: Joseph Hoffman, Buster Keaton, based on characters by Katharine Kavanaugh. Script: Joseph Hoffman, Stanley Rauh.

Cast:

Jed Prouty, Spring Byington, Ken Howell, June Carlson, Florence Roberts.

The Buster Keaton Story (1957)

Released: May 1957. Copyright: April 20, 1957. Length: 91 minutes. Distributed by: Paramount Pictures. Producer: Robert Smith, Sidney Sheldon.

Technical Credits:

Director: Sidney Sheldon. Script: Sidney Sheldon, Robert Smith. Photography: Loyal Griggs. Editor: Archie Marshek. Costumes: Edith Head. Technical Adviser: Buster Keaton.

Cast:

Donald O'Connor (Buster Keaton), Ann Blyth (Gloria), Rhonda Fleming (Peggy Courtney), Peter Lorre (Kurt Bergner), Larry Keating (Larry Winters), Richard Anderson (Tom McAfee), Dave Willock (Joe Keaton), Claire Carleton (Myra Keaton), Larry White (Buster, age seven), Jackie Coogan (Elmer Case), Cecil B. De Mille.

UNCREDITED FILM WORK

Splash! (1931)

Released: October 3, 1931. Distributed by: Metro-Goldwyn-Mayer. Director: Jules White, Zion Myers.

Uncredited Work:

Keaton supposedly worked one day on this short about swimming and diving.

Fast Company (1938) (TV Title: *The Rare Book Murder*)

Released: 1938. Distributed by: Metro-Goldwyn-Mayer. Producer: Frederick Stephani. Director: Edward Buzzell.

Cast:

Melvyn Douglas, Florence Rice, Claire Dodd, Louis Calhern, Douglas Dumbrille, Minor Watson.

Uncredited Work:

Keaton wrote a routine for Melvyn Douglas.

Too Hot to Handle (1938)

Released: 1938. Distributed by: Metro-Goldwyn-Mayer. Director: Jack Conway.

Cast:

Clark Gable, Myrna Loy, Walter Pidgeon, Johnny Hines, Leo Carrillo.

Uncredited Work:

Keaton gags.

Love Finds Andy Hardy (1938)

Released: 1938. Distributed by: Metro-Goldwyn-Mayer. Director: George Seitz.

Cast:

Mickey Rooney, Judy Garland, Lana Turner, Lewis Stone.

Uncredited Work:

Technical consultant.

At the Circus (1939)

Released: 1939. Distributed by: Metro-Goldwyn-Mayer. Director: Edward Buzzell.

Cast:

The Marx Brothers, Margaret Dumont, Kenny Baker, Eve Arden.

Uncredited Work:

Keaton gags.

Comrade X (1940)
Released: 1940. Distributed by: Metro-Goldwyn-Mayer. Director: King Vidor.

Cast:
Clark Gable, Hedy Lamarr, Felix Bressart, Eve Arden, Oscar Homolka, Sig Ruman.

Uncredited Work:
Keaton gags.

Go West (1940)
Released: 1940. Distributed by: Metro-Goldwyn-Mayer. Director: Edward Buzzell.

Cast:
The Marx Brothers.

Uncredited Work:
Keaton gags.

Tales of Manhattan (1942)
Released: 1942. Distributed by: 20th Century-Fox. Director: Julien Duvivier.

Cast:
Henry Fonda, Rita Hayworth, Ginger Rogers, Charles Boyer, Edward G. Robinson, Charles Laughton, Ethel Waters, Eddie Anderson, Thomas Mitchell.

Uncredited Work:
Keaton worked on a segment for W. C. Fields that was cut from the final film but still exists and is shown on occasion.

I Dood It (1943)
Released: 1943. Distributed by: Metro-Goldwyn-Mayer. Director: Vincente Minnelli.

Cast:
Red Skelton, Eleanor Powell, Lena Horne, John Hodiak.

Uncredited Work:
Keaton gags.

Note: Remake of Spite Marriage.

Bathing Beauty (1944)
Released: 1944. Distributed by: Metro-Goldwyn-Mayer. Director: George Sidney.

Cast:
Red Skelton, Esther Williams, Basil Rathbone, Bill Goodwin, Margaret Dumont.

Uncredited Work:
Keaton gags and suggested title of *The Fatal Breast Stroke*.

Nothing but Trouble (1945)
Released: 1945. Distributed by: Metro-Goldwyn-Mayer. Director: Sam Taylor.

Cast:
Laurel and Hardy, Mary Boland, Philip Merivale, Henry O'Neill.

Uncredited Work:
Keaton gags.

The Equestrian Quiz (1946)
Released: 1946. Distributed by: Metro-Goldwyn-Mayer. A Pete Smith Specialty.

Cast:
Dave O'Brian, Chistiani Brothers.

Uncredited Work:
Keaton directed the running gag.

Easy to Wed (1946)
Released: 1946. Distributed by: Metro-Goldwyn-Mayer. Director: Edward Buzzell.

Cast:
Van Johnson, Esther Williams, Lucille Ball, Keenan Wynn.

Uncredited Work:
Keaton gags and suggested title of *The Bride Wore Spurs*.

Cynthia (1947)
Released: 1947. Distributed by: Metro-Goldwyn-Mayer. Director: Robert Z. Leonard.

Cast:
Elizabeth Taylor, Mary Astor, James Lydon, George Murphy, S. Z. Sakall, Spring Byington.

Uncredited Work:
Keaton submitted five pages of script.

It Happened in Brooklyn (1947)
Released: 1947. Distributed by: Metro-Goldwyn-Mayer. Director: Richard Whorf.

Cast:
Frank Sinatra, Jimmy Durante, Kathryn Grayson, Peter Lawford.

Uncredited Work:
Keaton gags.

Merton of the Movies (1947)
Released: 1947. Distributed by: Metro-Goldwyn-Mayer. Director: Robert Alton.

Cast:
Red Skelton, Gloria Grahame, Virginia O'Brian, Leon Ames, Alan Mowbray.

Uncredited Work:
Keaton gags and technical adviser.

A Southern Yankee (1948) (My Hero)
Released: 1948. Distributed by: Metro-Goldwyn-Mayer. Director: Edward Sedgwick.

Cast:
Red Skelton, Arlene Dahl, Brian Donlevy, John Ireland, Joyce Compton.

Uncredited Work:
Keaton gags.

Neptune's Daughter (1949)
Released: 1949. Distributed by: Metro-Goldwyn-Mayer. Director: Edward Buzzell.

Cast:
Esther Williams, Red Skelton, Ricardo Montalban, Keenan Wynn.

Uncredited Work:
Keaton gags and suggested title of *Thar She Sews.*

Take Me Out to the Ball Game (1949)
Released: 1949. Distributed by: Metro-Goldwyn-Mayer. Director: Busby Berkeley.

Cast:
Frank Sinatra, Gene Kelly, Esther Williams, Betty Garrett, Jules Munshin.

Uncredited Work:
Keaton gags.

Watch the Birdie (1950)
Released: 1950. Distributed by: Metro-Goldwyn-Mayer. Director: Jack Donohoe.

Cast:
Red Skelton, Arlene Dahl, Ann Miller, Leon Ames, Pamela Britton.

Uncredited Work:
Keaton gags and loosely based on Keaton's *The Cameraman*.

The Yellow Cab Man (1950)

Released: 1950. Distributed by: Metro-Goldwyn-Mayer. Director: Jack Donohoe.

Cast:
Red Skelton, Gloria DeHaven.

Uncredited Work:
Keaton gags.

Excuse My Dust (1951) (Mr. Belden's Amazing Gasmobile)

Released: 1951. Distributed by: Metro-Goldwyn-Mayer. Director: Roy Rowland.

Cast:
Red Skelton, Sally Forrest, MacDonald Carey, William Demarest.

Uncredited Work:
Keaton gags.

TELEVISION WORK

Note: Television work is listed chronologically when air date is known. This results in multiple listings for shows on which Keaton appeared more than once.

The Ed Wynn Show (1949)

30-minute variety, CBS. Host: Ed Wynn. Air date: December 22, 1949.

Note: Keaton and Ed re-create a scene from The Butcher Boy.

The Buster Keaton Show (1949)

30-minute comedy, KTTV Hollywood. Premiered December 22, 1949. Producer: Joe Parker. Director: Philippe Delacy. Script: Clyde Bruckman, Henry Taylor.

Cast:
Buster Keaton, Alan Reed, Leon Belasco, Ben Weldon, Dick Elliot, Shirley Tegge.

Note: This was a local show that was not shown nationally due to poor kinescope quality. Some say there were 17 episodes followed by an additional 13, but it appears the 13 episodes may be part of a later filmed series from 1950–1951 also called The Buster Keaton Show *and syndicated as* Life with Buster Keaton.

Toast of the Town (1950) *(The Ed Sullivan Show)*
60-minute variety, CBS. Host: Ed Sullivan. Air date: November 5, 1950.

Note: Keaton appears in a sketch titled "Going Fishing." He was to appear many times with Ed Sullivan, including the first and second shows of 1951.

Four Star Revue (1950)
60-minute variety, NBC. Host: Ed Wynn. Air date: November 15 and December 13, 1950.

Note: Keaton appeared as a guest.

The Buster Keaton Show (1950–1951) *(Life with Buster Keaton)*
30-minute comedy, syndicated. Produced by: Consolidated Television. (Because of the number of episodes, people served in different capacities from show to show. The credits reflect those who worked on the show at one time or another.) Producers: Carl Hittleman, Clyde Bruckman, Jay Sommers. Directors: Arthur Hilton, Eddie Cline. Script: Carl Hittleman, Jay Sommers, Clyde Bruckman, Ben Perry, Harold Goodwin. Photography: Jackson Rose.

Cast:
Buster Keaton, Marcia Mae Jones, Dorothy Ford, Jack Reitzen, Philip Van Zandt, Eddie Gribbon, Eleanor Keaton.

Note: According to Variety, these shows were filmed in one day. There were 13 episodes with such titles as unimaginative as the shows. They are: "The Army Story," "The Bakery Story," "The Billboard Story," "The Collapsible Clerk," "The Detective Story," "The Fishing Story," "The Gymnasium Story," "The Haunted House," "The Little Theater," "The Shakespeare Story," "The Time Machine," "The Western Story," and "The Gorilla Story."

The Jack Carter Show (1951) *(Saturday Night Revue)*
60-minute variety, NBC. Host: Jack Carter. Air date: February 24, 1951.

Note: Keaton appeared as a guest.

All Star Revue (1951)
60-minute variety, NBC. Host: Ed Wynn. Air date: November 10, 1951.

Note: Keaton appears in bakery sketch.

The Colgate Comedy Hour (1952)
60-minute variety, NBC. Host: Donald O'Connor. Air date: March 2, 1952.

Note: Keaton does pantomime routine.

Ford Festival (1952)

60-minute musical variety, NBC. Air date: April 17, 1952.

Note: Keaton is guest.

Kate Smith Presents: Matinee in New York (1952)

NBC. Air date: July 15, 1952.

Note: Keaton appears as guest accompanied by his wife, Eleanor.

All Star Summer Review (1952)

60-minute variety, NBC. Air date: July 19, 1952.

Note: Keaton is guest.

All Star Review (1952)

60-minute variety, NBC. Host: Walter O'Keefe. Air date: December 27, 1952.

Note: Keaton is guest.

Douglas Fairbanks Jr. Presents: The Rheingold Theater (1954)

30-minute anthology, NBC. Air date: July 14, 1954. Episode title: "The Awakening" based on "The Overcoat" by Gogol.

Cast:

Buster Keaton.

Best of Broadway (1954)

60-minute anthology, CBS, color. Air date: October 13, 1954. Episode title: "The Man Who Came to Dinner." Producer: Martin Manulis. Director: David Alexander. Adaptation: Ronald Alexander from play by Kaufman and Hart. Music: David Broekman.

Cast:

Buster Keaton (Dr. Bradley), Sylvia Field (Mrs. Stanley), ZaSu Pitts (Miss Preen), Frank Tweddell (John), Margaret Hamilton (Sarah), Howard St. John (Mr. Stanley), Merle Oberon (Maggie Cutler), Monty Woolley (Sheridan Whiteside), Catherine Doucet (Harriet Stanley), William Prince (Bert Jefferson), Joan Bennett (Lorraine Sheldon), Reginald Gardiner (Beverly Carlton), Bert Lahr (Banjo).

This Is Your Life (1954)

30 minutes, NBC. Host: Ralph Edwards. Air date: November 3, 1954.

Note: Keaton appears with honored guest Joe E. Brown.

Make the Connection (1955)

30-minute quiz, NBC. Host: Jim McKay. Air date: August 18, 1955.

Note: Keaton is guest.

The Dunninger Show (1955)

30-minute mind reading-audience participation, NBC. Host: Joseph Dunninger. Air date: August 20, 1955.

Note: Keaton is guest challenging Dunninger.

Tonight (1955)

90-minute talk-variety, NBC. Host: Steve Allen. Air date: August 24, 1955.

Note: Keaton is guest.

The Sunday Spectacular (1955)

NBC, color. Air date: October 9, 1955. Episode title: "Show Biz."

Note: Keaton is featured guest.

Eddie Cantor Theater (1955)

30-minute variety, ABC. Host: Eddie Cantor. Air date: October 10, 1955. Episode title: "The Square World of Alonzo Pennyworth."

Note: Keaton plays the title character, a travel agent who has never traveled.

Screen Director's Playhouse (1955)

30-minute anthology, NBC. Air date: December 21, 1955 (rerun: March 21, 1956). Episode title: "The Silent Partner." Producer: Hal Roach. Director: George Marshall.

Cast:

Buster Keaton (Kelsey Dutton), Joe E. Brown (Arthur Vail), ZaSu Pitts (Selma), Evelyn Ankers (Miss Loving), Jack Kruschen (Ernie), Jack Elam (Shanks), Percy Helton (Barney), Joseph Corey (Arnold), Lyle Latell (Ernie's friend), Charles Horvath (barber).

The Adventures of Mr. Pastry (1955)

Director: Buster Keaton.

Cast:

Richard (Dickie) Hearne, Buster Keaton.

Note: Unsold pilot for British television. Supposedly received airplay in 1958. Buster's mother passed away in the U.S. during the making of this show.

The Martha Raye Show (1956)
60-minute comedy-variety, NBC. Host: Martha Raye. Air date: March 6, 1956.

Guests:
Buster Keaton, Paul Douglas, Harold Arlen, the Baird Marionettes.

Note: Depending on source, Keaton either re-creates scene from Limelight *or does a parody of the film.*

It Could Be You (1956)
30-minute quiz, NBC. Air date: June 7, 1956.

Note: Keaton is guest.

Today (1956)
News-talk, NBC. Air date: September 14, 1956.

Note: In a filmed segment at his California home Keaton is interviewed by Mary Kelly about his life as well as the film The Buster Keaton Story.

Producer's Showcase (1956)
90-minute anthology, NBC, color. Air date: September 17, 1956. Episode title: "The Lord Don't Play Favorites." Producer: Hal Stanley. Adaptation: Jo Swerling, based on story by Patrick H. Maloy. Music/Lyrics: Hal Stanley. Choreography: Tony Charmoli.

Cast:
Buster Keaton (Joey), Robert Stack (Duke), Kay Starr (Jessie), Dick Haymes (Doc), Louis Armstrong (Satch), Nejla Ates (Little Egypt), Mike Ross (Maxie), Arthur Q. Bryan (mayor), Oliver Blake (sheriff), Barry Kelley (Rev. Willis), Jerry Maren (Speck).

The Steve Allen Show (1956)
60-minute variety, NBC. Host: Steve Allen. Air date: December 30, 1956.

Note: Keaton appears in filmed interview at the Hollywood premiere of Around the World in 80 Days.

The Lux Show Starring Rosemary Clooney (1956)
30-minute musical variety, NBC.

Lux Video Theater (1956)
60-minute anthology, NBC.

Do You Trust Your Wife? (1956) (The Edgar Bergen Show)
30-minute quiz-audience participation, CBS. Host: Edgar Bergen.

The Johnny Carson Show (1956)
30-minute comedy-variety, CBS. Host: Johnny Carson.

Commercials (1956)
Colgate Toothpaste

It Could Be You (1957)
30-minute quiz, NBC. Air date: March 19, 1957.

Note: Keaton is guest.

This Is Your Life (1957)
30 minutes, NBC. Air date: April 3, 1957 (rerun: July 31, 1957). Host: Ralph Edwards.

Note: Keaton is honored guest. Buster is joined by his wife Eleanor, his sons, his sister Louise, his brother Harry, Red Skelton, Eddie Cline, and Donald O'Connor (dressed as Buster in an obvious plug for The Buster Keaton Story*).*

Today (1957)
News-talk, NBC. Air date: April 23, 1957.

Note: Keaton is interviewed about The Buster Keaton Story. *Old film clips are also shown.*

Tonight! America After Dark (1957)
105-minute talk-variety, NBC. Host: Jack Lescoulie. Air date: April 24, 1957.

Note: Keaton is interviewed by Hy Gardner on "Face to Face" segment.

Club 60 (1957)
NBC. Air date: May 2, 1957.

Note: Keaton is guest.

It Could Be You (1957)
30-minute quiz, NBC. Air date: December 23, 1957.

Note: Keaton is guest.

You Asked for It (1957)
30-minute audience request, ABC. Host: Art Baker.

Note: Keaton re-creates scene from The Butcher Boy *with the help of Eddie Gribbon.*

I've Got a Secret (1957)
30-minute quiz, CBS. Moderator: Garry Moore.

What's My Line? (1957)
30-minute quiz, CBS. Moderator: John Daly.

Note: Some sources say that Keaton appeared on this show four or five times. Perhaps as a panelist?

Truth or Consequences (1958)
30-minute quiz, NBC. Air dates: January 3, 1958, January 10, 1958, January 13, 1958, January 15, 1958.

Note: Keaton is guest (panelist?).

Playhouse 90 (1958)
90-minute anthology, CBS. Air date: June 5, 1958. Episode title: "The Innocent Sleep." Director: Franklin Schaffner. Script: Tad Mosel.

Cast:

Buster Keaton (Charles Blackburn), Hope Lange (Alex Winter), Dennis King (Clyde Winter), John Ericson (Leo), Hope Emerson (Mrs. Downey).

The Jack Paar Show (1958)
105-minute talk-variety, NBC. Host: Jack Paar. Air date: November 14, 1958.

Note: Keaton is guest.

The Donna Reed Show (1958)
30-minute sitcom, ABC. Air date: December 24, 1958. Episode title: "A Very Merry Christmas."

Cast:

Donna Reed, Carl Betz, Paul Peterson, Shelley Fabares, Buster Keaton (Charlie/Santa Claus).

The Betty White Show (1958)
30-minute variety, ABC. Host: Betty White.

Note: Keaton is guest.

Telephone Time (1958)
30-minute anthology, ABC. Host: Dr. Frank Baxter.

The Garry Moore Show (1958)
60-minute variety, CBS. Host: Garry Moore.

Commercials (1958)
Alka-Seltzer (plus print advertising)
Northwest Orient Airlines (six to eight)
Simon Pure Beer (six)

It Could Be You (1959)
30-minute quiz, NBC. Air date: October 26, 1959.

Note: Keaton is guest.

Masquerade Party (1959)
30-minute quiz, CBS. Moderator: Bert Parks.

Note: Keaton is guest.

Commercials (1959)
Shamrock Oil
7-Up
U.S. Steel (some with his wife, Eleanor)

Today (1960)
News-talk, NBC. Air date: January 20, 1960.

Note: Keaton is interviewed regarding his book, My Wonderful World of Slapstick.

Sunday Showcase (1960)
60-minute anthology/variety, NBC, color. Air date: February 7, 1960. Episode title: "After Hours." Director: Alex March. Script: Tony Webster.

Cast:
Buster Keaton (Santa Claus), Christopher Plummer (Steve Elliot), Sally Ann Howes (Susan Chambers), Robert Emhardt (Dr. Werner), Philip Abbott (Alan Buckman), Natalie Schafer (Edith Chambers), John Fiedler (congressman).

Masquerade Party (1960)
30-minute quiz, NBC. Air date: February 5, 1960. Host: Bert Parks.

Note: Keaton is guest masquerader.

It Could Be You (1960)
30-minute quiz, NBC. Air date: March 3, 1960.

Note: Keaton is guest.

Oscar Night in Hollywood (1960)
Special, NBC. Air date: April 4, 1960.

Note: Keaton in brief interview.

Play Your Hunch (1960)
30-minute quiz, NBC. Air date: August 19, 1960.

Note: Keaton is guest.

Officer Murphy (1960)

Cast:
Jim Davis.

Note: Unsold TV pilot. Buster's participation unknown.

The Jack Paar Show (1960)
90-minute talk-variety, NBC. Host: Jack Paar.

Note: Keaton was tied up and couldn't make it, so Eleanor took his place.

The Revlon Revue (1960)
60-minute variety, CBS.

Note: Keaton re-creates comic dueling scene from The Passionate Plumber *on this show that celebrates Paul Whiteman's seventieth birthday.*

Commercials (1960)
Wen Power Tools (also print ads)

It Could Be You (1961)
30-minute quiz, NBC. Air date: June 27, 1961.

Note: Keaton is guest.

Here's Hollywood (1961)
NBC. Air date: August 10, 1961.

Note: Keaton is interviewed at home.

Twilight Zone (1961)
30-minute sci-fi anthology, CBS. Air date: December 15, 1961. Episode title: "Once Upon a Time." Director: Norman Z. McLeod. Script: Richard Matheson. Photography: George T. Clemens. Host: Rod Serling.

Cast:

Buster Keaton (Woodrow Mulligan, janitor), Stanley Adams (Professor Rollo), Milton Parsons (Professor Gilbert), Jesse White (repairman), Gil Lamb, James Flavin, Michael Ross, George E. Stone, Warren Parker.

Note: According to Matheson, "the script was absolutely written with Keaton in mind. . . . I don't recall writing the trousers-in-a-wringer bit. I imagine that Keaton put it in himself" (Matheson to Marion Meade).

Candid Camera (1961)
30 minutes, CBS. Host: Allen Funt.

Note: Keaton appears as a man at lunch counter who has trouble eating without ripping his clothes or losing his toupee in his soup.

Commercials (1961)
Milky Way Candy Bar
Philips 66 Gasoline and Oil
Marlboro Cigarettes

Your First Impression (1962)
NBC. Air date: January 12, 1962 (guest). August 29, 1962 (on briefly with Eleanor).

The Scene Stealers (1962)
60-minute comedy-drama. Distributed by March of Dimes. Air date: Supposedly shown on CBS in April 1962 but may have been syndicated to local markets for airing during public service time. Director: Jack Shea. Script: Johnny Bradford. Filmed at Paramount Pictures.

Cast:

Buster Keaton, Ed Wynn, cameos by Jimmy Durante, David Janssen, Rosemary Clooney, Jack Lemmon, Ralph Edwards, Fritz Feld, James Garner, Jackie Cooper, Abby Dalton, Eartha Kitt, Nanette Fabray, Dan Blocker, Lorne Greene, Fabian, Dorothy Provine.

Route 66 (1962)
60-minute adventure, CBS. Episode title: "Journey to Nineveh." Air date: September 28, 1962.

Cast:

George Maharis (Buzz), Martin Milner (Todd), Buster Keaton (Jonah Butler), Joe E. Brown (Sam Butler), Gene Raymond (constable), Jenny Maxwell (Susie), John Astin (gas station attendant), John Davis Chandler (Frank), John Durren (Charlie).

Medicine Man (1962)

30-minute sitcom, Screen Gems. Episode title: "A Pony for Chris." Producer: Harry Ackerman. Director: Charles Barton. Script: Jay Sommer, Joe Bigelow.

Cast:

Ernie Kovacs (Doc), Buster Keaton (Junior, an Indian), Kevin Brodie (Chris).

Note: Pilot show that was almost not completed due to the death of Ernie Kovacs. It supposedly received airtime, but the date is unknown.

Commercials (1962)

Canadian Electric Razor (filmed in Los Angeles)
Ford Motor (five each year for three years)

Mr. Smith Goes to Washington (1963)

30-minute sitcom, ABC. Air date: January 19, 1963. Episode title: "Think Mink."

Cast:

Fess Parker (Mr. Smith), Buster Keaton (Si Willis), Jesslyn Fax (Abigail Willis), Sandra Warner (Pat).

Your First Impression (1963)

30 minutes. NBC. Air date: February 12, 1963.

Note: Keaton does special stunt.

Truth or Consequences (1963)

30-minute quiz, NBC. Air date: March 7, 1963.

Note: Keaton is a guest.

Today (1963)

120-minute news-talk, NBC. Air date: April 26, 1963. Episode title: "Buster Keaton Revisited." Host: Hugh Downs.

Note: The entire show is a tribute to Keaton, who is there as film clips are shown.

The Ed Sullivan Show (1963)

60-minute variety, CBS. Host: Ed Sullivan.

Commercials (1963)

Minute Rub
Beer (Buster did many beer commercials for many brewers. Not all have been identified.)
Bread (Minnesota)

The Greatest Show on Earth (1964)

60-minute drama, ABC. Air date: April 28, 1964. Episode title: "You're Alright Ivy." Director: Jack Palance.

Cast:

Jack Palance (Slate), Stuart Erwin (King), Buster Keaton (Pippo), Lynn Loring (Ivy Hatch), Ted Bessell (Loring Wagner), Joe E. Brown (Diamond "Dimey" Vine), Joan Blondell (T. T. Hill), Betsy Jones-Moreland (Louella Grant), Barbara Pepper (fat woman), Larry Montaigne (Felix).

Burke's Law (1964)

60-minute detective drama, ABC. Air date: May 8, 1964. Episode title: "Who Killed 1/2 of Glory Lee." Script: Harlan Ellison.

Cast:

Gene Barry (Amos Burke), Gary Conway (Tilson), Regis Toomey (Les), Buster Keaton (Mortimer Lovely), Joan Blondell (Candy Sturtevant), Nina Foch (Anjanette Delacroix), Anne Helm (Sable), Betty Hutton (Carlene Glory), Gisele Mackenzie (KiKi Lee).

Hollywood Palace (1964)

60-minute variety, ABC. Host: Gene Barry. Air date: June 6, 1964.

Note: Keaton and Gloria Swanson spoof Cleopatra. *Keaton also joins Gene Barry in a dance routine.*

Commercials (1964)

Georgia Oil
Ford Motor
U.S. Steel
Budweiser Beer
Salt Lake City Bank
Seneca Apple Juice

The Man Who Bought Paradise (1965) (Hotel Paradise)

60-minute comedy-drama, CBS. Air date: January 17, 1965 (filmed in 1963). Producer/Director: Ralph Nelson. Script: Richard Alan Simmons.

Cast:

Buster Keaton (Mr. Bloor), Robert Horton (runaway financial genius), Angie Dickinson (his wife), Paul Lukas (Colonel Von Rittner), Ray Walston (lawyer), Hoagy Carmichael (Mr. Leoni), Dolores Del Rio (Mona Meyerling), Cyril Ritchard (hotel keeper), Walter Slezak (Captain Meers).

The Jonathan Winters Show (1965)

Comedy-variety, NBC. Host: Jonathan Winters. Air date: March 29, 1965.

Note: Keaton does James Bond spoof.

The Donna Reed Show (1965)

30-minute sitcom, ABC. Air date: February 11, 1965 (filmed in 1964). Episode title: "Now You See It, Now You Don't." Director: Gene Nelson.

Cast:

Donna Reed, Ann McRea, Carl Betz, Bob Crane, Paul Peterson, Darryl Richard, Buster Keaton (Mr. Turner of Turner's Garage).

Truth or Consequences (1965)

30-minute quiz, NBC. Air date: April 6, 1965.

Note: Keaton is guest.

A Salute to Stan Laurel (1965)

60-minute special, CBS. Host: Dick Van Dyke. Air date: November 23, 1965.

Note: Keaton appears in sketch with Lucille Ball and Harvey Korman.

Commercials (1965)

Pure Oil
Pepsi-Cola (made in Madrid)

DOCUMENTARIES AND FILM COMPILATIONS

Ça C'Est du Cinema (1951 or 1952)

Length: 89 minutes. French compilation film. Includes Keaton in clips from his silent films.

When Comedy Was King (1960)

Released: March 1960. Copyright: December 31, 1959. Length: 81 minutes. Distributed by: 20th Century-Fox. Producer: Robert Youngson. Associate Producer: Herman Gelbspan. Assistant Producers: John E. Allen, Al Dahlem.

Technical Credits:

Script: Robert Youngson. Narrator: Dwight Weist. Music: Ted Royal. Sound Effects: Ralph Curtis.

Cast:

Buster Keaton, Laurel and Hardy, Charlie Chaplin, Ben Turpin, Fatty Arbuckle, the Keystone Kops, and more.

Note: Scenes from Cops.

The History of the Motion Picture (1960s) *(Silents Please)*
Length: 25–30 minutes. Distributed by: Sterling Educational Films. Producer: Saul J. Turell, Paul Killiam.

Technical Credits:
Director/Script: Saul J. Turell. Narrator: Paul Killiam. Research: William K. Everson. Film Editor: Ray Angus. Music Editor: Angelo Ross.

Note: Clips of Keaton's work appear in at least three segments of this series: "The Sad Clowns," "Clown Princes of Hollywood," and "The Buster Keaton Special" (title for segment released on home market).

The Great Chase (1962)
Released: December 20, 1962. Length: 79 minutes. Distributed by: Janus Films. Presented by: Saul J. Turell and Paul Killiam. Producer: Harvey Cort.

Technical Credits:
Script: Harvey Cort, Saul J. Turell, Paul Killiam. Editor: Harvey Cort. Narrator: Frank Gallop. Music: Larry Adler.

Cast:
Douglas Fairbanks, Sr., Lillian Gish, William S. Hart, Buster Keaton (abridged version of *The General*).

Note: In 1975, a Mack Sennett and Mabel Normand sequence was added.

30 Years of Fun (1963)
Released: February 12, 1963. Copyright: December 31, 1962. Length: 85 minutes. Distributed by: 20th Century-Fox. Producer/Script: Robert Youngson. Music: Bernard Green, Jack Shaindlin.

Cast:
Charlie Chaplin, Buster Keaton, Laurel and Hardy, Harry Langdon.

Note: Keaton clips include: Cops, Daydreams, The Balloonatic.

The Sound of Laughter (1963)
Released: December 17, 1963. Length: 75 minutes. Distributed by: Union Films. Producer: Barry B. Yellen, Irvin S. Dorfman.

Technical Credits:
Director: John O'Shaughnessy. Script: Fred Saidy. Music: Robert Waldman. Narrator: Ed Wynn.

Cast:
Buster Keaton, Shirley Temple, Danny Kaye, Bob Hope, Bing Crosby, Harry Langdon, Milton Berle, Andy Clyde.

Note: Keaton clips include: One Run Elmer, Grand Slam Opera.

MGM's Big Parade of Comedy (1964)

Released: 1964. Length: 89 minutes. Distributed by: Metro-Goldwyn-Mayer. Producer: Robert Youngson. Associate Producer: Alfred Dahlem.

Technical Credits:

Script: Robert Youngson. Narrator: Les Tremayne. Research Supervisor: Jeanne Keyes. Music: Bernie Green.

Cast:

Buster Keaton, the Marx Brothers, Abbott and Costello, Jimmy Durante, Laurel and Hardy.

Note: Keaton clip is from The Cameraman.

Buster Keaton Rides Again (1965)

Released: October 1965. Length: 56 minutes. Produced by: National Film Board of Canada. Producer: Julian Biggs.

Technical Credits:

Director/Photographer: John Spotton. Commentary: Donald Brittain. Editors: John Spotton (picture), Malca Gillsom (music), Sidney Pearson (sound).

Cast:

Buster Keaton, Eleanor Keaton, Gerald Potterton.

Note: Documentary filmed during the making of The Railrodder.

The Great Stone Face (1968)

Length: 93 minutes. Produced by: Funnyman, Inc. Productions. Producer: Vernon P. Becker, Mel May. Associate Producer: Michael Hyams.

Technical Credits:

Director/Script: Vernon P. Becker. Editor: William C. Dalzell. Music: T. J. Valentino. Narrator: Henry Morgan.

Note: Clips are from Fatty at Coney Island, Cops, The Balloonatic, Day-dreams, *and* The General. *Reedited to 60 minutes in 1981 and released on video through the Rohauer Collection. Video packaging calls this film* Buster Keaton, *but title on the screen is* The Great Stone Face.

The Four Clowns (1970)

Released: September 1970. Copyright: December 31, 1969. Length: 97 minutes. Distributed by: 20th Century-Fox. Producer: Robert Youngson. Associate Producers: Raymond Rohauer, Herbert Gelbspan, Alfred Dahlem.

Technical Credits:

Script: Robert Youngson. Narrator: Jay Jackson. Music: Manny Alban. Research: Jeanne Youngson.

Cast:
Stan Laurel, Oliver Hardy, Buster Keaton, Charlie Chase.

Note: Keaton clip is an abridged version of Seven Chances.

The Three Stooges Follies (1974)
Released: November 1974. Length: 116 minutes. Distributed by: Columbia Pictures.

Note: A compilation of shorts starring the Three Stooges but also includes other shorts produced by Columbia during the thirties and forties. Keaton is seen in Nothing but Pleasure.

Broadway Nights, Hollywood Days (1977)
Released: 1977 to the home market. Length: 9 minutes. Distributed by: Blackhawk Films.

Note: This film is a compilation of footage from Fox-Movietone newsreels. Keaton appears in the segment on a charity baseball game for Mt. Sinai Hospital with teams made up of Hollywood celebrities.

Life Goes to War: Hollywood and the Homefront (1977)
Produced by: Time-Life Television and 20th Century-Fox Television. Producer: Jack Haley, Jr. Coproducer: Malcom Leo.

Technical Credits:
Director/Script: Jack Haley, Jr. Editor: David Blewitt. Host/Narrator: Johnny Carson.

Note: Cesar Romero and Buster Keaton head up a volunteer station-wagon brigade.

Hollywood: The Pioneers (1980)
Released: 1980. Produced by: Thames Television. Producers: David Gill and Kevin Brownlow.

Technical Credits:
Director/Script: David Gill and Kevin Brownlow. Music: Carl Davis. Narrator: James Mason.

Note: 13-part series for television has clips of Keaton throughout and detailed coverage of Keaton in episode #8: "Comedy: A Serious Business."

The Golden Age of Buster Keaton (1982) *(Buster)*
Length: 100 minutes. Producer: Jay Ward, Raymond Rohauer.

Technical Credits:
Editor: Skip Craig. Technical Adviser: Mrs. Buster Keaton. Narrator: Bill Scott.

Buster Keaton: The Great Stone Face (1982)
Released: 1982. Produced by: S-L Film Productions. Producer: Gerald A. Shiller.

Technical Credits:
Director/Script: Gerald A. Shiller. Music: Richard Hieronumus. Narrator: Red Buttons.

Note: Keaton clips are from Coney Island, One Week, The Boat, The Playhouse, Cops, and The General.

Buster Keaton: A Hard Act to Follow (1987)
Released: September 1987. Produced by: Thames Television in association with Raymond Rohauer. Producers: David Gill, Kevin Brownlow.

Technical Credits:
Script: David Gill, Kevin Brownlow. Music: Carl Davis. Film Research: Cy Young. Research: Linda Philips. Additional Research: Joe Adamson, Robert S. Birchard, Bob Borgen, Jack Dragga (uncredited), Joel Goss, Alan Hoffman, Frank Holland, Mark Jungheim, Eric Sparks.

Note: Presented in three one-hour segments: "From Vaudeville to Movies," "Star Without a Studio," and "A Genius Recognized."

CARICATURES

Kuster Beaton (circa 1930)
Length: 10 minutes. Distributed/Produced by: Associated Sound Films Industries.

Note: Keaton appears in caricature as part of a British series called Little People Burlesques *starring the Ottorino Gorno Marionettes. Episodes were directed by John Grierson, Jack Harrison, and J. Elder Wills. Some of the American stars burlesqued are: Douglas Fairbanks, Sr. in* Don Dougio Fairbania, *Tom Mix in* Tom Mixup, *Clive Brook's portrayal of Sherlock Holmes in* Be-A-Live Crook, *and Buster Keaton in* Kuster Beaton.

Mickey's Gala Premiere (1933)
Released: July 1, 1933. Length: 1 reel. Distributed by: United Artists. Produced by: Walt Disney Productions. Director: Burt Gillett.

Note: Keaton, in caricature, attends the premiere of a Mickey Mouse cartoon. He sits next to Joe E. Brown and looks into his mouth. This scene is cut out of the version released to the home market under the title Movie Star Mickey.

The Soda Squirt (1933)

Released: 1933. Copyright: October 12, 1933. Length: 1 reel. Distributed by: Metro-Goldwyn-Mayer. Produced by: Ub Iwerks for Celebrity Productions.

Note: A Flip the Frog cartoon. Keaton is seen in caricature as one of many stars attending the opening of Flip the Frog's Soda Fountain. Parts resemble Disney's Mickey's Gala Premiere, *released a few months earlier.*

Hollywood Steps Out (1941)

Released: May 24, 1941. Length: 1 reel, color. Distributed by: Warner Bros. Directed by: Fred (Tex) Avery.

Note: Keaton appears briefly in caricature with other stars in this cartoon about a Hollywood nightclub. Academy Award nominee.

To Tell the Truth (1971)

30-minute quiz, NBC. Air date: January 4, 1971 (taped October 13, 1970).

Note: Garry Moore impersonates Buster Keaton in a comedy routine as a prelude to bringing out guest Raymond Rohauer, who was mounting a Keaton revival.

NOTES

Much of this biography is based on two types of primary sources: interviews with persons who knew Buster Keaton most intimately—his family and friends—as well as professional colleagues; and also his own words recorded in *My Wonderful World of Slapstick* and in countless interviews given in the course of his sixty-five-year career.

The main archival sources for Keaton materials are located at:

AFI   Louis B. Mayer Library, American Film Institute, Los Angeles (Myra Keaton Scrapbook)

AMPAS Margaret Herrick Library, Academy of Motion Picture Arts and Sciences, Beverly Hills, Calif. (clipping collections)

LC   New York Public Library of the Performing Arts at Lincoln Center (clipping collections and Robinson Locke Scrapbook of clippings, halftones, and reviews, 1904–1920, about the Keaton family in vaudeville)

ABBREVIATIONS

BK   Buster Keaton
JK   Joe Keaton
EK   Eleanor Keaton
NTK Natalie Talmadge Keaton
RA   Roscoe Arbuckle
RR   Raymond Rohauer
JS   Joseph Schenck
MM   Marion Meade

NYDM	*New York Dramatic Mirror*
NYTel	*New York Telegraph*
NYT	*New York Times*
P	*Photoplay*
PS	*Picture Show*
THMS	*Terre Haute Morning Star*
V	*Variety*

MWWS	*My Wonderful World of Slapstick,* Buster Keaton with Charles Samuels
NYSPCC	New York Society for the Prevention of Cruelty to Children

I. CHEROKEE STRIP

SOURCES

Books:

Allen, *Illustrated Atlas of Harrison County;* Andreas, *History of Kansas;* Blesh, *Keaton;* Bradsby, *History of Vigo County;* Cadbury, *Church in the Wilderness;* Flora, *Historical Sketch of Ancient Pasquotank County;* Hinshaw, *Encyclopedia of American Quaker Genealogy,* MWWS.

Articles:

JK, "Stage Career of Joe Keaton," *THMS,* May 30, 1904; JK, "The Cyclone Baby," *P,* May 1927.

Records:

Portrait and Biographical Album of Cass County, 1889; Noble County Genealogical Society, *History of Noble County;* Terre Haute City Directories 1881–1884.

Greenwood Centennial History Book; Magnolia Centennial History; Pride of Modale Centennial Book, 1974.

Keaton marriage, death, probate, cemeteries, military records, Vigo County, Ind.; U.S. Census, Vigo County, Prairie Creek Township, 1850–1880; North Carolina Abstracts of Wills, 1690–1760; State Census of North Carolina, 1784–1787.

Genealogies:

Cutler-Beebe genealogies: Hunt, *History of Harrison County;* Iowa State Census, Modale City, 1880, 1885.

Keaton genealogies: Bula Trueblood Watson, *The Trueblood Family in America, 1682–1963* (Naperville, Ill.: mimeo, 1964); Ruth Cline Ladd, *One Ladd's Family* (1974); Thomas D. Hamm and Mary Louise Reynolds, *The Works of Webster Parry with Additions by Edna Harvey Joseph* (1987); Lyle Williams, *The Batchelor-Williams Families and Related Lines* (1976) (earliest information on Henry Keaton); Bob and Elsie Emery genealogy (1981).

Transcript:
BK interview with Joan Franklin for Columbia University Oral History Collection, November 1958.

Interviews:
Terry Keaton.

NOTES

4 Oklahoma land run: all the applause, Ernest Jones quoted in Noble County Genealogical Society, p. 89; "I was a useful," JK, "Stage Career."

5 Burt Cutler: Myra's brother became a professional cornet player in vaudeville orchestras.

6 Joe's tall tales: JK's claim to have taken part in Jacob Coxey's famous crusade of the unemployed is a fabrication. The cross-country workers' march, a reaction to the 1893 depression, began months after Joe left California.

7 Cutler family history: Blesh, p. 4; *MWWS*, pp. 17–18; Cutler-Beebe genealogies above; Greenwood Centennial Book; Modale Public Library clipping collection; Woodbine (Iowa) *Twiner*, Woodbine, Iowa, clipping collection.

8 Keaton family history: Keaton genealogies; Vigo County Historical Society clipping collection; Vigo County records; Hinshaw; Bradsby.

9 Family origin: Some Keatons assume the surname is a derivation of Kenton. They believe their clan most likely originated in the English county of Kent. (Terry Keaton to MM, Jan. 7, 1990) In another version of the family history, BK's sister, Louise, believed that the Keatons intermarried with Native Americans. But there is no evidence of any such intermarriages; for more than 200 years, in fact until JK wed Myra Cutler, the Keatons strictly followed the rules of their faith and married only other Quakers. The Trueblood Cemetery near Prairie Creek, Indiana, is the burial place of BK's great-grandfather Joseph Zachariah Keaton and his wife, Margaret Trueblood, as well as many other family members.

10 Joe's temperament: JK, "Stage Career"; Joe's typewriter, *MWWS*, p. 45.

11 Marriage of Joe and Myra: "There's a lady," JK, "Stage Career"; "Joe afterward," Ernest Jones quoted in Noble County Genealogical Society, p. 89; he never laid a hand, Blesh, p. 21; a regular medicine show, JK, "Stage Career."

14 Accidents during pregnancy: Blesh, pp. 4–5.

2. THE TRAINS OF WOODSON COUNTY

SOURCES

Books:
Andreas, *History of Kansas;* Blackmar, *Cyclopedia of Kansas History;* Blesh, *Keaton;* Christopher, *Houdini;* Duncan, *History of Allen and Woodson Counties;* MWWS; Kellock, *Houdini: His Life Story.*

Articles:

JK, "Stage Career of Joe Keaton," *THMS,* May 30, 1904; JK, "The Cyclone Baby," *P,* May 1927; "News from Piqua," *Yates Center* (Kans.) *News,* Sept. 27, 1895; Bill Kennedy, "Mr. LA," *Los Angeles Herald-Examiner,* June 7, 1962; *Denver Times,* Jan. 1, 1921; *NYT,* Apr. 24, 1896; *NYDM,* Jan. 23, 1904; *New York Clipper,* Dec. 20, 1907; *Pittsburg Leader,* July 14, 1907; Elizabeth Peltret, "Poor Child!," *Motion Picture Classic,* Mar. 1921; Woodson County Historical Society, "History of Piqua," *In the Beginning,* July 1971; "Buster Keaton, Early Comedy Film Legend Was Born at Piqua," *Yates Center News,* Mar. 1, 1990; Harry Brand, "They Told Buster to Stick to It," *Motion Picture Classic,* June 1926.

Pamphlet:

Piqua, Kansas, Centennial Book, 1882–1982; A Century of Catholic Heritage, St. Martin of Tours, Piqua, Kansas, 1884–1984.

Unpublished Manuscript:

Brownlow, "The Search for Buster Keaton."

Clipping Collections:

Myra Keaton Scrapbook, AFI; clipping collections, LC and AMPAS.

Transcript:

BK interview with Columbia University Oral History Collection, 1958.

Interviews:

EK, Glenn Massoth, Richard Matheson, Sidney Radner.

NOTES

15 Piqua today: Like many Lake Wobegon towns whose time is past, Piqua was destined to fade and shrink—but nonetheless survive. About sixty people still live there, even though the rails haven't seen passenger service for years and people must drive seventy or eighty miles to find a shopping mall. Only three or four businesses remain. At the Piqua Tavern, people can exchange news with their neighbors and get themselves a beer, even eat lunch if they feel like it. "It's not a big deal, only sandwiches at the back," says Glen Massoth, the great-grandson of Jacob and Barbara Haen, who continues to work the land near Piqua but lives in the town of Yates Center with his wife, Peggy, and their three children.

    The Haen place was bulldozed shortly after Buster's visit, and the site is now occupied by the Piqua Farmers Cooperative Service Station, where locals can buy milk, bread, and tools, and can also get their hair cut.

Mohawk arrives in Piqua: *Yates Center News,* Sept. 27, 1895, Mar. 1, 1990.

BK birth: Based on Blesh, p. 3; JK, "Cyclone Baby"; Piqua Centennial Book.

17 Edison's Vitascope: *NYT,* Apr. 24, 1896.

Early accidents: "Before that," Kennedy, "Mr. LA"; "would just butt in," JK, "Stage Career."

18 Piqua blown away: JK's cyclone story ("Cyclone Baby") was invented. A search of 1895 issues of the *Yates Center News* by editor David Powls revealed that a month earlier Woodson County had suffered a severe storm with flooding and loss of livestock. But no cyclone took place. Also see: "Pickway itself," *MWWS*, p. 20.

How BK got nickname: based on unsourced clipping, AFI Scrapbook, ca. 1903; *NYDM,* Jan. 23, 1904; JK, "Stage Career"; *New York Clipper,* Dec. 20, 1907; *Denver Times,* Jan. 1, 1921.

19 George Pardey: An undated portrait of Pardey with Selden Irwin, manager of the Cincinnati Grand Opera House, shows him to have straight dark hair and a mustache (LC photo collection).

Apocryphal nickname story: "My, what a buster," *MWWS,* p. 20; Peltret; Brand.

20 Amputation of Buster's finger: based on Blesh, p. 7; *MWWS,* p. 21.

21 Keatons in Pittsburg: Guy G. Fritts letter to *Pittsburg Leader,* July 14, 1907, p. 7.

Keatons meet Houdinis: based on Kellock, p. 100; Christopher, p. 30; *Galena Republican,* Jan. 13, 1898; archives, Anderson County Historical Society, Garnett.

22 Misdated photo: Blesh, p. 17.

3. KEEP YOUR EYE ON THE KID

SOURCES

Books:

Blesh, *Keaton*; Gilliatt, *To Wit*; *MWWS*; Miller, *Untouched Key*; Sanford, *Strong at the Broken Places*; Shengold, *Soul Murder.*

Articles:

Harry Brand, "They Told Buster to Stick to It," *Motion Picture Classic,* June 1926; JK, "Stage Career of Joe Keaton," *THMS,* May 30, 1904; JK, "The Cyclone Baby," *P,* May 1927; *NYDM,* Nov. 17, 24, Dec. 2, 30, 1900, Mar. 2, 9, Apr. 6, 20, 1901; *New York Clipper,* July 20, 1901; BK, "Why I Never Smile," *Ladies' Home Journal,* June 1926; *NYTel,* Mar. 7, 1921; "Vaudeville Houses," *NYT,* May 21, 1903; Elizabeth Peltret, "Poor Child!," *Motion Picture Classic,* Mar. 1921; *Harrisburg Courier,* Jan. 17, 1915; "Buster's Bumps," *Detroit News,* Dec. 14, 1913.

Letters:

Joe Keaton–Harry Houdini letters, Harry Ransom Humanities Research Center, University of Texas at Austin.

Records:

BK files, NYSPCC.

Television:

Ralph Edwards's *This Is Your Life* television program, Apr. 3, 1957; *Do You Trust Your Wife?* television program, 1956.

Transcript:

BK taped interview with Herbert Feinstein, 1963.

Interviews:

Bert Cowlan, Edward Hutson, Susan Reed, Linda Sanford, Eileen Sedgwick, Leonard Shengold.

NOTES

23 Keatons' debut in New York: "act didn't go," *NYDM,* Nov. 17, 1900; "acrobatic comedy duo," *NYDM,* Dec. 30, 1899; Keaton ads, *NYDM,* Nov. 24, Dec. 22, 1900.

26 BK debut at Wilmington: "He's a handicap," unsourced clipping, 1904, Myra Keaton Scrapbook; "assisted by our little son," *NYDM,* Dec. 2, 1900.

27 BK makes New York debut: "I have a son," JK to NYSPCC, Dec. 27, 1900; "I must state," JK to NYSPCC, Jan. 5, 1901; "Keep your eye," *NYDM,* Mar. 2, 1901; "a ten-strike," *NYDM,* Mar. 9, 1901; BUSTER ad, *NYDM;* "The tiny comedian," *New York Clipper,* July 20, 1901.

29 Success at last: "Pop made me," *MWWS,* p. 31; "I was their partner," *MWWS,* p. 14; "Boots, old fellow," JK to Harry Houdini, Apr. 17, 1901.

30 Problems with NYSPCC: NYSPCC files, Mar. 7, 11, 1901. Also, in this way, BK, "Why I Never Smile."

32 Roughhouse comedy: "Of course the old man," Cowlan to MM; BK grabbed by ears, *NYTel,* Mar. 7, 1921; "When you go," Gilliatt, p. 4; "If I should chance," BK, "Why I Never Smile"; "Even people," *MWWS,* p. 32. For an idea of how Joe handled Buster onstage, watch *The Boat* (1921), in which the father picks up his little boy by the back of the collar like a shopping bag.

Joe bashes spectator: Based on JK, "Cyclone Baby"; *MWWS,* p. 27; Blesh, p. 46. When BK tried to recall this experience for *MWWS,* he must not have remembered the place exactly and set it at Poli's New Haven. According to JK's recollection, written some thirty years earlier, it happened in Syracuse. Also, "Tighten up," Reed to MM; "had no fear," Blesh, p. 47; "Now, look here," JK, "Cyclone Baby."

33 Joe's aggressive behavior: "THE LITTLE BOY," *NYDM* ads; "Father threw me," BK quoted on *Do You Trust Your Wife?*

Act toned down: "You're a blockhead," "Vaudeville Houses," p. 7.

34 BK describes rough treatment: "Dad has had," "Buster's Bumps."

35 Psychoanalytic opinions: "To survive," Sanford to MM; "praise for not crying," Shengold to MM; in spite of remembering, Miller, p. 40. Also see, Sanford, *Strong at the Broken Places,* and Shengold, *Soul Murder.*

4. JINGLES JUNGLE

SOURCES

Books:

Blesh, *Keaton*; *MWWS*; Stein, *American Vaudeville*; Lee, *Gypsy*; Dardis, *Man Who Wouldn't Lie Down.*

Articles:

Margaret Reid, "The Child Who Was 'Abused,'" *PS*, Feb. 1928; *New York Post*, July 3, 1941; JK, "London: 'Mr. Butt and Co.,'" *V*, Dec. 11, 1909; *New York Clipper*, Apr. 8, 1905; *NYT*, Nov. 19, 1907; *NYDM*, Jan. 4, 1908; *NYTel*, Mar. 22, 1906, Feb. 21, Mar. 23, 1913; misc. clippings, *Muskegon Chronicle.*

Pamphlets:

Bluffton Historical Committee, "Shifting Sands," Muskegon, Mich., 1976; Bluffton School P.T.A. Historical Committee, "Sand in Their Shoes: A Story of the Bluffton Area," Muskegon, Mich., 1970.

Records:

BK case files, NYSPCC; Louise Keaton birth certificate, Lewiston, Maine, Oct. 30, 1906; Joseph Z. Keaton, certificate of death, Perry, Okla., July 20, 1909; U.S. Census, Michigan, 1920.

Transcript:

RR filmed interview with Kevin Brownlow and David Gill, 1986, transcript.

Interviews:

Mary Anderson, Marcia Engle, Eddie Foy 3d, Richard Freye, EK, Eloise Munz, Audrey Reberg, Susan Reed, Eileen Sedgwick, Dorothy Dana Walton.

NOTES

37 Rough handling: "about six weeks," Williams quoted in Stein, p. 246; Bernhardt story, BK quoted in Reid, p. 25.

BK attends school: based on *MWWS*, pp. 24–26; Blesh, p. 45; Reed to MM. Also, *New York Post*, July 3, 1941.

38 Reading problems as adult: "I trust you," RR transcript; child, Weingarten to Pierre Sauvage, quoted in Dardis, p. 158; "I don't need to grow," EK to MM.

40 Myra's pregnancies: "not many children," *MWWS*, p. 14; "Pullman babies," Blesh, p. 48; "I thank you," unsourced article, ca. Sept. 12, 1907, LC clipping collection.

41 Jingles kidnaping hoax: "A bold attempt," *NYTel*, Mar. 22, 1906.

42 Birth of Louise: Louise Keaton birth certificate. In 1942, Myra and Joe filed a request for "delayed return" birth certificate for Louise. Her middle name was given as Josephine, not Dresser.

Lynchburg accident: *NYTel,* ca. June 1906, LC clipping collection.

Keatons banned in New York: "Young though he is," *New York Clipper,* Apr. 8, 1905; NYSPCC case file #216252; *NYT,* Nov. 19, 1907; "cruel setback," *MWWS,* p. 68.

43 Parental neglect: "first-class governess," *NYDM,* Jan. 4, 1908.

44 BK as baby-sitter: *NYTel,* Feb. 21, 1913.

Louise joins act: "looked filthy," Walton to MM.

Siblings exhibit problem behavior: Jingles's backstage fights, unsourced articles, Nov. 27, 1910, Dec. 30, 1914, LC clipping collection; photo of Louise and Jingles in boxing gloves, *NYTel,* Mar. 23, 1913; visit to Modale, photocopy courtesy of Margaret Louden and Edna Beebe Cherry; Louise at Ursuline, Anderson to MM.

45 Power of Gerries: "The only place," Sedgwick to MM.

Keatons visit London: based on Blesh, pp. 60–63; *MWWS,* pp. 58–63; JK, "London: Mr. Butt and Co."

46 Summer home in Muskegon: based on "Shifting Sands" and "Sand in Their Shoes"; Anderson, Freye, Munz, Engle, Reberg to MM; Louise and Harry Keaton letters to Anderson; Mary Anderson historical notes on Actors Colony. Love of Keaton children for Actors Colony: "most wonderful little town," Louise Keaton to Mary Anderson, Aug. 13, 1975.

5. THE PROVIDENCE FURNITURE MASSACRE

SOURCES

Books:
Blesh, *Keaton; MWWS.*

Articles:
NYTel, May 8, 1910. *New Republic,* Mar. 20, 1915; George Pratt, "Anything Can Happen—and Usually Did," *Image,* Dec. 1974; *V,* Oct. 4, Dec. 18, 1909, Apr. 28, 1916.

Interviews:
James Karen.

NOTES

48 Buster turns 16: "Today," *V,* Oct. 4, 1909; Buster improves, *V,* Dec. 18, 1909, p. 20.

BK buys first car: photo of Browniekar, *NYTel,* May 8, 1910.

49 First sexual experiences: "cute as a bug's ear," Blesh, p. 73.

50 Joe rejects movie offer: "What are you *saying?*" *MWWS,* p. 90.

52 Influenced by *Birth of a Nation:* "aggressively vicious," *New Republic;* "From then on," Pratt, p. 24.

53 JK out of control: "not an enlivening spectacle," *NYDM,* ca. 1912; Joe arrested, *MWWS,* p. 82.

54 Keatons play the Palace: Palace Theatre program, week of Apr. 24, 1916, Chris Carmen collection; *V,* Apr. 28, 1916, p. 19; "Okay, Keaton," *MWWS,* p. 83.

55 BK breaks up act: "terrible, disastrous drunk," Karen to MM; "We didn't even leave," *MWWS,* p. 89.

6. TOYS

SOURCES

Books:

Blesh, *Keaton;* Brownlow, *Parade;* Edmonds, *Frame-Up!;* *MWWS;* Herman, *How I Broke into the Movies;* McNamara, *Shuberts of Broadway;* Yallop, *Day the Laughter Stopped;* Talmadge, *Talmadge Sisters;* Wagner, *You Must Remember This.*

Articles:

Christopher Bishop, "Interview with Buster Keaton," *Film Quarterly,* Fall 1958; Alan Hynd, "The Rise and Fall of Joseph Schenck," *Liberty,* June 28, July 5, July 12, 1941; *NYT,* Mar. 4, 1917; "Joe Keaton Is Lonesome," *NYTel,* Feb. 12, Apr. 8, 1917, Mar. 9, 1921; *NYDM,* Mar. 7, 1917; BK, "Why I Never Smile," *Ladies' Home Journal,* June 1926; *Chicago Post,* Mar. 3, 1917; *V,* Mar. 23, 1917; Henry F. Pringle, "Business Is Business," *New Yorker,* Apr. 30, 1932.

Television:
This Is Your Life.

Interviews:
Maryann Chach, James Karen.

NOTES

57 *The Passing Show:* "a fine boy," *NYTel,* Mar. 9, 1921; "spun nostalgic tales," *NYTel,* Feb. 12, 1917.

59 Arbuckle arrives in New York: "tired big boy," *NYDM,* Mar. 7, 1917; *NYT,* Mar. 4, 1917. Also see LC clipping collection.

62 BK meets RA: BK could not remember the exact circumstances of his first contact with Arbuckle. In *MWWS* and other interviews, he said that he met RA, or RA with Lou Anger, on the street. Talking to Blesh, however, he recalled that it was Anger alone whom he saw in Times Square. In my opinion, the most likely scenario is his first running into Anger on the street and then meeting RA later that day at Colony Studio.

Butcher Boy: "tear that camera," *This Is Your Life;* "things just started happening," Bishop; "the first time," BK quoted in Movieland Wax Museum press release; "You're late," Blesh, p. 89; "put my head," *This Is Your Life;* "slam him about," *NYTel,* Apr. 8, 1917.

65   Arbuckle childhood and early career: based mainly on Yallop and LC's Arbuckle clipping collection. Also, Minta Arbuckle quoted in Wagner, p. 32.

67   Joseph Schenck early career: called husband Daddy, Talmadge, p. 141; Hynd; Pringle, p. 22; "I had a visit," BK, "Why I Never Smile"; and Herman p. 111.

68   *Butcher Boy* praised: *NYDM*, May 26, 1917; "Newcomer Keaton," Edmonds, p. 109.

69   Parsley girls party: based on Yallop, p. 69.

70   BK joins Comique: "Why doggone it," RA quoted in Paramount Pictures press release, Apr. 1917; "I directed," BK quoted in Brownlow, p. 479.

7. THREE SISTERS

SOURCES

Books:

Blesh, *Keaton*; Goldwyn, *Behind the Screen*; *MWWS*; Loos, *Talmadge Girls*; Ramsaye, *Million and One Nights*; Talmadge, A., *The Talmadge, Tallmadge and Talmage Genealogy*; Talmadge, M., *Talmadge Sisters*; Talmey, *Doug and Mary and Others*.

Articles:

Boston Post, Aug. 3, 1919; Karl Kitchen, "Meet the Movie Mamas," *Cleveland Plain Dealer*, Aug. 14, 1919; Alan Hynd, "The Rise and Fall of Joseph Schenck," *Liberty*, June 28, July 5, July 12, 1941; Norma Talmadge, "Close-Ups," *Saturday Evening Post*, Mar. 12, 1927; *V*, Jan. 25, 1918; *PS*, Jan. 24, 1920, p. 3; Ruth Hummel, "Author's Visit to Plainville Spurs Interest in Silent-Era Actress Sisters," *New Britain* (Conn.) *Herald*, Feb. 23, 1991; Hazel Simpson Taylor, "That Tantalizing Talmadge," *Motion Picture Magazine*, n.d., 1917; *P*, Jan. 1929; "Buster Keaton on His Way," *Motion Picture World*, Aug. 18, 1918; David Balch, "Alice Lake from High School Amateur to Screen Favorite," *Photo-Play Journal*, Mar. 1920.

Pamphlet:

Ruth Hummel, "Our Plainville Heritage," 1973.

Records:

John Tallmadge Affidavit, Declaration for Pension Claim, 1892; John Tallmadge certificate of death, Middletown, Conn., June 7, 1915; correspondence, Martha Talmadge and U.S. Bureau of Pensions; U.S. Census, Muskegon County, Mich., 1920; U.S. Census, Kings County, Brooklyn, 1900; Norma Talmadge certificate of death, Las Vegas, Nev., Dec. 24, 1957; Natalie Talmadge certificate of death, Santa Monica, Calif., June 19, 1969; BK Military Personnel records.

Interviews:

Melissa Talmadge Cox, Ruth Hummel.

NOTES

73 Ages of sisters: Peg Talmadge doctored the ages of all three daughters by subtracting four years across the board. The 1900 census for Kings County, Brooklyn, lists their true ages: Norma was born in May 1894, Natalie in April 1896, and Constance in April 1898.

Natalie's personality and appearance: "I told her," Kitchen; duties at Comique, Loos, p. 125; "harbored same genes," Loos, p. 5.

74 Peg Talmadge conceals history: Jersey City plumber, Loos, p. 11; Peg's birthdate and place, Norma Talmadge death certificate.

75 Fred Talmadge family history: Saxon descent, A. Talmadge; "another Democrat," John Tallmadge pension claim; death, Ruth Hummel, Plainville Historical Society; traveling salesman, M. Talmadge, p. 6.

Talmadge surname: Fred Talmadge deleted one of the *l*'s from his name.

Talmadge marriage: "arrived by accident," Loos, p. 83.

76 Norma meets JS: Goldwyn, p. 211; "Joe, you wouldn't make," Hynd, p. 55.

77 Alice Lake: Balch, p. 18.

79 BK in Army: Military Personnel records (National Personnel Records Center) indicate BK enlisted; in *MWWS*, p. 96, and Blesh, p. 112, BK said he was drafted; farewell party, *Motion Picture World*, Aug. 31, 1918; "She looked gorgeous," *MWWS*, p. 98; Jingles and Louise in public school, U.S. Census, Michigan, 1920; "Give 'em hell," *MWWS*, p. 96; friend, Blesh, p. 116.

81 Natalie's film debut: "Natalie doesn't want," Kitchen; "motherly type," *Boston Post*, Aug. 3, 1919; Natalie "possesses the talent," *PS*, p. 3.

82 Peg opinion of BK: "He used to come home," M. Talmadge, p. 133.

8. HOLLYWOOD

SOURCES

Books:

Blesh, *Keaton*; Brownlow, *Parade*; Fussell, *Mabel*; Loos, *Girl Like I*; *MWWS*; St. Johns, *Love, Laughter and Tears*; *The Movie Mirror Book*.

Article:

DeWitt Bodeen, "Where Did All the Fun Go?: Viola Dana and Shirley Mason," *Films in Review*, Mar. 1976.

Unpublished Manuscript:

Hoffman, "Buster."

Records:

BK contracts with Comique, 1920–1924.

Transcript:

BK interview with Herbert Feinstein, 1963.

Interviews:
Sheila Kaufman, Sid Taylor.

NOTES
83 BK returns to Hollywood: "best friend," *MWWS*, photo caption; "square shooter," *MWWS*, p. 109; "When she stopped laughing," *MWWS*, p. 120; "Life was good," St. Johns, p. 126.

88 BK romance with Viola Dana: Flugrath family, Kaufman, Taylor to MM; Bodeen, p. 141: Viola's career, *Movie Mirror Book;* Vi was quite a cutup, Kaufman to MM.

89 Vernon Country Club: *MWWS*, p. 152, and Loos, p. 116; Normand cocaine addiction, described in Fussell.
    BK succeeds RA at Comique: "just turned me loose," Hoffman, p. 23; "never knew," BK quoted in Feinstein; "So I had a city lot," BK quoted in Brownlow, p. 480; Comique contracts, Joel Goss collection.

92 Keaton family leaves Muskegon: "Keatons all agree," Harry Keaton letter to Mary Anderson, July 27, 1976.

9. HOME TEAM

SOURCES

Books:
Blesh, *Keaton*; Capra, *Name Above Title;* MWWS.

Articles:
V, July 9, 1920; *NYT*, Oct. 27, 1919; Elizabeth Peltret, "Poor Child!," *Motion Picture Classic*, Mar. 1921; Herb Stein, "Harry Brand: Another Brilliant Publicist," *New York Morning Telegraph*, May 9, 1959.

Unpublished Manuscript:
Brownlow, "Search for Buster Keaton."

Transcript:
BK interview with Columbia University Oral History Collection.

Interviews:
Douglas Fairbanks, Jr., Fred Gabourie, Jr., Sheila Kaufman, EK, Patsy Ruth Miller, Darrylin Zanuck Pineda, Sid Taylor, Bartine Burkett Zane.

NOTES
94 Work methods: "The way we worked," LC clipping collection.
    Unhappiness with *High Sign*: Blesh, p. 139.

95 BK acts in *Saphead*: "That could have been," Fairbanks to MM; "cyclone," V, Feb. 18, 1921.

96 Inspiration for *One Week*: In the 1980s Kevin Brownlow accidentally discovered *Home Made* in a vault at Teddington Studios in England. He was surprised to recognize the sixty-year-old educational film as the inspiration for *One Week,* whose simple construction of seven parts had retained the gimmick of the calendar pages.

97 Opening of *One Week:* In New York City, the picture opened at the Rivoli Theatre on the same bill with a prison story, *The Great Redeemer,* and a nature film, *As Fancy Paints.*

Natalie's picture career: "The third of the Talmadge sisters," *V,* July 9, 1920.

98 BK's leading ladies: "supposed to be the costar," Zane to MM; Virginia Fox chosen, Virginia Fox Zanuck scrapbook; "a rose," Pineda to MM.

BK's "Buster" character: Keaton "*suffered,*" Capra, p. 62; "all his own," EK to MM.

100 BK social life: breakup with Viola Dana, Kaufman to MM; he went upstairs, Zane interviewed on Johnny Carson TV show; "But, Buster," Zane to MM.

101 Brand hired as publicist: Brand career, Stein; Keaton family mythology, Peltret, p. 64.

10. HONEYMOON EXPRESS

SOURCES

Books:

Blesh, *Keaton;* Brownlow, *Parade;* Brundidge, *Twinkle, Twinkle;* Gish, *The Movies, Mr. Griffith, and Me; MWWS;* Loos, *Talmadge Girls;* Talmadge, *Talmadge Sisters.*

Articles:

Robert DeRoos, "Biggest Laugh in Movie History," *Coronet,* Aug. 1959; Christopher Bishop, "Interview with Buster Keaton," *Film Quarterly,* Fall 1958; Karl Kitchen, "Meet the Movie Mamas," *Cleveland Plain Dealer,* Aug. 14, 1919; *P,* May, Dec. 1921; Hazel Taylor, "That Tantalizing Talmadge," *Motion Picture Magazine,* ca. 1917; Willis Goldbeck, "Only Three Weeks," *Motion Picture Magazine,* Oct. 1921; *V,* Feb. 10, 1921; *New York Star,* Feb. 25, 1921; *Los Angeles Evening Herald,* June 15, 1921; *Chicago Exhibitors Herald,* Sept. 10, 1921; *NYTel,* Feb. 7, 1921.

Interviews:

Melissa Talmadge Cox, Carol De Luise, EK, Susan Reed.

NOTES

103 JK at Continental: AMPAS clipping collection, Mar. 28, 1928.

Keaton's relations by marriage: One of Keaton's cousins, Bertie Jones, married into the theatrical Lyman family, which included her husband, Mike, a well-known Hollywood restaurateur, and his brother Abe, a popular orchestra leader. Through another cousin, Rose Jones, Keaton was related to the Lupinos, a famous English theatrical family. Rose married actor Wallace Lupino and lived in England. The Hollywood branch of the family included Wallace's brother, the popular comedian Lupino Lane (known for his role in the musical *Me and My Girl*), and actress-director Ida Lupino.

104 Success of BK comedies: "greatest thrill," Brundidge, p. 211; "They laughed so hard," DeRoos, p. 98; "biggest laughing," Bishop.

105 Alice Lake career: Despite a successful transition to sound films, Alice's career slowly foundered during the early thirties; she made her last picture in 1934 and died in 1967 (obit, *V,* Nov. 22), having spent her final years working in a candy factory, packing chocolates.

Connie elopes: Gish, p. 239; *P,* May 1921, p. 74; "curse of many," Kitchen; "Merrily yours," Loos, p. 125; "She had a demure," Cox to MM.

106 BK engagement: "if you still care," *MWWS,* p. 165; "butter and eggs man," Loos, p. 39; consent of Mama Talmadge, *V,* Feb. 10, 1921; "Yes, the report," *New York Star,* Feb. 25, 1921; broken leg, *NYTel,* Feb. 7, 1921.

108 Marriage: based mainly on AMPAS and LC clipping collections. Also, "spent motoring," Talmadge, p. 175; BK not ready for marriage, Blesh, p. 157, *MWWS,* p. 166; "one of the most interesting," Goldbeck, p. 28; "mail-order romance," Talmadge, p. 173.

110 Early weeks of marriage: "didn't develop," Loos, p. 124; two sides, *Los Angeles Evening Herald,* June 15, 1921; "I've only been married," Goldbeck, p. 28.

111 Ingenuity of *The Playhouse*: "audience laughed," Keaton quoted in Brownlow, p. 491; Keaton ranks third, *P,* Dec. 1921, p. 62.

Leaves Metro: In the summer of 1921, BK switched his distributor from Metro to First National Pictures. First release was *The Playhouse.*

112 BK technical innovations: BK was the first comedy director to abandon the 16-frames-per-second camera speed and film at the now standard 22 frames per second. This eliminated the jerky quality seen in Keystone comedies and used a more natural tempo that did not destroy a gag's timing.

BK distaste for Chaplin: "But, Charlie," *MWWS,* p. 269; "when people praised him," De Luise to MM.

113 *The Blacksmith*: "another button-buster," *Chicago Exhibitors Herald,* Sept. 10, 1921.

115 BK learns bridge: based on *MWWS,* pp. 185–86.

II. LABOR DAY PARTY

SOURCES

Books:

Blesh, *Keaton*; Brownlow, *Pioneers*; Brundidge, *Twinkle, Twinkle*; *MWWS*; Loos, *Talmadge Girls*; Yallop, *Day the Laughter Stopped*; Edmonds, *Frame-Up!*

Articles:

Marion (Ind.) *Chronicle,* Sept. 30, 1921; *Camera,* Oct. 8, 1921; *P,* July 1921, Jan., Feb. 1922, May 1923; "Clean from Pittsburg," *Motion Picture Classic,* ca. Dec. 1921.

Transcript:

BK interview with Columbia University Oral History Collection, 1958.

Interviews:

Lina Basquette, James Karen, Irene Mayer Selznick.

NOTES

117 Marital difficulties: "Peg had schooled," Loos, p. 4.

118 Labor Day party: "He told me," Karen to MM; several weekend dates, *MWWS,* p. 156; "Shut up," Yallop, p. 116.

121 RA arrested: "Now listen, kids," Dana quoted in Brownlow, p. 108; "My mother snatched," Basquette to MM; "Hello, folks," *Marion Chronicle,* Sept. 30, 1921; "beast," "murderer," *MWWS,* p. 160; "learned his lesson," Edmonds, p. 209; "Half the people," Blesh, p. 180; "Certainly Fatty," BK quoted in Columbia Oral History; "damn him," Edmonds, p. 211.

123 NTK's pregnancy: "Speaking of the Talmadges," *P,* Jan. 1922; "None of the Talmadge women," Selznick to MM.
BK and Talmadge women: "Peg came," Blesh, p. 204; Connie and Pialogiou, *P,* July 1921, p. 74; "so large," *P,* Feb. 1922, p. 88.

124 Talmadges in Hollywood society: "much in evidence," *P,* May 1923, p. 90; "None of the Talmadges," Selznick to MM; "show yellow," Brundidge, p. 210.

125 Repercussions of RA trials: "happiest couple," Virginia Fox quoted in "Clean from Pittsburg," p. 37, Virginia Fox Zanuck scrapbook.

12. COPS

SOURCES

Books:

Blesh, *Keaton;* Edmonds, *Frame-Up!;* Freeman, *American Testament; MWWS;* Loos, *Talmadge Girls;* Talmadge, *Talmadge Sisters.*

Articles:

Seattle Post-Intelligencer, Jan. 1, 1922; Sylvain du Pasquier, "Buster Keaton's Gags," *Journal of Modern Literature,* Apr. 1973; *P,* Aug. 1922, May, June 1923, Mar. 1924; Christopher Bishop, "Interview with Buster Keaton," *Film Quarterly,* Fall 1958; Alma Whitaker, "Sparklers or Stardust," 1923; unid. clipping, Zanuck scrapbook; *New York World,* Sept. 25, 1923; *Motion Picture World,* Oct. 27, Nov. 24, Dec. 15, 1923; Arthur Friedman, "Buster Keaton:

An Interview," *Film Quarterly,* Summer 1966; *Sierra Sun,* Aug. 27, 1981; *Truckee Republican,* 1922–1923; *NYT,* Dec. 10, 1923; Robert Sherwood, "The Silent Drama," *Life,* Oct. 25, 1923; George Pratt, "Anything Can Happen—and Generally Did," *Image,* Dec. 1974; "Studio Lights Injure Keaton's Little Son," *New York World,* Aug. 19, 1923; *V,* Dec. 13, 1923.

Unpublished Manuscript:
Brownlow, "Search for Buster Keaton."

Transcripts:
BK taped interview with Joe Laitin, 1956; BK interview with Columbia University Oral History Collection, 1958; BK taped interview with Studs Terkel.

Interviews:
Douglas Fairbanks, Jr., Elaine St. Johns.

NOTES

127 BK films *Cops:* "abounding with gags," *Seattle Post-Intelligencer;* French film semiologist, du Pasquier, "BK's Gags," p. 268; "Well, just running," BK quoted in Laitin interview, 1956; "hit and miss," BK quoted in Terkel interview.

128 RA exoneration and aftermath: "entirely innocent," Edmonds, pp. 247–48; conversation with Hearst, BK quoted in Columbia Oral History.

130 Shooting in Truckee: *Truckee Republican,* 1922; RA scenario for *Frozen North*—his writing credit would go to BK and Eddie Cline.
His in-laws: "walls were bulging," Blesh, p. 204; "Just plain Norma," *P,* Aug. 1922, p. 66; "If so," Loos, p. 129.

131 Birth of son: *P,* Oct. 1922, p. 51; "Blue is for boys," *MWWS,* p. 185.

132 Marital relations: "all monies due," contract, Oct. 30, 1922, Joel Goss collection.
Keatons in Tijuana: racehorse, *P,* May 1923, p. 90; Blesh, p. 327.

135 Margaret Leahy background: Whitaker; "Comic leading ladies," Blesh, p. 218; "Talmadge English importation," article, Zanuck scrapbook; "scenes we threw in trash," BK quoted in Blesh, p. 218. Margaret Leahy dropped out of films to became an interior decorator at Bullock's department store. Her husband sixty years later told Joel Goss that she hated the motion picture business. She once collected her movie scrapbooks and burned them in the yard. Leahy died in 1967 after drinking drain cleanser.

136 Role of women in BK films: Women may appear unimportant because he seldom takes the focus off himself. "Buster" also tends to treat women only slightly less methodically than machinery. But Keaton the filmmaker is not Buster the character. Keaton's women never behave like objects, no matter how Buster treats them. There are no lovesick bimbos or naive masochists in BK films, although a few of them are terrifying (*Seven Chances*), or amazons who toss him over cliffs (*The Three Ages*). Keaton's women snatch their independence and dance away from him.

Success of *The Three Ages*: "funniest picture," *New York World*, Sept. 25, 1923; national treasure, Sherwood; Lenin's analysis, Freeman, p. 592; American navy, *Motion Picture World;* "all right," Pratt, p. 24.

Peg publishes book: "the fabulous three," St. Johns to MM; Norma Talmadge, *P,* June 1923, p. 74; "I used to be," Fairbanks to MM.

137 Success of *Our Hospitality*: "a frustrated actress," Keaton, *MWWS,* p. 183; Truckee river, *Sierra Sun;* "Did Nate see it?," Blesh, p. 253; son's eye problem, "Studio Lights."

140 Critical raves: "Keaton is a comedian," *San Francisco Call* quoted in *Motion Picture World*, Dec. 15, 1923; "*Our Hospitality* classes," *V,* Dec. 13, 1923; "quite good," *NYT,* Dec. 10, 1923.

141 New Year's Eve, 1923: *P,* Mar. 1924, p. 78.

13. HEARTS AND PEARLS

SOURCES

Books:
Blesh, *Keaton*; Brownlow, *Parade*; MWWS.

Articles:
Arthur Friedman, "Buster Keaton: An Interview," *Film Quarterly*, Summer 1966; Christopher Bishop, "Interview with Buster Keaton," *Film Quarterly*, Fall 1958; *NYT,* May 26, 1924; John Gillett and James Blue, "Keaton at Venice," *Sight and Sound,* Winter 1965–66; *Picture Play*, Sept. 1924; *V,* May 28, 1924, Oct. 28, 1925; Edmund Wilson, *New Republic*, "Chaplin and His Comic Rivals," Dec. 16, 1925; *Motion Picture World*, June 16, 1923; *Los Angeles Mirror News,* Oct. 21, 1955; *Motion Picture Magazine,* July 1925; *New York American,* Mar. 13, 1925; *P,* May, July 1924; George Pratt, "Anything Can Happen—And Generally Did," *Image,* Dec. 1974; Robert Sherwood, "The Silent Drama," *Life,* Nov. 19, 1925.

Unpublished Manuscript:
Brownlow, "Search for Buster Keaton."

Transcript:
BK interview with Columbia University Oral History Collection, 1958.

Interviews:
Douglas Fairbanks, Jr., EK, James Talmadge.

NOTES

142 *Sherlock* special effects: "This was the reason," Gillett and Blue.

143 RA's blacklisted career: Since so few of RA's films were preserved, filmgoers today have difficulty accepting his greatness. In 1994 the American Museum of the Moving Image, Astoria, N.Y., presented a retrospective. Announce-

ments noted that a sensationalized scandal had caused his banishment from movies but failed to explain the nature of the scandal.

144 BK fires RA: "flushed and mad," Brownlow, *Parade*, p. 486.

Baptism of son: "no use for religion," Talmadge to MM; "Wanta be kept!" *P,* May 1924.

Separate beds: "I'm not going without sex," EK to MM; "Gals used to," Blesh, p. 165; "I was always delighted," Fairbanks to MM.

145 Broken neck: "When did you break?" Brownlow, "Search for Buster Keaton," p. 86.

146 Stunt injuries: "get a thrill," Friedman, p. 3.

Problems with *Sherlock*: "We spent," Bishop; "rare and refreshing," *P,* July 1924; "one of the best," *NYT,* May 26, 1924, p. 21; "devoid of ingenuity," *Picture Play,* Sept. 1924; "hospital operating room," *V,* May 28, 1924; "machinery and stunts," Wilson, *New Republic,* Sept. 2, 1925; "all right," BK quoted in Brownlow, *Parade,* p. 488.

148 Developing *Navigator* story: "Set fire to it," Columbia University Oral History; "he turned gagman," BK quoted in Brownlow, *Parade,* p. 489; "the $3.5 million," *Motion Picture World,* June 16, 1923.

150 Blacks in *Navigator*: For the role of the cannibal chief, BK cast Noble M. Johnson, a leading black actor who portrayed many different racial types in his dozens of films (in *King Kong* he appears as the chief of Skull Island).

151 BK's children: "very good mother," Collier to Brownlow, "Search for Buster Keaton," p. 135.

152 Keatons buy homes: "refueling," Blesh, p. 237; "It has no room," *MWWS,* p. 182.

153 BK's debts to JS: "Whenever I made investments," AMPAS clipping collection, *Los Angeles Mirror News,* Oct. 21, 1955.

155 *Seven Chances* premiere: "hoping the children," *New York American,* Mar. 13, 1925; "he wrote his name," *Motion Picture Magazine,* July 1925.

157 Reviews of *Go West*: "I didn't care," Pratt, p. 27; "cow is the whole show," *V,* Oct. 28, 1925; "soul-stirring," Sherwood; p. 26; "not entirely," Wilson.

14. POMP AND CIRCUMSTANCE

SOURCES

Books:

Anobile, *Buster Keaton's The General;* Blesh, *Keaton;* Cassidy, *Civil War Cinema;* MWWS; Loos, *Talmadge Girls;* Thompson and Christie, *Scorsese on Scorsese.*

Articles:

P, Feb. 1925; George Pratt, "Anything Can Happen—And Usually Did," *Image,* Dec. 1974; Robert Sherwood, "Silent Drama," *Life,* Sept. 16, 1926; *V,* Aug. 25, 1926; *NYT,* Aug. 23, 1926; *Cottage Grove* (Ore.) *Sentinel,* June 10, July 26, 1926.

Unpublished Article:
Joel Goss, "The Making of *The General,*" 1990.

Clipping Collections:
MGM press book for *Battling Butler;* United Artists press book for *The General.*

Interviews:
Gene Woodward Barnes, Joe Bricher, Kieth Fennell, James Karen, Harold Terry.

NOTES
159 Fred Talmadge funeral: based on Peg's reports to Anita Loos, p. 120. Also
see *P,* Feb. 1925, p. 98.
160 Production of *Battling Butler:* "for seven reels," Pratt, p. 200; "The only
person," Thompson and Christie, p. 80; BK's legs, Karen to MM; "biggest
Keaton," MGM press book, *Battling Butler;* "just as funny," Sherwood;
"equal to the prominence," *V.*
161 BK releases through United Artists: *Battling Butler* would be the last film
BK released through Metro. In 1924, JS was elected chairman of the board
of United Artists, the organization formed five years earlier to distribute the
films of Pickford, Fairbanks, Griffith, and Chaplin. BK's first film for UA was
The General.
Pittinger book: Pittinger's widow felt Keaton used the book unfairly and
threatened to sue for copyright infringement. Keaton had no written script.
Lou Anger gave an oral synopsis, saying the picture followed the same plot
as all Keaton films; it was about a "fellow in love with a girl." The suit was
dropped.
163 BK arrives in Cottage Grove: This section is based on interviews, clippings,
photographs, archival material from Laura Hall and Cottage Grove Museum;
and Goss. Also see: "ignored and slighted," Marion Mack to RR, quoted in
Anobile, p. 15; "one of best shortstops," Bricher to MM.
164 Ballplayers in cameo roles: Keaton cast ex-major league baseball players from
the New York Giants and Cleveland Indians.
Expenses mount: United Artists press book for *The General.*
165 Forest fires: Goss.
Blows up bridge: "happy as a kid," *Cottage Grove Sentinel,* July 26, 1926;
"put 'em in blue uniforms," Pratt, p. 28.

15. ITALIAN VILLA

SOURCES

Books:
Anobile, *Buster Keaton's The General;* Blesh, *Keaton;* Brundidge, *Twinkle,
Twinkle;* Fitzgerald, "Magnetism," in *Stories of F. Scott Fitzgerald;* MWWS;
McDowall, *Double Exposure.*

Articles:
Richard W. Bann, "An Italian Villa for the Great Stone Face," *Architectural Digest,* Apr. 1990; *P,* Nov. 1926, May 1927; *New York Herald Tribune,* Feb. 8, 1927; *V,* Feb. 9, 16, Sept. 14, 1927; Robert Sherwood, "The Silent Drama," *Life,* Feb. 24, 1927; John Gillett and James Blue, "Keaton at Venice," *Sight and Sound,* Winter 1965–66; *Motion Picture Herald,* July 14, 1928; *New York Evening Journal,* Sept. 28, 1936.

Unpublished Paper:
Jason D. Scott, "The Selling of the Stone Face: Studio Marketing Practices and Keaton's *The General.*"

Transcript:
BK interview with Herbert Feinstein, 1963.

Interviews:
Larry Breslow, John Coyle, Francisco "Chico" Day, Pamela Mason, Julie Randall, Dean Reisner, Gilbert Roland, Rose Rufman, Irene Mayer Selznick, Sam White.

NOTES
167 Opulence of Italian Villa: based on MM tour of house, Mason to MM, and Bann, p. 140. Also: "My father was impressed," Coyle to MM; "very ornate," Mason to MM.
169 *General* wrapped: celebration, Bricher to MM.
170 BK's angry mood: "He pretended," Marion Mack quoted in Anobile, p. 17; "stop acting like," White to MM.
    Norma in love: "Clara was my first love," Roland to MM; "My brother," Day to MM; Joe's guilt, LC clipping collection, Mar. 7, 1928.
171 *General* opens in New York: preopening publicity, Scott; "long and tedious," *New York Herald Tribune,* Feb. 8, 1927; "flop," *V,* Feb. 9, 1927; "vaulting ambition," Sherwood; "although Miss Mack," *V,* Feb. 16, 1927; "I was more proud," BK to Feinstein.
173 Shooting *College*: "I could not do the scene," Brundidge, p. 209; "because the Keaton name," *V,* Sept. 14, 1927.
174 BK hostility toward Brand: "jumped out of my seat," Blesh, pp. 284–85; publicity man, Gillett and Blue, p. 28.
175 On location for *Steamboat Bill*: JS kills flood, Gillett and Blue, p. 28.
176 JS dismisses talkies: *Motion Picture Herald,* July 14, 1928, p. 26.
    Social life at Italian Villa: "I hope Buster," *MWWS,* p. 183; "Natalie was not sophisticated," Selznick to MM; "He went about each project," Brooks quoted in McDowall, p. 161; "magnificent playpen," McDowall, p. 161.
178 NTK's spending spree: "Who Is Hollywood's," *P,* May 1927, p. 106; Natalie's clothes allowance, *New York Evening Journal,* Sept. 28, 1936.
179 The falling-wall stunt: BK describes to Gillett and Blue; people praying, Reisner to MM; "I was mad," Brundidge, p. 209.

180 BK in New York: based entirely on Blesh, pp. 298–99.

181 Keaton studio closes: "worst mistake of my life," *MWWS*, p. 201; "still young enough to believe," Fitzgerald, p. 227.

16. KEATON'S KENNEL

SOURCES

Books:
Blesh, *Keaton;* Brownlow, *Parade;* Dardis, *Man Who Wouldn't Lie Down; MWWS;* Marx, *Mayer and Thalberg;* Paris, *Louise Brooks.*

Articles:
Los Angeles Herald Examiner, June 7, 1962; *New York Sun,* Jan. 11, 1930; *P,* Nov., Dec. 1930; *V,* Mar. 27, 1929, Nov. 5, 1930.

Unpublished Manuscript:
Brownlow, "Search for Buster Keaton."

Interviews:
Lina Basquette, Edward Bernds, J. J. Cohn, Carol De Luise, Frank Dugas, Leatrice Gilbert Fountain, Fred Gabourie, Jr., Edward Hutson, EK, Sam Marx, Anita Page, Gilbert Perkins, Maurice Rapf, Linda Santos, Betty Goulding Saunder, Eileen Sedgwick, Irene Mayer Selznick, James Talmadge, Jim Talmadge.

NOTES

183 Location shooting in New York: "Hey, *Keaton!,*" *MWWS*, p. 209; "People were enchanted," Dugas to MM; "They sat," Dugas to Brownlow, "Search for Buster Keaton"; "They can kiss," Dugas to MM; *Cameraman* script, Frank Dugas recalls a ten-page shooting script, ideas mostly, the majority BK's.

184 BK contract with MGM: In addition to his salary, MGM agreed to pay 25 percent of the net profits from BK's films to shareholders of Buster Keaton Productions. BK also continued to receive 25 percent of the profits from the features he had completed as an independent. MGM to Joseph Moskowitz, Oct. 9, 1928, Oct. 14, 1930, June 19, 1931, Joel Goss collection.

185 BK affection for Ed Sedgwick: based on interviews with Sedgwick and Hutson.
BK relations with Mayer and Thalberg: "I learned," Selznick to MM; "piss ice water," Marx, p. vii.

186 Problems with Weingarten: "If he hadn't been," Selznick to MM; "He never listens," Saunder to MM; "a child," Weingarten to Pierre Sauvage, quoted in Dardis, p. 158; "holy war," Marx, p. 84.

187 Special treatment ends: MGM promoted Fred Gabourie, Keaton's art director, to superintendent of construction. He continued to work at the studio until his death in 1951.

Weingarten objects to gag: BK describes in Blesh, p. 311; "a salvo," *V*, Mar. 27, 1929; "in a place," Weingarten quoted in Dardis, p. 187; "He had cocktails," Goodwin to Brownlow, "Search for Buster Keaton," p. 37; "I wasn't aware," Cohn to MM.

188 Restrictions on BK: "I swung my bat," *Los Angeles Herald Examiner*, June 7, 1962.

189 Early career of Dorothy Sebastian: "disappeared," Brooks to Brownlow and Gill, quoted in Paris, p. 72. See also AMPAS's and LC's Sebastian clipping collections.

190 BK moves to studio lot: dressing-room dispute, Blesh, p. 311; "all of the MGM stars," *MWWS*, p. 214; "revolutionary headquarters," Marx, p. 122.

191 Sound ends Talmadge sisters' careers: poor reviews, *V*, Nov. 5, 1930; "Talmadge sisters epitomized," Basquette to MM.

192 BK switches to talkies: Weingarten on BK's voice, Weingarten quoted in Dardis, p. 178; "a lighter voice," Bernds to MM.

194 High stakes card games: "What did it matter," Brownlow, *Parade*, p. 474; "break out," Brooks quoted in Dardis, p. 169.

Remote figure to sons: "not around," James Talmadge to MM; "not really aware," Jim Talmadge to MM; "threw liver," James Talmadge to MM; "Keaton was absent," *New York Sun*, Jan. 11, 1930. Also see *MWWS*, pp. 184–85.

195 Louise and Harry flounder: Louise "could have become," EK to MM; "female version," De Luise to MM.

196 Shooting *Doughboys*: Keaton and Sedgwick, Nealis to MM; frustrated director, Perkins to MM.

17. HIGH CRIMES AND MISDEMEANORS

SOURCES

Books:
Blesh, *Keaton*; *MWWS*; Rotha, *Celluloid*; White, *White Brothers*.

Articles:
NYT, Feb. 6, 1931; *P*, Feb., May 1931, June 1932; *V*, Apr. 4, 1931, Aug. 23, 1932; *New York Sun*, Apr. 5, 6, June 27, 1932; *New York Herald Tribune*, Apr. 5, 1932; *Movie Classic*, June 1932; "John Corbett's Historic Photo Album," *Sierra Sun*, Apr. 19, 1984.

Clipping Collections:
MGM press books for *The Passionate Plumber, Speak Easily*, 1932.

Television:
MGM: When the Lion Roars, Turner Pictures documentary, 1992.

Transcript:
Marion Mack taped interview with Rick Vanderknyff, 1987.

Interviews:
William Bakewell, Andy Nealis, Maurice Rapf, Gilbert Roland, Irene Mayer Selznick, Willard Sheldon, James Talmadge.

NOTES
199 BK in Tahoe City: *Sierra Sun,* Apr. 19, 1984; "Well, he was brilliant," Roland to MM.
BK's drinking: Alcoholism ran in both the Keaton and Talmadge families.
200 Sebastian weds: "wanted desperately," Page to MM.
Kathleen Key career: Key clipping collection, LC.
BK–Key brawl: "Flag your ass," Blesh, p. 323; headlines, *NYT,* Feb. 6, 1931; payoff, Loeb, Walker and Loeb letter to C. K. Stern, Mar. 13, 1931, Joel Goss collection; "For farces," *V,* Apr. 4, 1931; "L. B. Mayer gave her a trip," Bakewell to MM; "floozy," BK quoted in Blesh, p. 324, and *MWWS,* p. 224; "Closed for repairs," *P,* May 1931, p. 84.
202 NTK threatens divorce: BK describes in Blesh, p. 324, and *MWWS,* p. 224; "only for the sake," *MWWS,* p. 225.
203 BK pranks: Cody's vase, *P,* Feb. 1931, p. 48; party at Lewyns' house, Mack to Vanderknyff.
204 Quality of BK work criticized: Rotha, p. 101.
205 *Sidewalks of New York:* "Nevertheless," Rapf to MM; "After lunch," Sheldon to MM.
206 BK teamed with Durante: "Very seldom," Rapf to MM; "Buster was supposed to," Nealis to MM; "100 percent turkey," *MWWS,* p. 237.
207 Air trip to Mexico: BK comments to reporters, *New York Herald Tribune,* Apr. 5, 1932, *New York Sun,* Apr. 5, 6, 1932; "forlornly waiting," *Movie Classic,* June 1932, p. 32; "She's home," *P,* June 1932, p. 88.
208 *Speak Easily* completed: "practically self-educated," MGM press book, *Speak Easily,* 1932; "much more satisfying," *V,* Aug. 23, 1932; "love gift," *New York Sun,* June 27, 1932.
209 BK invites woman home: based on *MWWS,* pp. 227–29.
210 Separation: James Talmadge to MM.

18. DOWN AND OUT IN CHEVIOT HILLS

SOURCES

Books:
Blesh, *Keaton;* Brownlow, *Parade;* Brunel, *Nice Work;* Chaplin, *My Father;* *MWWS;* Marx, *Mayer and Thalberg;* Rooney, *Life Is Too Short;* Sinclair, *Spiegel.*

Articles:
Dale Stevens, "Buster Keaton Looks Back at Vaudeville, Silent Films," unsourced article, 1961; *Los Angeles Herald Examiner,* June 7, 1962; *NYT,* Oct. 18, 22, 1933; *V,* Feb. 14, 1933, Mar. 25, 1936; *New York Evening Journal,*

Sept. 28, 1936; *New York Herald Tribune,* Oct. 5, 1935; *New York Post,* Oct. 23, 1935; *New York American,* Oct. 22, 1935.

Unpublished Manuscripts:

Brownlow, "Search for Buster Keaton"; Jewel Elizabeth Steven, a.k.a. Mae Keaton, "Satan! Pull Up a Chair," 1942.

Records:

Joseph Frank Keaton and Mae Scriven Hawley certificate of marriage, Ventura, Calif., Oct. 21, 1933; *Keaton* v. *Keaton,* Case No. #D–134150, Los Angeles Superior Court; Mae Keaton and William Walter Gassert certificate of marriage, Carson City, Nev., Aug. 2, 1937.

Interviews:

J. J. Cohn, Melissa Talmadge Cox, Fred Gabourie, Jr., Samuel Goldwyn, Jr., John Jennings, James Karen, Lupita Tovar Kohner, Charles Lamont, Maurice Rapf, Dean Reisner, Irene Mayer Selznick, Addie O. Sheldon, Willard Sheldon, James Talmadge.

NOTES

211 BK buys mobile home: St. Francis hotel, *Los Angeles Herald Examiner,* June 7, 1962; "That trailer," Marx to Brownlow, "Search for Buster Keaton," p. 165; "You studio people," Marx, p. 122.

212 Divorce suit: Natalie's testimony, Los Angeles County Superior Court. Also, Complaint, Keaton vs. Keaton, Aug. 5, 1932, Docket No. D–105469.
Attempts to stop drinking: "Every studio," Selznick to MM; "studio was run," Rapf to MM.

214 Marriage to Mae Scriven: Based on AMPAS's BK clipping collections; *NYT,* Oct. 18, 22, 1933; *MWWS,* p. 246; Blesh, pp. 336–37.
Mae's family: U.S. Census, 1900, Wilmington Township, Los Angeles County; U.S. Census, 1920, Judicial Township No. 8, Amsterdam Village, Merced County, Calif.
Mae falls for BK: "every girl," Steven, "Satan."

215 MGM fires BK: "dominates nearly every," *V,* Feb. 14, 1933; "Go ahead," Marx, p. 122.

216 BK and Mae second wedding: marriage certificate.

217 RA dies suddenly: out of touch, Addie O. Sheldon to MM. Also see LC's Arbuckle clipping collection.
BK in Florida: St. Petersburg research by Chris Carmen and Lisa Bradberry. Based on articles in *St. Petersburg Evening Independent* and *St. Petersburg Times,* May–July 1933; "History of Filmmaking in St. Petersburg," notes from exhibit, St. Petersburg Historical Museum, "Lights, Camera, Florida! Ninety Years of Moviemaking and Television Production in the Sunshine State." Also see, "empty taxicab," Brownlow, *Parade,* p. 422.

218 Tries vaudeville comeback: unsourced article, Sept. 23, 1933, AMPAS clipping collection.

Blackballed in Hollywood: "You'd never be able," *MWWS*, p. 188; "Mayer gave me such," Stevens.

219 MGM films *Broadway to Hollywood*: Twelve-year-old Mickey Rooney played Ted Hackett as a child but never connected the role with BK; "nothing to do with Buster," Marx to Joel Goss.

220 BK and Mae in Paris: "indulging in extravagant," Keaton vs. Keaton, Affidavit, Los Angeles Superior Court, Sept. 9, 1935.

221 Spiegel's *The Invader*: "they didn't tell me," Kohner to MM. Also see Brunel, p. 177, and Sinclair, pp. 23–28.

222 Shorts at Educational: "pretty near good enough," *V*, Mar. 25, 1936; "Despite that dumb look," Lamont to MM.

NTK changes sons' names: "Maybe it shouldn't," James Talmadge to MM.

223 Sons attend Black-Foxe: "In those days," Goldwyn to MM; "a prison," James Talmadge to MM; "everyone knew," Jennings to MM.

BK bankrupt: *New York Sun*, July 14, 16, 1934; Cadillac dealer, Karen to MM.

224 Money battles between BK and NTK: "for the best interest," Keaton vs. Keaton, Los Angeles Superior Court, Docket No. D–105469, Oct. 29, 1936; by the conduct of defendant, Keaton vs. Keaton, Affidavit, Docket No. D–105469, Dec. 8 1936; "We were very close," James Talmadge to MM; "I don't see why," *New York Evening Journal*, Sept. 28, 1936.

225 BK and Leah Sewell: unsourced articles, AMPAS clipping collection.

226 Mae divorces BK: based mainly on Los Angeles Superior Court divorce records. Also see, "very abusive," Keaton vs. Keaton, Amended Divorce Complaint, Docket No. D–134150; BK denies allegations, Keaton vs. Keaton, Answer, Aug. 16, 1935; "Buster just kidding," unsourced articles, AMPAS clipping collection, July 18, 29, 1935; "He criticized," *New York Herald Tribune*, Oct. 5, 1935.

BK hospitalized: AMPAS and LC clipping collections. Also see *New York Post*, Oct. 22, 23, 1935; "I nursed him," *New York American*, Oct. 22, 1935.

19. THE LEMON-MERINGUE BLONDE

SOURCES

Books:
Agee, *Agee on Film*; Blesh, *Keaton*; MWWS; Okuda and Watz, *Columbia Comedy Shorts*.

Articles:
Philadelphia Bulletin, Oct. 10, 1966; Paul Gallico, "Circus in Paris," *Esquire*, Aug. 1954; "Gloomy Buster Is Back Again," *Life*, Mar. 13, 1950, p. 145; *Albany Times Union*, June 22, 1949; Eileen Foley, "Mrs. Keaton Looks Back on Her Life with Buster," *Philadelphia Evening Bulletin*, Oct. 6, 1966;

Ashton Reid, "Strictly for Laughs," *Collier's,* June 10, 1944; "Mrs. Buster Keaton Wed to Sam Fuller," *New York Sun,* Jan. 24, 1936; "Mrs. Keaton Weds Again," *New York Herald Tribune,* Aug. 3, 1937; "Fresnan Marries Ex-Wife of Film Comedian," *Fresno Bee,* Feb. 2, 1940.

Unpublished Manuscripts:
Brownlow, "Search for Buster Keaton"; Hoffman, "Buster."

Records:
Mae Keaton and William Walter Gassert, certificate of marriage, Carson City, Nev., Aug. 2, 1937; Dorothy Sebastian Shapiro, certificate of death, Los Angeles, Apr. 8, 1957; Joseph H. Keaton certificate of death, Ventura, Calif., Jan. 13, 1946. Polk's City Directory, Fresno, 1940–1.

Transcript:
U.S. v. Schenck, U.S. Court of Appeals, Second Circuit, C–107–440, 1941.

Interviews:
Jayne DuFrayne Abbott, Iris Adrian, Billy Beck, Rudy Behlmer, Ed Bernds, Frank Biro, Frank Buxton, Harry Joe Brown, Jr., Bert Cowlan, Arlene Dahl, Jane Dulo, Douglas Humble, Janet Humble, William E. Hunt, Seaman Jacobs, Hal Kanter, James Karen, EK, Jane Norris Kelly, Walter Kerr, Ralph Levy, Trudi Maizel, Jean Pearson, Gil Perkins, Nat Perrin, Dean Reisner, James Talmadge, Jim Talmadge, Shirley Tegge.

NOTES

228 Meeting Eleanor Norris: "quiet, well-mannered," Brownlow, p. 188; "Lord," EK to MM; "beautiful," EK quoted in Hoffman; "He just bowled her over," Humble to MM; EK treated like an interloper, ibid.

230 BK hostility toward Mae: "the nurse," *MWWS,* p. 245; marriage meaningless, Dulo to MM; "my grandmother," Jim Talmadge to MM.
   Mae's marriages and divorces: This section is based on: "Mrs. Buster Keaton Wed to Sam Fuller," "Mrs. Keaton Weds Again," "Fresnan Marries Ex-Wife of Film Comedian," Zengel clippings, *Fresno Bee,* 1939–1953; Polk's City Directory, Fresno; Keaton–Gassert marriage certificate.

231 BK breaks off with Sebastian: "I sat there," EK to MM; "organized Dorothy," EK to MM; boyfriend for Sebastian, *MWWS,* p. 259. Sebastian's marriage, Sebastian death certificate.

232 BK weds Eleanor Norris: *Keaton, MWWS,* AMPAS and LC clipping collections; "I don't know," Kelly to MM.
   BK's employment difficulties: "if I'm worth more," Brownlow, p. 181; "pretty dull," Charles Lamont quoted in Brownlow, p. 176; "By the time I met him," Humble to MM; "I think that he," Maizel to MM; "happy-boy personality," EK to MM.

234 Columbia comedy shorts: Bruckman and White quoted in Okuda, p. 139; "X number of dollars," EK quoted in Brownlow, p. 185; "He was good," Bernds to MM.

235 Reunion with sons: "A friend," James Talmadge to MM; "thrills of my life-time," *MWWS*, p. 277.

236 Relationship with Eleanor: "We never argued," EK to MM; "a queer house-hold," Humble to MM.
Resumes drinking: *MWWS*, pp. 257–58; Blesh, p. 348; "favorite songs," Kelly to MM.

237 Schenck in prison: urges BK to call Zanuck, Blesh, pp. 354–55; Schenck trial, *U.S. v. Schenck*; LC clipping collection.

238 War years: death of JK, death certificate, LC clipping collection.

239 BK as MGM writer: "Whatever ideas," Dahl to MM.
Cirque Medrano: "fantastic physical shape," Beck to MM; "What difference," Kelly to MM; BK's elegant tastes, Cowlan to MM; "have it for breakfast," Karen to MM.

240 Early TV career: "first TV set on our block," James Talmadge to MM; "remarkable physical comedy," Kanter to MM; "He did things," Levy to MM; BK's pratfalls, *Life*, p. 145; "Buster just winged it," Tegge to MM; "He had a little too much," Goodwin quoted in Hoffman, p. 176.

242 *Three Men on a Horse*: "I thought he was the kind," Hunt to MM.
Agee's admiration: "most wonderful comedies," Agee, p. 229; "early American archetype," Agee, p. 15.

20. KEATON'S ANGELS

SOURCES

Books:

Bacon, *Hollywood Is a Four Letter Town*; Bloom, *Limelight and After*; Epstein, *Remembering Charlie*; *MWWS*; Kline, *Complete Films of Buster Keaton*; Swanson, *Swanson on Swanson*.

Articles:

La Revue du Cinema, Nov. 1972; John Baxter, "The Silent Empire of Raymond Rohauer," *London Sunday Times Magazine*, Jan. 19, 1975; Don McGregor, "An Interview with Raymond Rohauer," *Buster Keaton Festival Album*, 1982; Stefan Kanfer, "Great Stone Face," *Time*, Nov. 2, 1970; *New York Post*, Sept. 11, 1956; Milton Shulman, "Then and Now," *NYT*, May 9, 1954.

Brochure:

RR, "The Films of Buster Keaton" (1969).

Unpublished Manuscripts:

Hoffman, "Buster"; *Limelight* shooting script for BK scene, courtesy of Jerry Epstein.

Transcripts:

BK interview with Columbia University Oral History Collection, 1958; RR filmed interview with Kevin Brownlow and David Gill, 1986.

Interviews:

Iris Adrian, Larry Austin, Stan Brakhage, Jack Dragga, Jane Dulo, Jerry Epstein, Kenneth Fiebelkorn, Joel Goss, Albert Hackett, James Karen, EK, Gene Kelly, Jane Kelly, Norman Lloyd, Pamela Mason, Jonas Mekas, Berni Schoenfeld, Anthony Slide, Jim Talmadge, Billy Wilder.

NOTES

244 BK as MGM writer: "Buster usually played," Gene Kelly to MM.

BK in *In the Good Old Summertime*: "You're gonna be in," EK quoted in Hoffman.

245 BK in *Sunset Boulevard*: "looking for faces," Wilder to MM; "Waxworks is right," Swanson, p. 483; "Just watch," Wilder to MM.

246 BK and Chaplin in *Limelight*: "our production manager," Epstein to MM; "Then Calvero," *Limelight* shooting script; "But the moment," Epstein to MM; "reticent," Lloyd to MM; "sort of postcard," Bloom, p. 112; "Stunt men," Bacon, p. 26; "acutely aware," Schoenfeld to MM; "physical and mental wreck," *MWWS,* p. 271; "greatest of all comedy directors," BK quoted in *La Revue du Cinema;* "like two masters," Lloyd to MM; "good and lazy," BK quoted in Columbia University Oral History.

248 BK meets RR: "watching my grandson," Karen to MM; "save a lot of old junk," RR quoted in McGregor, p. 30.

249 Importance of film preservation: "Film Preservation 1993: A Study of the Current State of American Film Preservation," Library of Congress, reported that less than 20 percent of feature films made in the 1920s and about 10 percent made between 1910 and 1920 survive in complete form.

RR visits BK's garage: "if I save these films," McGregor, p. 30; "No danger," BK quoted in *Time*, p. 94; visit to film lab: RR quoted in McGregor, p. 30.

250 RR reputation: "wasn't particularly interested," RR transcript; "give the devil," Brakhage to MM; "Even then," Austin to MM; "You see," Slide to MM.

251 RR early years: Fiebelkorn to MM.

252 BK and RR become business partners: "He was the postman," Jim Talmadge to MM; "He distrusted," Dragga to MM; "clearly defined set," Goss to MM; "Raymond knew," EK to MM; "It must be done," RR transcript.

255 Masons discover BK films: "Mason wouldn't come to door," BK quoted in *New York Post,* p. 35; "I ruined," Mason to MM.

256 Prints found at Italian Villa: BK films in the cutting room shed were working copies, not release prints ready for distribution to theaters.

21. SCHENCK REDUX

SOURCES

Books:

Bacon, *Hollywood Is a Four Letter Town*; Capra, *Name Above the Title*; Eyman, *Mary Pickford*; Perelman, *Don't Tread on Me;* Todd and Todd, *Valuable Property*; White, *White Brothers.*

Articles:

James Karen, "My Friend Buster Keaton," *Hollywood Studio Magazine,* Sept. 1978; "Buster at Bay," *Life,* Dec. 12, 1955; "Film Pioneers Roll Off Their Living Immortals," *Life,* Jan. 23, 1956; Don McGregor, "An Interview with Raymond Rohauer," *Buster Keaton Film Festival Album,* 1982.

Records:

RR will, probate proceedings, petition for letters of administration, New York Surrogates Court; RR certificate of death, New York, Nov. 10, 1987; Clyde A. Bruckman certificate of death, Santa Monica, Jan. 4, 1955; Myra Keaton certificate of death, Los Angeles, July 21, 1955.

Transcripts:

RR filmed interview with Kevin Brownlow and David Gill, 1986; BK interview with Columbia University Oral History Collection, 1958.

Interviews:

Mary Anderson, Larry Austin, Ed Bernds, Stan Brakhage, Jack Carter, Bert Cowlan, Carol De Luise, Jane Dulo, Helen Fiebelkorn, Joan Franklin, Richard Gordon, Joel Goss, James Karen, EK, Jane Kelly, Walter Kerr, Jonas Mekas, Harry Moore, Anthony Slide, Linda Santos, James Talmadge.

NOTES

257 JS as elder statesman: Capra, p. 268; "this stuff can't wait," Bacon, p. 127.

258 BK business relations with JS: On Sept. 20, 1948, JS gave BK a six-month option on *The Navigator* because MGM was considering remaking the film with Danny Kaye.
JS illness and death: "Buster always thought," Louise Keaton letter to Mary Anderson; "He would never say," Karen to MM.

259 BK relations with RR: "that genius bullshit," EK to MM; "average man," De Luise to MM; "Christ!" Karen to MM; "He got crazy," EK to MM; "Raymond's reputation," Goss to MM; "one good deed," Brakhage to MM; "Buster tolerated," Jane Kelly to MM; "Eleanor Keaton told me," RR transcript; "Before Rohauer," Kerr to MM.

260 Bruckman suicide: death certificate. Santa Monica police returned Keaton's Colt automatic, now owned by James Talmadge.

261 Louise and Jingles problems: "pure parasite," confidential source; "crackbrained scheme," James Talmadge to MM; "He always held Buster's coat," Anderson to MM. Louise Keaton appeared in several Educational Films: *Trimmed in Furs* (1934) and *Way Up Thar* (1935), and also in *Li'l Abner* (1940). Harry Keaton appeared in two Columbia comedy shorts: *Uncivil Warriors* with the Three Stooges (1935) and *Peppery Salt* with Andy Clyde (1936).

262 *Mr. Pastry* pilot: "He never flew," James Talmadge to MM.

263 Myra's death: EK to MM; Myra Keaton death certificate.
Breaking up household: "Either Buster said it": EK to MM.

264 BK's TV appearances: "A lot of people," Jane Kelly to MM; *Silent Partner,*

"Buster at Bay," p. 132. Other interviews: Jack Carter, Garry Moore, Johnny Carson, Douglas Fairbanks, Jr., Ray Walston.

Shooting *80 Days*: "I must have been," BK quoted in Columbia University Oral History; "psychopathic little bastard," Perelman, pp. 176–77; "There's no mistake," Todd and Todd, p. 296.

265 Eastman Awards: awards described, "Film Pioneers," p. 119, and Eyman, p. 289.

266 BK near death: EK to MM.

22. WOODLAND HILLS

SOURCES

Books:

Eyman, *Mary Pickford*; Fitzgerald, "Crazy Sunday," *Stories of F. Scott Fitzgerald*; Gill, *New York Life*; Niven, *Bring on the Empty Horses*; Perelman, *Vinegar Puss*.

Articles:

"Film Pioneers Roll Off Their Living Immortals," *Life*, Jan. 23, 1956; "Wistful Reunion at Pickfair," *Life*, Apr. 16, 1956; *V*, June 5, June 20, 1957; *Hollywood Reporter*, June 22, 1955; *New York Post*, Sept. 16, 1956; Bill Kennedy, "Mr. LA," *Los Angeles Herald-Examiner*, June 7, 1962; Arthur Friedman, "Buster Keaton: An Interview," *Film Quarterly*, Summer 1966; Rex Reed, "Keaton: Still Making the Scene," *NYT*, Oct. 17, 1965; Aline Mosby, "Buster Keaton Sneers at Today's Big Bosoms," *El Paso Herald-Post*, June 23, 1956; Don McGregor, "An Interview with Raymond Rohauer," *Buster Keaton Festival Album*, 1982.

Interviews:

Mary Anderson, Francisco "Chico" Day, Arthur Friedman, Eddie Hodges, Arthur Josephson, James Karen, EK, Jane Kelly, Joe Laitin, Harry Moore, Jean Pearson, Susan Reed, Linda Santos, Sidney Sheldon, James Talmadge, Jim Talmadge.

NOTES

267 BK at Sawtelle: "hurt himself," "Film Pioneers," p. 119.

Life story sold: announcement, *Hollywood Reporter*; "Yeah, I made a deal," RR quoted in McGregor, p. 32; "check the contracts," EK to MM. In 1948, Warner Bros. paid Keaton and his mother $3,500 for story rights to the Three Keatons' vaudeville career. *April Showers* starred Ann Sothern and Jack Carson.

269 Recuperation: UCLA interview, Friedman to MM.

Purchase of real estate: "The chickens," BK quoted in Kennedy.

Pickfair reunion: "great emotional moments," Fitzgerald, p. 404; "sad, over-furnished," Niven, p. 208; "wistful reunion," "Wistful Reunion," p. 163;

"Poor Buster!" Lloyd quoted in Gill, p. 281; "cry myself," Pearson quoted in *V*; "tried to have fun," BK quoted in Reed.

273 Louise and Harry independence: "He stayed there," EK to MM; "reputation as fisherman," Moore to MM; "He lives in a hotel," Anderson to MM.

274 Shooting *Buster Keaton Story*: "I had him there," Sheldon to MM; "Buster's face," Day to MM; bosoms interview, Mosby.

275 Sheldon party: "There were maybe sixteen," Sheldon to MM; "During other people's conversations," Josephson to MM; "incapable of socializing," Day to MM.

276 BK watching TV: "The man never left," Jim Talmadge to MM; *"Cut!"* Karen to MM; "What Buster called his den," Pearson to MM; "One time he looked," Jim Talmadge to MM; "I had had my fill," Hodges to MM.

277 *Buster Keaton Story* preview: "By sheer osmosis," Pearson quoted in *V*, June 20, p. 3.

23. FAMILY GHOSTS

SOURCES

Books:

DiMucci, *Wanderer*; Gilliatt, *Holy Fools*; Lahr, *Notes on a Cowardly Lion*; Loos, *Talmadge Girls*; Riefenstahl, *Memoir*.

Articles:

Mae Elizabeth Keaton a.k.a. Jewel Steven, "I Am Being Blackmailed!," *Confidential*, Dec. 1958; *New York Herald Tribune*, Apr. 22, 1957; *NYT*, Apr. 22, 1957; *V*, Apr. 1957; Rex Reed, "Keaton: Still Making the Scene," *NYT*, Oct. 17, 1965; "Keaton Movie Libel Charged," *New York Daily News*, Aug. 29, 1957, p. 20; Joe Schoenfeld, "Time and Place," *V*, June 5, 20, 1957; Murray Schumach, "Keaton Receives Special Film Prize," *NYT*, Apr. 6, 1960; N. C. Chambers, "Industry's Third Oscarcast," *Films in Review*, May 1960, p. 257; "Buster Keaton Hopes for a Revival," *London Times*, Aug. 17, 1960; Richard Schickel, "Happy Pro," *New Yorker*, Apr. 27, 1963.

Unpublished Manuscripts:

Brownlow, "Search for Buster Keaton"; Jewel Elizabeth Steven and Victor Dwyer, "Six Feet Under," © Apr. 23, 1941 (Library of Congress # DU 74607); Jewel Elizabeth Steven, "Mother Please Behave," © Aug. 18, 1942 (DU 81704); Jewel Elizabeth Steven, "Satan! Pull Up a Chair," © Jan. 22, 1942 (DU 79215); Jewel Elizabeth Steven, "Desk Clerk," © May 13, 1943 (DU 84324); Jewel Elizabeth Steven, "The Traitor Prayed," © Jan. 30, 1945 (DU 92385). Also the following songs: Betty Sisson Willsey and Jewel Steven, "Something's Going Wrong," © Mar. 24, 1946 (EU 18190); Jewel Steven, Larry Lane, and J. Albert Harris, "There's a Message in a Song," © May 6, 1946 (EU 26729), "We'll Do the Things We Said We'd Do," © May 28, 1946 (EU 52323); Jewel Steven and Harold Potter, "Arms in Armijo,"

© July 1, 1958 (EU 531394), "No News Is Good News," © July 10, 1958 (EU 532703).

Records:

Mae Elizabeth Keaton a.k.a. Jewel Steven v. State of New York and City of New York, New York Superior Court 13570-1959; *Keaton v. Keaton,* Case # D–134150, Los Angeles Superior Court; *Mae Elizabeth Keaton v. Paramount Pictures,* New York Superior Court 10066-1957; BK Freedom of Information Act file, U.S. Department of Justice, Federal Bureau of Investigation, Washington.

Television and Film:

This Is Your Life television program, Apr. 3, 1957; Ray Muller, *The Wonderful, Horrible Life of Leni Riefenstahl,* documentary film, 1994.

Transcript:

RR filmed interview with Kevin Brownlow and David Gill, 1986.

Interviews:

John Baylis, Fritzi Burr, Imogene Coca, Bert Cowlan, Melissa Talmadge Cox, Francisco "Chico" Day, Carol De Luise, Dion DiMucci, Jane Dulo, John Fiedler, Eddie Foy 3d, Joe Franklin, Allen Funt, Brendan Gill, Penelope Gilliatt, Marvin Ginsky, Dody Goodman, Alan Harper, Kenneth Hume, Arthur Josephson, James Karen, EK, Stanley Kramer, Diane Lampert, John Lyons, Jan Miner, Gerald Potterton, Tony Randall, Susan Reed, Leni Riefenstahl, John Sebert, Sidney Sheldon, Ruth Silva, Willy Switkes, Jack Sydow, James Talmadge, Jim Talmadge, Richard Lyle Thomas.

NOTES

278 *This Is Your Life* program: "The little man," *This Is Your Life*; "a great guy," Bobby Talmadge quoted on *This Is Your Life*; "a lot of presents," EK to MM. Ralph Edwards promised to erect a commemorative plaque on the site of Keaton's old studio on Lillian Way. When the promise was finally fulfilled decades later, the plaque was placed at the wrong corner.

279 Critics roast *Buster Keaton Story*: "Apparently pure fiction," *New York Herald Tribune*; "very vindictive," James Talmadge to MM.

BK relations with sons and grandchildren: "living on Victoria Avenue," James Talmadge to MM; "When Grandpa played," Jim Talmadge to MM; "On Christmas," Cox to MM.

281 NTK lifestyle in middle age: "She just hated," Jim Talmadge to MM; "She never went out," Cox to MM; "not an ounce of truth," EK to MM.

282 Mae Keaton committed to Creedmoor: "actress, producer," Keaton a.k.a. Steven, *Confidential*; "prepared for death," *Steven v. New York State*; "Buster told me," Reed to MM.

283 BK's new friends: "Go ahead," Potterton to MM; "She took over," Switkes to MM; "Call me Buster," Sydow to MM; "utterly delicious," Burr to MM; "Buster was always," Goodman to MM; "big box of chocolates," Thomas to MM; "like a stepdad," Silva to MM; "We'd play bridge," Dulo to MM; "I

knew Buster," confidential source; "He was hoping," Dulo to MM; "They could have changed their names," confidential source; "pedestrian children," confidential source. In the 1980s, Robert Talmadge's son Robert, Jr., changed his name to Keaton. More recently, the sons of Harry Moore (born Harry Keaton) began using the Keaton name.

286 Mae Keaton v. Paramount: "married him for his name," "Keaton Movie Libel"; "decent-looking," Ginksy to MM.

287 BK and grandchildren: "We'd go to his house," Jim Talmadge to MM.
BK concern for posterity: "I wanted Buster," Kramer to MM; "He had no artistic ego," EK quoted in Brownlow, p. 283.

288 Academy Award: "all choked up," EK to MM.
BK tours Germany: "He had to duck," EK to MM; "What are they laughing at?," RR quoted in Brownlow, p. 277; "complete and delightful surprise," Riefenstahl to MM; Riefenstahl and Nazis, RR transcript; "We only managed," Riefenstahl to MM.

290 RR and Riefenstahl: In 1986, RR told Brownlow and Gill that Riefenstahl agreed to give him U.S. distribution rights for *Olympia,* even promising to personally prepare a thirty-five-mm print from the original. But Riefenstahl denies it and said only a lack of money kept her from suing him. Though she refused him the rights, he took them anyway and "never paid a penny" (Riefenstahl to MM).
Ten Girls Ago: "Did you bring the cocaine?" Lahr, p. 225; "They seemed ancient," DiMucci to MM; "would knock at my door," Lampert to MM.

291 BK in Woodland Hills: "good until midnight," EK to MM; "had a little train," O'Connor quoted in Brownlow, p. 242; "terrifying," Gill to MM; "We have aisle seats," EK to MM, also quoted in Gilliatt, p. 53.

24. BOTTOM OF THE NINTH

SOURCES

Books:

Bair, *Samuel Beckett;* Beckett, *Film;* Funicello, *A Dream Is a Wish Your Heart Makes;* Mostel and Gilford, *170 Years of Show Business;* Ginsberg, *Collected Poems;* Kline, *Complete Films of Buster Keaton;* Schneider, *Entrances;* Wolf, *Landmark Films.*

Articles:

"Buster Keaton in Beckett's First Film," *NYT,* July 21, 1964; Glenn Collins, "Hang On! It's the Drive-in Thriller King!!," *NYT,* Oct. 23, 1990; Andrew Sarris, "Buster Keaton and Samuel Beckett," *Columbia Forum,* Winter 1969; "Beckett," *New Yorker,* Aug. 8, 1964; Jerry Tallmer, "The Film That Pairs Beckett and Keaton," *New York Post,* May 5, 1984; "Richard Lester," *Sight and Sound,* Spring 1973; Rex Reed, "Keaton: Still Making the Scene": *NYT,* Oct. 17, 1965; John Gillett and James Blue, "Keaton at Venice," *Sight and Sound,* Winter 1965–66.

Pamphlet, Unpublished Manuscript, and Letters:

"Vision Is My Dwelling Place," Sydney Meyers memorial pamphlet, n.d.; Brownlow, "Search for Buster Keaton"; Piqua, Kansas, Centennial Book, 1882–1982; three unpublished letters from Samuel Beckett to Sydney Meyers, Sept.–Oct. 1964.

Records:

Joseph Frank Keaton Last Will and Testament, July 11, 1962.

Film:

John Sebert, *Buster Keaton Rides Again,* documentary film, 1964.

RR filmed interview with Kevin Brownlow and David Gill, 1986.

Interviews:

William Asher, Sid Avery, Joe Coffey, Mick Dillon, Madeline Gilford, Roberta Hodes, James Karen, EK, Tom Kirk, John Kobler, Kenneth Koch, Jane Kramer, Richard Lester, Glen Massoth, Edna Meyers, Gerald Potterton, Susan Reed, Jean Schneider, John Sebert, John Spotton, Irene Tsu.

NOTES

293 BK and baseball: BK preferred the National League. When the Dodgers were still in Brooklyn, he rode the subway to Ebbets Field to attend games.
St. Moritz meeting: Conversation reconstructed from EK to MM, Schneider autobiography, and Beckett interview with Brownlow. "Did you have," Schneider, p. 358; "art picture," EK to MM; "no good," Beckett quoted in Brownlow, p. 252; "no sense," EK to MM.

294 Shooting *Film*: red suspenders, Ginsberg, "Today," p. 345; "ass backwards," Hodes to MM; "he wasn't interested," Beckett quoted in Brownlow, p. 253; "a man may keep away," *NYT*, July 21, 1964; "It's about a man," Beckett quoted in Brownlow, p. 253; "What Buster didn't get," Karen to MM; "magnificent," Schneider, p. 358.

296 BK 1964 visit to Piqua: EK to MM; Piqua Centennial Book.

297 Reaction to *Film*: "catastrophic," Sarris, p. 42.
Arkoff films: "Somehow he had dignity," Kirk to MM; "older, established actors," Funicello, p. 141; "We all knew," Tsu to MM; "worst acting," Kline, p. 206.

298 Filming *Railrodder*: "Sounds crazy," Potterton to MM; "No, no," Potterton to MM; "The bridge," BK quoted in *Buster Keaton Rides Again*; "public speaking," BK quoted in *Buster Keaton Rides Again*; "bloody cold," Spotton to MM; "guess who directed," Potterton to MM.

300 Wedding anniversary: "There's a night club," BK quoted in Hedda Hopper interview, AMPAS collection.

Venice Film Festival: "You know how much," RR transcript; "even the most sedate journalists," *Films in Review,* Oct. 1965, p. 470.

301 *Forum*: "true envy," Lester to MM; "breath away," Dillon quoted in Brownlow, p. 270; "They would shoot quite late," Gilford to MM; "wasn't good," EK to MM.

303 BK shoots *Scribe*: Sebert to MM.

FADE OUT

SOURCES

Articles:

"Buster Keaton, 70, Dies on Coast," *NYT,* Feb. 2, 1966; Bosley Crowther, "Keaton and the Past," *NYT,* Feb. 6, 1966.

Records:

Joseph F. a.k.a. Buster Keaton certificate of death, Woodland Hills, Calif., Feb. 1, 1966.

Transcript:

RR filmed interview with Kevin Brownlow and David Gill, 1986.

Interviews:

This chapter is mainly based on interviews with EK. Also Bill Cosby, Melissa Talmadge Cox, James Karen, Ruth Silva.

NOTES

304 Cancer diagnosis: "When he gets dressed," EK to MM; "You might like to know," Nov. 2, 1965 letter, Hedda Hopper collection, AMPAS; Levy's Rye Bread: When BK died, the advertiser killed the ad. "This medication," EK to MM.

Cosby visit: Bill Cosby to MM. Cosby's collection of Keaton memorabilia includes a suit and hat, donated by EK. It is preserved in a specially constructed glass case. "Buster is all over the joint in my house," Cosby said. EK bestowed other items on family and friends: BK's Oscar statuette to his son Bobby and JK's pocket watch to Jimmy.

305 Keaton's death: Joseph Frank Keaton death certificate. Also, "okay," RR transcript; "he became more irrational," EK to MM.

Planning funeral: "We're not going to spend," EK to MM.

CODA

307 Louise Keaton: "movies were so awfully old," Bob Borgen to MM.

Harry Keaton: "he left small amount," Harry Moore to MM.

KEATON'S KITCHEN

SOURCES

Book:
Beverly Hills Woman's Club, *Fashions in Foods in Beverly Hills.*

Articles:
Helen Bower, "Buster Keaton Remembers Old Summers at Muskegon," *Detroit Free Press,* Jan. 11, 1961; Richard Pollak, "How to Launch Keaton Missiles," *Baltimore Evening Sun,* Feb. 10, 1961.

Press Release:
Movieland Wax Museum, 1964.

Interviews:
Bert Cowlan, EK, Ruth Silva.

NOTES
310 Lobster Joseph: Bert Cowlan to MM.
   Fried perch: *Detroit Free Press.*
311 Chipped beef: Bert Cowlan to MM.
   Chop suey: Bert Cowlan to MM; earlier version appeared in *Fashions in Foods in Beverly Hills,* p. 85.
312 Custard pie: *Baltimore Evening Sun.*
   Porkpie hat: Movieland Wax Museum.

SELECTED BIBLIOGRAPHY

BOOKS

Allen, C. R., comp. *Illustrated Atlas of Harrison County, Iowa*. Logan, Iowa: C. R. Allen and Co., 1884.

Agee, James. *Agee on Film: Reviews and Comments*. Includes reprint of "Comedy's Greatest Era," *Life*, Sept. 3, 1949. Boston: Beacon Press, 1964.

Andreas, Alfred T. *History of Kansas*. 2 vols. Chicago: A. T. Andreas, 1883.

Anger, Kenneth. *Hollywood Babylon*. New York: Dell, 1975.

Anobile, Richard J. *Buster Keaton's The General*. New York: Darien House, Universe Books, 1975.

Bacon, James. *Hollywood Is a Four Letter Town*. Chicago: Henry Regnery, 1976.

Bair, Deirdre. *Samuel Beckett*. New York: Harcourt Brace, 1978.

Balio, Tino. *United Artists: The Company Built by the Stars*. Madison, Wisc.: University of Wisconsin Press, 1976.

Bart, Peter. *Fade Out. The Calamitous Final Days of MGM*. New York: Willliam Morrow, 1990.

Beckett, Samuel. *Film*. New York: Grove Press, 1969.

Benayoun, Robert. *The Look of Buster Keaton*. London: Pavilion Books, 1982.

Bergreen, Laurence. *As Thousands Cheer: The Life of Irving Berlin*. New York: Viking, 1990.

Beverly Hills Woman's Club. *Fashions in Foods in Beverly Hills*. Beverly Hills, Calif.: 1931.

Blackmar, Frank W. *Cyclopedia of Kansas History*. 3 vols. Chicago: Standard Publishing Co., 1912.

Blesh, Rudi. *Keaton*. New York, Macmillan, 1966.

Bloom, Claire. *Limelight and After*. New York: Harper & Row, 1982.

Bradsby, Henry C., *History of Vigo County, Indiana, with Bibliographical Selections*. Chicago: S. B. Nelson and Co, 1891.

Brooks, Louise. *Lulu in Hollywood*. New York: Alfred A. Knopf, 1982.

Brownlow, Kevin. *Behind the Mask of Innocence.* New York: Alfred A. Knopf, 1990.

———. *Hollywood: The Pioneers.* New York: Alfred A. Knopf, 1979.

———. *The Parade's Gone By.* Berkeley: University of California Press, 1968.

Brundidge, Harry T. *Twinkle, Twinkle Movie Star!* New York: Dutton, 1930.

Brunel, Adrian. *Nice Work.* London: Forbes, Robertson, 1949.

Cadbury, Henry J. *The Church in the Wilderness: North Carolina Quakerism as Seen by Visitors.* Guilford College, N.C.: North Carolina Friends Historical Society, 1948.

Capra, Frank. *The Name Above the Title.* New York: Macmillan, 1971.

Cary, Gary. *Anita Loos.* New York: Alfred A. Knopf, 1988.

———. *All the Stars in Heaven: Louis B. Mayer's MGM.* New York: Dutton, 1981.

Cassidy, John M. *Civil War Cinema: A Pictorial History of Hollywood and the War Between the States.* Missoula, Mont.: Pictorial Histories Pub. Co., 1986.

Chaplin, Charles, Jr. *My Father, Charlie Chaplin.* New York: Random House, 1960.

Christopher, Milbourne. *Houdini: The Untold Story.* Mattituck, N.Y.: Aeonian Press, 1969.

Crowther, Bosley. *Hollywood Rajah: The Life and Times of Louis B. Mayer.* New York: Holt, Rinehart and Winston, 1960.

Dardis, Tom. *Keaton: The Man Who Wouldn't Lie Down.* New York: Charles Scribner's Sons, 1979.

DiMeglio, John C. *Vaudeville USA.* Bowling Green, Ohio: Bowling Green University Press, 1973.

DiMucci, Dion, with Davin Seay. *The Wanderer.* New York: Beech Tree Books/William Morrow, 1988.

Drew, William M. *Speaking of Silents: First Ladies of the Screen.* Vestal, N.Y.: The Vestal Press, 1989.

Duncan, L. Wallace. *History of Allen and Woodson Counties, Kansas.* Iola, Kans.: Iola Register, Printers and Binders, 1901.

Edmonds, Andy. *Frame-Up! The Untold Story of Roscoe "Fatty" Arbuckle.* New York: William Morrow, 1991.

Eisele, Fannie L. *A History of Noble County, Oklahoma.* Pamphlet, 1958.

Epstein, Jerry. *Remembering Charlie: A Pictorial Biography.* New York: Doubleday, 1989.

Eyman, Scott. *Mary Pickford, America's Sweetheart.* New York: Donald Fine, 1990.

Fields, W. C. *W. C. Fields by Himself.* Englewood Cliffs, N.J.: Prentice-Hall, 1973.

Fitzgerald, Daniel. *Ghost Towns of Kansas.* Lawrence, Kans.: University of Kansas Press, 1988.

Fitzgerald, F. Scott. *The Stories of F. Scott Fitzgerald.* New York: Charles Scribner's Sons, 1951.

Flora, Jerome B. *A Historical Sketch of Ancient Pasquotank County, North Carolina, 1586–1793.* Pamphlet. Elizabeth City, N.C.: 1953.

Fox, Charles Donald, and Milton Silver. *Who's Who on the Screen*. New York: Ross Publishing Co., 1920.

Freeman, Joseph. *An American Testament: A Narrative of Rebels and Romantics*. New York: Octagon Books, 1973.

Friedrich, Otto. *City of Nets*. New York: Harper & Row, 1986.

Funicello, Annette, with Patricia Romanowski. *A Dream Is a Wish Your Heart Makes*. New York: Hyperion, 1994.

Fussell, Betty Harper. *Mabel*. New York: Ticknor & Fields, 1982.

Gabler, Neal. *An Empire of Their Own: How the Jews Invented Hollywood*. New York: Crown, 1988.

Gilbert, Douglas. *American Vaudeville: Its Life and Times*. New York: Dover Publications, 1940.

Gill, Brendan. *A New York Life*. New York: Poseidon Press, 1990.

Gilliatt, Penelope. *To Wit: Skin and Bones of Comedy*. New York: Charles Scribner's Sons, 1990.

———. *Unholy Fools: Wits, Comics, and Disturbers of the Peace*. New York: Viking Press, 1979.

Ginsberg, Allen. *Collected Poems*. New York: Harper & Row, 1982.

Giroux, Robert. *A Deed of Death*. New York: Alfred A. Knopf, 1990.

Gish, Lillian, with Ann Pinchot. *The Movies, Mr. Griffith, and Me*. Englewood Cliffs, N.J.: Prentice-Hall, 1969.

Goldwyn, Samuel. *Behind the Screen*. New York: George H. Doran, 1923.

Green, Abel, and Joe Laurie, Jr. *Show Biz from Vaude to Video*. New York: Henry Holt, 1951.

Gussow, Mel. *Don't Say Yes Until I Finish Talking*. New York: Doubleday, 1971.

Harris, Marlys. *The Zanucks of Hollywood*. New York: Crown, 1989.

Heimann, Jim. *Hooray for Hollywood: A Postcard Tour of Hollywood's Golden Era*. San Francisco: Chronicle Books, 1983.

———. *Out with the Stars: Hollywood Nightlife in the Golden Era*. New York: Abbeville Press, 1985.

Herman. Hal C., ed. *How I Broke into the Movies: Signed Autobiographies of Sixty Famous Stars*. Hollywood: Hal C. Herman, 1928.

Hinshaw, William W. *Encyclopedia of American Quaker Genealogy, vol. 1*. Baltimore: Genealogical Publishing Co., 1978.

Hughes, Laurence A., ed. *The Truth About the Movies by the Stars*. Hollywood: Hollywood Publishers, 1924.

Hunt, Charles W. *History of Harrison County, Iowa*. Indianapolis: Bowen Co., 1915.

Jessel, George. *So Help Me*. New York: Random House, 1943.

Kanin, Garson. *Hollywood*. New York: Viking Press, 1967.

Kauffmann, Stanley, with Bruce Henstell. *American Film Criticism: From the Beginnings to Citizen Kane*. New York: Liveright, 1972.

Keaton, Buster, with Charles Samuels. *My Wonderful World of Slapstick*. New York: Doubleday, 1960.

Kellock, Harold. *Houdini, His Life Story, from the Recollections and Documents of Beatrice Houdini*. New York: Harcourt Brace, 1928.

Kerr, Walter. *The Silent Clowns.* New York: Alfred A. Knopf, 1975.

Kline, Jim. *The Complete Films of Buster Keaton.* New York: Citadel Press, 1993.

Lahr, John. *Notes on a Cowardly Lion.* New York: Alfred A. Knopf, 1969.

Lahue, Kalton C., and Terry Brewer. *Kops and Custards: The Legend of Keystone Films.* Norman, Okla.: University of Oklahoma Press, 1968.

Lamparski, Richard. *Hidden Hollywood.* New York: Simon & Schuster, 1981.

———. *Whatever Became of . . . .* New York: Bantam, 1976.

Lebel, J. P. *Buster Keaton.* P. D. Stovin, trans. London: A. Zwemmer, 1967.

Lee, Gypsy Rose. *Gypsy.* New York: Simon & Schuster, 1957.

Lockwood, Charles. *Dream Palaces: Hollywood at Home.* New York: Viking, 1981.

Loos, Anita. *A Girl Like I.* New York: Viking, 1966.

———. *Kiss Hollywood Good-by.* New York: Viking, 1974. circ.

———. *The Talmadge Girls.* New York: Viking, 1978.

McDowall, Roddy. *Double Exposure.* New York: Delacorte, 1966.

McNamara, Brooks. *The Shuberts of Broadway.* New York: Oxford University Press, 1990.

———. *Step Right Up: An Illustrated History of the American Medicine Show.* Garden City, N.Y.: Doubleday, 1976.

Maltin, Leonard. *The Great Movie Shorts.* New York: Crown, 1972.

Marx, Samuel. *A Gaudy Spree.* New York: Franklin Watts, 1987.

———. *Mayer and Thalberg: The Make-Believe Saints.* New York: Random House, 1975.

Miller, Alice. *The Untouched Key: Tracing Childhood Trauma in Creativity and Destructiveness.* Garden City, N.Y.: Doubleday, 1990.

Moews, Daniel. *Keaton: The Silent Features Up Close.* Berkeley: University of California Press, 1977.

Mordden, Ethan. *The Hollywood Studios: House Style in the Golden Age of the Movies.* New York: Alfred A. Knopf, 1988.

Morley, Sheridan. *James Mason: Odd Man Out.* New York: Harper & Row, 1989.

Mostel, Kate, and Madeline Gilford. *170 Years of Show Business.* New York: Random House, 1978.

The Movie Mirror Book / Viola Dana. New York: Ross Publishing Co., 1920.

Niven, David. *Bring on the Empty Horses.* New York: G. P. Putnam's Sons, 1975.

Noble County Genealogical Society, comp. and ed. *History of Noble County, Oklahoma.* Norman, Okla.: Type Traditional, 1987.

Okuda, Ted, and Edward Watz. *The Columbia Comedy Shorts.* Jefferson, N.C.: McFarland & Co., 1986.

Paris, Barry. *Louise Brooks.* New York: Alfred A. Knopf, 1989.

Perelman, S. J. *Don't Tread on Me: The Selected Letters of S. J. Perelman.* Prudence Crowther, ed. New York: Viking Press, 1987.

———. *Vinegar Puss.* New York: Dell, 1975.

Ramsaye, Terry. *A Million and One Nights.* New York: Simon & Schuster, 1926.

Rapf, Joanna, and Gary L. Green. *Buster Keaton. A Bio-Bibliography.* Westport, Conn.: Greenwood Press, 1995.

Reed, Rex. *Do You Sleep in the Nude?* New York: NAL, 1968.

Riefenstahl, Leni. *Leni Riefenstahl: A Memoir.* New York: St. Martin's Press, 1993.

Robbins, Jhan. *Inka Dinka Doo: The Life of Jimmy Durante.* New York: Paragon House, 1991.

Robinson, David. *Buster Keaton.* Bloomington, Ind.: Indiana University Press, 1969.

———. *Chaplin: His Life and Art.* London: Collins, 1985.

———. *Hollywood in the Twenties.* New York: A. S. Barnes & Co., 1968.

Rooney, Mickey. *Life Is Too Short.* New York: Villard, 1991.

Rotha, Paul. *Celluloid: The Film Today.* London: Longman's, 1931.

St. Johns, Adela Rogers. *Love, Laughter and Tears: My Hollywood Story.* Garden City, N.Y.: Doubleday, 1978.

Samuels, Charles, and Louise Samuels. *Once Upon a Stage. The Merry World of Vaudeville.* New York: Dodd, Mead, 1974.

Sanford, Linda T. *Strong at the Broken Places: Overcoming the Trauma of Childhood Abuse.* New York: Random House, 1990.

Schatz, Thomas. *The Genius of the System. Hollywood Filmmaking in the Studio Era.* New York: Pantheon, 1988.

Schickel, Richard. *D. W. Griffith: An American Life.* New York: Simon & Schuster, 1984.

———. *Schickel on Film. Encounters Critical and Personal with Movie Immortals.* New York: William Morrow, 1989.

Schneider, Alan. *Entrances: An American Director's Journey.* New York: Viking, 1986.

Selznick, Irene Mayer. *A Private View.* New York: Alfred A. Knopf, 1983.

Shengold, Leonard. *Soul Murder: The Effects of Childhood Abuse and Deprivation.* New Haven: Yale University Press, 1989.

Sinclair, Andrew. *Spiegel: The Man Behind the Pictures.* Boston: Little, Brown, 1987.

Slide, Anthony. *Selected Vaudeville Criticism.* Metuchen, N.J.: Scarecrow Press, 1988.

Snyder, Robert W. *The Voice of the City: Vaudeville and Popular Culture in New York.* New York: Oxford University Press, 1989.

Starks, Michael. *Cocaine Fiends and Reefer Madness: An Illustrated History of Drugs in the Movies.* New York: Cornwall Books, 1982.

Stein, Charles W., ed. *American Vaudeville, as Seen by Its Contemporaries.* New York: Alfred A. Knopf, 1984.

Swanson, Gloria. *Swanson on Swanson.* New York: Random House, 1980.

Talmadge, Arthur White. *The Talmadge, Tallmadge and Talmadge Genealogy.* New York: Grafton Press, 1909.

Talmadge, Margaret L. *The Talmadge Sisters, Norma, Constance, Natalie: An Intimate Story of the World's Most Famous Screen Family by Their Mother.* Philadelphia: J. B. Lippincott, 1924.

Talmey, Allene. *Doug and Mary and Others.* New York: Macy-Masius, 1927.

Thompson, David, and Ian Christie, eds. *Scorsese on Scorsese*. London: Faber & Faber, 1989.

Todd, Michael, Jr., and Susan McCarthy Todd. *A Valuable Property: The Life Story of Michael Todd*. New York: Arbor House, 1983.

Wagner, Walter. *You Must Remember This*. New York: G. P. Putnam's, 1975.

Walker, Alexander. *The Shattered Silents: How the Talkies Came to Stay*. New York: William Morrow, 1979.

Wead, George, and George Lellis. *The Film Career of Buster Keaton*. Pleasantville, N.Y.: Redgrave Publishing Co., 1977.

White, Jack, Jules White, and Sam White; Interviewed by David Bruskin. *The White Brothers: Jack, Jules and Sam*. Directors Guild of America. Metuchen, N.J.: The Scarecrow Press, 1990.

Wolf, William. *Landmark Films*. New York: Paddington Press, 1979.

Yallop, David A. *The Day the Laughter Stopped: The True Story of Fatty Arbuckle*. New York: St. Martin's Press, 1976.

Zolotow, Maurice. *Billy Wilder in Hollywood*. New York: G. P. Putnam's, 1977.

UNPUBLISHED MANUSCRIPTS

Brownlow, Kevin. "The Search for Buster Keaton." 1990.

Goss, Joel. "The Making of *The General*." 1990.

Hoffman, Alan. "Buster." 1978.

Scott, Jason D. "The Selling of the Stone Face: Studio Marketing Practices and Keaton's *The General*." 1989.

DEBTS

While writing can be a solitary business, making biography is anything but, especially if your subject lived during recent times. Reporting the life of Buster Keaton has meant asking help from scores of people and incurring plenty of debts.

Extraordinarily generous has been one person in particular, Eleanor Keaton, who sat for tape-recorded sessions in her home, took endless telephone calls, introduced me to friends, and signed all sorts of permissions. For the past four years I put to her questions about almost every facet of her husband's personal life. I cannot think of an instance when she failed to give a frank answer, even to what must have struck her as the dopiest queries in the world.

Keaton's son James Talmadge spoke with admirable candor about his father, even though it could not have been easy to lay aside his privacy and confide in a stranger asking questions that opened up painful memories. Melissa Talmadge Cox and Jim Talmadge were also wonderful about sharing amazingly clear memories of their grandfather. Their understanding of his character and his relationships with his sons and grandchildren permitted me unique insights into his family life.

Several close friends of Keaton gave me the benefit of vivid reminiscences, especially James Karen, Carol De Luise, Ruth Silva, the late Jane Dulo, and the late Jane Kelly. In addition to contributions to the project, I could always count on inspiration from Bob Borgen and Minako Saki.

In large part the material in these pages was obtained from interviews. I am immensely indebted to those who shared information and their individual perspectives on Buster Keaton. The names of those who talked to me appear both in the text and also in the detailed notes for each chapter.

It was my good fortune to meet Keaton scholars who had done research before me. From the earliest days of this project, Joel Goss has been a stalwart friend. Among numerous favors to me over the years, he provided documents and photographs from his Keaton collection, made available his interviews with people who figured in Keaton's life, and screened many of the films for me. At the end he read the manuscript for errors and offered many helpful suggestions.

Kevin Brownlow deserves a special thank-you for his expert advice and unstinting support throughout this undertaking. My job would have been far more difficult without access to his unpublished manuscript on Keaton.

Enormously helpful was Alan Hoffman, who permitted me to see his unpublished work on Keaton. Others who graciously shared unpublished material were Joanna Rapf for an early draft of her Keaton bio-bibliography; Jason Scott for his paper on the marketing of *The General*; and Mary Anderson for her historical notes on the Actors Colony in Bluffton, Michigan.

I am especially grateful to Jim Kline, whose generous sharing of information from his own book on Keaton's films improved mine.

My appreciation to Chris Carmen, who first directed me to important contacts in California. Later on, in St. Petersburg, his expert research enabled me to track Keaton's short-lived Florida film career. Lisa Bradberry's exemplary library work unearthed material from the 1930s in St. Peterburg newpapers.

Among my essential archival sources was the New York Society for the Prevention of Cruelty to Children, whose Buster Keaton files were opened to me by Anne Reiniger, executive director. Joe Gleason facilitated my viewing of the documents.

My gratitude to Pamela Mason for inviting me into the Italian Villa in Beverly Hills, Keaton's home for six years, hers for forty-six.

In Palos Verdes Estates, Darrylin Zanuck Pineda extended gracious hospitality and permitted me to drive off with her mother's scrapbook.

For access to interview tapes, I am indebted to Randy Vanderknyff for a transcript of his Marion Mack interview, to Joseph Laitin for a transcript of his 1956 Keaton interview, and to B. J. Davenport for her 1990 interview with Gene Woodward Barnes.

In California, Mark Jungheim loaned me a tape of Bartine Burkett's appearance on *The Tonight Show*; David Weddle alerted me to valuable leads; Gwendolyn Brown faciliated my research trips to Los Angeles; and Frances Feldman supplied guidance on Los Angeles geography in the 1950s.

At the Rohauer Collection in Columbus, Ohio, the late Alan Twyman and later on Ty Kistler arranged for me to view videos of Keaton's work.

Extraordinary help in my research was provided by dozens of librarians and archivists in New York, California, Kansas, Oregon, Indiana, Connecticut, Michigan, Nebraska, Nevada, Iowa, Washington, D.C., Oklahoma, Ohio, North Carolina, Texas, Wyoming, and Massachusetts.

New York City

Maryann Chach and Reagan Fletcher, the Shubert Archive; Joel Buckwald, National Archives—Northeast Region; Joe Van Nostrand, Hall of Records, New York Surrogates Court; Barry Dougherty, Museum of Broadcasting; Charles Silver and Ron Magliozzi, Film Study Center, Museum of Modern Art; staff, New York Family History Center, Church of Jesus Christ of Latter-Day Saints; Ron Grele, Oral History Research Collection, Columbia University; Bernard Crystal, Rare Book and Manuscript Library, Columbia University; Hilary Bosch,

William E. Weiner Oral History Library, American Jewish Committee; Nadia Shtendera, Anthology Film Archives; Joan Franklin, Cinema Sound Ltd.; and Bruce Goldstein, New York Film Forum. Also: Paolo Cherchi Usai, George Eastman House, Rochester.

California
I owe a special debt of gratitude to Ruth Spencer of the Louis B. Mayer Library, American Film Institute, Los Angeles, and to Samuel Gill at the Margaret Herrick Library, Academy of Motion Picture Arts and Sciences, Beverly Hills.

Other help was provided by Selise Eiseman, Directors Guild of America, L.A.; Brigitte Kueppers, Theater Arts Library, UCLA; Ned Comstock, Doheny Library, University of Southern California; Eddie Cress, private clipping collection; Jon Torkelson and Marigrey Fish, Truckee Library, Truckee; Ruth Everingham, Truckee-Donner Historical Society; Miriam Biro, North Lake Tahoe Historical Society, Tahoe City; and Sally McManus, Palm Springs Historical Society, Palm Springs.

My investigation of Mae Keaton's life in California and Nevada was assisted by John Panter, archivist, Fresno Historical Society; John Kallenberg, Fresno County Free Library; Jane Nowak, History Dept., Los Angeles Public Library; and the immensely helpful Carolyn Thomas, Merced County Library.

Kansas
Carl Rauch, Coffeyville Historical Society, Coffeyville; David Powls, *Yates Center News*; Sondra Updike-Allen, Allen County Historical Society, Iola; Cindy Adams, Yates Center Public Library, Yates Center; Ray Willson, Iola Public Library, Iola; Dan Fitzgerald, Kansas State Historical Society, Topeka; Pam Stillwell, Woodson County Clerk Office, Yates Center; Juanita Kellerman, Anderson County Historical Society, Garnett; and Jerry Derfelt, Galena Mining and Historical Museum, Galena.

Oregon
Laura Hall, news director, Station KPNW, Eugene, deserves special mention for her painstaking help in arranging interviews. Others who assisted were Isabelle Woolcott, Cottage Grove Museum; and Dan Kaye, Cottage Grove Library.

Indiana
Ruth Dorrel, Indiana Historical Society, Indianapolis; Nancy Sherrill, Vigo County Public Library, Terre Haute; Joyce E. Oehler, Clay County Genealogical Society, Brazil; David Buchanan, Vigo County Historical Society, Terre Haute; Billie Peters, Board of Cemetery Regents, Terre Haute.

Ohio
Richard Abell, Public Library of Cincinnati; and Barbara Dawson, Cincinnati Historical Society.

Connecticut

Ruth Hummel, Plainville Historical Society, was an indefatigible sleuth in researching the Talmadge family, and also treated me to cookies and tea and a delightful tour of Plainville. Others were Ella Noack, Plainville Public Library; Judith Johnson, Connecticut Historical Society, Hartford; and Carolyn Picciano, Connecticut State Library, Hartford.

Michigan

Russ Fairfield, Muskegon Elks Lodge No. 274, Muskegon; and Barbara Martin, Muskegon County Museum.

Nebraska

Andrea Paul, Nebraska State Historical Society, Lincoln; and Donald Hall, Cass County Historical Society, Plattsmouth.

Iowa

Darlene Vergamini, Historical Society of Pottawattamie County, Council Bluffs; Elaine Ehlert, Harrison County Genealogical Society, Woodbine; Karen Laughlin, State Historical Society of Iowa, Iowa City; and Margaret Vittitoe, Modale Public Library, Modale.

For valuable genealogical material on the Cutler family, special thanks to Edna B. Cherry, Margaret Louden, Hart Beebe, and Henry C. Beebe.

Nevada

James Hayes, Clark County Library, Las Vegas; Earl C. Brunner, Jr., Family History Center, Church of Jesus Christ of Latter-Day Saints, Las Vegas; Office of the County Recorder, Carson City; and John McDonald, Washoe County Library, Reno.

Washington

Glenna Broderick, Servawan Massey, Anthony J. Bogucki, U.S. Copyright Office, Library of Congress; Madeline Matz, Motion Picture, Broadcasting and Recorded Sound Div., Library of Congress; and Jeff Flannery, Manuscript Reading Room, Library of Congress.

Elsewhere around the country I received assistance from Kaye Bond, Cherokee Strip Museum, Perry, Okla.; Augusta Benjamin, Friends Historical Society, Greensboro, N.C.; Jamie C. Duke and Cathy Henderson, University of Texas at Austin; David Horan, American Heritage Center, University of Wyoming, Laramie; Margaret Goostray, Mugar Library, Boston University, and Mara Thomas, Houdini Historical Center, Appleton, Wisc.

A number of individuals kindly responded to my requests for information: Steve Allen, Samuel Z. Arkoff, Sid Avery, Polly Bergen, Pandro Berman, Ted Bessel, Guy Roop for Eleanor Boardman, Heywood Broun, Anna and Regina

Brzoska, June Mohney for Frank Capra, Johnny Carson, Maurine Christopher, Gary Conway, Fred de Cordova, Edna Ross for Hugh Downs, Ralph Edwards, Rudi Fehr, Fritz Feld, Rhonda Fleming, Nina Foch, Arlene Francis, Allen Funt, Betty Fussell, John Gallagher, Ira Gallen, George Giannini, Allen Ginsberg, Lillian Gish, Mark Goodson, Lois Laurel Hawes, Robert Horton, Betty Hutton, John Kobler, Dorothy Lamour, Loyal Lucas, John Lyons, Richard Matheson, Gisele Mackenzie, Garry Moore, Charles O'Neill, Sidney Radner, Mrs. Thomas J. Reis, Cesar Romero, Mickey Rooney, Barney Rosset, Natalie Schafer, Richard Schickel, Oscar Shefler, Red Skelton, Robert Stack, Charles Stecy, Micki Vincent, Deborah Walley, Jim Watters, Max Wilk, and Charles Wolfe.

Many writers gave me help in my research. For their generosity in contributing precious leads, I should like to thank Deirdre Bair, David Bruskin, Gary Carey, Tom Dardis, Erwin Dumbrille, Scott Eyman, Mike Foster, Ron Hutchison, Peter Kramer, David Macleod, Barry Paris, Anthony Slide, and David Stenn.

My thanks as well to colleagues in the Biography Seminar of the New York Institute of Humanities, in particular Joan Mellen, Carl Rollyson, Nancy Dougherty, Carol Stanger, and William Luhr. Kenneth Silverman deserves special recognition for supplying material on Harry Houdini and Dona Munker for contributions on Los Angeles history.

For editorial assistance I thank the capable Elizabeth Gold. For expert advice on the game of baseball, among other subjects, I am indebted to Joseph and Mary Epifanio.

Good friends gave me unwavering support throughout the preparation of this biography, by offering not only encouragement and insights but also various kinds of tangible help. I was lucky to have the interest of Minda Novek, Dorothy Herrmann, Carole Klein, Barbara Foster, Ruth Webb Olgachild, Marlene Coburn, Joan Concannon, Friedl Stremnitzer, Thetis and Larry Reeves, Lois Battle, the late Ann Sperber, Myron Brenton, Gordon Sander, Pamela Taylor, Kyle Gallup, and Philip Turner.

I owe a special debt of gratitude to Janet Gardner, who accompanied me on a research trip from one end of California to the other and who was amazing tolerant of the inconveniences that cropped up along the way.

With her unique wit and style, and the highest-quality representation in matters large and small, my literary agent, Lois Wallace, has stood by me through the writing of another book. Invariably she has been there to offer friendship and astute counsel.

I am most fortunate to have Diane Reverand as my editor on a third book, in a relationship that extends back to 1979. As always Diane has brought to my manuscript sensitivity, perceptive judgment, and a keen editorial eye. I am pleased to work with her again.

And finally my thanks to my daughter, Alison Sprague. During the period of entering the tapestry of another's life and times, life simultaneously happens to the biographer, bringing moments of great joy and equally great anguish. On all occasions I have been able to turn to her for love and strength.

INDEX